Want to know more about the hidden architecture of the global economy? Roger Moody takes readers on a perilous tour of the shadow world of Political Risk Insurance and Export Credit Guarantees. He focuses on the mining industry, including projects that the World Bank routinely classifies as posing the greatest social and environmental risks. From controversial submarine tailings disposal in Papua New Guinea, to allegations of human rights abuses in conjunction with gold mining in Tanzania, and to the Omai cyanide spill in Guyana, Moody and his co-authors show how problematic development projects receive multilateral and state support. Drawing on detailed NGO reports, *The Risks We Run* reveals the hit-and-run tactics of political risk insurers and export credit agencies who make the world safe for investors, but fail to protect the people and environments affected by these projects. This is a story that the World Bank, the International Monetary Fund, and other multilateral agencies don't want you to hear! – STUART KIRSCH
Assistant Professor of Anthropology, the University of Michigan.

In memory of my brother Pete,
who ran more risks,
with greater fortitude, than most.

Roger Moody

The Risks We Run

Mining, Communities and Political Risk Insurance

Foreword by Robert Goodland

Contributions by Al Gedicks; S. Dennison Smith; Bank
Information Center; Peter Bosshard; Jacklyne Membup,
Matilda Koma & Augustine Hala; Shanna Langdon and
Project Underground; Tindu Lissu and LEAT

IB
INTERNATIONAL BOOKS, 2005

This publication was made possible with the support of Novib, The Hague (member of Oxfam International).

ISBN 90 5727 006 4

Cover design: Karel Oosting
Desk Top Publishing: Trees Vulto
Printing: De Boekentuin

International Books, Grifthoek 151, 3514 JK Utrecht, the Netherlands
phone +31 30 2731 840, fax +31 30 2733 614
e-mail: i-books@antenna.nl; website www.antenna.nl/i-books

US-orders to: IPG books, frontdesk@ipgbook.com,
or phone tollfree 800-888-4741
UK-orders to: Jon Carpenter Publishing, carpenter@oxfree.com
or phone/fax 01689 870437

Contents

Acknowledgements

Without the dedication and persistence of Jan van Arkel, and his staff, this book would never have seen the light of day. Jan cajoled and complimented his mercurial and dilatory author in almost equal measure. Thanks also to Lin Pugh for proposing this project in the first place; to Novib for part-financing my research; to Nick and Susan at The Cornherhouse; Robert Goodland and Stuart Kirsch for their comments; and to my dear friend Richard for his personal support.

Last but certainly not least, my gratitude goes to those who made statements and analyses which have been incorporated into the case studies at the heart of this book. The responsibility for any errors in editing or incorporating these contributions lies with myself.

Roger Moody, Chennai, March 2005

Websites

The following websites should be of interest to readers who want to follow up the issues in this book.

Mines and Communities – www.minesandcommunities.org
A regularly updated site covering the impacts of mining on people throughout the world

Berne Declaration – www.evb.ch
A longstanding Swiss NGO using research, public education and advocacy to promote more equitable, sustainable and democratic North-South relationships

Lawyers Environmental Action Tanzania – www.leat.org.tz
The first public interest environmental law organisation to be set up in Tanzania

CEE Bankwatch – www.bankwatch.org
Keeps a close and continuing watch on World Bank programmes and policies as they affect peoples in Central and Eastern Europe

Cooperaccion – www.cooperaccion.org
Leading community and workers' rights organisation in Peru which has taken up the issues around the Newmont mine

Project Underground – www.moles.org
Though sadly defunct, its valuable archival material is still accessible

Mineral Policy Institute – www.mpi.org
The most important Australian mining advocacy group which also maintains a close watching brief on Papua New Guinea

Contact Roger Moody
To contact Roger Moody on any aspect of this book, please email him at:
info@minesandcommunities.org

Foreword

In this illuminating and thoroughly researched study, Roger Moody guides the general reader through the relatively unknown – and sometimes distinctly murky – world of Political Risk Insurance (PRI).

His starting point (which might surprise some) is the Enron scandal, which marked a massive collapse of public confidence in the ability of huge corporations to account for themselves, let alone deliver meaningful "development" to communities at large. One key device lodged within Enron's financial underbelly was this form of insurance that, with savage paradox, has enabled the company to claim against some of its victims (e.g. the Indian and Indonesian governments), even while itself performing distinctly illegal acts.

Political risk insurance is a crucial tool in the armory of export credit guarantees. Both are designed to boost the private profits of generally North-based companies, while leaving much of the liability with governments in the South. While state-based export credit agencies are among the biggest providers of PRI, in many cases the most important single provider has been the World Bank, through its Multilateral Investment Guarantee Agency (MIGA). Nor should we neglect (the author doesn't) the increasing role in providing PRI being played by private insurance companies, which are often even less accountable. *The risks we run* does not pretend to be a comprehensive critique of PRI, but it deals with what may be the most dangerous and damaging part it plays – by bolstering huge mining projects with critical social and environment consequences for thousands of people.

Roger Moody is an accomplished analyst of mining and he comes to this issue through intimate knowledge of how the industry works, and long experience of working with communities affected by it. Ten years ago one specific mining project outraged the author.

This was the Grasberg copper-gold mine, carved out of a sacred mountain, in West Papua, by the US Company Freeport, and (after 1995) the UK-based Rio Tinto. Several features marked out this project from other "bad" mines. First, its size (by the turn of the century it was to become the world's single biggest mine). Second, the fact that it produces more mine wastes than any other on the planet – at more than 200,000 tonnes a day thrown directly into a major river system. Third, the extreme repression exercised by the armed forces against the Indigenous Peoples around the minesite, and on whose land it was constructed: repression which has continued to this day.

Underpinning this unacceptable project was the PRI issued by the World Bank in the early 1990s (actually the Bank's first use of this form of insurance). It soon became clear that, without PRI, Freeport would have found it difficult to raise finance in international markets for the vast and destructive project on which it was to embark. In effect, by providing PRI, the World Bank granted Grasberg its seal of approval, rather than the "thumbs down" it surely merited.

As he dug further into the mechanics and politics of PRI, Roger Moody discovered a large number of other mines which had been kick-started by PRI and which, though not as devastating as Grasberg, evinced some highly worrying aspects. Indeed, he came to the conclusion that there was virtually no mining project, backed by PRI, which had served the needs of local communities; on the contrary. In demonstrating this, the author has drawn together six case studies from around the world, using compelling eyewitness accounts to back his assertions.

In essence, he claims, PRI is a massive confidence trick, designed to bulwark dubious and risky ventures, while transferring the social and environmental costs away from relatively rich corporate backers, to those least able to bear them.

You, dear Reader, be the judge as you read this exposé. I find it difficult to disagree with his conclusion.

*Robert Goodland**

---

* Robert Goodland advised His Excellency Dr Emil Salim's Independent Extractive Industry Review (2001-2004) of the World Bank Group's oil, gas and mining portfolio.

Introduction

A Risky World

The 1999 collapse of US power trader, Enron was the most spectacular in corporate history – until WorldCom fell into the abyss only a few months later. Both companies were built on sand or rather the shifting of a myriad different grains, to give the illusion of plenty where there was actually dearth. Enron's operations encompassed a variety of financial risks, as well as victims. Among the latter were the many staff and shareholders who thought the company had enormous wealth when it was merely repackaging losses. Add to this, the third world governments (notably India and Indonesia) which were inveigled into adding further major costs to their massive foreign debt servicing. There were those board members and staff kept in the dark about the true extent of Enron's own indebtedness. And there was the accountancy company, Arthur Andersen, which went under carrying innocent staff and investors with them, all suffering a finite "loss" of one kind or another.[1] (See box "Enron's End Run")

Those too-closely involved with Enron ran other risks as well. The company's former chair and chief executive face possible life imprisonment. At least one government representative on the board (Britain's Lord Wakeham) was disgraced and forced to resign. Those who promoted investment in Enron forfeited shards of their reputation, even if much of the company still remains intact.

Enron's End Run

It wasn't just another energy conglomerate, in the mould of numerous oil and gas outfits that have sequestered much of the literal and fiscal landscapes of Texas and California for well over a century. Instead, Enron was designed by its prime architects, Jeffrey Skilling, Andrew Fastow and Kenneth Lay, to be a "trading powerhouse". It would employ the most sophisticated financial instruments, to cash in on the 1990s de-regulation of the energy industry in the south western USA. The Harvard Business School put it more prosaically, describing Enron's rise as "transformation from Gas Pipeline to New Economy Powerhouse".

The strategy was formulated and backed by America's high elite, notably Dick Cheney of Halliburton Services – soon to become vice-president in the Bush cabinet.[2] Lay himself (known fondly as "Kenny Boy" to president George W Bush) repaid his political supporters with generous donations, loaning his private jet to the future president for his 2000 election campaign.[3]

Then, in 2001, Enron crashed. Its managers were accused of massive fraud, using concocted subsidies and "partnerships" in off-the-books debt, recondite hedging techniques, and other devices to cover up vast losses sustained by its trading. When the true origin of these massive debts began to emerge, Enron sold its stock at high profit to the company's upper echelons, while the majority of ordinary employees (6,000 in Houston alone) came close to ruin.

The conglomerate's accountancy firm, Arthur Andersen – one of the world's five biggest – was charged with destroying vital documents to conceal complicity in the frauds, and it too got submerged, never to resurface.

Enron proved to be the thin edge of a thoroughly rotten wedge. Further investigations by the US Securities and Exchange Commission led, like the toppling of a line of dominoes, to the downfall of WorldCom (which had deliberately overstated its earnings, in the one and a quarter years after June 2001, by US$39 billion) and HealthSouth.[4]

In July 2004 Kenneth Lay was finally brought to trial on eleven criminal counts of securities, bank and wire fraud. If found guilty he could be sentenced to a maximum of 175 years in jail, and have to pay up to US$5.7 million in fines. He has denied all charges.[5]

It has been estimated that seventeen trillion dollars of the proceeds which were kept in pension funds and administered by these recalcitrant companies, have been wiped off the books. This is an estimated quarter of all the financial assets held by ordinary US citizens.[6]

Some of these dangers were foreseeable and were insured against: notably the lost employment of thousands of Enron workers worldwide, prescient enough to sign up to private insurance schemes. The losses for many others – of pension funds, sub-contracts and direct employment – is probably incalculable. There were many other less visible victims, too: those who placed their faith in cheap energy supplies, only to find it disappear like a mirage in the desert; and the governments and communities in the South, left holding the direct and indirect liabilities for the company's collapse and the corrosive consequences of corrupt dealings between Enron and foreign officials.

PRI Provision

But worse than this (and contrary to popular perception), although Enron was brought to its knees as an energy trader, it has nonetheless continued as a business (albeit as a shell of its former self). Shockingly, the company has also been able to make its own claims for compensation. This is primarily due to use of a specific type of insurance, granted solely for operations in "lesser developing countries", and which carries implicit political endorsement from Northern governments and – in some key cases – from the World Bank.

"Political Risk Insurance" (PRI) underwrites industrial and commercial projects and enterprises. Indeed, without PRI, major ventures in many regions would simply not materialise, since their proponents would not attract the debt financing necessary. Enron's Dabhol power project foisted on India is one example; the Lihir mine – dealt with in Chapter 7 of this book – being another.

Enron got its PRI for Dabhol from OPIC, the United States' Overseas Private Investment Corporation. Later, the World Bank's MIGA (Multilateral Investment Guarantee Agency) afforded similar insurance to another flawed Enron venture in Indonesia. Like many other companies, the US power ranger ostensibly required the PRI in order to cover putative losses from doing business outside its own corporate jurisdiction. Precisely because OPIC is an arm of the US state department and treasury, it has come under heavy fire for uncritically supporting Enron in its criminal endeavours. Why didn't OPIC examine the company's books properly and consistently? Was it overly influenced by the US administration's distinct partiality for Enron's top management into not probing thoroughly into its financial structure? What "due diligence" studies did OPIC make of the company's huge "white elephant" schemes before committing to them? Did it ever question the probity of some top employees of Arthur Andersen, Merrill Lynch, Citibank and other Enron "groupies" who later proved to have been, at the least naïve if not rampantly corrupt?

We may never get convincing answers to these questions in the Enron case. But what the unprecedented "scandal" *should* have triggered is an urgent and thorough examination of the criteria used by OPIC in granting PRI *per se*. More (much more) the Enron fall-out ought to have sounded a huge wake-up call to those other government agencies which promised indemnity against losses from the company's enterprises. But little has happened on this front. Although the US administration introduced the Sarbanes-Oxley Act to tighten domestic corporate accountability, other governments have failed to follow suit. (In fact the British government actively lobbied for British companies operating in the USA to be excluded from the provisions of Sar-banes-Oxley.)

European counterparts to OPIC were equally involved in bulwarking Enron, using what are called Export Credit Guarantees (ECGs). In this case alone, their losses ran into hundreds of millions of dollars. However it wasn't Enron, or the majority of its directors and advisors, which suffered (or will suffer) the brunt of these costs. Nor was it the stock exchanges on which the company was allowed to raise its equity funding. The blunt reality is that the burden of paying out on defaulted ECGs ultimately lies at the feet of the governments of the countries where the failures occurred; sometimes, less painfully, on taxpayers in the states providing it.

Political risk insurance is integral to the granting of Export Credit Guarantees. While a PRI policy may be written for a project without the provision of an ECG, the reverse is rarely true (see Chapter 1). Within the past five years, governments, as well as multilateral and bilateral agencies offering both the guarantees and the insurance, have come under increasing pressure from human rights and development NGOs to modify – if not do away with – them altogether. Yet communities profoundly affected by major projects backed by ECGs and PRI are often not even aware that guarantees have been provided or by whom. In 2003 the Canadian development agency, CoDev, examined "stakeholders'" perceptions of mining projects covered by World Bank-MIGA PRI over the previous ten years. Not one of these ventures had enjoyed even limited public scrutiny.[7]

Certainly the mechanics of granting PRI appear more complex than those used for other forms of fiscal guarantee. Arguably this is an effect rather than a cause of widespread public ignorance. As spelt out in Chapter 2 of this book, PRI covers a large gambit of possible events. Taken collectively they comprise a startling portfolio of "risk avoidances" for those who – like Enron – speculate at the shadier edges, and ride the dizzier curves, of venture capital investment.

Anomalies

How, then, do "political" risks differ from those affecting ordinary citizens, and how is the insurance cover provided? In answering these questions we come up against three apparent anomalies. First, despite the name, the risks covered by PRI are not run by governments; on the contrary they often derive from acts of (ill) governance. Nor do states themselves obtain PRI, although state export credit guarantee agencies (ECAs) are key providers of it. PRI is granted businesses for the performance of projects (and transactions) in "developing" countries which lack the standards and norms of investment, property and peoples' protection, supposedly common to the "developed" world.

A second anomaly is that, if we take a broad view of project failure – including what is euphemistically termed "third party" liability – the consequences can be far greater for those who are not insured than for those holding the policy. At the core of this book are case studies graphically demonstrating that mining and mineral enterprises insured under PRI often do fail, sometimes calamitously. Yet the burden of calamity and collapse – loss of arable land, poisoning of vital water supplies and at worst death and serious injury – is bourn, not by project investors, managers and insurers, but by mineworkers and local people. Adding insult to injury, local people have been kept in the dark about potentially adverse outcomes; never being consulted on alternative means to implement a project, nor given the right to veto any of its components. The ECAs responsible for PRI supposedly carry out social and environmental risk assessments before signing a contract with an operator. As we will see, not only are these studies rarely adequate; in no way do they bind the insurer to compensate third parties for any physical, cultural, or ecological damage.

Even if this critical element were included from the outset, the worst impacts of large scale, open-pit, mining are often not sustained until some time after the PRI cover has expired (as with the Lihir project in Papua New Guinea – see Chapter 7).

Arguably the very term "political risk" is a chimera; a hold-all into which almost any happenstance can be thrown, including the appropriation or devaluing of assets, the sabotage of an electricity power plant, attacks on staff, restrictions on profit transfers, a company's expulsion from a host country. Such events, and more, do get covered by many PRI policies. Yet – and this is the third anomaly – the premiums paid rarely seem to reflect the magnitude of possible risks. Equally curious is that companies may fail to make a claim, following an interruption to their work or an operational failure, although these occurrences are manifestly covered by their PRI policy. Conversely, insurance cover is sometimes continued, even when project design has been demonstrably changed for the worse. It becomes clear why this happens if we regard PRI, not so much as an insurance instrument, as a political tool used to maintain a project or sustain a company's debt finance.

Where claims do arise they are often settled through mediation. The more contentious the enterprise, the more likely are its proponents to seek a swift extension of PRI, rather than squabble over figures, thereby risking cancellation of the insurance; not to mention costly delays in finding a new insurance provider.

For those whose experience of insurance is limited to the aftermath of an accident, robbery or freak of nature, PRI's *modus operandi* does seem peculiar, if not actually perverse. Should a driver lose control of his vehicle on the high street, crash into a shop window and destroy thousands of dollars worth of goods, we would expect him or his insurers to pay various types of compensation. This would cover replacement value of the goods, damage to the premises, loss of business during repairs, and possibly the psychological impacts on those in the shop at the time.

There would be public outrage if the driver were found drunk at the time of the accident, injuring pedestrians in his wild trajectory. Many folk would declare that imprisonment itself was "too good for him".

But, when the Omai mine's tailings dam in Guyana collapsed in mid-1995, resulting in massive, if short term, loss of potable water and fish for communities dependent on the Essequibo river, only derisory and desultory payments were made to the victims by Cambior, the operator. As for the company's PRI (obtained from the World Bank and Canada's ECA Export Development Canada – the EDC), this was renewed without proper public review, and apparently without penalty, when the mine reopened several months later (see Omai case, Chapter 5).

Just once in its first seventeen years history of issuing PRI did the world's largest single public provider, the World Bank's MIGA, ever pay out on a claim. This was a modest US$15 million given to Enron in 2000, to cover its equity investment in an abandoned power project on the Indonesian island of Java, operated by the P.T. East Java Power Corporation. (In fact, MIGA suspended all PRI for Indonesia after its 1997 "economic crisis", a decision partly provoked by the country's wilful extension of insupportable credit facilities.) The loss to MIGA was recuperated within a year. Commented the agency's General Counsel (lawyer) and World Bank vice President, Luis Dodero, at the time:

> "While we understand the circumstances that led to the project's suspension, international law dictates that the cancellation be compensated. We are pleased that the claim has been resolved and we can now resume our guarantee operations in the country."[8]

Added MIGA in a press statement:

> "Over the past 13 years, MIGA has successfully resolved disputes between investors and host governments in developing countries through its dispute

mediation services, enabling the agency to prevent formal claims from arising in a number of cases."[9]

In the case of West Papua's Grasberg mine, the joint venturers Freeport and
Rio Tinto jettisoned PRI cover by MIGA just as they appeared to be most in
need of it. The probable trigger for this was the announcement of a long-
overdue environmental investigation of the mine (particularly its riverine
tailings dumping) by a MIGA-sponsored team. The two companies were
already benefiting from a secret contract with the Indonesian military, ostensibly to safeguard the mine lease area against attacks by the independence
organisation, Operasi Papua Merdeka (OPM). Avoiding further unwelcome
public exposure of its dubious practices may well have been more important
to Freeport-Rio Tinto than continuing with an insurance policy which may
never be invoked. After junking MIGA, it is likely that the partners negotiated
a private PRI policy (see Chapter 2) which would have excluded any mandatory vetting of Grasberg's practices.[10]

MIGA and OPIC had both laid down initial environmental safeguards
before granting PRI, and OPIC temporarily pulled its cover when these were
violated by the two companies. For this reason some environmentalists urged
continuance of the World Bank's "involvement" in Grasberg while acknowl-
edging that the mining operation was unacceptable (see Chapter 4). There
seemed little logic to this argument. Grasberg's PRI was intended to give the
mine an essential "kick-start" and stamp of respectability. Withdrawing it,
once operations were well underway, thus made little – if any – difference
to what took place on the ground (and above all in the water). Certainly, in
the period following withdrawal of PRI, the mine's ore throughput expanded
enormously; wastes delivered to the Ajkwa river system have doubled, and
disaster has succeeded disaster with appalling regularity. But the mine had
been a social and environmental calamity for many years. Any influence the
World Bank or OPIC might have exerted to forestall these consequences could
only have come from their refusing insurance at the outset. Once PRI was
secured, Freeport-Rio Tinto hubristically went its own way, cocking a snook
at the external agencies and starkly revealing their impotence to do anything
about it.

If we join the Grasberg experience together with similar outcomes at
mines in Peru, Guyana and Papua New Guinea, we discover overwhelmingly
that PRI has provided no cover for the most vulnerable of project-affected
people, or other species and their biosphere. On the contrary, it has abet-
ted the cover-up of unacceptable practises and served only to reassure those
responsible for them.

Rejecting PRI

This book is an introduction to those who provide political risk insurance and the criteria they adopt, concentrating on one crucial industrial sector. Case histories, drawing on a large amount of source material, reveal the dereliction by insurers of fundamental safeguards and, in most cases, the complete absence of any project-related bonding, let alone recognition of the principle that "the polluter pays". We seek to discover whether multilateral, government, or private, agencies are the most important in dispensing PRI. The impacts of PRI-insured projects on local communities and the environment are graphically described – in several instances by people directly affected. Finally, the book argues that these projects are so detrimental to what is now broadly understood as "sustainable development" that we should reject the entire concept of PRI forthwith.

Targeting Mines

But why specifically mines? At first sight they do not seem intrinsically more damaging to people and ecology than big dams (such as the Three Gorges in China, granted PRI and ECG by Export Development Canada) or power plants like Enron's. Nonetheless, mineral extraction has profound effects upon, and beneath, a specific piece of territory; while its "footprint" (the anodyne term commonly employed to describe impacts beyond an immediate operational area) may sprawl over many square miles. From the moment of first entry (exploratory drilling) mining companies create problems for those living, or dependent, on that territory and its resources. This is implicitly acknowledged by the World Bank which classifies most mining projects that it insures as Category A, denoting the highest social and environmental risk.

There are few commercially attractive mineral deposits on earth which are not occupied or claimed by a self-identified community or communities. Moreover, the proportion of specifically Indigenous and traditional peoples' territory, now being explored and exploited for its mineral riches, far outstrips that which sourced the huge iron, copper, lead-zinc, nickel, coal and gold mines from the 1940s to the early 1990s. Twenty years ago, many of these impacted Peoples felt ill-informed about the consequences of mineral extraction. Today almost all them understand at least some of its profound effects. With the exception of a few ventures in Australia and Canada, community opposition to new mine projects is a foregone conclusion. In turn, their outcries have had a marked effect on the rate at which the large mining multinationals actually proceed. The minerals industry has responded by adopting a new linguistic patina, backhandedly recognising the existence of resistance, while actively seeking to deflect it. Since 1997 (or so) a bout of "good neighbour programmes" and exercises in civil society "engagement", have invoked the supposed principles of "sustainable mining", "stakeholder democracy", business "charters" and "corporate social responsibility". These modern mantras appear to acknowledge the right of territorial custodians to reject extractive projects they consider damaging. But for the most part, their legal or political power to do so is as weak as ever and, in some instances, being eroded irrevocably.

Whether it be from the coalfields of Bihar, the gold fields of Guyana, Indonesia, Peru, or the killing fields of Sierra Leone, Congo (RC) and former Zaire (DRC), we hear the same basic demand: Show us how we will be better off if a big, open-pit mine is constructed where we live, work, play and have our understanding! Unfortunately, there is rarely a remotely convincing response.[11]

Notes

1   The demise of Arthur Andersen reduced the number of world class accountancies from five to the current "big four", which then promptly "carved up and assimilated" its assets: see Andrew Simms "Accounting for the accountants" in *Third World Resurgence,* Penang, January 2003, p. 45.

2   Gerry Wills, "The tragedy of Bill Clinton", *New York Review of Books,* August 12 2004, p. 64.

3   Graydon Carter, *What we've lost,* Little Brown, 2004.

4   John Micklethwait and Adrian Wooldridge, *The Company: A short history of a 'Revolutonary Idea',* Wiedenfeld and Nicholson, London 2003, pps. 149-50.

5   *Financial Times* (FT) July 10 2004; *FT* July 15 2004.

6   Mickelthwait and Wooldridge, op cit, p. 149.

7   Ginger Gibson, *Community Perspectives on the Extractive Industries: A report for the Extractive Industries Review, CoDevelopment Canada,* Vancouver, 2003, p. 20.

8   MIGA press release, Washington DC, February 21 2001.

9   MIGA press release, op cit.

10   I asked MIGA's chief lawyer to provide me with the terms of its PRI policy for the Grasberg mine but he was not forthcoming. It is quite likely that the contract did not include indemnification against civil disturbance or damage attributed to local agitation, thus making it even less vital for the company to maintain.

11   Indicatively, the one example of a sustainable, community-endorsed project that is provided by the world's biggest mining company, BHPBilliton, is of a smelter not a mine – namely the Mozal aluminium complex in Mozambique. And this too has come under criticism from local people.

PART I

Behind Political Risk Insurance

CHAPTER I

The Export Credit Curse

Back in the late 1960s, the World Bank commissioned Lester Pearson and others to assess the causes of global poverty. In its noteworthy study "Partners in Development" Pearson's eponymous commission expressed alarm that private banks had become "less concerned about [a] borrowing country's credit worthiness because of the facility of export credit insurance". Expanded use of this tool could, said the commission, cause "very real dangers". Not only was export credit a particularly expensive form of external finance; often the only project feasibility studies available were those undertaken by its promoters. Reckless schemes were being launched because export credit agencies (ECAs) failed to enforce "rigorous tests of economic desirability".

For the previous fifteen years such guarantees had become "a major reason for the need to reschedule the debts of a number of countries, notably Argentina, Brazil, Chile, Ghana, Indonesia and Turkey". The commission warned that debt rescheduling would become "more difficult in the future if export credits are imprudently used".[1]

Over the following two decades Pearson's fears were amply borne out. Commercial banks became even more unwilling to loan to South-based countries, even as export credit guarantees (ECGs) proliferated. The result was a crisis in both hemispheres: debts piled up for "lesser developed" countries, while lending states tried to disguise the extent to which defaults in repayment blighted their own exchequers.[2] The main winners, it seemed, were those whose projects – however skimped, irrelevant or downright pernicious – got supported by the ECAs.

In a rational world, informed by a thorough understanding of sustainable development, the use of export credit would have become redundant long ago. Instead the practice has merely been refined – primarily to safeguard the guarantors, serve guaranteed firms, and even further exploit the dependencies of indebted countries.

Today seventy six ECAs operate out of sixty two nation states. The majority are members of the Berne Union (International Union of Credit and Investment Insurers) set up in 1984 and based in Switzerland. The Union's stated aim is to promote uniform principles for export credit and investment (including political risk) insurance, both with state support and among its own membership. Fledgling members of the Union, mainly from the Middle East, Eastern Europe and "lesser developed" countries are grouped in the Prague Club, a "pre-membership training group" for the Berne Union.[3] One of these new entrants, South Africa's ECIC (Export Credit Insurance Corporation) was set up just a few years ago in 2001. It deals with both exporters of capital goods and home grown financial institutions, providing political risk insurance against an exporter being "prevented or restricted" from importing goods or services into a foreign country. No doubt learning from recent experience, cover is also granted in the event of a boycott, or the institution of sanctions, against South African goods or the country itself.[4]

For its part, the Organisation for Economic Cooperation and Development (OECD) has its own export credit benchmarks (the "OECD Consensus") which purportedly fosters competition based on quality and prices of exported goods, rather than the most favourable conditions offered by individual states. The OECD's Working Party on Export Credits and Credit Guarantees is charged with determining a common policy on insurance rates.

In terms of their global reach and investment capabilities, these are the eight most important government ECAS:
— Ex-Im Bank (US)
— OPIC (US)
— EDC (Export Development Canada)
— JBIC (formerly EXIM) Japan
— ECGD (Export Credit Guarantee Department, UK)
— COFACE (Compagnie Française d'Assurance pour le Commerce Extérieur, France)
— Hermes (Germany)
— Istituto per I Servizio Assicuratai per il Commercio Estero (formerly Sace) Italy

The World Bank's MIGA (Multilateral Investment Guarantee Agency) between 1994 and 2004 signed Memorandums of Understanding (MoUs) enabling it to partner two of these key agencies (COFACE and Sace), along with other ECAS based in Australia, Brazil, China, India, Europe, Africa and the Middle East.[5]

Currently, ECGS are used to underwrite ("underpin" may be the more apt term) around 10 per cent of global exports from Northern countries, primarily for private sector projects.[6] Already by 1996, ECAS had become the "single largest public financiers of large-scale infrastructure projects in the developing world".[7] Their huge financial and political leverage can be gauged from the fact that, in the year 2000, almost as much (US$58.8 billion) was dispensed in the form of ECAs as in global development aid (US$60 billion), while this was considerably more than all the loans provided by multilateral development banks (US$41 billion).

Between 1995 and 2001 the British ECGD regularly paid out more than twice (in some instances up to three times) as much in claims as it had ostensibly received in premium payments. To do this it relied on counter-guarantees from the countries which imported the underwritten goods and services. For example, in the financial year 2001-2002 the ECGD recovered just over five million pounds; a little less the following year. Since the ECGD doesn't have to make a profit, it can maintain its premium fees at below-market rates.[8] In effect, this was issuing cut-price insurance for the private sector or – put bluntly – screwing the poor while feather-bedding the relatively rich.

According to Dr Susan Hawley, a researcher with the British social research group, The Cornerhouse, some 95 per cent of southern country debt to the UK government is export credit debt.[9] It may be true that only 8 per cent of the poorest countries receive ECGs, the majority going to so-called "middle income" states like Brazil, China, the Philippines, Mexico, Turkey and Indonesia.[10] Nonetheless, this is precisely where the worst damage can be done to the biggest expanse of territory or the greatest number of people. For example, between 1992 and 1996 a clutch of ECAs targeted Indonesia despite (or because) it then suffered under the iron rule of the Suharto oligopoly. During that period an estimated 24 per cent of the country's external debt was in the form of export credit guarantees. Some of these covered damaging logging projects and were provided by EXIM, the Finnish Guarantee Board, Swedish Export Credit and Debit, and Export Development Canada (EDC). Destructive palm oil plantations were backed by the Danish ECA and the EDC, while the US$4.2 billion Pailton coal power plants earned the support of EXIM, US Ex-Im and OPIC.[11] The political backing for Pailton was astonishing, even by the standards of the time and place: those riding this particular gravy train included President Clinton, ex-vice president Dan Quayle, ex-secretary of state Warren Christopher and (almost inevitably) Henry Kissinger.[12]

For their part, companies know that ECGs can render them relatively immune from facing the negative consequences of their own decision making; being bailed out by the public purse with few questions asked. Thus they may be more reckless in making investments, or less pre-cautionary in risk assessment, than a competitive investment market would require. (As *Euromoney* magazine in 2002 whimsically enquired: "What could be nicer in time of turmoil than having the risk picked up by the public purse?")

Evidence of such profligacy abounds, as we can see from a more detailed examination of decisions taken in recent years by three of the world's leading ECAS: the USA's OPIC, Canada's EDC and Britain's ECGD. Although globally less influential, Australia's EFIC is equally important in terms of its backing for unacceptable mining-related ventures.

OPIC and US Ex-Im

Squandered Opportunity

The US government's Overseas Private Investment Corporation, or OPIC, has a better reputation for what it's not done than for what it has. Its 1995 decision to cancel US$100 million in PRI cover for Freeport-Rio Tinto's Grasberg mine met with approval from many social activists[13] for whom political risk insurance had, until then, been at best a fuzzy concept. Citing a breach of the US Foreign Assistance Act, in 1997 OPIC's lawyers again produced compelling environmental arguments against Rio Tinto's Lihir gold venture.[14] In both instances, OPIC was well ahead of the World Bank, whose guidelines and rules on pollution prevention abatement it pledges to follow. It looked then as if the corporation might develop further critiques of unacceptable extractive ventures.

The promise remains demonstrably unfulfilled. By the new millennium, OPIC was subscribing to Enron's highly dubious ventures in India and Indonesia, and a wilfully ill-judged gas pipeline project through Bolivia and Brazil. In 2003, it handed Unocal a cool US$350 million in political risk insurance for the oil company's potentially dangerous West Seno offshore oil and gas exploitation in Indonesia. Unocal's intention is to drill forty new offshore wells and lay two 60 kilometre pipelines beneath the sea and across the land. Ninety four Indonesian and international NGOs, headed by the Environmental Defense Fund (EDF) argued that the project "appears to be in violation of Indonesia's environmental law requiring full citizen input into the structure and production of an environmental impact assessment prior to the commencement of new activities". There are, declared EDF, "strong indications of serious environmental and human rights abuses associated with this project".[15] Only a year before, local communities in East Kalimantan had been kept in the dark for several weeks about a major oil spill.[16]

Again in 2003 OPIC stepped in where at least one doubtful angel – the World Bank – feared to tread, by joining the European Union in providing a US$50 million investment guarantee to Sierra Rutile Ltd, for the re-start of its troubled and troubling mineral sands mining in Sierra Leone. (See Chapter 3.) The anodyne justification for this decision, given by OPIC president and chief executive, Peter Watson, was that "...as Sierra Leone emerges into peace, restoring its primary industries – like rutile mining – will be critical to its economic development... OPIC is pleased to help a US company restart a business that has contributed so importantly to the Sierra Leone economy."[17] In fact, although originally managed by Nord Resources of the US, Sierra Rutile has since passed through the clutches of a partnership headed by the mercenary Jean Boulle; followed by a joint ownership by Boulle's MIL Investments SARL and US Titanium; before ending up in the hands of Idaho-based WGI Heavy Minerals Inc in mid-2004.[18] As for Sierra Rutile's pretended contribution to the country's well being, a UN investigation in the early nineties accused the company (at the time supplying a quarter of the world's rutile), along with fellow multinationals based in Sierra Leone, of robbing the government of around half the income due from mineral extraction.

In the last years of his presidency (when he could spare time from socialising with market manipulators like Marc Rich) Bill Clinton identified OPIC and US Export Import Bank (Ex-Im) as the two key government agencies for promoting overseas sales by US companies. Stasticis in 1995 had shown that the US government was the least munificent of export credit guarantors, charging up to four times the fees imposed by ECAS in Japan, Germany, France and Britain. Ex-Im was then providing less than 3 per cent of total US export funding, while Japan's provision to its domestic businesses was more 30 per cent.[19]

Clinton's boost to export credits was a success: 1996 proved a record year for OPIC, with 169 projects covered by loan guarantees and PRI, generating nearly ten billion dollars in US exports. The administration promptly proposed a doubling of the corporation's liabilities exposure to a ceiling of US$45 billion. The move would have given OPIC unrivalled financial (and political) muscle but provoked strident protests from rightwing congressmen and consumer groups, which defeated the move in September that year. A researcher for the Competitive Enterprise Institute said it was "inappropriate for large, profitable corporations to continue receiving... benefits from organisations like OPIC": he demanded the agency cease transacting new government-guaranteed business. One congressional spokesman commented that Congress was "finding it quite easy to generate support... to get rid of [OPIC]".[20]

The attacks failed to bring OPIC to its knees. If anything, PRI and loans were now tailored even more to serve US foreign policy. OPIC re-opened the doors to investment in Vietnam, abandoning twenty four years of trade sanctions.[21] It initiated a US$350 million infrastructure fund to serve southern Africa. In order to revive confidence in Asia, following the widespread credit collapse of 1997, political risk cover was offered for new bonds aimed at securing better returns for US financiers of major global infrastructure projects, such as pipelines, power stations and toll roads. The terms were more flexible than ones normally laid down by other export credit agencies.[22]

Parlous Precedents

OPIC's recent "bad history" dates at least to 1991 when,[23] along with the UK government's Commonwealth Development Corporation (CDC) and the World Bank's International Finance Corporation (IFC), it first approved joint financing for expansion of the Sierra Rutile mine.[24]

That year, too, the corporation began tailoring its portfolio to lure extractive businesses to Russia and the Newly Independent States of the former USSR (the CIS).[25] No clear environmental protection polices had until then emerged in post-communist Russia, and OPIC did little to change the situation for the better. On the contrary, it set about contributing further to the worst environmental legacy on earth. In 1994 alone it approved more than US$1.5 billion of finance for fifty projects in the region. Most of this money went towards logging ventures, including one encompassing a million acres of virgin forest in the Khabarovsk area of the Russian Far East. OPIC and the Agency for International Development (USAID) also sponsored a privately-operated Fund for Large Enterprises in Russia, doling out US$20 million bonuses to each new project.[26]

The US-backed Russian exploits were "shrouded in secrecy".[27] OPIC ignored the terms of the US Freedom of Information Act and refused open access to the documents which purportedly guided its decisions. Nor would it entertain public comment on its policies, whether from Russian or American citizens.[28] With hardly any public lobby groups aware, in 1995 OPIC and the European Bank for Reconstruction and Development (EBRD) backed the US-based Cyprus-Amax's Magadan-based Kubaka gold and silver mining project.[29]

But, as David Gordon noted in early 1996, it was the KAMGOLD joint venture between Canada's Kinross Gold Corporation (25 per cent), US-based Grynberg Resources Inc. (25 per cent) and Russia's Kamgeo (50 per cent) that lay "at the center of the region's mining debate".[30] In 1994 KAMGOLD gained mining rights to central Kamchatka's very rich Aginskoye gold deposit, as well as the neighbouring Solotoye lode. Like Cyprus-Amax, the company looked for investment support to the EBRD and OPIC. Aginskoye lies within the vast, 3.5-million-acre, Bystrinsky Regional Park which sustains "a wealth of pristine rivers, brown bears, bighorn sheep, eagles, salmon, reindeer, more than 120 volcanoes and a number of endangered animals and plant species, as well as around a thousand aboriginal people,..."[31] But, in summer 1995 Kamchatka's governor, Vladimir Biryukov, promised to effectively excise the mine from the park, in order that construction could proceed.

"Much of Kamchatka's population is opposed to multinational gold mining plans" commented David Gordon. "Aginskoye... is located on areas that the indigenous Itel'men people claim as traditional lands. They, along with other indigenous Kamchatka peoples, have expressed opposition to gold mining and concern about potential environmental impacts. The Kamchatka fishing industry is also opposed to gold mining, with the fishing union voting unanimously against it."[32]

Indigenous opposition gathered strength through 1996, supported by Russian, Asian and American environmentalists, including the Pacific Environment and Resources Center, the Environmental Defense Fund (EDF) and the Sierra Club. In October the World Conservation Congress passed a resolution opposing any finance, insurance or support activities for Aginskoye and Solotoye, stating that the mine sites lay within the headwaters of nine principal wild salmon spawning rivers.[33]

That year the Bystrinsky park was designated a UNESCO World Heritage Site; shortly afterwards OPIC withdrew its offer of PRI to the Kinross Corporation. (See box "Rushing for gold".)

The reprieve was short lived. After Vladimir Putin came to power, Russia's Natural Resources ministry was designated the pretended guardian of the nation's environment – a blatant example of foxes being put in charge of chickens. The ministry in 2000 rebuffed a United Nations Development Program (UNDP) proposal, to include the Bystrinsky park in a series of four Kamchatka nature reserves where the UNDP "would help strengthen management and safeguard the environment".[34] According to the ministry some US$600 million could be generated in revenues from a nickel mine near Bystrinsky, compared with just $10 million in new funds offered by the UNDP. One ministry official, Igor Petrenko, openly denounced the UN agency, blaming "foreign-funded environmentalists" for the "well-organized sabotage" of the mining industry.[35]

The Aginskoye mine went ahead; Kinross did not sell its shares in the project until August 2002.[36]

Rushing for Gold

"Mining companies [in Russia] say that they are finding bonanzas of gold and other precious minerals that are similar to the deposits found in the Gold Rush days of 19th-century California. Yet in their rush to extract these

mineral resources and in the Russian government's race for quick cash investments, it appears that basic environmental standards are being forgotten.

With the financial backing of the US and other governments, major international mining corporations are focusing their attention on Siberia and the
Russian Far East. Canada's TVX Gold is preparing documents to mine the
Asachinskoye site in Kamchatka. Kinross Gold, also from Canada, has been
trying to develop Kamchatka's Aginskoye site for more than two years now,
despite its proximity to a UNESCO World Heritage Site and a protected nature
park. The US company Cyprus Amax is already pouring gold at the Kubaka
site in Magadan Region, home to much of Russia's worst mining pollution.

Mine plans in Russia... fall short in their engineering and design of tailings impoundments and their assurances that groundwater and surface
water will not be polluted. Technical mining specialists point out that such
mines in the US would not be allowed to move forward without meeting significantly higher standards to ensure that an accident will not occur.

Proposed mine sites in Kamchatka... where the local economy is almost
entirely dependent on fishing and... the protection of salmon spawning
grounds... have proven to be especially controversial.

Kinross Corporation's proposed Aginskoye mine has thus far been
blocked while environmental officials with the Kamchatka Committee for
the Protection of the Environment and Natural Resources demand that the
company meet strictest applicable environmental standards. Local scientists
are especially concerned that the proposed Aginskoye mine will negatively
impact the Bystrinsky Nature Park and the newly created UNESCO World
Heritage Site... They point out that President Clinton blocked plans to
develop a gold mine on the border of Yellowstone National Park and they
suggest that the Aginskoye mine would similarly damage neighboring Bystrinsky Park.

Bilateral and multilateral finance agencies among the other industrialized nations continue to promote the development of environmentally dangerous mines in Russia. The US Overseas Private Investment Corporation
recently withdrew its proposed support to Kamchatka's Aginskoye project
only after intense pressure from environmental groups, UNESCO's declaration
of World Heritage status for Kamchatka, and a resolution from the International Union for the Conservation of Nature."

(From a press release issued at the Summit of Eight *conference in Russia, by the
Pacific Environment and Resources Center (PERC) and Friends of the Earth-
Japan (FoE-J), June 1997.)*

The Enron Factor

OPIC's sponsorship of the most morally deficient US company in recent history dates to the mid-nineties when it underwrote the Dabhol power plant in Maharashtra, then projected to be the biggest electricity generating utility in India. Dipping their fingers into the venture were some of the world's most powerful banks and multinationals, supported by export credit guarantees, with PRI from at least five ECAs, including OPIC and ECGD. Enron's own partners were the world's biggest public corporation, General Electric, and – after Halliburton – America's most notorious engineering and construction company, Bechtel.[37]

When Enron collapsed in late 2001, Dabhol went into mothballs and its global backers into overdrive as they sought to make good the pretended losses on their investments. In reality it was the people of India who had been the most spectacularly screwed. They not only paid well over the odds for the power which was delivered, but hundreds of millions of their tax dollars may ultimately end up in the pockets of companies (including the disgraced Enron) which exploited their labour and natural resources (See box "Power without power".)

While promoting Dabhol, OPIC also provided guarantees for other dubious Enron schemes. In 1996 four hundred million dollars went towards the company's joint venture with Uzbekneftagaz to open up several major gas fields in Uzbekistan: it was the largest OPIC commitment in Central Asia to that date.[38]

Although OPIC by 1999 had tightened its environmental permitting criteria, it promptly signed yet another loan agreement with Enron, worth US$200 million. The Bolivia-Brazil gas pipeline was aimed at exporting cheap power to the USA; Enron's partners were Royal Dutch/Shell and Transredes.[39] OPIC justified the project as "green" on the decidedly shaky grounds that it would avoid further damage to Brazilian Amazonia. Some sixty citizens' groups from twenty countries argued that, on the contrary, the scheme violated President Clinton's own undertaking to ban new infrastructure in primary rain forests. According to a former OPIC environmental officer (who later joined Friends of the Earth) a report, commissioned by Enron at the insistence of OPIC, showed that, although "standards look good on paper... in reality this project will destroy the environment".[40]

Citizens' revulsion at what amounted to a wholesale giveaway of Bolivian natural resources rose to fever pitch in late 2003. At least sixty people died during bloody street battles between thousands of pipeline opponents and forces loyal to President "Goni" Lozado who was finally forced to flee the country. In May 2004 his successor, Carlos Mesa, dropped the project (at least for the time being) promising to consider a partial re-nationalisation of the country's energy sector, among other options.[41] Just over two months later, OPIC granted US$135 million PRI to Coeur D'Alene's San Bartolome silver project in the historical Bolivian mining region of Potosi.[42]

Meanwhile, the sorry legacy of Dabhol continues. In 2003, Enron, General Electric (GE) and Bechtel sought to recover around US$200 million by suing OPIC, arguing that the Indian government had expropriated the plant after Enron invested in it more than a billion dollars. A US arbitration court awarded just under thirty million dollars against OPIC to GE and Bechtel in September that year: OPIC in turn accused the Indian government of political machinations which caused the project to collapse.[43]

For good measure the two companies sued the Indian government, seeking US$600 million in forfeited dues.[44] The Bank of America received compensation from OPIC on like grounds.[45] No doubt fired up by this success, Bank of America's fellow banks, Standard Chartered, ABN Amro and ANZ, in 2004 revived a £60 million claim against the ECGD, first made in 2001. The three banks argued that Dabhol had been appropriated by the Indian government and that the British export credit agency, ECGD, was responsible by proxy.[46] GE and Bechtel also won approval from a US bankruptcy court to buy two thirds of Enron's stake in Dabhol. However, far from re-opening the abandoned power plant, they wished to sell their stakes for at least US$400 million.[47]

Power Without Power

At least five ECAs were involved in financing the Dabhol Power Plant in India's Maharashtra state. The US OPIC and Ex-Im provided $640 million in loans and guarantees for the project, while Japan's JBIC and Belgium's OND also provided backing. The UK's ECGD provided Overseas Investment Insurance for three investing banks (ANZ Bank, Standard Chartered Bank and ABN Amro). It also supplied re-insurance in early 2000 for a UK company, Kier International, to build a liquefied petroleum gas port terminal for the power plant. Banks from Austria, France, the Netherlands and Switzerland, including Erste Bank, Credit Lyonnais, BNP Paribas and PSFB, made further loans.

At US$2.9 billion in estimated costs, Dabhol was India's biggest-ever foreign investment project and destined to be one of the most important electricity generating plants on earth. The Dabhol Power Company (DPC), which built and ran the plant until it closed in June 2001, was initially a joint venture between three US energy companies (the now-collapsed Enron, General Electric and Bechtel Corporation), until the Maharashtra State Electricity

Board (MSEB) took a stake in the project, signing a Memorandum of Understanding (MoU) with Enron in June 1992. Notwithstanding this, a World Bank review, commissioned by the Maharashtra government, found many irregularities in the MoU and concluded that the Memorandum was very one-sided in Enron's favour. Questioning its economic viability, in April 1993 the World Bank refused to provide funds for the plant. According to documents released under the US Freedom of Information Act, staff at US Ex-Im were also not convinced about the viability of the project. But, in 1994, Ex-Im came under intense pressure from the former chair of Enron, Kenneth Lay. The then-chair of Ex-Im, Kenneth Brody, personally helped to hurry through a finance package.

The MSEB got locked into a Power Purchase Agreement (PPA) with Enron, signed in 1993, which was anomalous to say the least. The Agreement ensured that the state would pay for power, even if it didn't need it, and even if electricity was not produced by the plant. The MSEB was required to pay between $1.2 and $1.3 billion a year for Dabhol's electrical power – a tariff India's Central Electricity Authority declared to be more than double what it should be.

The haste with which the project was agreed, the lack of transparency and the absence of competitive tendering, resulted in a plethora of corruption allegations. In September 1995, a newly-elected Maharashtra government filed a court case against both the Dabhol Power Company and MSEB, alleging that bribes had been made to influence the awarding of the contract and demanding that it be voided. But, early the following year, following extensive negotiations with Enron, a newly-elected Maharashtra government withdrew the case. It accepted a renegotiated deal for an even larger power plant than originally planned, with almost equal haste and on equally, if not more, disadvantageous terms.

By the end of 2000, power from Dabhol was four times more expensive than that sold by other domestic producers. The state of Maharashtra was spending more on Dabhol's supply than its entire budget for primary and secondary education. It had to pay the company 8 rupees per unit, but could sell it on for only a quarter of the cost.

In June 2001, the Dabhol Power Company shut down the plant after the MSEB decided the Company had failed to provide power at full capacity or within the time-frame agreed under the Power Purchase Agreement. Nonetheless, the Company carried on billing the MSEB $21 million a month and, in September, Enron demanded that the Indian government pay it $2.3 billion for its investment and debts on the project.

After Enron's collapse following its bankruptcy in December 2001, Dabhol was put up for sale. Among the foreign bidders were BP, British Gas, Royal Dutch/Shell and Gaz de France, alongside four Indian companies. But disputes, between domestic lenders and the Indian government on the one hand, and foreign lenders on the other, have left the plant standing idle since.

Foreign banks have a total exposure on Dabhol of $372 million. Most of the foreign finance is guaranteed by domestic Indian banks, while the Indian government gave a counter-guarantee for the project. Foreign investors have been blocking ideas presented by domestic lenders and the Indian government as to what to do with Dabhol, while at the same time aggressively pursuing compensation for their investment losses. They claim that Dabhol has been effectively expropriated by the Indian government, even though the problems arose because the plant did not perform adequately, and foreign lenders are implicated in the failure to find a solution to the plant's problems.

In September 2003, a US arbitration panel ruled that OPIC should pay GE and Bechtel compensation of $28.57 million each. A month later, OPIC paid compensation of $30 million to Bank of America under its political risk insurance cover (its total exposure to the project being $340 million). Ex-Im also coughed up $298.2 million to Enron. The US government, represented by top officials such as Vice President Dick Cheney, was meanwhile exerting strong pressure on the Indian government to come to a solution that would benefit Enron and protect US taxpayers' money. The US government reportedly threatened to withdraw aid to India; deplorably warning that, if there were no accommodation, this would "spell death to potential investment".

It is not just US investors who are seeking compensation. In November 2003, ANZ Bank, Standard Chartered Bank and ABN Amro filed claims for political risk insurance with the UK's ECGD for about $60 million. Six European banks, including those backed by the ECGD, filed claims worth $200 million with the Indian government. Belgium's OND has been approached by three banks for $90.8 million worth of insurance compensation.

OPIC, Ex-Im, OND, the ECGD and other ECAs involved will seek to recover the expenses of any pay-outs from the Indian government. That government, and ultimately the Indian people, therefore face a huge compensation bill for a project that has brought far more harm than good.

(Main source: Underwriting Bribery: Export Credit Agencies and Corruption, *The Corner House December 2003, pps.14-15.)*

The prospect of legal claims for damage, caused by adverse climate change "events", has increased alarmingly over recent years. Not surprisingly OPIC's failures to safeguard against these changes have come in for attack. In August 2002 Greenpeace and Friends of the Earth (FoE) USA, several individuals and the cities of Boulder, Oakland and Arcatas, filed a lawsuit against both OPIC and Ex-Im, accusing them of not conducting adequate environmental reviews, before supporting projects which contribute to global warming.[48]

Business as Usual at the EDC

In early 2001, Canada's Auditor-General revealed that EDC, the country's export credit agency (then the Export Development Corporation, now Export Development Canada) had implemented its own governance framework correctly in only two out of the twenty-six projects that the government reviewed.

Doubtless the Auditor-General had before him a report produced the previous year by the NGO Working Group on the EDC, convened by the Halifax Initiative, a coalition formed in 1994 to press for reforms in international financial institutions. Among EDC-sponsored projects criticised by the Working Group were the Marcopper mine, part-owned by Placer Dome, which was responsible for a massive tailings discharge in 1996[49], and Papua New Guinea's Ok Tedi copper-gold mine, in which Canada's Inmet Corporation had an 18 per cent share at the time. For a decade and a half, tailings from this operation had been dumped directly into two major rivers, at the rate of 80,000 tonnes a day.[50]

These were not the only precarious mines which enjoyed EDC's provision of political risk insurance. There was also Placer's gold project on Misima Island in Papua New Guinea, insured by EDC in 1988.[51] By the year 2000 a 75 metres thick carpet of piped wastes from this mine was smothering all marine life across twenty square kilometres of seabed.[52] Above all, there had been the massive tailings dam collapse at Guyana's Omai mine in 1995. (See chapter 5.)

Succumbing to public pressure, in October 2001 Canada's International Trade Minister, Pierre Pettigrew, announced amendments to the Export Development Act to give the EDC new policies on disclosure and environmental review. But, although Canada's NGO Working Group on the EDC declared the proposed changes "good", they were "not good enough". They would improve EDC's environmental and public accountability, but fail to ensure the Export Credit Agency's adherence to the country's Environmental Assessment Act and the Access to Information Act.[53]

A year later, the NGO Working Group discovered that EDC's practices were essentially unchanged. (See box below.)

"Canadian companies may be wreaking havoc with public lending; EDC remains secretive" – Ottawa, January 8, 2003

Export Development Canada (EDC) may be helping to finance a number of projects under development by Canadian companies without the necessary environmental and social due diligence, reveals a new report issued today by the NGO Working Group on the EDC. EDC continues to hide the environmental and social risks of its investments from the public, despite a report from the Auditor-General calling for disclosure and transparency, said Fraser Reilly-King, Coordinator for the NGO Working Group on the EDC.

As of October 2001, EDC has started to list projects it may be supporting – although releasing the name of the Canadian companies involved is not mandatory – on its web site. EDC has also begun listing projects before consideration, if the company agrees.

However, there is still no reporting on the implementation of the Environmental Review Directive, and disclosure of the full environmental impact assessment (EIA) remains at the discretion of the company involved. Last week, Trade Minister Pettigrew revealed that EDC would guarantee $328 million in loans to complete the Cernavoda 2 nuclear reactor in Romania, said Shawn Patrick Stensil of the Campaign for Nuclear Phase-out.

Yet, to date, a full environmental impact assessment has never been made available to the public. This is unacceptable, especially given the serious risks involved. This is also in direct contrast to international standards.

Both the World Bank and EDC's US counterparts make the public disclosure of EIAS for controversial projects a prerequisite of project approval. While US export credit agency the Export-Import Bank requires the public availability of this information at least sixty days prior to Board approval, EDC has neither a requirement for disclosure, nor a minimum number of days for doing so.

This is setting a double standard, said Melanie Quevillon of Mining Watch Canada. The Canadian public would be outraged if the government backed a mining project that had potentially devastating impacts on local livelihoods and the environment, without consulting groups prior. Yet in Patagonia, Chile, despite significant opposition and expected environmental impacts, Noranda is still scheduled to go ahead with its Alumysa aluminum smelter. The Working Group has twice asked EDC whether they are involved in Alumysa. On both occasions, their disclosure policy prevented them from saying.

The EDC has also shown interest in backing projects that private investors are hesitant to support, such as Inco's Goro mine project in New Caledonia, says Catherine Coumans of MiningWatch Canada. If the EDC backs this project, Canadian public funds will be put at risk.

EDC is a public financial institution, whose credit rating is guaranteed by the government and whose capital base is derived from taxpayer dollars. In spite of the changes to EDC policy, it seems to be business as usual one year on from the adoption of its Environmental Review Directive, says Mr. Reilly-King. EDC as a crown corporation should be setting the high standards we would expect Canadian companies to follow.

The Working Group's report documents Inco's involvement in a nickel mine in Indonesia, Gabriel Resources' involvement in a gold mine in Romania, Encana's role in the OCP oil pipeline in Ecuador, and Manhattan Mineral's interest in developing a gold mine in Peru.

(Seven Deadly Secrets: what EDC does not want you to know: www.halifaxinitiative.org)

Arms and the Men: Britain's ECGD

"Most of the [British] arms deals and construction projects to build Saddam Hussein's palace were backed by the Export Credit Guarantee Department. It underwrote the loans with which Hussein armed his state and created his chemical weapons. When Saddam didn't keep up with the payments, the ECGD stepped in to pay the companies and banks with taxpayers money. The debt for these deals has been quietly left in the ECGD's spending file for some time... If the interest rate is 8 per cent... payable since 1990... then Iraq owes the ECGD £1,685,760,440.

Unless that debt is cancelled, Iraq, one of the poorest nations on earth, must pay for the arms and palaces that caused its peoples' oppression. This is liberation."[54]

Britain's Export Credit Guarantee Department (ECGD) is the oldest government agency, anywhere in the world, granting credit and political risk insurance to foreign deals by home-based companies. Founded in 1919 it grew to the point where, in the last five years of the twentieth century alone, it issued 17 billion pounds worth of insurance, with between two and ten years cover each.[55] During that period, 6,659 British companies requested an export guarantee, although only just over eight hundred such guarantees were eventually issued. British taxpayers in the meantime have had to pay out between £148 million and £750 million a year when a project collapses, or a country has defaulted on repayment.

ECGD provides PRI cover for both principal and interest value of loan financing, up to 85 per cent of a contract's value. However, it only protects lenders against non-payment directly caused by what the Department (somewhat archly, if not tautologically) terms "reason of political causes of loss" which are "to be specified at the outset, case by case". A policy may be framed, not only to protect against customary losses caused by war, revolt or failure to honour a contract, but also by the "prevention of, or delay in, the payment of external debt by the host government or by that of a third country through which payment must be made".[56]

Despite boasting an "ethical foreign policy" when it came to power in 1997, the "New Labour" government took three more years before stepping back in any way from its traditional export credit backing for arms sales. Until 2000 an estimated one third of issued guarantees went on war-related purposes, the main beneficiaries being Turkey, the Russian Federation, China, Saudi Arabia and Oman.

During the 1980's and 1990's, ECGD's most controversial investments were in Saudi Arabia, Malaysia, and provision made for the sale of Hawk fighter aircraft to Indonesian dictator, Suharto, primarily to attack the people of East Timor. The department supported the Saudi Arabian company Al Yamanah in a deal where between 5 per cent and 25 per cent of the contract payments allegedly ended up in the pockets of middlemen and government officers.[57] Investment in Malaysia's Pergau dam was also linked to an arms deal with the host government. The project would have burdened the British taxpayer with an estimated £100 million more than the likely cost of an alternative electricity supply.[58] The proposal brought down upon the Conservative Party's administration the wrath of many environmental and human rights NGOs. In 1994 the London-based World Development Movement successfully challenged the deal in court, helping establish a government's "fiduciary duty" to refuse investment in uneconomic foreign projects.[59]

Meanwhile the ECGD had been squandering more funds on two manifestly corrupt overseas ventures. Bangladesh's Kafco fertiliser plant was indemnified in 1990 by export credit guarantees secured from ECGD, JBIC (Jexim) of Japan and Italy's Sace. The scheme became dogged by charges of corruption, bribery, overpricing, cost overruns and outright theft. During Kafco's hapless "development" the Bangladesh government was forced to use precious foreign exchange to buy its fertiliser at international prices. Adding insult to injury, the government also had to subsidise the plant's gas supplies while Bangladesh's own citizens paid double the unit cost.[60]

From 1994 (until late 2003), ECGD also supported the Lesotho Highlands Water Project, along with France's Coface, Germany's Hermes and – yet again – Sace. Intended to divert water to South Africa, the project was distinguished more for its ability to siphon money into the pockets of various politicians and middlemen.[61]

Failing to learn from these gross errors of judgment, the ECGD went on to promise backing for the construction company, Balfour Beatty's £200 million participation (also backed by US Ex-Im) in the Asea Brown Boveri (ABB)-led consortium behind the Ilisu dam on Turkey's Tigris river. The dam would have put at risk the livelihoods of thousands of the country's Kurdish farmers and the irrigation of parts of Iraq and Syria.[62]

Ilisu's financial package was to be arranged by the Union Bank of Switzerland (UBS), with roughly half the construction costs met by imports from Western Europe and the USA. Underwriting the potentially disastrous undertaking were Britain's usual prospects: Hermes, Sace and Jexim, along with ECAS from Portugal, Sweden, Switzerland and the USA. Already, by November 1998, the Swiss export credit agency, Exportrisikogarantie (ERG), had approved provisional export credit support of 470 million Swiss francs for Ilisu contracts concluded by two domestic companies, Sulzer Hydro and ABB. Sace also approved a US$152 million guarantee for the Italian company Impregilo, although this had to be confirmed by the Interministerial Committee on Economic Planning of having SACE formally requested an opinion on its financial involvement in the project.[63] Finally, public pressure forced Balfour Beatty to withdraw from the Ilisu project and, in November 2001, ECGD cancelled its cover.[64]

Summer 2000 found nearly thirty British development, human rights and other NGOs, demanding that the ECGD limit its support to projects consistent with poverty reduction, promotion of human rights and mitigation of adverse climate change. In response, the British government's Department of Trade and Industry provided ECGD with a "mission statement" which trotted out the familiar concerns about promoting sustainable development, buttressing smaller companies and "beefing up" environmental monitoring.[65] Although short-term contracts were "privatised", day-to-day control of export insurance reverted to the ECGD (control having been passed to the

Treasury in 1998, as a result of massive Asian and Russian defaults on international loans that year.)[66]

The first year of the new millennium saw the publication of a report by two British research groups which concluded that the department was still providing an average annual subsidy of no less than £227 million to the "defence sector".[67] Although the government promised no longer to cover arms sales to the worlds sixty-two poorest nations, it continued to back British Aerospace (BAe)'s supply of Hawk fighter aircraft and spare parts to Suharto's successors in Indonesia.[68] (In 2003 Blair's administration allowed the signing of another contract between BAE and Al Yamanah, the Saudi Arabian company accused of corruption two decades earlier.)[69]

By 2004 it was not only critics of the very concept of export credit guarantees who were taking issue with ECGD. In March that year John Tyler, chair of the British Exporters Association, complained to a government trade and industry select committee of a general lack of business confidence in the department. The ECGD was no longer willing to invest in "risky" countries such as Libya and Serbia, declared Mr. Tyler, while other export credit agencies – specifically of old friends from Germany, the US and Italy – were proving more amenable to British corporate needs – and were cheaper too.[70] The Department of Trade and Industry also concluded that ECGD was more expensive than its rivals, with less cover available than "most other countries' equivalent agencies";[71] a parliamentary enquiry in June considered this was due to the ECGD's refusal to finance exports (such as arms).

Under attack from all sides, it seemed as if the world's oldest government-supported export credit agency couldn't win. On the one hand it was driving away its business clientele; on the other, virtually every one of its major investments triggered outrage from British civil society groups.

A Pipeline to Disaster

Nowhere was this better demonstrated than in regard to one of the biggest projects ever backed by the World Bank's MIGA and – to the tune of £83 million – by the ECGD. The 1,020 mile Baku-Tbilisi-Ceyhan pipeline is currently being constructed by BTC, a consortium led by Britain's largest company, BP, to carry oil to Turkey from the Caspian Sea. It is the world's largest export pipeline, boasting a production capacity of nearly four millions barrels a day by 2010.

From its inception in 2002, the project ran up hard against Turkish and British environmental and human rights campaigners.[72] Two years later, there was a profoundly alarming checklist of potentially disastrous consequences stemming from Baku-Tbilisi-Ceyhan's construction and operation. These included large scale toxic spills adding to contamination of the already-blighted Caspian Sea; the scarring of existing national parks; threats to hundreds of Turkey's endemic species, including vertebrates living within, or near, the pipeline corridor; and earthquakes or terrorist attacks resulting in massive and uncontrollable pollution.[73] Not least, there was a high probability that the human rights of communities in conflict-ridden Azerbeijan, Georgia and Turkey would be further violated by "security" forces employed to push the project through.

In response to these widely-canvassed fears, BP set up a Caspian Development Advisory Panel (CDAP) in 2003. This made BP the effective government over the pipeline corridor. Some have praised the British oil giant for its readiness to apply human rights norms to its operations, and getting the Turkish government to abide by them.[74] Others – including Amnesty International – argued that, on the contrary, the deal subverts the civil rights of those living or working within the project's ambit.[75]

A private dossier, compiled by four experienced professionals working on the pipeline, was sent to *The Independent* newspaper in summer 2004, exposing what the British national newspaper called "an environmental time bomb".[76] Allegedly BP's contractors and subcontractors had been guilty of a series of major botches, cost-cutting and dangerous, shoddy, workmanship, in an effort to get the project completed on time. The company had made a "major mistake" in handing control of the Turkish section of the pipeline to a Turkish government-owned company, Botas, on a fixed-price contract. The whistle-blowers' document recounted a familiar litany. Builders had severed villages water supplies, flooded farmland and allowed oil seepages. Insufficient checks were being made to prevent the pipe buckling in earthquake zones; crucial welding work often failed inspections; workers handled toxic coating materials without proper health and safety equipment.

Perhaps worse, those who complained of these delinquencies were sacked or made to leave. Dennis Adams, a Briton who quit unpaid after six weeks, said pipes were left exposed far longer than specifications allowed, and trenches filled with materials which might allow uncontrolled movement of the pipes. "Safety violations were occurring at all times, including [against] workers in deep unprotected and unstable areas... It is quite obvious that [BP] are not in control of the Turkish section of this pipeline."[77] Several other engineers were sacked after making complaints. One – with 35 years experience – highlighted a problem with the drainage system at Ceyhan terminal, that allowed toxins to flow straight into the ground. Another, employed as a weld-coatings inspector, claimed that "numerous" welds had to be redone while many others had been laid before inspection.[78]

In 1995, ECGD had provided re-insurance for a US$64.8 million MIGA policy covering the development of a gas field in Tunisia. This marked the first time the World Bank concluded a reinsurance agreement with the British government. (In fact it was also the first time MIGA had insured a gas project, or any venture in Tunisia.)[79]

Seven years later, in 2002, the ECGD re-insured a coal mine (linked to a steel project), with first-line insurance coming from Sace. This was to be constructed by a British company in Iran, close to the Afghanistan border, with £17 million worth of contracts to British companies expected to follow. Diplomatic relations had been resumed with the Iranian government following New Labour's attempts to confront the "war on terrorism" alongside its European partners.[80]

Dubious Efficacity

In a typically antipodean "no nonsense" fashion, the Australian Export and Finance Insurance Corporation (EFIC) states clearly that its "mission" is to "increase Australia's exports". There are no namby-pamby assertions of assisting poorer countries to trade domestically-produced goods, or boosting sustainable development for the poor.[81] Like the World Bank (whose pollution and abatement rules it follows as "guidelines") the Corporation classifies environmental risks under three categories, claiming to insure on average only one high-risk "A" class project per year. These are operations "likely to have significant adverse impacts that may be irreversible, affect vulnerable groups, involve large scale displacement and resettlement or affect significant cultural or natural heritage sites".[82]

Papua New Guinea's Lihir mine (see chapter 7) clearly meets all these high-risk criteria. Once OPIC had "declined" to insure the project – a fact well-publicised by Sydney's Mineral Policy Institute (MPI) among others[83] – and the World Bank had expressed its own misgivings – Rio Tinto (RTZ-CRA) would doubtless have stressed how important the project was to EFIC's mission. After all, it was potentially the biggest gold mine in Australasia. Nonetheless, one insider has reported that, when Rio Tinto first approached EFIC, the agency refused to provide insurance cover unless the company hired an anthropologist to monitor "gender issues".[84] Soon afterwards an anthropologist, Martha McIntyre, was taken on to perform the task. and PRI was granted.

Papua New Guinea's annual 2002 "Country Risk Assessment", as gauged by EFIC, was distinctly alarming and alarmist. Self-evidently PNG was suffering the classic "curses": over-dependency on long lines of credit and income from natural resource extraction; economic "overheating" through spurts of internal spending; high inflation and massive devaluation of the local currency, the kina. From the late 1980's until the turn of the millenium, the gulf between early promise and actual performance gaped wider and wider. The Ok Tedi, Misima and Tolukuma mines were plagued by community discontents, prompting both legal and direct action by local villagers. All three mines are due to close by 2011 and only Lihir "will still have a life ahead of it," pronounced EFIC's Chief Economist, Roger Donnelly in 2001.[85]

PNG's "asset risk" – a key component of PRI assessment – was unacceptably high, said EFIC, partly because "several projects have got dragged into either tribal feuds (sic), landowner/miner disputes or secessionist disputes". The "main risk" from now on was "creeping" expropriation, characterised by EFIC as "the appropriation of income and market value through arbitrary and retrospective change of taxes and regulations".[86] (Or, in plainer English, an attempt by successive PNG governments to claw back what they were forced to surrender under the very policies endorsed and enforced by EFIC and the World Bank.)

Latching onto Lihir, as the (only) bright star in a gloom-laden firmament, left EFIC increasingly exposed. On June 30 2000, the Mineral Policy Institute (MPI) announced that the mine had "spilt cyanide into the ocean... This is the third cyanide accident by Australian mining companies operating overseas in less than half a year" said MPI's Director, Geoff Atkins. "In this case the government actually supported the development of an unsound mine... Lihir's [waste disposal] practices are totally unacceptable in Australia. The Lihir proposal approved by EFIC uses 1,800 tonnes of highly toxic sodium cyanide annually to extract gold at the mine site. The process leaves considerable cyanide concentrations in the tailings... EFIC's loans are characterised by a veil of secrecy masquerading as a commercial in-confidence policy.

"Scandal surrounding many of EFIC's loans has forced the government to consider new regulations for its loans. The Australian government must apply the same environmental and social standards for lending on overseas Australian projects as would apply to them if they were proposed within the country."[87]

A Future Unsecured

In mid-2001 a number of Export Credit Agencies collectively decided not to back what they called "unproductive expenditure". Ostensibly the term describes guarantees which do not contribute to social or economic development, poverty reduction and sustainable development. In practice it means precious little (as the case histories in this book graphically illustrate); indeed, we might well ask what it *could* mean, given current practices. Export credit remains wedded to the exploits of multinational enterprises, with profit as the impregnable bottom line; or to projects (especially extractive ones) of limited "life" and fluctuating, market-dependent, returns. Vague "social licences" are affixed to dubious ventures, without any insistence on community-control or absolute transparency in project concept and design.[88] In almost every instance, the principle of prior, fully informed consent (or more appropriately "dissent") is denied.

Looking forward another five years, it may be that some ECAs will be persuaded to step back from certain types of cover, notably for armaments export and manufacture. However, the collapse of Britain's "ethical foreign policy" in 2002 showed that, even where the mandate exists to cancel unacceptable contracts, it will be undermined by threats of legal action for breach of contract and the pervasive demand of "jobs for the boys".

Export Credit Guarantees and political risk insurance cover, for extractive industries and power projects, may also decline. But this is less likely if the World Bank continues refusing to accept the findings of its own 2004 Extractive Industries Review (EIR). (See Chapter 3.) Nor would such a major public policy swing deter many private insurers from continuing to back highly dubious projects in the field. It is to these that we now turn.

Notes

1   Lester B Pearson, Chairman, *Partners in Development: Report of the Commission on International Development*, Praeger Publishers, New York, 1969.

2   Patricia Adams, *Odious Debts: Loose Lending, Corruption and the Third World's Environmental Legacy*, Probe International, Toronto, and Earthscan, London, 1991, p. 90.

3   Susan Hawley, *Underwriting Bribery: Export Credit Agencies and Corruption*, Briefing 30, The Corner House, Sturminster Newton, UK, 2003.

4   *South African Business Week*, exact date unknown, 2002.

5   *MIGA Draft Annual Report 2004*, Washington DC, May 24 2004, p. 11.

6   *Underwriting Bribery*, op cit, p. 2.

7   Bruce Rich, *Export credit agencies: the need for more rigorous common policies, procedures and guidelines to future sustainable development*, Environmental Defense Fund, Washington, 1998, p. 6.

8   *Underwriting Bribery*, op cit, pps. 6-7.

9   *Underwriting Bribery,* op cit, p. 13.

10   *Underwriting Bribery,* op cit, p. 15.

11   Titi Soentoro (Bioforum) and Stephanie Fried (EDF), *Case study: Export Credit Agency finance in Indonesia,* Washington DC, 2002; see also *Pulping the people,* Down To Earth, London, 1997.

12   Soentaro and Fried, ibid.

13   *Mining Journal* (MJ), London, November 10 1995, *Financial Times* (FT), London, November 8 1995.

14   OPIC, *Overseas Private Investment Corporation Environmental summary of Lihir Gold Project, Papua New Guinea,* Washington DC, August 8 1997.

15   Soentaro and Fried, op. cit.; Tracy Glynn, *Letter to Harvey Himberg, OPIC, JATAM,* Jakarta, February 2 2002.

16   *Report on Unocal in East Kalimantan,* Down to Earth, 2002 *www.gn.apc.org//dte/480+G.html;* see also: www.gn.apc.org/dte/470+G.html; Press statement, Environmental Defense Fund, USA, April 2 2003.

17   *MJ,* April 4 2003.

18   *MJ,* June 7 2002; *MJ,* August 13 2004.

19   *FT,* May 8 1997.

20   *FT,* March 6 1997.

21   *FT,* March 20 1998.

22   *FT,* November 6 1998.

23   OPIC also supplied PRI to the Ok Tedi mine in 1983, a project many observers viewed with trepidation at the time. The mine's operator, BHPBilliton, was belatedly to confess that it should never have been built – a view apparently shared by at least one staff member of OPIC at the time: source:personal communication.

24   Sullay Kamara, *Mined Out,* FOE UK and Orient, Freetown, 1997 page 8; see also Chapter page 3 of this book.

25   *FT,* March 6 1997.

26   David Gordon, *Kamchatka at Risk: Gold and the Struggle for Sustainability, Multinational Monitor* (MM), Washington DC, January-February 1996, page 21.

27   *MM,* ibid.

28   *MM,* ibid.

29   *MM,* ibid.

30   *MM,* ibid.

31   *Globe and Mail,* Toronto, August 8 2000.

32   *MM,* ibid.

33   Pacific Environment and Resource Center Press release, December 18 1996.

34   *Globe and Mail,* op cit.

35   *Globe and Mail,* ibid.

36   *Kinross Annual Report* 2003.

37   See Arundhati Roy, *Peace and the new corporation liberation theology,* Sydney Peace Prize lecture, delivered at the University of Sydney, Australia, November 4 2004.

38   *Oil and Gas Journal*, US, July 8 1996; *Drillbits and Tailings*, August 2 1996, Project Underground, San Francisco, page 11.

39   Friends of the Earth US and Amazon Watch, Press release, December 10 1999; San Francisco Chronicle, December 16 1999.

40   *FT*, June 16 1999.

41   *FT*, May 22-23 2004.

42   *MJ*, August 6 2004.

43   In May 2001 OPIC also sued the Indonesian government for breach of an undertaking to supply electricity from the power utility, PLN, and to construct a second plant. Since the contracts had actually been signed with the notoriously corrupt Suharto regime, the newly-democratised government claimed – surely with justification – that the suit was redundant. The argument did not prevail and the Indonesians had to fork out US$260 million in compensation. See *Underwriting Bribery: Export Credit Agencies and Corruption,* The Corner House, 2003 page 5. For background see the *Wall Street Journal,* May 15 2000; also S Fried and T Soentoro, *Export Credit Agency Finance in Indonesia: Ecological Destruction and Corruption,* Environmental Defense Fund and Bioforum, December 2000.

44   *Frontline*, Mumbai, August 21 2004.

45   *FT*, February 29 2004.

46   *FT*, ibid.

47   *FT*, ibid.

48   *FT*, July 14 2003.

49   Ré Marcopper, *Undermining the forests: the need to control transnational mining companies: a Canadian case study*, Forest Peoples Foundation, et al pps.56-70, Moreton in Marsh, January 2000.

50   See NGO Working Group on the Export Development Corporation, *Reckless Lending: How Canada's Export Development Corporation Puts People and the Environment at Risk,* Halifax Initiative, Ottawa, March 2000, pps. 6-7 & 9.

51   *MJ*, February 26 1988.

52   *New Scientist*, London, November 11 2000.

53   See *Miningwatch Canada Newsletter* 5, Spring-summer 2001; www.miningwatch.ca

54   Mark Thomas, *New Statesman*, London, April 21 2003.

55   *Guardian*, January 26 2000.

56   ECGD website, June 26 2004.

57   *Guardian,* November 27 2003.

58   *Report of the National Audit Office,* UK, October 2003, p. 5.

59   *Underwriting Corruption*, op cit p. 10.

60   *Underwriting Corruption*, op cit p. 9.

61   *Underwriting Corruption*, op cit, p. 10.

62   *FT*, July 14 2000.

63   Ilisu Dam Campaign, *Who's behind the Ilisu dam,* London, 2000

64 ECGD website, op cit.

65 *FT*, July 25 2000.

66 *FT*, ibid.

67 Saferworld and Oxford Research Group, *The Subsidy for British government financial support for Arms Exports and the Defence Industry*, Oxford, July 2000.

68 *The Independent*, July 27 2002.

69 *Guardian*, November 27 2003.

70 *FT*, March 31 2004.

71 *FT*, June 16 2004.

72 See, *Some Common Concerns: imagining BP's Azerbeijan-Georgia-Turkey Pipelines System*, The Cornerhouse, Sturminster Newton, UK, 2002.

73 *The Independent*, July 26 2004.

74 Personal communication from London-based class action lawyer to author, 2003.

75 *The Independent*, ibid.

76 *The Independent*, ibid. The newspaper had exposed the likely "havoc" of the world's biggest oil pipeline eight months earlier in its edition of October 28 2003.

77 *The Independent*, July 26 2004, ibid.

78 *The Independent*, ibid.

79 MIGA, *Annual Report*, 1995.

80 *FT*, February 8 2002.

81 *EFIC Environmental Policy*, EFIC website 2002.

82 *EFIC Environmental Policy* op cit.

83 Email from Mineral Policy Institute, Sydney, December 3 1997.

84 Personal communication, July 15 1998.

85 *Papua New Guinea Country Risk Assessment*, EFIC, Sydney, December 21 2001.

86 *Country Risk Assessment* EFIC, ibid.

87 Press release: *Oz Government Shares Responsibility For Cyanide Kill; Australian Government Financed Lihir Mine Cyanide Dumping*, Mineral Policy Institute, Sydney, June 20 2002.

88 On transparency, see Geoff Evans, James Goodman, Nina Lansbury, Politicising Finance, in (eds Evans, Goodman, Lansbury) *Moving Mountains: Communities confront mining & globalisation*, Zed Books, London, 2001, p. 41.

CHAPTER 2

The Providers

"Not much happens without risk, so not much happens without insurance. Roads and buildings wouldn't be constructed, goods and services wouldn't be produced and our world wouldn't develop." (From a statement by The Reinsurance Research Council, Toronto, 1998.)

As the world grows perceptibly more insecure, and political instability increases, so insurers are confronted with previously unforeseen dilemmas. Should a recently-elected democratic government be obliged to honour an unacceptable construction contract signed by a former dictator? Who will compensate the hundreds of thousands victimised by preventable industrial diseases, the vast dimensions of which have only lately been revealed? It is reasonable to expect such bucks to stop with the insurance industry. Certainly public and private insurers, brokerages, and specialised insurance companies are developing "products" to forestall their being overwhelmed by new types of compensation claim in the future. An example of this is Royal & Sun Alliance's Environmental Impairment Liability (EIL), offered against "specified environmental risks, often related to contaminated land in the US".[1] Definitions of "political risk" have also become more refined, while merging with older concepts of liability. (See box "Redefining PRI".)

Redefining PRI
The following are some of the "political risks" against which a company or contracting firm can insure themselves:

Asset Expropriation
Those who buy this type of insurance cover reside, and stow their valuables, in the North – while transacting deals in the South where they have their money-spinning assets: real estate, tradable commodities, and access to raw materials, labour forces, plants, refineries and mines.

The expropriation of these assets can take many forms, from the burning down of your south Asian godown (storehouse); discrimination against your business by local people (boycott); a government identifying your firm as belonging to, or serving, the wrong ethnic group – to outright state take-over. Then there is "creeping expropriation," described by the Meridian Finance Group, a key provider of PRI, as "a series of individual government actions which, taken together, effectively result in expropriation".

Insurers include in this category the failure by an "owner" to secure their dividends, royalties or other funds, following the sale of an asset, or disposal of an investment, in the country of ownership.[2] It is this definition of "ownership" that lies at the heart of what insurees are most afraid of losing (apart from their own lives). Others might assert that these are precisely the assets which should be surrendered to their "true" owners.

Currency inconvertability
Two main types of political risk attach to the conversion of local into foreign currency (sometimes called "hard currency"). Depending on the prevailing exchange rate, buying local goods and services, and paying for them in local denominations, can make huge savings for the overseas company. But, it may also result in major losses: for example, when wages and other running costs are priced in national currencies (such as the South African Rand or the Australian dollar), which then rise against the US dollar as the currency used to pay production costs. Insurers don't provide cover against this; such risks are intrinsic to the global financial architecture.

However, insurance may be provided where a government refuses to exchange a currency, or where hard currency is short, and firms therefore cannot convert their locally-held cash.

Political violence
This particular field is wide open to the application of PRI, used to cover non-payment of dues, loss of income and equity investment, "business interruption," or the damage and destruction of political assets due to war, expropriation, civil unrest, rioting, strikes, armed uprising, insurrection, terrorism, sabotage, and "other politically motivated violence or acts of malice".[3]

Contract Repudiation...
... not only covers the reneging of payments made under contract with a foreign government, but also alleged failures by a private party in the respective country to provide goods or services.

Licence cancellation

A contract may be cancelled by a government, while other parties (such as groups of workers or civil society protestors) could, *de facto*, make it impossible to implement one.

Wrongful Calling of Guarantees...

... is a policy, purchased by exporters, to guarantee that their contracts will be observed by foreign governments or public sector buyers. It protects the insured against the buyer's unilateral extension of contract terms, or an "unfair calling" of the guarantees.

Non-delivery by foreign supplier

This applies in a "high-risk" foreign country, where contracts are frustrated due to political events, government actions outside the suppliers' control, and the government's seizure of goods in transit or in the country of origin.

The Pyramid of Provision

At the same time, insurance agencies are having to play several different games. Not only must they aggregate sufficient funds from individual policies in order to pay out directly on personal claims. They also have to invest those funds (effectively their clients' money) so as to make a profit in "the market". This is that vast, but often nugatory, matrix of companies, banks, investment institutions, hedge funds, government instruments – all of which promise cake tomorrow in return for the bread put into their stomachs today. These investments are also exposed to increasingly higher risk (companies collapse, banks become bankrupt, governments renege on bonds, corporate and other taxes leap upwards). This requires the insurers themselves to find safeguards (as the Netherlands' government did recently by launching a government sponsored claims' "terrorism pool" for the Dutch bank and insurer, ING).[4] We might usefully picture this process as "climbing down the pyramid".

At the top of this schematic edifice are the hundreds of millions of people taking out life and property insurance with companies like AIG (see *Who Dares Profits* below), Travelers, Allianz and AXA, or who subscribe regularly to corporate pension funds. In turn those funds invest for profit in the "matrix" just mentioned. At the bottom of the pyramid – and holding much of it together – are the re-insurers. While the needs of global insurers for reinsurance may fluctuate according to circumstances, it has become a vital tool for smaller, specialised, insurance companies.[5]

Admittedly, this is a considerable oversimplification of what happens in practice. Insurers themselves often offer reinsurance, or join a reinsurance consortium (as Allianz did with Swiss Re). They also grant banks specific project financing, or facilitate co-insurance with both government and multilateral agencies on behalf of a policy holder. As a result, projects in emerging markets may attract lower lending rates because the "Country Risk" has been transferred to a highly rated insurer.

Occasionally, too, the state-based Export Credit Agencies (examined in the previous chapter) act as reinsurers. Brokers (like Marsh & McLennan) may offer PRI. And, of course, the huge reinsurance outfits must invest in banks, funds and companies in order to "grow" their capital. But one thing is certain: without solvent, dedicated, reinsurance companies, various blocks within the global financial structure would fast become dislodged.

This is not to say that reinsurance companies are transparent institutions whose workings are obvious to all. Reinsurance, it has been argued, is substantially a "hedging vehicle" or a derivatives' instrument. Such gambling can become as speculative, mysterious – and grotesquely profitable – as placing money on a race-course tote.[6]

John Kay, iconoclastic financial journalist and author of *The Truth About Markets* has gone further, arguing that trading in risks (the essence of reinsurance) has become "more and more disassociated from the real uncertainties in society". Risks may appear to be transferred from vulnerable people to those more capable of dealing with them – often making huge profits for those engaged in risk dealing. Most of us, however, find the benefits are illusory since "most risks traded in securities markets are manufactured by those markets themselves".[7]

As a graphic example of such chicanery, Kay takes us back to July 1998, soon after a huge explosion shattered the North Sea oil rig, Piper Alpha, operated by Occidental Petroleum (Oxy) – an old client of Lloyds, the British reinsurance veteran. (See *Titan Going Under: Lloyds* below.) According to Kay the oil company had been re-insured many times over, thanks to the practice of reinsurers passing policies among themselves. Scandalously, Lloyds failed to make its own trading agents, or syndicates ("Names"), who did the reinsuring, aware that they were being used in this fashion. Although Occidental's initial insurance claim was "only" a billion dollars, the Names had to fork out sixteen times this amount, "nearly destroying the Lloyds market"[8] and ruining a number of the Names themselves. A savage irony was that Oxy could have found the whole US$16 billion out of its own annual profits.[9]

This chapter tours the reader briefly around the base of our pyramid. Along the way we meet key re-insurers (including the discredited Lloyds), the insurance market giant AIG, some specialist insurance companies particularly relevant to the minerals industry, and the leading global consultancy supposedly advising insurers and others on the nature of risks – but sometimes going beyond that brief. The chapter ends with a discussion of "surety bonding," a safeguard increasingly demanded by environmental and community groups as the *sine qua non* for any new mining project, but which seems to be fast fading as a viable insurance tool.

Reinsurance

"Selling insurance to insurers," is how Walter Kielholz, Swiss Re's CEO, in 2002 pithily described the function of his company, the world's second biggest reinsurer. Reinsurance has also been characterised as business gained from investing against future claims, much of it obtained through aggregated life insurance premiums.[10] There are four basic forms of reinsurance, dubbed "treaty", "facultative", "program" and "finite". (The last two are not relevant to our discussion). The first covers a portfolio of risks, such as thousands of car insurance policies attached to billions of dollars worth of property. The second (also known as "individual risk") covers part of a large-scale liability under a single policy, such as a mine, smelter, chemical or fireworks factory.[11]

Globally, reinsurance is a US$140 billion industry, managed by around twenty companies, based predominantly in Europe and the US (the Korean Reinsurance Company seems the exception that proves the rule). General Electric, the world's biggest multinational, has three reinsurance subsidiaries: the Employers Reinsurance Corporation, GE Reinsurance and GE Frankona Re.[12] However, smaller insurers may also offer reinsurance, and some of these are listed below.

Without reinsurance, according to Forbes Global, "big scale business could hardly take place".[13] Until the Lloyds scandal of 1996 the industry stayed liquid and largely buoyant. Nonetheless, despite its gravity, the Lloyds "meltdown" appeared at the time to be an anomaly, deriving from the company's unique use of its individual re-insurers, the so-called "Names". It was not until the US stock market crash in 2000, followed by the fatal attacks on US citizens of September 11 2001, the perfidy of Enron, and similar accounting scandals, that leading reinsurers became seriously alarmed about their solvency. Previously they had dealt with other peoples' crises and profited from a growing sense of the pervasiveness of uncertainty. Now they had an overwhelming crisis of their own, hardly mitigated by the climate change-related droughts and floods of 2002; nor an accusation that some life insurers had been cooking the books, using more accountancy glutamate than Enron itself. Independent consultant, Neil Cazalet, told the *Financial Times* in late 2003 that these insurance companies had also been listing future profits as current assets and thereby "hid[ing their] liabilities by reinsuring them".[14]

If there were a specific alarum, it sounded in 2001 when Gerlin Global Reinsurance – then enjoying sixth place in the global hierarchy – went into liquidation, raising "numerous questions" among primary insurers about the stability and credit worthiness of its big brothers.[15] Gerlin's collapse, announced Kielholz of Swiss Re in 2002, "...destroyed so much capital in the insurance industry that there is now severe imbalance between supply and demand".[16] By late 2002, Standard & Poor's had downgraded five life insurers in Japan alone.[17] Reinsurance rates shot up by at least 30 per cent and so did the claims. The months between early 2002 and late 2003 were anxious times for the likes of Munich Re and Swiss Re: the anxiety has diminished only fleetingly since.

Munich Re/Allianz/Ergo/American Re

The world's biggest reinsurer is Germany's Munich Re, until recently heading a consortium with Allianz and the HVB bank, which distributed primary insurance products through Ergo. In the *Annus Horribilis* of 2002, Munich Re lost its triple-A credit rating bestowed by Moody's Investors Services,[18] following claims for damage caused by unprecedented flooding over much of Europe that year.[19] The world's second major assessor of creditworthiness, Standard & Poor's (S&P) also downgraded Munich Re, from AA to A the following year, just as the company suffered (like other insurers) from a fall in share prices of the key companies in which it invests. True, it became the first re-insurer to gain entry into China but, for the foreseeable future, the world's most populous country is likely to account for only a minor part of its business.[20]

In late 2003, Munich Re tried to convince the market that it was once more in the ascendant and would recoup its AA status with S&P. But Standard & Poor's viewed Munich's minimum rights issue of Euro 3.8 million that year with marked scepticism.[21] A little later, the company was indeed "dragged down by hurricanes... typhoons" and power failures across north America.

As a result the company suffered its first net loss in a century, an estimated Euro 100 million (us$118 million).

Allianz is Europe's biggest insurer in terms of its premium base, as well as the owner since 2000 of Dresdner, Germany's second major bank. Thanks to both "natural" catastrophes and asbestos-related claims, Allianz also suffered considerable losses in 2002[22] for which it had to find an additional us$750 million in reserves.[23] In November 2003 Allianz and Munich Re began "ripping up" their century-old pledge to maintain cross-stakes in each other's businesses. Allianz had to start selling shares in its brother company in order to recapitalise itself.[24] Apparently, by mid 2004, Munich Re had returned to "the black", but it seemed possible that the German giant would soon lose rank to its closest rival, Swiss Re.

Meanwhile American Re, Munich's us subsidiary, found its income falling as it withdrew cover against terrorism, and stopped underwriting professional indemnity, company directors' and officers' liability, and worker's compensation.[25]

Swiss Re: the Innovator

Visitors to the heart of London's business district ("the City") are often startled by the gherkin at its heart. This is the new British headquarters for the world's second largest reinsurer, Swiss Re. Shaped like an unprepossessing vegetable in order to capture sunlight, improve ventilation and reduce fuel consumption, sceptics may view the edifice merely as a sop to environmentalism. Arguably, however, Swiss Re is more than just a blast of hot (or cool) air. Among Sustainablebusiness.com's top twenty "sustainable" businesses for 2003 (in terms of internal functioning and environmental standards) Swiss Re was included alongside more demonstrably "green" candidates.

In June 2004 the company identified global warming as one of the top three global risks (alongside "terrorism" and "demographic change").[26] It earnestly favours an enforceable treaty to curb greenhouse gas emissions – to which end it has set up The Climate Group, jointly with the Rockefeller Brothers. Obviously, the initiative is self-serving, as are the company's policies to insure wind farms and support carbon emissions' trading. Swiss Re's great fear is of unmanageable exposure to climate-related health risks, especially in its Chinese, Indian and South African developing markets.[27]

As the last millennium got bowed out, Swiss Re began offering insurance contracts (essentially as credit facilities) directly to companies in order that they could safeguard against adverse events.[28] This was intended to avoid the uncertainties of raising new capital in the market. The practice has since been followed by Munich Re. But, like its German cousin, Swiss Re was downgraded from its Triple A rating by Standard and Poor's in late 2002. The firm struggled to make ends meet during early 2003,[29] shortly after Credit Suisse sold its remaining shares in the company,[30] sullied by claims that it hid away hundreds of millions of dollars purloined from the Philippine exchequer by the late dictator, Fernando Marcos.[31]

In mid 2003, Swiss Re and Mitsui Sumitomo Insurance of Japan launched one of the world's first "catastrophe risk swaps" at a cost of US$100 million. The two groups pledged to bail each other out in the event of overwhelming but "unlikely events," such as a typhoon or hurricane. Ten swaps had been negotiated by August that year.[32]

Zurich Financial Services Group/Converium/Centre Re/zna

Zurich Financial Services is one of Europe's biggest insurance companies; it includes British subsidiaries Allied Dunbar, Eagle Star, Threadneedle Asset Management, as well as the US-based Farmer's Insurance. The majority of its income derives from non-life insurance provision[33] although, in early 2004, it announced a plan to return to life insurance as a "core business".[34] Centre Re is its US-based reinsurance subsidiary.

Like the other insurance majors Zurich recently suffered from a lack of "liquidity" (dwindling ready cash) and falling share prices.

By late 2002, this triggered speculation that the company might even have to freeze its businesses.[35] The company managed to generate a billion dollars of risk-based capital within the first nine months of 2003, but this was at the cost of a significant number of jobs, the sale of half its Zurich Life subsidiary to Bank One in the US, and a reluctant re-focussing on property and casualty cover.[36]

Until 2001, Converium was Zurich's reinsurance arm, before being spun off on its own. A brief two years later, the company had to bid for new capital to "shore up its battered balance sheet".[37] Hardly did this strategy appear to succeed (Spring 2004 saw a loss of US$3.4 billion turned into a US$2 billion profit)[38] than Converium chalked up a record second quarterly loss of US$660 million and, once again, had to seek further capital.[39]

Zurich North America (zna) is a member of the Zurich Financial Services group, through its subsidiary Zurich Emerging Markets (zems). zna wrote US$13.6 billion in premiums in 2002. Along with other PRI providers it offers project developers, financial institutions and contractors, "protection that can help control losses associated with political risk in emerging markets".[40] It transacts PRI business in some seventy "developing" countries in Latin America, Asia, Africa, the Middle East and eastern Europe, based on what the company calls "flexible underwriting": cover is available up to US$100 million per insured risk, for a maximum of 15 years.

A ZNA affiliate, Remediation Stop Loss (RSL), enables insured parties to mitigate the "inherent risk and uncertainty of environmental remediation projects by securing coverage for remediation costs that exceed a designated self-insured retention (SIR) for the covered project". In other words, if a company cannot make good its damage through its own insurance policy, RSL will ride to the rescue. It also promises to meet the "special needs of commercial real estate owners, managers, investors, developers and others who have to address the consequences of environmentally impaired property (so-called brown field sites)". Coverage in these cases can reach $300 million "subject to reinsurance availability".[41]

In effect (or so it claims) ZNA "transfer[s] environmental risk to a financially secure company" (namely itself), providing borrowers with an alternative to traditional environmental impact assessment. The policy covers "historical contamination, regulatory re-openers of remediated conditions (sic) and new pollution events," including first-party on-site cleanup costs as well as third-party bodily injury, property damage and "defence costs".

Claiming to be "one of the broadest environmental forms in the industry," ZNA also allows the actual, or putative, contaminator to meet third-party claims arising from "pollution events" at insured project sites, including those designated under the US government Superfund and those affected by asbestos, lead and radioactivity. Taken at face value, Zurich's environmental coverage promises a form of rescue for those who would otherwise fall victim to mining companies that go bankrupt, while leaving toxic time bombs in their wake. Cynics may argue, however, that it substitutes ill-defined, and only partial mitigation, for impacts which should have been prevented from the outset.

General ReCologne

The General Re Corporation is a subsidiary of Berkshire Hathaway Inc., owned (around 40 per cent) by the highly successful "market-killing" investment broker, Warren Buffett and his wife. It acts as a holding company for global reinsurance and related risk assessment, risk transfer and risk management operations, priding itself on being a "direct reinsurer" – which simply means it has a relationship with its corporate clients. Berkshire Hathaway uses the so-called "float" – cash collected before claims are paid out – to invest in a growing stable of businesses which, besides General Re, includes National Indemnity and the GEICO Corporation.

General Re holds a controlling interest in Kölnische Rückversicherungs-Gesellschaft AG (Cologne Re). Together, General Re and Cologne Re conduct business as Gen ReCologne, the fourth largest reinsurer worldwide, with a global network of seventy offices, employing over 2,700 staff. It is also the US reinsurance leader.

In March 2003 General ReCologne issued its *Loss and Litigation* report, naming specific corporate offenders in twenty selected countries. Particularly striking in this summary is the enormous recent rise in chemical pollution cases, logged by the European Union's MARS (Major Accident Reporting System). According to the report there was a more than fourfold increase in such cases (up from a dozen to fifty seven, with minor annual fluctuations) between 1985 and 1998. This was despite the dramatic increase over the past fifteen and more years of supposed preventative measures.

Equally alarming was the high proportion of mining failures which have unleashed major chemical pollution during the previous decade. The fourteen cases cited in the report comprised a quarter of the total.

Titan Going Under: Lloyds

Until the late 16th century, when European ships got sunk by weapons, sabotage or sheer carelessness, their owners also often metaphorically sunk without trace. The Venetian Republic then fostered the new concept of sharing the consequences of such catastrophic risks among a group of rich merchants. Thus "marine insurance" was born and, soon afterwards, what we know as "underwriting", an early form of re-insurance or "hedging" against risks.[42] For three hundred and fifteen years Lloyds of London (not to be confused with LloydsTSB, the British high street bank) was the best known and most successful re-insurer anywhere in the world. Indeed, it doesn't regard itself as a company – rather as a "market".

But the "market" almost collapsed in 1996, and again in 1998, following the Piper Alpha disaster. By the end of the century Lloyds had surrendered its pre-eminence, probably for all time. Despite lately scraping towards recovery, its losses in 2001 still topped three thousand million pounds.[43] After corporate reforms the following year, Lloyds re-capitalised itself to the tune of over £14 billion. Its 2003 profits ran close to two billion pounds.[44]

In essence, Lloyds had fallen on its own swords. Vast losses, resulting from ill-judged and fraudulent deals, had threatened to bankrupt many of its 15,000 "Names".[45] The Names were sophisticated speculators: although they faced unlimited liability they safeguarded themselves against it by joining together in their syndicates – a sort of modern equivalent of the medieval guild. Or so they thought. Many were soon ruined and some driven to suicide. One of the victims, a well-known journalist called Adam Raphael, in 1994 published a scathing denunciation of Lloyd's abject failure to assess its true risks, and described the active connivance of some of its upper management in concealing those liabilities.

Lloyds today expresses confidence that it has weathered the storms of the eighties and nineties. It was the biggest single insurer hit by pay-outs, due to the attack on New York's Twin Towers on September 11 2002, but the company claims to have paid all its outstanding dues, to be well set up for future business,[46] and to have limited total premiums to £15 billion.[47] Inevitably, the influence of the legendary Names, Lloyds' financial backbone throughout three centuries, has considerably weakened, though they are still 2,500 strong in number. Less than two decades ago, they provided 100 per cent of the company's capital while today it has drifted to just 13 per cent.[48]

Not that this has prevented some Names from continuing to protest what they believe is the company's abject betrayal of their interests. Some have been taking legal action. Others say that the vast losses, caused by payments in asbestosis damages, had not been guarded against because Lloyds was insufficiently regulated. At Lloyds annual general meeting in June 2004, Sally Noel, who signed up as a Name in 1978, alleged that she and others had been wilfully deceived into taking on liabilities for asbestos claims dating back to the 1940s.[49] The sixty six remaining syndicates (defined by the Financial Times as "mutually-supportive, medium-sized entrepreneurial companies")[50] have been luckier: they now benefit from a central fund, set up by Lloyds to protect against future defaults.

Whatever the truth of allegations relating to asbestos, during the 1950s and 1960s Lloyds had undeniably written thousands of insurance policies for us companies, failing to include clauses relating to environmental damage. After 1970 it tried to limit the damaging consequences of this, by introducing an exclusion clause precluding such claims, other than for "sudden and accidental" events. The us courts, by and large, refused to take Lloyds side.

In 1978 Lloyds was vicariously struck by the fall-out from one of the worst industrial crimes in us history. A subsidiary of Occidental Petroleum (Oxy) had, between 1942 and 1953, dumped 21,800 tons of toxic chemicals in New York state's Love Canal waterway. The detritus polluted residential neighbourhoods and contaminated a landfill site used by children as a playground.[51] This was the trigger for thousands of similar claims across the country,[52] probably the most important of which related to a little-known site that for many years, was at the heart of the US military mass destruction project: the Rocky Mountain Arsenal in Colorado.

It was not until 1980 that the US public belatedly woke up to the appalling damage caused by this closely-guarded operation. Royal Dutch/Shell, among other companies, had manufactured on-site a wide range of pesticides and insecticides, while tapping adjacent freshwater resources to cool its reactors. Contributing to the cocktail were nerve gas, blistering agents and chemical warfare and incendiary devices (components of the "Weapons of Mass Destruction" supplied by the US, Britain and other former allies to the Saddam Hussein regime in Iraq). In response to public exposure of the deadly morass at Rocky Mountain, the US Congress passed the Comprehensive Environmental Response Compensation and Liability Act (CERCLA) – usually known as "the Superfund" – to be administered by the US Environmental Protection Agency (EPA). A cartload of criticisms has been dumped upon the act in intervening years (not least because of the huge fees earned by lawyers, often with no apparent return on the expenditure of public funds). Nonetheless, this was the first piece of national legislation anywhere, to embrace the *diktat* that the "polluter pays". The rules apply even if a company has contributed in only a minor way to identified contamination, or done so after the operations were officially closed.[53] (The biggest and most problematic single category of affected sites has proved to be abandoned mines, especially in the Clark Forks area, also in Colorado.)

In many cases, establishing specific responsibility under CERCLA has proved enormously time-consuming, if not impossible. Even when culprits become identified, debate over who bears the costs, and how extensive should be the remediation, has engaged the EPA and polluting industry in seemingly endless debate. Notable was Rio Tinto's refusal during the nineties to clean-up water pollution, caused by its Kennecott copper-gold mine in Utah, according to a formula produced by the EPA. The British company finally got away with implementing its own plan.

As Adam Raphael points out in his engaging 1994 history of Lloyds, after CERCLA "it was inevitable that companies would seek to shift the burden and look to their insurers for compensation. The result has been an avalanche of litigation, at the heart of which stands Lloyds, one of the major insurers and re-insurers of North American liability policies."[54]

In 1970 the US Army, owner of the Rocky Mountain site, had priced Shell's responsibility for neutralising the contamination at 85 per cent of the total costs.[55] Yet the Dutch/British company continued to use the leaking evaporation basins for another eight years. Finally, when the EPA told Shell in 1983 to clean up at a cost of US$ 2 billion, the oil giant promptly commenced legal action against no less than 220 insurance companies and 400 Lloyds syndicates, which had acted on its behalf during the previous thirty seven years.[56] At the root of Shell's defence was its assertion that Lloyds (as well as the other insurers) – even while charging huge premiums – had failed in its duty to inspect the site and meet its policy obligations. Lloyds produced a robust counter-argument: Shell had been fully aware of the consequences of its activities at the arsenal; there was palpable evidence in the shape of thousands of dead ducks and polluted aquifers which stretched over many miles. For thirty years, said Lloyds, the Anglo-Dutch company had consciously added to the contamination.[57]

Arguments about specific responsibility got tossed between various US courts, until California's Court of Appeal ruled that Shell could not collect on some eight hundred policies issued after 1969 – the date when insurers introduced a clause limiting their responsibilities for pollution. Round one went to Lloyds and its fellow companies. However, the court reserved judgment as to whether Shell had knowingly caused the pollution while both "expecting and intending" it.

For another decade Lloyds managed to staunch the flood of claims by citing its pollution exclusion clause. In 1992, however, it lost a case filed against it by a company guilty of PCB contamination of Lake Michigan. The Illinois Supreme Court declared that Lloyds could only use the exclusion defence if the polluter actually knew – rather than "should have known" – that its discharges would cause damage.[58]

It may be ironic – if not distinctly perverse – that a multinatioal corporation, directly culpable for damaging unsuspecting citizens, should hail a victory against those whose main sin was ignorance and negligence, rather than hands-on criminal activity. But, by the 1990s – and in the US at least – a manifest paradox had become evident: the polluter did not need to pay for its misdeeds, so long as it could pass the bill to its insurers. On discovering this Achilles heel, Lloyds set up an environmental group which sought to alert and inform others belonging to the insurance and reinsurance markets. The company warned that, were insurers and reinsurers to bear the full costs of galloping US claims against pollution, the entire industry might collapse. Surely the US government could not possibly allow this to happen? Lloyds did not believe it would.

According to Adam Raphael, in 1994 the British company was confident that "sooner or later the White House will be forced to intervene" to forestall such a financial disaster.[59] Lloyds' optimism proved well-founded. Not surprisingly, the "adjustment" resulted from the torrent of suits laid by victims of asbestos, the twentieth century's most insidious industrial killer. In late 2003 the Bush administration, backed by insurers and former asbestos product manufacturers, launched a bill to cap these claims at a derisory US$114 billion.[60]

The Asbestos Toll

It was precisely the sudden explosion in asbestos-related claims, during the 1980s and 1990s, that almost sunk the Lloyds ship without trace. By 1994 these claims, in the US alone, were estimated at around US$50 billion dollars – ten times the net asset value of US asbestos producers at that time, and equal to the liquidity of the entire US liability insurance industry.[61] Lloyds had already been forced to pay out an estimated five billion pounds, at an average loss of £170,000 for each of its Names, plunging many of those once-secure and profitable re-insurers into ruin. One lawyer, specialising in asbestos cases, considered that the company's liabilities would rise to more than £30 billion by 2023.[62] And rise they did.

 The year 2002 saw predicted asbestos liabilities shooting up to between US$200 and US$275 billion in the US, and Euro 60 billion in Europe. Two years later the figure of likely deaths from asbestos-related cancer climbed to 100,000 a year in the US, with a peak predicted between 2015 and 2020.[63]

Lloyds had already set about re-insuring itself through Equitas, a vehicle created in 1996 to shoulder its pre-1993 liabilities. By March 2000 the new outfit had set aside £1.7 billion for the purpose.[64] In 2004, Equitas settled two major asbestos-related claims: the first with En-Pro of the US, a manufacturer of industrial products; and the second with the insurance company Travelers.[65] Three years later, however, Equitas came under renewed pressure – as did the Lloyds syndicate Brian Smith, and another global re-insurer, Zurich Financial Services[66] – from compensation suits mounted by former employees of Britain's largest recent manufacturer of asbestos products, Turner & Newall (T&N).

The deadly association between mesothelioma and asbestos was widely confirmed by the 1950s. (In fact, a British parliamentary committee had established asbestos as a cause of cancer in 1931.) But, for many years, T&N continued producing its goods in cavalier disregard of the evidence.[67] When the huge US asbestos producer, Johns-Manville, was forced into bankruptcy in 1982, T&N changed its management and ceased working with the toxic material. But the move came far too late – and not just for thousands of sufferers. As John Kay put it in 2001: "Asbestos proved damaging not only to the lungs of asbestos workers but to the wealth of Lloyds Names. But little of the misery of the latter is helping to relieve the agony of the former."[68]

In 1996 T&N set up its own re-insurance scheme, in order to limit compensation payouts.[69] Shortly afterwards it was "saved" through a takeover by the US-based Federal-Mogul corporation which, in turn, filed for bankruptcy in its home country and for administration in the UK, thus rendering the British subsidiary insolvent.[70] T&N then reconstituted itself as a car-parts manufacturer.

T&Ns plaintiffs finally went to court in early 2003, having secured a favourable ruling from Britain's highest court, the House of Lords.[71] This shouldered the country's second largest general insurer, Royal Sun & Alliance (RSA), alongside the Lloyds syndicate and Equitas, with liabilities potentially reaching £8 billion.[72] The struggle for justice had been protracted. Despite the Lord's unanimous verdict, the Association of British Insurers still took three months before agreeing to launch a packaged "rescue" deal[73] that forced RSA to double its compensations "kitty" to nearly £700 million.[74] Nor is the battle necessarily over. Although RSA had written out employees' liability cover for T&N between 1968 and 1977, it argues that these policies contained certain "get out" clauses. It says that the British manufacturer had also failed to divulge the full extent of its deadly operations.[75]

Meanwhile, because Federal Mogul went into bankruptcy, the 40,000 current and former workers at T&N in Britain fell victim to yet another disgraceful lacuna. Creditors of Federal Mogul had offered only £64 million to the employees pension fund, although it sustained a £875 million deficit on the company's wind-up.[76] The UK government in May 2004 set up an *ad hoc* Pension Protection Fund, but its total funding was only £400 million and, in any case, this had to be shared with 60,000 workers from other companies.[77]

Lloyds may have put parts of its sorry history behind it. But once again, in mid-2004, the company unexpectedly found itself the subject of a multi-million dollar lawsuit with little apparent relevance to its recent travails. Ed Fagan is a US lawyer, renowned for filing lucrative and successful class-action suits against Swiss banks on behalf of Jews robbed of gold during the holocaust. Fagan has now taken up the cudgels on behalf of descendants of African-Americans, seeking massive compensation from Lloyds as the underwriters of vessels which transported millions of slaves in the infamous triangular trade of the 18th-19th centuries.[78]

It seems that the world's oldest, furthest-flung and most deeply compromised re-insurance company, may never fully escape its past.

Who Dares Profits: AIG

> The greatest risk is not taking one... It takes courage to do something that's never been done before. To attempt a feat that goes beyond conventional thinking... No one has better understanding of the inherent risks of daring enterprises than we do.[79]

Late in 2004, the US Justice department accused the American International Group (AIG) of using a "special purposes vehicle" in 2001, to move US$762 million in bad loans, run up by a firm called PNC Services, "off its books". The result of AIG's actions was a boost in PNC's earnings by 52 per cent that year – virtually a carbon copy of Exxon's manoeuvres at roughly the same time. AIG claimed it did nothing wrong; the Justice department was convinced the company committed fraud.[80] Hot on the heels of this accusation came another, and then another. AIG was put under a federal grand jury investigation for rigging insurance quotes;[81] and the US Securities and Exchange Commission claimed it had performed yet another "Exxon", by assisting mobile phone operator, Brightpoint, to hide US$12 million of the latter's losses.[82] AIG declared the allegations "outrageous", while its *primo genitur*, Maurice "Hank" Greenberg, was "sickened" by them.[83] But this was by no means first time that the world's largest insurance provider has been at the centre of controversy – to put it mildly.

AIG's endorsement of, and exposure to, mining and the minerals industry is probably more extensive than that of any other private insurer. This is scarcely surprising, considering its size and the fact that (in 2002) it could call on US$155 billion in capital reserves. Of late it has gone further than most of its rivals in crafting "innovative products" to serve the mining industry. Its AIG Environment subsidiary has its own "Mine Reclamation Program" which provides mine-owners with a financial bond to cover post-mine reclamation expenses, and protect against cost overruns, without increasing the premiums.[84] For example, in 2003, AIG Environmental underwrote a US$2.7 million financial assurance programme, managed by IMA Environmental Insurance of Denver, which enabled Golden Phoenix Minerals Inc to acquire a bond already filed with Nevada's Bureau of Land Management. Without the bond, Golden Phoenix would not have been allowed to proceed with gold heap-leaching at its Mineral Ridge mine. Thanks to IMA and AIG, the company got a more favourable rate of bond repayment than available from other insurers, thus "provid[ing] for stabilized cash flow and better use of working capital".[85]

AIG's political risk insurance has been supplied through AIG Global Trade & Political Risk Insurance Company (AIG Global) since the mid-1970s. The company is also linked to that of another provider, the Corporacion Andina de Fomento (CAF), through their joint Latin American Investment Guarantee Company (LAIGC). Together they offer conventional protection "...against confiscation, expropriation, nationalisation, inconvertibility and transfer of foreign exchange, political violence, and risks associated with foreign trade operations".[86]

In common with MIGA, and government-run Export Credit Agencies (ECAs), AIG Global claims to have the expertise and capacity to support heavy injections of PRI for large project-related transactions, including mining infrastructure, oil, gas, telecommunications and power generation. It is ready to grant cover up to US$80 million, per project, over fifteen years (a "very long time to speculate on any country's fortunes," according to Ann Russell-Cook, AIG's political risk regional manager in Australia), and arrange co-insurance when necessary. The company also says it can factor "project dynamics such as location, environmental impact and net benefit to local communities" into its premium charges. Thus, in the recent past, rates have been increased for Papua New Guinea while, in 2003, AIG was "off cover for Zimbabwe at the moment".[87]

However, AIG is not very forthcoming about the projects it underwrites. One of only two examples cited by AIG Global of its minerals-related PRI is of a "small but experienced mining company with highly productive acreage in an African country" using the cover for an equity interest in, and bank financing of, an unnamed project.[88] (This company may have been First Quantum Minerals which, in 2003, got coverage from AIG's Infrastructure Fund LLC for an equity deal worth C$22,400,000 of First Quantum shares. The investment came shortly after the Canadian miner had been indicted by the UN for illegal activities in the Democratic Republic of Congo).[89]

An equally contentious company was Australia's Ross Mining, whose Gold Ridge mine on Guadalcanal in the Solomon Islands, was recently dubbed "infamous" by a journalist on the Sydney Morning Herald.[90] Around 1998, Ross appears to have signed an insurance contract with AIG, enabling the giant US insurer to acquire equity in Gold Ridge, should the project founder and premiums fail to be repaid. Founder the project did, when local "militiamen" from Guadalcanal overran the mine site in 2000. Three years later (after Ross had sold out to Delta Gold, itself later taken over by Placer

Pacific), Australia sent troops to the Solomons at the request of the corrupt prime minister, Sir Alan Kamekeza, in an invasive action which was deplored across the south Pacific. A major aim of the "intervention" was to secure Australian investments in the islands, including re-opening Gold Ridge.[91] By mid-2004, AIG and the British government's Commonwealth Development Corporation (CDC) – which had inherited Delta/Placer's debt burden for Gold Ridge – clearly believed that "stability" had been re-installed on the islands. They put the mine up for sale and had soon attracted bids from South African, US and Australian companies.[92]

The China Connection

AIG started life some sixty years ago in Shanghai as American Asiatic Underwriters. It was forced out of China in 1940 but, almost fifty years later, once again established an office complex in the Peoples Republic. In 1992, through its Asia Infrastructure Fund, AIG became the first US insurance company permitted to operate in the country.[93]

(At this time, says Indonesian researcher George Aditjondro, the Asia Infrastructure Fund loaned US$41 million to Manila Tollways, which was itself 55 per cent owned by Indonesian dictator Suharto's daughter, Siti Hardyanit Rukmans.[94])

For many years this sprawling financial services' provider has operated under the aegis of the Greenberg family – first Evan, then his son Maurice ("Hank"). According to the *Wall Street Journal*, Evan Greenberg "transformed [the company]... from an overseas-focussed life insurer into a hugely profitable financial services powerhouse with subsidiaries operating in more than 130 countries".[95] Described by London's *Financial Times* in 2000 as "one of the few insurers that would be able to acquire banks or brokers,"[96] it has never relinquished its determination to dominate what is soon bound to become the world's single most lucrative insurance market. In 2003 AIG secured nearly 10 per cent of PICC, China's biggest property insurer, and took the lead in a consortium that acquired South Korea's second biggest broadband operator.[97] A few months later it bid for a stake in Minshen, China's only private bank.[98]

By August 2002, AIG found itself among those life insurance companies with the greatest exposure to the consequences of the Twin Towers tragedy of September 11 2001, and investment in those "troubled companies", WorldCom and Enron, Kmart, Dynegy and Tyco. At that time, declared Moody's Investors Services, the insurers collectively faced current and potential losses of US$23 billion.[99] Less than three months on, however, AIG had actually benefited from the unprecedented destruction on September 11th. The company was not only able to increase premiums as a result of the "war on terrorism"; it also introduced new "lines of business".[100]

The following February, Greenberg's business had to take a US$2.8 billion pre-tax charge, to bolster policies designed to protect company directors from billion dollar class action lawsuits, mounted primarily by asbestosis and mesothelioma sufferers. This pushed Greenberg into a swingeing attack on alien tort legislation, which he made vicariously, by damning US states that had failed to cap the size of payouts determined by juries to asbestos victims.[101] Little wonder that he was soon being dubbed by the *Financial Times* "probably the most outspoken critic of the US legal system". Greenberg's special outrage was reserved for the Sarbanes-Oxley Act, introduced to prevent corporate ill-governance of the type which wrecked Enron and WorldCom; he claimed it was now costing AIG US$300 million a year, to meet its new obligations under the legislation.[102]

Dog Bites Dog

Nonetheless, AIG's wheeling and dealings are so diverse that it has sometimes ended up on both sides of the fence. One of its closest recent partners was the US law firm, Milberg Weiss Bershad Hynes Lerach, a leading exponent of the class action litigation that Greenberg – and AIG – ostensibly abhor. In fact, AIG itself employed the strategy when trying to recover millions of dollars of lost bond investment which it had purchased from WorldCom.[103] Just as the Enron meltdown pressed export credit agencies, international banks (notably Merrill Lynch and Citigroup), and the accountancy firm Arthur Andersen, into massive mutual recrimination, so the WorldCom debacle set AIG against some of its erstwhile partners. In trying to cope with the consequences of what has proved to be the biggest bankruptcy in corporate history, AIG took former allies, Citigroup, JP Morgan Chase, Goldman Sachs and Lehmann Brothers to court for damages.[104]

A comparable dispute in India matched AIG against Tata, the country's leading industrial conglomerate, with which it had an earlier partnership. AIG was one of the first foreign companies prepared to invest in India during the 1980s, when it bought up 16.46 per cent of BPL, a major national telecommunications company. Then, in 2004, along with CDC (now known as Actis), it was hauled before the London Tribunal of Arbitration and sued, to the tune of US$400 million, for alleged unwarranted interference in BPL's strategic development.[105]

Kissinger Associates

The notorious Henry Kissinger was on the board of AIG, and chair of its international advisory board[106] at the same time the former US Secretary of State was a director of the huge US mining company, Freeport McMoran.[107] Kissinger travelled with Maurice Greenberg in 1989, as they tried to bring in new business from the far east. Kissinger Associates was seeking contracts for clients which included food giant HJ Heinz, the telecommunications empire of ITT, the oil and mining corporation Atlantic Richfield and, not least, Freeport. Greenberg wanted to consolidate AIG's business in China; Freeport and Kissinger were interested in new mining ventures in the country.[108]

Both men had set up China Ventures in early 1989, with Greenberg as a principal. Six months later, Chinese troops opened fire on hundreds of unarmed demonstrators in Beijing's Tiananmen Square, as they gathered to protest countrywide, human rights-violations. Although Kissinger vigorously opposed sanctions against the regime, US revulsion at the massacres killed off the joint venture later that year. (The connections between Kissinger and Greenberg seem to have endured, however: if Freeport did indeed get private PRI, after cancelling its cover with MIGA and OPIC in 1997, it is likely AIG provided it.)

Despite its name, the vast majority of AIG's business is outside the US.[109] In 1998 it became Japan's largest life and non-life assurer,[110] as well as the premier life insurer for Southeast Asia as a whole. Among its recent acquisitions are HSB (the largest US insurer against equipment breakdown);[111] American General Insurance (formerly in the lap of Britain's Prudential Assurance); a Lloyds' syndicate which includes some reinsurance liabilities;[112] and the brokerage firm, Hyundai Securities, part of a consortium led by AIG that recently engineered the biggest foreign acquisition in South Korea's history.[113]

Nor has AIG neglected opportunities in Africa: it is linked with the World Bank's IFC, the African Development Bank and Norfund[114] in attempts to bring new infrastructure to the continent through the African Infrastructure Fund, set up in 1999 under the chairmanship of South Africa's then-president, Nelson Mandela.[115]

For once, a company's own hype may be an accurate reflection of reality: AIG is indeed an "...organisation with more ways to manage risk and more financial solutions than anyone else".[116]

Specialist Insurance Brokers

Marsh & McLennan: Keeping it in the (Greenberg) Family

In a recent advertisement carried by the Financial Times' Insurance: Risk Management supplement[117] "the world's number one risk specialist" (and its biggest insurance brokerage) boasted that "Only one thing's certain. Nothing's certain." The comment is reminiscent of George Bernard Shaw's much more profound dictum: "We only learn one thing from history – that we learn nothing from history!" Marsh & McLennan have certainly taken one history lesson on board: in its huge range of policies and combative self-promotion, it is well-versed in promoting fear of risks, without implying they may be impossible to contain.

Unfortunately, it has also failed to learn another lesson. In October 2004, New York Attorney General, Eliot Spitzer (that scourge of corporate ne'er-do-wells), sued the company for illegally demanding kick-backs and commissions from insurance companies for which it landed business with major corporations. The charge was identical to that laid at the same time against AIG and another insurance company called Ace. But this was hardly surprising: Marsh & McLennan until this point had been run by Hank Greenberg's son, Jeffrey, while Jeffrey's brother, Evan junior, also headed up Ace.[118] No doubt the Greenbergs found it quite acceptable to "keep business in the family"; others might be tempted to use a less flattering description.

Marsh and McLennan's Political Risks division advises both companies and financial institutions, seeking protection against various elements of "country risk". It claims to have "access to all the major international insurance markets," covering confiscation of fixed, overseas and mobile assets, "contract frustration" and protection of contracts against "the risk of political actions over which you [the client] have no control"; as well as losses on foreign exchange transactions, through trade disruption, or from other unspecified activities overseas "for a variety of reasons".[119]

Emphasising this omnibus approach to client requirements, in 1998 (before they merged) J&H Marsh, and fellow brokerage firm McClennan, granted Canada's Placer Dome mining company five years PRI cover to the tune of US$470 million, for "various investments" in different countries.[120] Marsh Canada Ltd has its "own mining practice offering tailored solutions to the mining industry".[121]

The prospect that a client is "unable to repatriate dividends from overseas subsidiaries or payment of loads from overseas companies" is covered by Marsh's exchange transfer risks policy. It promises to insure loan repayments "against the inability to remit on due dates, for example due to the rescheduling of [a] country's debts".

Other specialised insurance brokers

Also worth noting among specialised insurance brokers are the Structured Trade Group LLC, "providing solutions to Global Trade Finance and International Investment Risk Challenges"; the Meridian Finance Group, and London-based Miller, both of which grant insurance against terrorism risks, as well as more general PRI. Sovereign Risk Insurance Ltd, a subsidiary of ACE Ltd, claims to be "only one of three private political risk insurers that are approved" by the Berne Union (the International Union of Credit and Investment Insurers).[122]

Mining Insurers

AON

US-based "risk services provider" AON (the name means "oneness" in Gaelic) claims to be "the world's premiere centre for raising mining finance" and packed "with personnel who have actually worked in the mining industry".[123] It focuses on all aspects of the sector, including smelting, refining and tailings management. Offering PRI for both "tenders and borrowers investments," AON additionally undertakes "alternative risk financing for the environmental risks of mine/site reclamation".[124]

After Marsh & McLennan, AON is the second biggest insurance broker anywhere, with "the largest group of natural resource professionals in the [insurance] industry". It offers a wide range of conventional insurance "products", but its services merge (almost imperceptibly) with those of so-called security specialists such as the Control Risks Group, or the newly-established Vanguard Response System Inc., registered on the Toronto Stock Exchange, which promises "counter measures against weapons of mass destruction".[125] While AON may not have gone that far, it nonetheless offers dubious Kidnap and Ransom Protection, Evacuation and Repatriation, among more conventional products such as Contamination/Recall Insurance, "Catastrophe Modelling" and security consulting.[126] AON has also been condemned by opponents of the regime in Burma, where its two offices issue re-insurance for some of the military's contracts.[127]

Mining Insurance Ltd./the American Mining Insurance Company

Mining Insurance Ltd (MIL) is a subsidiary of UK-based Strategic Risk Management, set up by two former Rio Tinto employees.[128] Domiciled in Bermuda, MIL claims to be the "first mutual... non-profit" facility established for mining companies. Its members all belong to the "natural resources" industry, including smelting and refining. They pool both the costs and benefits of their insurance contracts, as well as developing "financial, engineering and environmental products" for their needs.[129] Among other services, customers are offered PRI, "claims handling" and specialised reinsurance "solutions".[130]

The American Mining Insurance Company is the principal operational arm of CGH Insurance, based in the US state of Alabama. Its staff are supposedly "the most experienced in the United States in providing mining-related insurance," which includes workers' compensation and pollution liability cover.

"Controlling" Risk – CRG

The rise in number and status of risk consultancies is one of the key signifiers of our parlous times. It is the inevitable corollary of institutional failures to pre-empt catastrophic happenings – and actually provoke them. When business confidence in government as a barometer of bad events evaporates, who can companies call upon but private agencies with no obvious vested interest in, either downplaying or inflating, the dangers? That's the theory at any rate.

The best known and arguably most influential of these organisations is the Control Risks Group (CRG) based in London. With consultants in almost every nation state, and the claim to have worked for 91 of the Fortune 100 companies – in particular to counteract kidnapping and extortion[131] – CRG is unrivalled for the breadth of advice it makes available, albeit priced well beyond the reach of average citizens.

While it has attempted to disassociate itself from the rougher, more venal and self-serving end of the market in risk-related data, CRG has not escaped allegations that it indirectly feeds demand for armed responses to threatened investments, or the outright takeover of disputed mineral leases (so long as it is on behalf of "the state").

Founded in 1975, CRG was bought out by a management team in 1981, comprising ex-SAS officers, Jim Johnson and David Walker, along with their colleague, Arish Turle. Walker and Johnson went on to establish the private military company, KMS (probably an abbreviation of Keenie Meenie Services, SAS slang for covert operations[132]) and its subsidiary, Saladin Security.[133] A new investigative division was added in 1995.[134]

Along with British based mercenary outfits, such as Defence Systems Ltd (DSL) and Sandline, CRG again offered its services in the mid-nineties to the embattled Sierra Leone government, as it vied with murderous rebels of the RUF (Revolutionary United Front) for control of the diamond fields.[135]

Despite contending that private "security" forces will "never have the remit to run a private army," CRG has performed just such a role. A year after the New Labour government in Britain launched its 2003 armed intervention in Iraq, CRG was providing armed escorts to UK Foreign Office officials and others from the Department for International Development (DFID).[136] In its *Riskmap 2004*, the Group identified US foreign policy as the "single most important factor driving the development of global risk" – creating the "paradox" that the administration of George W Bush (and his New Labour crony across the pond) were undermining the very global stability they purported to create.[137]

An additional paradox derives from the fact that CRG's ranking of risks – from country to country and business to business – deters investment in the very fields (sustainable employment, universal social welfare, publicly available clean water, essential infrastructure, village-based savings schemes), and among the very states, which require it in order to achieve "good governance".

CRG fixes attention on the most visible forms of disorder: high crime rates, inability to maintain civil order and (in the case of resource extraction) community aggression directed against specific companies or personnel. But it fails to recognise that most projects to which local communities object are, in the long run incompatible with a country's overall stability. In 1995 CRG ranked Argentina and Bolivia as "low risk" countries, while India and the Philippines were considered to be of medium risk to mining investors. One of the justifications for this is self-evident: while the first two countries had already embraced free market "principles", major debates had erupted in India and the Philippines over the wisdom of opening their borders to private investment, specifically in mining.[138] Nonetheless, local antagonism to major mining projects was scarcely less strident in Bolivia and Argentina at the time: CRG simply failed to comprehend its significance. Resistance was to grow at an equal pace in all four countries over the succeeding eight years. Indeed, by 2004 no mining company could move an inch in Argentina without evoking a critical, if not hostile, response.[139]

CRG has become closely allied with the London-based Mining Journal (MJ). Together, MJ and CRG organised a conference on mining risk and opportunities in Africa, during November 1996. Two years later, CRG's annual survey, *Outlook '98*, was given pride of place in the MJ, where two of the Group's conclusions were considered "of prime relevance to the mining industry". The first conclusion was frankly banal: "poverty impacts on businesses throughout the world". More startling was CRG's observation that "every (sic) aspect of political risk stems from the growing divide between rich and poor".[140]

Martin Stone, head of CRG's research department at the time, was concerned at the widespread perception that wealth lay in the hands of a few, while the many couldn't acquire it. But, far from concluding that mineral extraction *ipso facto* extrapolated and deepened these divisions in poor countries, *Outlook '98* dished out the old prescriptions. Among the mineral-dependent countries promoted by CRG that year was Colombia. CRG admitted that investment there carried a high political risk, but the country would still "attract companies prepared to manage [the risk]". No mention was made of the alarming growth in paramilitary forces, to enforce that illusory "security" on behalf of extractive companies. Zambia was rated low risk, despite government corruption, poor infrastructure and bad communications. CRG welcomed the 1997 World Bank-brokered privatisation of assets owned by the state company Zambia Consolidated Copper Mines (ZCCM). Alas, the privatisation exercise was to fall completely on its face and regeneration of ZCCM's major asset, Konkola Deeps, was still in considerable doubt some seven years later.

CRG had failed to predict the virulent – and sometimes violent – reactions within Colombia to increased foreign penetration, and the likelihood of a collapse of the ill-conceived privatisation in Zambia. Yet, in both cases, warning signs were blatantly obvious.[141] This lack of foresight seems all the more puzzling in light of CRG's 1997 publication of a report with the evocative title *No Hiding Place*. The work quickly became one of the most quoted documents challenging the lack of meaningful "engagement" between extractive companies and their critics. Author John Bray recognised that some oil, gas and mining companies – notably Royal Dutch/Shell and Rio Tinto – had tried to deflect criticism by reasoned "dialogues"; nonetheless the exercises were ill-conceived.

According to Bray, the extractive sector was the least responsive of any industrial sector, to NGO pressure. "None of [these] companies had evaluation procedures, even though they believed that they were particularly vulnerable to pressure groups."[142] *No Hiding Place* selected flashpoint clashes between NGOs and corporate power (genetically modified foods, Shell's activ-

ities in Nigeria, foreign investment in Burma), which remain burning socio-
political issues, eight years on. A brief chapter on the rise in opposition to
Freeport-Rio Tinto's Grasberg mine was especially well-timed. It traced the
origin of global campaigning against the mine to 1995, with the re-capitali-
sation of the US company by Rio Tinto, which "had the dubious privilege
of being tracked by Partizans... [for whom] the mine became fair game for...
protests".[143]

CRG did not consider that OPICS' withdrawal of political risk insurance,
followed by kidnappings and riots around the mine site in early 1996, would
permanently damage Freeport-Rio Tinto's reputation among investors. Nonetheless, it concluded that the mining operations had been employed by the
Suharto regime "to control local dissent without having to enter into debate
with local leaders". The advent of international action (the UK-based World
Development Movement is specifically mentioned) "brought the debate to
the attention of the world at large," showing that "NGOs are as much a part of
the mine's political risk profile as Amungme tribespeople".[144]

No doubt the CRG report played a small role in prompting eight global
mining companies (headed by Rio Tinto) to launch the Global Mining Initiative (GMI) shortly afterwards and – somewhat later – the large scale "civil
society" exercise, Mining, Minerals and Sustainable Development (MMSD).

The GMI was aimed at cogent, pre-emptive risk analysis of the type recommended in *No Hiding Place*. Yet this has been noticeably lacking in CRG itself
over recent years, as the agency has moved towards advising companies how
to deflect, rather than address, NGO criticism.

Out of Bondage

> "The cumulative impacts of the financial distress in the surety market and
> the decrease in available reinsurance have been accentuated by circumstances
> particularly unique to the mining industry."[145]

Although decidedly a form of insurance, "surety bonding" is both a specialist
tool and an increasingly problematic one.

It is used (or rather not used) by mining companies to pre-empt their
being called to account for a disastrous project outcome. The problem is that
surety reinsurers have not been reinsuring as once they did, while surety providers have been losing business hand over fist.

For years, US states – as well as some other jurisdictions – have demanded
that companies make financial guarantees to cover future liabilities, such as

tailings dam collapses, acid rock drainage, cyanide and heavy metals contamination, and failure to implement closure plans. Surety bonds allow mining companies to satisfy these obligations without producing the cash upfront. They are, in effect, "a means for mining companies to free the significant amounts of capital needed to develop a mining project".[146]

Nonetheless, bonding has become much more costly of late. Recent hundred-fold (sic) increases in bond costs by state and federal agencies are not atypical, says one commentator. In coal-rich Wyoming during 2003, a surety company increased its rate to us$50 per thousand dollars insured, although it had earlier been as low as us$3.[147]

Like other insurance contracts, offers of surety bonding are based on a company's financial health and "the nature and complexity of the obligation during the term of the bond".[148] As the obligation stretches further into the future, so assessment of credit worthiness becomes more uncertain, and perceived risks extrapolate. Those agencies that provide bonding (known as "sureties") have always been hesitant to underwrite such long term obligations. Today, they will underwrite only "the most benign obligations and for a short duration".[149] According to the Surety Association of America, loss ratios for mining bonds have typically been well below those for all other surety bonding. But the large amounts of required coverage, the duration of the obligations, and the lack of any reinsurance support, have left the mining industry wanting for surety capacity at any price.[150]

The crisis had been brewing in the us for several years, even before the cataclysmic events of 2001. It reached its apogee that year when sureties reported a $2.5 billion loss, or an 80 per cent-plus loss ratio, compared to a previous average of around 30 per cent. Six of the top fifteen surety providers dropped out of the market in 2002-2003, while others announced their intention to withdraw.[151] For many us mining companies, surety bonding was no longer an option. As a result they have been forced to curtail existing operations, or discontinue plans for new and expanded ones.[152] Understandably, the associated "credit crunch" has prompted mining companies to seek and post alternative forms of collateral, including cash and letters of credit.[153]

Nonetheless, these options have not proved feasible for most operators: cash is beyond the reach of many smaller mining companies, while banks have sometimes required up to 200 per cent of the surety amount as collateral. Mining regulators may allow partial bond releases for concurrent reclamation, so long as a site has been "successfully backfilled, regraded, and stabilized as necessary to conform to the operator's reclamation plan". But this, too, is of limited value to a cash-strapped company, or where reclamation proves impossible to undertake.[154]

So it is scarcely surprising that the "bonding crisis" has stimulated a search for innovations such as "self bonding" (sic), tying payments to mineral production, the "potential innovative use of liens or the acceptance of property pledges (including water rights, equipment, or other valuable assets)," and drawing on state insurance funds.[155] All these are ways of circumventing the precept of "polluter pays". If the operator cannot insure fully against worst case scenarios we may well ask why they are allowed to operate in the first place.

It is difficult to disagree with the comment by Lisa Kirschner and Edward B Grandy in 2003 that "[t]he surety challenges facing the mining industry are symptomatic of the tension between federal and state policies that, on the one hand, promote economic development including mining, and on the other hand, require that the mining operators protect the government authorities from every conceivable financial risk."

What Kirschner and Grandy do not appear to acknowledge is that financial risks must be related directly to putative worst events. However remote a disaster may seem, the very fact that it cannot be predicted with accuracy is sufficient reason to fully insure against it at the outset. This in essence is the precautionary principle.

Nor is it those sitting comfortably in state capitols or Washington DC who bear the negative social costs; rather it is humans and other life-forms, whether they be local residents, farmers, consumers of water and vegetation, or taxpayers at large.

Notes

1   Royal & Sun Alliance, *Annual Report*, 2001.

2   See *Meridian Political Risks Insurance* web page.

3   Meridian, op cit.

4   See ING, *Shareholders Bulletin* No.3, October 2003, p. 23.

5   Deborah Orr, "Risk Buster", *Forbes Global* magazine, January 21 2002.

6   See James R Graven and Joan Lamm Tennant, "Economic and Financial Perspectives on the Demand for Reinsurance", in *Rational Reinsurance Buying*, Nick Golden (ed), London Risk Publications, December 2002, p. 170. The authors define reinsurance contracts as "a type of hedging contract whereby the ceding company puts the losses on the reinsurer subject to some trigger event". They suggest that "the very motive for purchasing reinsurance is entangled with both financial and cultural organisational characteristics," (p. 17).

7   John Kay, *Financial Times* (*FT*), London, May 1 2003.

8   John Kay, *FT* ibid.

9   John Kay, FT ibid.

10   Deborah Orr, op cit.

11   *Statement by The Reinsurance Research Council,* Toronto, 1998.

12   About, Inc., website "Reinsurance Companies", 2004.

13   About, Inc., ibid.

14   FT, September 21-22 2003.

15   Frank Schaar, "Who is profiting from the boom in the reinsurance business?", *WirtschaftsKurier,* May 27 2003.

16   Deborah Orr, op cit.

17   FT, September 9 2002.

18   FT, September 20 2002.

19   FT, November 27 2002.

20   FT, July 11 2003.

21   FT, October 19 2003; FT, December 12 2003.

22   FT, March 21 2003.

23   FT, August 14-15 2002.

24   FT, February 25 2004.

25   FT, August 6 2004.

26   "Businesses pledge change on threats from climate change, biodiversity loss", *UNDP press statement,* New York, June 15 2004.

27   FT, April 27 2004.

28   Deborah Orr, op cit.

29   FT, May 2 2003.

30   FT, October 16 2002.

31   *Multinational Monitor,* Washington DC, March 2003.

32   FT, August 5 2003.

33   FT, September 6 2002.

34   FT, April 7 2004.

35   FT, September 3 2002; *Guardian,* September 5 2002.

36   FT, February 16 2003.

37   FT, September 3 2003.

38   FT, April 7 2004.

39   FT, July 28 2004.

40   ZNA website 2004.

41   ZNA Product Information, October 10 2003.

42   FT, May 1 2003.

43   *Le Monde,* Paris, March 29 2003.

44   FT, April 5 2004.

45   Adam Raphael, *The Ultimate Risk: The Inside Story of the Lloyd's Catastrophe,* Bantam Press, London, 1994, p. 48.

46   FT, May 15 2003.

47   FT, April 8 2004.

48   *Le Monde,* op cit.

49   *FT*, June 22, 2004.

50   *FT*, April 8 2004.

51   Stuart Gold, *Occidental Petroleum: Pollution*, Profits and Petroleum, *Multinational Monitor*, Washington DC, July-August, 1989; News & Letters, Detroit, May 1984.

52   Raphael, op cit, p. 158.

53   Raphael, op cit, pps.150-154.

54   Raphael, op cit, p. 151.

55   Raphael, op cit, pps.154-5.

56   Raphael, op cit, p. 152.

57   Raphael, op cit, pps.156-157.

58   Supreme Court of Illinois, Docket 71753, November 1991, quoted in *FT*, December 23 1992.

59   Raphael, op cit, page 172.

60   PlanetArk, Reuters, November 12 2003.

61   Raphael, op cit, p. 3; see also Raphael, op cit, pps.99-124.

62   Raphael, op cit, p. 149.

63   *British Medical Journal*, quoted in *FT*, February 4 2004; see also *the Independent*, London, February 6 2002.

64   *FT*, December 6 2001.

65   Travelers Property Casualty Corp, *PlanetArk*, London, July 21 2004.

66   *FT*, May 17 2002.

67   Geoffrey Tweedale, *Magic Mineral to Killer Dust*, Oxford University Press, 2000; see also Alan J P Dalton, *Asbestos: Killer Dust*, London Work Hazards Group, 1978.

68   John Kay, *FT*, June 13 2001.

69   *FT*, November 28 1996.

70   *FT*, January 1 2003; see also Professor Laurence, University of London, *Letter to the Guardian*, September 2 2003.

71   *FT*, May 8 2002; *FT* May 17 2002; *the Independent*, May 17 2002.

72   *FT*, May 10-11 2003.

73   *FT*, August 6 2002.

74   *Evening Standard*, London, February 5 2002.

75   *FT*, May 10-11 2003, op cit.

76   *FT*, July 24 2004.

77   *FT*, July 25 2004.

78   *FT*, April 5 2004.

79   From an AIG advertisement published in the *Financial Times*, London, July 17 2000.

80   www.ethicalcorp.com, October 2 2004.

81   *The Independent*, October 22 2004.

82   *The Independent*, ibid.

83   *The Independent*, ibid.

84   Advertisement by AIG, *Mining Environmental Magazine*, September 2003.

85   Stock Talk, *Gold Mining and Natural Resources,* Golden Phoenix Minerals, reply 388, on www.biz.yahoo.com/prnewsw'030623/lam101.1html.

86   CAF website, June 30 2003.

87   AIG website, http://aigglobal.aig.com.

88   AIG website, ibid.

89   *MJ*, March 28 2003.

90   James Chessell, *Sydney Morning Herald*, September 8 2004.

91   The Australian Strategic Policy Institute in early 2003 called for armed intervention in the Solomons. See *No troops to the Solomons! People aid, not military aid!*, Statement by ASAP (Action in Solidarity with Asia and the Pacific), July 8 2003. According to a background paper published by ASAP in July 2003, the intervention was "fundamentally aimed at restoring the stable conditions for Western – primarily Australian – economic interests. Specifically, it (sic) wants the neo-liberal restructuring continued, the Gold Ridge mine and... oil plantations reopened, the reentry of 100 Australian companies which have departed, and the resumption of Australian imports.", *Australia in the Solomons: Security in whose interests?*, ASAP Background paper, July 6 2003.

92   James Chessell, *Sydney Morning Herald*, op cit.

93   *FT*, May 22 1998; see also *FT*, January 8 2004.

94   George Aditjondro, personal communication, July 16 1998.

95   *Wall Street Journal*, September 20 2000.

96   *FT*, February 1 2000.

97   *FT*, October 22 2003.

98   *FT*, March 5 2004.

99   *FT*, August 2 2002.

100 *FT*, October 25 2002.

101 *FT*, April 8 2003.

102 *FT*, May 12 2004.

103 *FT*, ibid.

104 *FT*, ibid.

105 *Hindustan Times*, Delhi, April 4 2004.

106 Walter Isaacson, *Kissinger: A Biography,* faber and faber, p. 748.

107 George Aditjondro, private communication July 16 1998.

108 Walter Isaacson, ibid.

109 *FT*, May 15 2001.

110 *FT*, March 2 1998; see also *FT*, March 24 2004.

111 *FT*, August 20 2000.

112 *FT*, May 11 2000.

113 *FT*, August 23 2001; *FT*, September 9 2002.

114 Norfund is supported and part-funded by Aureos, the main private investment arm of Britain's CDC, which is itself associated with the CDC's Actis, AIG's partner in the 2004 bid to sell the Solomons' Gold Ridge mine.

115 Aureos website, UK, September 2004.

116 From an AIG advertisement published in the *Financial Times supplement on World Insurance*, May 24 2002.

117 *FT*, October 1 2003.

118 *The Independent*, October 22 2004; Jeffrey Greenberg was forced to resign from Marsh & McLennan in late October 2004, and seeral senior executives were fired from the brokerage: *the Independent*, October 26 2004.

119 Welcome to Marsh, Marsh website 2003.

120 *MJ*, November 11 1998.

121 *MJ*, Exploration special, March 2004, p. 29.

122 ACE, website 2004.

123 AON Mining, website 2004.

124 AON Mining, website, 2004.

125 *Stockwatch E-blast*, December 19 2003.

126 AON Mining, website 2004.

127 Burma Campaign UK, *The Dirty List – Companies supporting the Regime in Burma*, London 2004.

128 *MJ*, Februry 28 1997; *MJ*, May 1 1998.

129 www.mininginsurance.com.

130 *MJ*, May 1 1998, op cit.

131 *FT*, April 10 2001.

132 Abdel-Fatau Musah and J Kayode Fayemi (Eds.), *Mercenaries*, Pluto Press, 2000 p. 47.

133 *Daily Telegraph*, March 27 1997; *Mercenaries*, op cit, p. 47.

134 *FT*, April 10 2001.

135 *Janes Intelligence Review*, London, January 1996.

136 *FT*, September 10 2003.

137 *FT*, November 11 2003.

138 *MJ*, November 26 1995.

139 See the Mines and Communities website (www.minesandcommunties.org) for bilingual postings on these struggles.

140 *MJ*, March 13 1998.

141 Ré Zambia see Patricia Feeney's illuminating analysis: *The Limitations of Corporate Social Responsibility in Zambia's Copperbelt*, Oxfam, November 2001.

142 CRG, *No Hiding Place: Business and the Politics of Pressure*, London 1997.

143 *No Hiding Place*, ibid, p. 44.

144 *No Hiding Place*, ibid, p. 45.

145 Lisa A Kirschner and Edward B Grandy, "Mining and the Vanishing Surety Bond Market", in *Natural Resources & Environment*, Winter 2003, volume 17, number 3.

146 Kirschner and Grandy (ibid*.)* summarise US surety bonding practice in mining as follows:

"*The* Surface Mining Control and Reclamation Act (SMCRA), applicable to surface coal mining on public and private lands, requires performance bonds to cover the estimated costs of reclamation. Additionally, regulations implementing the Mineral Leasing Act, applicable to coal, oil, gas and certain other minerals located on public lands, require lease bonds. In the case of recent federal coal leases, the bonds also are required to cover deferred bonus amounts, which can amount to many millions of dollars. Many states have enacted statutes with respect to state and private lands that substantially parallel the bonding requirements of federal law. The procedure for developing the amount of the financial guarantee varies depending on the jurisdiction. A number of agencies have used guidelines that establish presumptive surety amounts or ceilings based on the acreage of the project, ranging from approximately \$2,000 to \$5,000 per acre. [However] the trend in recent years has been to move away from acreage calculations toward regulators' estimates of what they would be required to pay to third-party contractors to perform the reclamation. Recently, the cost projection approach has often resulted in financial guarantee obligations in the tens of millions of dollars. Surety companies, in turn, have typically set premiums based on a percentage of the bond amount; for example, 1 per cent of the bond amount per year, which percentage has varied significantly depending on the financial strength of the operator."

147 Wanda Burget, Powder River Coal Company, *Testimony to the US House of Representatives Committee on Resources, Subcommittee on Energy and Mineral Resources, Field Oversight Hearing*, Washington DC, November 2 2003.

148 National Mining Association (NMA), *Surety Bonding Crisis*, NMA website 2004, Washington DC.

149 NMA, ibid.

150 NMA, ibid.

151 NMA, ibid.

152 NMA, ibid.

153 Kirschner and Grandy op cit.

154 Kirschner and Grandy ibid: "The partial bond release provides one means of freeing some capital prior to closure and most often corresponds with the regrading of waste rock and the stabilization of tailings facilities. The benefits of partial bond release are often limited, however, by regulations or policies that require a relatively large percentage of the total financial guarantee (often 30 per cent to 40 per cent) to remain in place until all reclamation has been completed successfully. See, e.g., 43 C.F.R. § 3809.591. Moreover, in practice, concurrent reclamation takes time to implement and does not typically serve to return capital to a self-bonded operator in the early phases of an operation, when capital is needed most. Additionally, significant portions of an operating mine cannot be backfilled or regraded while operations are ongoing, thereby constraining the funds available for release. As a consequence, many operators have not viewed cash bonding and similar forms of financial assurance as acceptable replacements to surety bonding."

155 Kirschner and Grandy ibid.

CHAPTER 3

A Bank Without Backing

Just when many staff were packing their valises, to vacation from the World Bank (also called "the Bank") in summer 2004, its board of directors pronounced upon their future involvement in extractive industries. Almost three years earlier the Bank had launched its *Extractive Industries Review* (EIR) to determine whether mining, oil and gas investment squared with its historic "mission" to abolish global poverty. In essence, the Bank's conclusion was affirmative: yes, it could and it did. In a stroke, the world's largest development agency set aside the opinions of numerous analysts (including some of its own), hundreds of community and non-governmental organizations; not to mention Emil Salim, the "eminent person" entrusted with performing the Review itself.

Salim is a former Indonesian Minister for the Environment, and was chair of all four preparatory committees for the 2002 Johannesburg World Summit for Sustainable Development (WSSD). At the outset he was far from convinced the Bank should significantly reduce its commitment to extractive industry. Many critics of mining were equally sure he would pay scant attention to their experiences, and initially refused to participate in the EIR.[1]

But, by the time he had taken evidence from civil society groups in Central and Eastern Europe, Africa and the Asia-Pacific,[2] visited some Bank-aided mining projects, and finally heard testimony from Indigenous communities,[3] Salim was a firm critic of the status quo. Presented in its final form in late 2003, the Review called on the Bank to phase out commitments to oil and gas within four years, and withdraw all support for the extraction of coal. Meanwhile, said Salim, the institution should urgently address the injustices, inequities and liabilities, typified by other forms of mining, re-directing its resources to making good the damages already done.[4]

Some EIR demands bore the imprimatur of its progenitor; in particular Salim's unequivocal rejection of mine tailings' dumping into rivers, and onto the seabed (STD). These are practices that have blighted his native land and, he said, clearly breached the "Precautionary principle".[5] The Bank should only support projects which benefit local groups, especially vulnerable ethnic minorities, women, and the poorest, assuring them "[a]n equitable share of the revenues". The Bank should also promote "rights based" development. Indigenous communities must be granted the right to exercise "fully informed prior consent" (FIPR) before any proposal got nodded through. Core ILO labour standards had to be endorsed and support given to workers laid-off by mine closures. Ecologically critical habitats should count as "no go areas," and a new emphasis placed on promoting sources of renewable energy.[6]

The Bank's chairman, James Wolfensohn, bridled at these demands. His management declared them "not consistent with the World Bank Group mission of helping to fight poverty and improve the living standards of the people in the developing world".[7] While "recognizing" the legitimacy of benefit-sharing, the Bank failed to commit to a guaranteed redistribution of profits; promising merely to "help ensure that affected groups are not harmed by developments and, where possible, are better off". Although agreeing to increase renewable energy output by 20 per cent annually, it set a base line target for such investment in 2005 which was in fact "lower than the bank loans for renewables in 1994".[8]

The insistence that mining-affected communities should be entitled to give "free, prior informed consent" (FPIC) to a minerals project was rejected by the Bank in favour of a "commitment" to "consultation," aimed at "broad acceptance of the project by the affected community". This, claimed the Bank, would result in "informed participation," thereby granting communities the opportunity to "understand projects that will affect them".[9]

Wolfensohn's intransigence – and that of his directors – was greeted with anger and dismay by a raft of civil society groups and prominent individuals. Cooperaccíon, a leading Peruvian NGO working with miners and Indigenous peoples, pointed out that "[t]he resettlement of communities to make way for extractive industry projects is intimately connected to the issue of consent... The Bank's failure to unequivocally ban involuntary resettlement, a practice that *de facto* violates the economic, social and cultural rights of communities, reveals its unwillingness to make substantive change in the governance of extractive industry projects".[10]

Scores of Indigenous and environmental organisations joined Oxfam, virtually all the Green party members of the European Parliament, and Nobel Peace prize winners, Desmond Tutu and Jody Williams (*inter alia*), in backing the EIR.[11] In an exceptionally strident opinion, Nadia Martinez of the US-based Institute for Policy Studies (IPS) condemned the Bank for failing "to distinguish its goals and standards from the likes of Halliburton, Exxon, Mobil, Shell, and other profit-driven institutions. US taxpayers' contributions to the World Bank are supposed to constitute international development assistance, not corporate handouts".[12] According to IPS' research "82 per cent of oil projects that the Bank has invested in since 1992... are primarily designed for export of oil to the United States and Europe, Canada, Australia and Aoteaora/New Zealand and Japan".[13]

Three years earlier campaigners, led by Friends of the Earth International (FOEI), had already urged the Bank to withdraw completely from large-scale mining.[14] Midway through the EIR process, FOEI's Carol Welch pointed out the Bank's "vested financial interest in staying engaged in the extractive industries: [they] are among [its] most lucrative investments... In fact, the Director of the Oil, Gas and Chemicals Department, Rashad Kaldany, is so confident that the EIR will not affect his department's activities that he has stated publicly, 'What we see looking forward is large investments in the oil sector.'"[15]

Just as the Bank dismissed the EIR, a leaked World Bank/International Finance Corporation report confirmed FOEI's prognosis. During the first nine months of its 2004 financial year (FY 2004), half a dozen oil, gas and mining investments accounted for less than 56 per cent of all dividend and related returns to the International Finance Corporation (IFC). Put bluntly, the extractive sector is a money spinner the Bank cannot afford to snub, let alone abandon – at least so long as the IFC remains an integral part of its operations.[16] (See box: "Arms of the Bank.") Kaldany returned to the offensive in October 2004, speaking of a "new climate of optimism as global metal prices reach record levels". The Bank would increase its investments in mining, so long as companies came up with environmental safeguards and "more transparent book keeping".[17]

Arms of the Bank

The World Bank has four operational arms. The IBRD (International Bank for Reconstruction and Development) lends to governments at market rates, backed by government guarantees. The International Development Association (IDA) makes long term, below market-rate, loans to the poorest countries. While the IBRD and IDA initiate programmes ostensibly to reform state mining sectors, the International Finance Corporation (IFC) and its Multilateral Guarantee Agency (MIGA) are the Bank institutions most supportive of specific mining endeavours, both promoting private firms operating in "developing" countries. At root, the IFC must meet a "profitability test" by purchasing equity (shares) in companies, offering commercial loans and advising governments and private sector clients on privatisation.

MIGA, set up in 1984 and guided by the IFC, provides companies with political risk insurance (PRI): its first cover was issued in 1991 to Freeport for the Grasberg mine in West Papua. By the end of 2004, mining was the sixth most important sector in its portfolio. The agency derives its income from member governments (the most important single provider being Austria) and, while making provision against claims for failed projects, has in fact paid out very little over the past two decades. It has working partnerships with a number of other PRI agencies, and cooperative underwriting programmes primarily with Lloyds Syndicates, as well as ACE, among others. Of late MIGA has also provided "Facultative Reinsurance" for guarantees issued by North-based reinsurers, and ECAs, including Coface, Sace, ECGD, EDC, EFIC, Global Re, Lloyds and ACE Global Markets. (See Chapter Two.)

Projects directly funded by the Bank are appraised under three categories of environmental review, depending on what Bank staff consider will be their likely impacts. Category A encompasses virtually all mining ventures, since they "may result in diverse and significant environmental impacts" and they require "a detailed environmental assessment, involving a site visit by the Environment Unit or a consultant appointed by the Unit as well as a desk review of the issues involved".

The Bank has appointed an Ombudsman (initially a woman) and "beefed up" its Inspection Panel – the independent group of experts, dating from 1993, supposed to assess the negative consequences of a project once underway. However, as demonstrated by local community experiences (see box "The Golden Fleece") the Ombudsman's recommendations may arrive too late or not be implemented. This is also true of conclusions reached by the Inspection Panel (as in the case of Indian coal mining; see box "Coal Sores").

Skewed Commitments

In terms of shares held in mining companies, and the amount of debt finance it provides the minerals industry, the IFC may seem "a relatively small player from a global perspective". From 1993 to 2001, it financed thirty-three mining projects with US$681 million in funds: only 18 per cent of the total project costs. Annually, out of around US$30 billion invested in mining world-wide, less than 2 per cent has come from the IFC.[18]

But simple statistics undervalue the Bank's crucial, twenty year old, role in "reforming" rules of entry to mineral-endowed states in the South on behalf of hundreds of external private minerals companies and investors. The Bank's structural adjustment programmes (SAPs) have driven nations like Guyana, Peru and Zambia, into high-risk privatisation processes or over-dependency on mineral extraction. A significant number of damaging mines would never have been constructed, had it not been for IFC investment or MIGA's political risk insurance cover.

World Bank "standards" and "guidelines" have also become the benchmark which other banks, multilateral institutions, export credit agencies, private investment managers, the OECD and the so-called Equator Principles Banks purportedly observe. Yet, precisely during this period, key principles have been betrayed by the institution itself. Prompting most alarm of late have been the Bank's proposals to transfer responsibility for environmental and social safeguards onto nation-states,[19] and substitute "principles and guidelines" for its ten previous "enforcement standards," thus "deviat[ing] from the clarity attached to the decade-long effort to distinguish mandatory from discretionary action".[20] In fact, the de-regulatory rot had set in several years before. As the UK-based Forest Peoples' Programme (FPP) commented in May 2003 "...almost all of the World Bank's original safeguard policies... have been compromised, or are not implemented. Under revised safeguards, the old mandatory guidelines have been whittled down and divided into two categories: a set of new Operational Policies (OPs), whose provisions are mandatory; and Bank Procedures (BPs) which are non-binding. In the process, the mandatory guidelines have been reduced to a bare minimum."[21]

The Bank's 2002 Operational Policy on Involuntary Resettlement (OP 4.02),

"allows removal of communities from their land, even if this would have 'significant adverse impacts on their cultural survival.' It contains provisions which permit the curtailment of the traditional resource rights of indigenous peoples in legally recognised national parks and protected areas. Fundamentally, there is no requirement that standards of living or livelihoods are improved by the resettlement programme... The prior policy did have such provisions, although they were rarely, if ever, adhered to. It did however provide leverage and space for affected communities to obtain some kind of redress through the [Bank's] Inspection Panel."[22]

In particular, said FPP, the 2002 Operational Policy on Indigenous Peoples "seriously undermines the Bank's social standards, failing to require Bank staff and borrowers to take action to safeguard internationally-recognised rights of Indigenous Peoples' to own, control and manage their lands... there is no requirement for detailed baseline studies to determine Indigenous Peoples' priorities and concerns, or provision for the monitoring, tracking and evaluation of projects by Indigenous Peoples themselves. A social assessment is only prepared if the Bank's staff unilaterally decide that a project may have adverse impacts."[23]

The latest version of the Operational Policy on Indigenous Peoples (OP 4.10, May 2004) was set out in draft by the Bank shortly before it rejected the main findings of the EIR.[24]

Coal Sores

When he called on the World Bank to withdraw from all coal-related projects, Emil Salim was particularly mindful of communities affected by the 1997 Bank-funded expansion of twenty five mines belonging to Coal India Ltd (CIL) – the world's single biggest coal producer. The Coal India Rehabilitation Project (CSRP) was granted an IBRD loan of US$530 million. An additional US$63 million was loaned by the IDA for the Coal Sector Environmental Social Mitigation Project (CSESMP), to assist CIL's efforts in mitigating the environmental and social impacts of the expansion. After being tested and revised during the five-year time period, CIL would apply its new environmental and social mitigation policies to no less than 495 mines.

The twin loans were the largest ever made by the Bank to a specific extractive enterprise; they proved, at best useless and at worst disastrous. Chotanagpur Adivasi Seva Samiti (CASS), an NGO working among the Project Affected Peoples (PAPs) of the Parej Coal India Project (Hazaribagh, Jharkhand), patiently went through the cumbersome process of getting the Bank's Inspection Panel to come to Parej to do an inspection and present their Report to the World Bank. After delays and obfuscation by the Bank, in November 2003 following a visit to Parej, the Inspection Panel found that all 70-plus families interviewed complained of a decrease in incomes after being displaced. When this drama is over, the 174 PAP's families of Parej will get some incentives to increase their incomes. This is being done, not as a measure of justice, but as a face-saver for the Bank. The other hundreds of thousands of PAP's from dozens of Coal India Projects and the Big Dam Projects and projects yet to come, will have to remain content with the fact that all the International Financial Institutions and Corporations that have taken their lands and displaced them, are having a sound sleep.

(Source: Xavier Dias, World Bank Creates Poverty in India, *Adhikar, Ranchi, June 2004.)*

Code Breakers

Between 1955 and 1990, the Bank concentrated its mining-related IBRD and IDA public sector grants on five areas: "reform and rehabilitation" (in Guyana, Bolivia and Ghana); "green field" mine construction (as in China and Jordan); mineral processing (eg. Jamaican bauxite-alumina), technical assistance (such as that given to Gecamines in Zaire/Congo) and engineering work.[25] Over these thirty five years, nearly 50 mining or mineral processing projects were supported with loans and credits totaling just under US$2 billion. The most widely criticised venture was undoubtedly Ferro Carajas, initiated in 1981. This huge iron ore mine lay at the centre of Brazil's Grande Carajas resource colonisation programme, which was ultimately to cover more than 10 per cent of the country's land mass and 16 per cent of Amazonia alone.[26]

Until the late 1980s, the Bank also implemented seventy one Structural Adjustment Programmes (SAPs) and "sectoral adjustment loans," but left state-owned mining companies largely intact. However its 1992 review, *The Strategy for African Mining* indicated a sea-change, with the aggressive view that most publicly-owned mining enterprises were ineffectual and corrupt. From now on these laggards should conform to "market discipline" (for which read privatisation or dismantlement), thus reducing risks to private capital. New projects would aim primarily at production for export, rather than value-adding at home. Funding for exploration and development would be redirected to "qualified firms" – almost exclusively from north America, Europe, Australia and Japan. Investment legislation, foreign exchange regulations, taxation and labour laws in poorer, mining-dependent, countries would all be "streamlined". Above all, the Bank would "improve" state mining codes "where issues refer to the access by the investors to mining rights, the politics (sic) with respect to mining rights, and the role and scope of the state owned enterprises".[27]

Backing for these "reforms" had already been obtained four years earlier, in 1988, when the Bank's Mining Unit invited forty five major mining companies (with combined mineral sales of US$40 billion) to prescribe how Southern states should behave towards them in future. The companies urged "the reduction of personnel, and even mine closure in response to economic reasons [sic] and to regulate the right of strike in order to avoid unnecessary conflicts where confrontations could be avoided". But "greatest importance" was bestowed on the Bank's "work with individual countries to update and reform existing mining investment codes".[28, 29]

The first batch of revised mineral rules was imposed by the Bank and the International Monetary Fund (IMF) upon sub-Saharan Africa in the 1980s and 1990s. Thirty five African nations were forced to implement 162 structural adjustment packages (SAPs) – more than all other SAPs put together – and start privatising their mining companies. Extraordinarily, it was not until 2003 that an objective analysis was published on the impacts of these revisionary codes, by the Groupe de recherche sur les activités minières" (GRAMA), based at the University of Quebec in Montreal. GRAMA cited Ghana's experience as most indicative of the retrograde changes. The new legislation had stimulated a Ghanaian "mining boom", conceded GRAMA. However the sector had only limited capacity to generate additional local employment; meanwhile at least 71 per cent of the country's mineral value had been siphoned into foreign-held accounts. Since 1992, mining had represented around 40 per cent of Ghana's total merchandise export earnings, yet less than 3 per cent in earnings actually contributed to the nation's Gross Domestic Product.[30]

From 1989 further codes were impressed, not only upon other African states, but also eastern and central Europe, Latin America and the Asia-Pacific region, proving most contentious in Peru, Brazil, Bolivia, India and the Philippines. In some instances the codes supplanted laws dating back several decades (Venezuela's legislation went back to 1945, India's to 1947). According to GRAMA, this second tranche of regulations was "characterised by such an absence of regulatory mechanisms that the situation came to be recognized as largely detrimental to the mining industry itself". The Bank was now obsessed with re-defining the role of the state, in the interests of "good governance," but interpreted this primarily as "creating a favourable environment for investment". Consequently "[D]evelopment objectives, ...were given little emphasis" while, in some countries (like Guinea) the state's former role, as protector of social and environmental rights, was weakened at precisely the point it should have been strengthened.[31]

The latest phase of "encoding" kicked-off in the late 1990s, as the World Bank released its 1997 document *Assistance for Mineral Sector Development and Reform in Member Countries*.[32] This third set of codes did purport to pay attention to the views of project-affected peoples, and to insist on mandatory environmental impact assessments. Unfortunately, says GRAMA, more than a decade's emphasis on inward private investment had left government bodies with precious little structural capacity to enforce improvements. Together, the Bank and the mining industry had ruthlessly driven down the costs of exploiting Southern-based mineral deposits; very little was returning to the exchequer for "development", while profits continued to flow offshore.

The liberalisation of mining regulations has become a "cumulative" process, as more recent legislation has drawn on earlier precepts.[33] Nor has the "picking and mixing" stopped: for example, in 2004, the Central African Republic promulgated rules "aimed at curbing corruption and re-launching the lucrative mining industry," only after first submitting them for approval to the World Bank.[34]

What the Mining, Minerals and Sustainable Development (MMSD) Report in 2002 euphemistically termed "relaxed laws on the repatriation of profits and foreign ownership"[35] have, in reality, been savagely prescriptive. Although application differs from country to country, they may include: tax holidays of up to ten years; the abolition of customs duties on imports of equipment; the reduction of withholding taxes and income tax rates (usually to 30 per cent or lower); tax relief for operating losses and mine closure costs (as in Indonesia);[36] charging for a state's former free minority equity in a project (as in Botswana);[37] and relief for any charge on prospecting rights. In Papua New Guinea, the Bank also tried to remove price controls and dispense with government approval for private mining investments.[38]

Of most concern to local communities, and many politicians, has been the frequent licensing of huge new expanses of territory to overseas companies, and extension of lease rights for twenty five years or more, as laid down by the Philippines 1995 Mining Act.[39] (In this instance opponents took their case to the country's Supreme Court which, in February 2004, ruled that 100 per cent foreign ownership of minerals was "unconstitutional": a decision that the government and mining companies overturned later that year.[40] Civil society organisations were not the only ones to vociferously oppose the new codes. Several governments, particularly in the Asia-Pacific and Latin America, became increasingly doubtful of their validity and have belatedly tried to clawing back what they lost, by increasing royalties and charging higher rates for concessions – though with mixed results.[41] Nor are the World Bank and IMF the only agents behind these neo-liberal fiscal and labour regimes. Mining companies share the Bank's agenda and actively promote it globally. As the United Nations World Investment Report pointed out: "Transnational Corporations are increasingly shaping the conditions under which they can operate in foreign countries."[42] As far back as 1981, a Rio Tinto (RTZ) lawyer warned the Panamanian government that, if his company was unable to "get round" the country's hard-won, pro-trade, union Labour Act, "we'll get rid of it".[43] Fourteen years later, in 1994, 30,000 indigenous Papuan landowners sued BHP (now BHPBilliton) for damages caused by riverine tailings dumping at its Ok Tedi mine. In response, company lawyers drafted legislation for the Papua New Guinean government, criminalising citizens pursuing compensation claims in foreign courts. Only widespread outrage on the part of national organisations to prevent the law from being passed.[44] Trade unionists in Colombia have not been so fortunate. Their efforts prevented the privatisation of Minercol in 2003-2004 triggered death threats against their leadership after it accused lawyers acting for overseas companies, notably Cemex and Holcim, of framing the legislation at the behest of the World Bank.[45]

Dividing the Spoils

In April 1997 more than a thousand Brazilians took to the streets of Rio de Janeiro in protest at the government's planned privatisation of Companhia do Vale Rio Doce (CVRD), Latin America's biggest state-owned mining company. They were fearful of losing hard-earned pension funds, and of economic power becoming concentrated even further in the hands of "oligopolistic" institutions. The demonstrators were greeted, not by government or World Bank mediators, but police firing tear gas and water cannon. Critics of the sale included former presidents, Jose Sarney and Itamar Franco, and the Workers' Party senator, Ms Benedeta da Silva, who called it "a theft against the Brazilian people". Meanwhile, more than a hundred injunctions, seeking to block de-nationalisation, piled up in the courts;[46] the outcry fell on death ears and the sell-off went ahead.

As we have seen, the privatization of mines and mineral assets has been central to the Bank's long term strategy of attracting foreign investment to the sector. However, the process has not proceeded evenly, nor at the same pace everywhere. In some cases, such as Morocco, no-one wanted to buy what was on offer.[47] The government of India has resisted wholesale off-loading – although a few companies were made to succumb. Elsewhere, state enterprises have proved to be too cumbersome, or run-down, for other than a messy re-distribution of its components. (See box "Zambia's experience of privatisation".)

The Bank's overt intention was to rescue "failed states", blighted by corruption, nepotism, over-employment, mismanagement and high grading (the exploitation of richer ores for profit in the short term, while abandoning lower grade, but economically recoverable, reserves). These factors, claimed the Bank, had resulted in indebtedness and impoverishment. By gearing to competitive markets, bloated and subsidised workforces would be cut back, commodities tailored to global demand, safer technologies made available by the private sector, and sustainable incomes generated for all.[48]

In reality, almost none of these promises have been fulfilled. There is no evidence that corruption has significantly diminished: in Peru, for example, the US company Newmont paid bribes to secure its huge Yanacocha concession.[49] The practice of "high-grading" seems as extensive today as it was under state oversight. Above all, as Canadian researcher Bonnie Campbell points out: "In the absence of a central power which holds internal and local political legitimacy, the process of privatisation in favour of foreign companies may affect not only certain functions of the state but entire regions of the country."[50] It could be argued, says Campbell, that "state-owned mining interests are more likely [than private companies] to embrace the long term management of regional, amorphous, environmental degradation".[51] In particular, enforced reductions of organized workforces and their substitution for casual ("contract") labour has, in some countries, deepened endemic poverty while eroding worker's rights to strike, arbitrate and benefit from welfare provisions.

Far from failing, some disposed-of state companies were actually making healthy profits at the time of privatization. Such was the case with Balco, India's third largest aluminium company, "disinvested" in 2001 to Sterlite Industries (now Vedanta), at what some critics claimed was only a tenth of its true asset value.[52] The same was true of Brazil's CVRD, causing Brazilian commentator, Flavio E N Hegenberg, to declare: "In practice privatisation has been used more to highlight the commitment to market oriented reforms than to redeem debt or increase efficiency."[53]

Zambia's Experience of Privatisation

In 2000, the IFC embarked on what was essentially the asset-stripping of Zambia Consolidated Copper Mines, one of Africa's legendary state enterprises. Konkola Copper Mines plc (KCM) emerged from the wreckage, with its major shareholding in the hands of Anglo American Corporation (AAC), and smaller equities owned by the British Commonwealth Development Corporation (CDC) Capital Partners, and the Zambian government. Within eighteen months, however, KCM appeared on the brink of dissolution, unable to meet production targets and reduce costs, in the teeth of a deteriorating market.[54] Much to the Bank's alarm, Anglo American ditched the enterprise, leaving the Zambian government determined to pull together another corporate "rescue", which the IFC and CDC considered they must support. In mid-2004, Vedanta – a London-listed, upstart, enterprise owned by Indian mine financier, Anil Agarwal – finally secured KCM from the Zambian government for under US$50 million,[55] but with no guaranteed capital to improve workers' wages and construct safer plant.

This cut-price deal revived concerns, eloquently expressed by researcher Patricia Feeney in 2001, that workers health, safety, and rights to compensation, as well as urgently required environmental improvements at the mine, would be sacrificed to expediency.[56]

Sustained Non-Development

In January 1999, Peter van der Veen, the Bank's head of mining, expressed confidence that, though states had largely ceased being "owner/operators" of mining assets, they had nonetheless become "regulators/administrators" operating alongside companies. Now they could "increasingly negotiate with indigenous peoples, local communities, and NGOs, any of which can influence, even stop, the development of a mining project". Added van der Veen: "The old enclave model for development is rarely going to be considered a viable alternative for large mining projects."[57] The Business Partners for Development initiative (BPD), conceived by the Bank the previous year, was intended to demonstrate that governments, businesses and civil society could indeed work together, brokering projects of benefit to them all. However, the extractive industries component of the BPD proved an almost unmitigated disaster. (See box "Partners in Grime".)

Partners in Grime

Conceived in 1998 by World Bank president, James Wolfensohn, the Business Partners for Development programme (BPD) contained four "clusters", of which "Natural Resources" (NRC) was the first. Supposedly it would demonstrate the Bank's faith in "tri-sectoral, stakeholder" partnerships between business, civil society and governments.

Although the three other clusters (water and sanitation, road safety and youth development) functioned fairly effectively, the NRC was little short of a travesty. Three mining companies quit the exercise in its early days and a key case study was abandoned altogether. Only one international NGO and one government department (Britain's Department for International Development or DFID) participated.

The project was packaged as "action research," but essentially degenerated into a desk exercise. The steering committee had two public sector and eight corporate representatives, with CARE International as the sole NGO. (Other NGOs refused to join, believing CARE's close association with private companies would "damage their reputations".)

Four out of the seven chosen NRC projects were functioning or putative mines: Sarshatali (coal, India); Las Cristinas (gold, Venezuela); Kelian (gold, Indonesia); Konkola (copper, Zambia). A fifth – Utkal Alumina International Ltd. (UAIL)'s planned bauxite-alumina complex in the Indian state of Orissa – was hastily (and without explanation) withdrawn in 2001, shortly after police shot dead three villagers during a non-violent protest. Substituted for UAIL was the Transredes Bolivia-Brazil pipeline, owned by Enron. The project became the object of massive protests in Bolivia in 2003, causing the downfall and abdication of President "Goni" Lozado.

PriceWaterhouseCooper, in its final evaluation of the BPD, admits that the number of study visits to the extraction sites was "not up to expectations". In fact there were none: "Secretarial requests to Steering Committee members to facilitate field based study visits were unsuccessful..." After three years, and the expenditure of more money than most NGOs can dream of in a lifetime, only Las Cristinas and Sarshatali were claimed to "demonstrate the value added for tri-sector partnerships".

All the mining, oil and gas projects had provoked community or workers' resistance; only at Las Cristinas and Sarshatali were NGOs sufficiently enthused to join the BPD. It was therefore axiomatic that these projects would be most successful in meeting the programme's criteria. But the successes were minimal. While a health center was established by Placer Dome to serve 12,000 people at Las Cristinas, the project as a whole became overshadowed by bitter conflicts over the mine's ultimate ownership.[58] The major achievement attributed to the Sarshatali partnership in West Bengal was the construction of an access road to the mine. Ironically it was this very feature which most angered local people, since the road invaded fields and affected property that villagers were emphatically refusing to cede to the company. Compounding the irony, the IFC itself pulled out of the project in November 2002, since it "did not conform" to Bank criteria: in other words Sarshatali's private sector operators had failed to meet their legal and social obligations.

The BPD closed down in 2002 but was succeeded by an amorphous programme (not connected with the Bank) confusingly re-named "Building Partnerships for Development." Concentrating on water and sanitation issues, one of the new BPD's ventures is between a private water company, local villagers and employees of the Kahama Mining Company at the Bulyanhulu gold mine in Tanzania.[59] Bulyanhulu had been covered by PRI from MIGA in 2000, despite claims by Tanzanian lawyers and Amnesty International that major human rights abuses were inflicted on local people during the construction of the mine.[60] (See Chapter 9.)

In reality, almost every major IFC/MIGA funded mining project since 1990 has ignored key demands by local people and failed to adequately address their grievances. Far from being integrated with local communities, more often than not mining operations have been the source of bitter conflicts (see box "A Sorry History".)

A Sorry History

This is a selective list of mining projects supported by the IFC/MIGA, or programmes backed by IBRD/IDA, since 1991, which have attracted significant opposition from local communities and national NGOs.

Project/programme	Year and type of World Bank investment	Strong opposition
Grasberg (West Papua)	MIGA 1991	YES
Sierra Rutile (Sierra Leone)	IFC 1991	YES
Omai (Guyana)	MIGA 1992	YES
Kasese Cobalt (Uganda)	MIGA 1993	
Sieromco (Sierra Leone)	IFC 1993	
Peru: Energy and Mining privatisation	IBRD/IDA 1993	YES
Buenaventura (Peru)	IFC 1993	YES
Yanacocha (Peru)	IFC 1992, MIGA 1994	YES
Sadiola Hill (Mali)	IFC 1994	
Tintaya (Peru)	MIGA 1994	YES
Cyprus Climax (Peru)	MIGA 1994	
Comsur (Bolivia)	IFC 1994	YES
Zaravshan-Newmont JV (Uzbekistan)	MIGA 1994	
Cayeli (Turkey)	IFC 1994	
Ghana Mining Sector Development & Environment Project	IDA 1995	
Tanzania Mining Sector Development	IDA 1995	
Kumtor (Kyrgyzstan)	IFC 1995, MIGA 1996	YES
Lihir (Papua New Guinea)	MIGA 1996	YES
Sierra Rutile (Sierra Leone)	IFC 1996	YES
Ghana-Australian Goldfields Ltd (Ghana)	IFC 1996	YES
India: Coal Mining Environment and Social Protection	IDA 1996	YES
Alumbrera (Argentina)	MIGA 1997	YES
La Loma (Colombia)	MIGA 1997	

Project/programme	Year and type of World Bank investment	Strong opposition
Loma do Niquel (Venezuela)	IFC 1997	
India Coal Sector Rehabilitation Project	IBRD 1997	YES
Fasomine (Burkina Faso)	IFC 1998	
Ashanti Goldfields (Ghana)	IFC 1998	YES
Antamina (Peru)	MIGA 1999	YES
Sarshatali (India)	IFC 1999	YES
Dukat (Russia)	IFC 1999	
Juliettta (Russia)	MIGA 2000[a]	YES
Bulyanhulu (Tanzania)	MIGA 2000	YES
Konkola Copper (Zambia)	IFC 2000[b]	
PT Arutmin (Indonesia)	IFC 2000[c]	
PT Adaro (Indonesia)	IFC 2000[d]	
Quellavaco (Peru)	IFC 2001	YES
Sopon (Laos)	IFC 2001[e]	YES
Carbones del Car (Colombia)	IFC 2001	
Sierra Rutile (Sierra Leone)	IFC 2001[f]	YES
Kolwezi/American Mineral Fields (Congo DR)	IFC 2003	
MDL/BHPBilliton (Botswana)	IFC 2003	YES
Kenmare Resources (Mozambique)	MIGA 2003	
Glamis Gold (Guatemala)	IFC 2004	YES

a IFC sold its shares at a fourfold profit in 2002.
b IFC transferred its equity in KCM to Zambia Copper Investments Ltd et al in 2002.
c Project placed "on hold" in 2001 due to "country consideration" (sic), IFC *Monthly Operations Report*, August 2001, page 34.
d Project put on hold in 2001.
e The IFC cancelled its loan in early 2003.
f The loan was withdrawn in October 2002. OPIC provided a new investment guarantee in April 2003.

The naive optimism expressed by van der Veen in 1999 was shattered in 2003 by a consultant to the Bank's own Operations Evaluation Department (OED). M A Thomas was asked to determine how far the Bank had been "factoring governance" into its extractive industries "approach" to Chile, Ecuador,

Ghana, Kazakhstan, Papua New Guinea and Tanzania, between 1993 and 2002.[61] "Paradoxically," concluded Thomas, "although a few countries have bootstrapped themselves to higher incomes through the judicious exploitation of such resources, an abundance of natural resources is more often associated with poor economic performance... Most EI [Extractive Industry] projects are not the result of a governance-informed sector assistance strategy." Even the projects which did pursue such a strategy evinced "no indication that the decision to support increased investment was preceded by an analysis that considered the likely benefits and risks of such investment in light of the quality of governance".[62]

"Historically," said Thomas, "the Bank's approach to the EI sector appears to treat increased private investment as the primary goal and a good in itself".[63] However, "increased EI investment is likely to lead to bad development outcomes for many if not most of the Bank's clients".[64] In the worst case, "the EI sector can bring little public benefit and leave long-term costs behind in the form of environmental destruction and war".[65] Local communities "bear the brunt of accompanying environmental damage, health risks, property takings and damage, and changes to traditional life and culture".[66] The Bank "risks facilitating the wastage of the country's non-renewable resources, as well as contributing to environmental damage, violence, and weakening of the quality of governance itself".[67] Strangely, the OED's own 2002 annual review ignored Thomas' findings completely, as well as one graphic example of the Bank's operational failures earlier that year. (See box "The Golden Fleece".) Meanwhile the IFC was touting an elliptical definition of "sustainable development" as one which ensured "the financial viability and economic soundness of all new projects and a proactive strengthening of their environmental and social sustainability including transparency and good corporate governance".[68] However, even by these weak indices, projects supported by the IFC have performed poorly and, as the IFC admitted, their standards actually worsened between 1999 and 2001.[69]

The Golden Fleece

The Yanacocha gold mine, operated by Newmont of the US in Peru's Cajamarca province, is Latin America's premier gold producer[70] and supposed to be the IFC's minerals' flagship on the subcontinent. In practice the World Bank has demonstrated a woeful lack of project oversight, failure to evaluate the project's liabilities, and contempt for local Indigenous Peoples' rights.[71] The mine's "development" outcome is one even Bank consultants have acknowledged to be defective.

The enterprise had already been opposed by Cajamarca's Indigenous communities long before its first gold was poured in 1993. Opposition mounted between May that year and June 1999 when IFC funding and undertakings reached US$151.7 million.[72] In fact, the IFC did not regard either the mine or its host country as risk-free. On the contrary, its investment was specifically aimed at providing "political comfort" (sic) to Newmont and its domestic partner, in the face of marked investor reluctance to back Peruvian mining.[73]

In June 2000, shortly after the IFC made its heaviest investment in the project, 151 kilos of mercury spilled from a truck leaving the Yanacocha site, causing eight people to be hospitalised.[74] Some 1,000 residents, along with the municipal authorities, filed lawsuits against Newmont in its home state of Colorado, alleging injury as a result of the disaster.[75] The company was also fined half a million US dollars by Peru's Mining and Energy Ministry. Meg Taylor, the Bank's newly-appointed Compliance Advisory Officer ("ombudsman"), acknowledged that the company had failed to avert the disaster – startlingly adding that the Peruvian government had "no relevant... regulations regarding the transportation of mercury or other hazardous materials (sic)".[76]

While the IFC continued to assert that Yanacocha promoted large scale employment, two Bank personnel threw strong doubt on some of its other claims. Consultants Gary McMahon and Felix Remy pointed out in late 2001 that, though "substantial taxes from a mining operation... should go to the local and regional levels" it was "unclear if they actually have [in the case of Yanacocha]".[77] Examining rises in mining-related prostitution, "related diseases", and alcohol abuse, at six major mines, McMahon and Remy found that these problems were "most evident in Cajamarca".[78]

Bad Marks

Not to be deterred by mounting criticisms, the Bank continues to claim that investment in large scale extractive industry can turn around a company's bad environmental performance, compelling it to raise its game. This is perhaps the greatest single fallacy, as can be demonstrated by many failed enterprises.

Guyana and Sierra Leone

In two important instances, the IFC or MIGA have "rolled over" their finance, despite massive previous failure. Following a spectacular breach of the Omai mine's tailings dam in August 1995 and against demands by affected Guyanese residents that the project be permanently closed, MIGA renewed its political risk insurance. The dam collapse resulted in some four billion cubic litres of mine effluent cascading into a local creek, then into the Essequibo river – the country's main waterway. President Cheddi Jagan called it "the country's worst environmental disaster". (See chapter 5.)

MIGA, together with Canada's Export Development Corporation had provided critical political risk insurance cover (worth US$49.8 million) for the mine's Canadian partners, Cambior and Golden Star Resources. It adequately scrutinised neither the mine's standards of construction nor its operation. The partners had failed to line the dam with HDPE (high density polyethelene) to protect groundwater resources. Worse, they allowed the dam wall to rise far above limits set in the original Environmental Impact Assessment. Several observers had warned that a dam collapse was virtually inevitable[79] and three cyanide "spills" had already occurred during the previous six months, poisoning scores of fish. Cambior acknowledged that the dam was filling close to its brink, prompting a company petition to the government, in early 1995, for a permit to discharge "treated wastes" directly into the river. The government refused on environmental grounds, but the mine continued to function. Throughout this critical period, MIGA failed to monitor the mine's safety, let alone insist on closure as a basic precaution. Later, the United Nations Development Programme (UNDP) concluded that "baseline and continuous monitoring at Omai have largely been inadequate".

The mine was re-opened in 1996, albeit with several technical improvements, but before a parliamentary sub-commission on the disaster had delivered its final conclusions. Having promoted Omai as a prime example of large-scale minerals-related investment critical to a highly-indebted third-world state, the Bank was certainly not going to argue against its re-opening.[80]

The IFC in 2001 resumed funding for Sierra Rutile Ltd (SRL)'s ilmenite mine in Sierra Rutile, following its closure when besieged by forces of the murderous Revolutionary United Front (RUF) between 1994 and 1995. The loan was withdrawn in late 2002 because SRL found alternative finance.[81] The first tranche of IFC funding was agreed in Financial Year 1991, three years after the mine came on-stream, and backed by Britain's Commonwealth Development Corporation (CDC) in order to expand SRL's production from 150,000 to 200,000 tonnes a year. This was despite the fact that OREINT, an environmental rights NGO based in the capital Freetown, had already damned SRL's performance, claiming that no adequate Environmental Impact Assessments were carried out before the loans were agreed.

OREINT's report *Mined Out* was circulated in draft in 1994 and published (revised) under the auspices of Friends of the Earth UK in 1997.[82] It detailed land degradation, flooding and pollution, with associated risks to health caused by the wet dredging methods used by SRL, alongside the "complete relocation of villages and their inhabitants, often against their wishes".[83] In 1992, a dam constructed by SRL collapsed, destroying ten villages and leaving 10,000 people homeless, as well as intensifying water-bourne diseases, such as malaria, cholera and polio. By 1997, 5,300 villagers had been forced to move. Representatives of the company themselves acknowledged that "some villages were resettled in places where... water and farmland were grossly inadequate and where the general sanitation... was critical". In addition, villagers complained that (under a community resettlement and health programme managed by CARE) they were dumped on inadequate and inferior land, resulting in the depletion of freshwater fish and bush meat. Restoration of mined-out land, in the absence of topsoil, was severely limited while "damage to the original ecosystem will probably be irreversible".[84]

After five years of conflict, SRL in 1996 approached the IFC for further finance to repair war damage and complete the mine's expansion. The Bank commissioned a more comprehensive EIA which nonetheless failed to address the critical issues in the OREINT-FOE report. It also ignored SRL's continued employment of the services of the notorious South African mercenary force, Executive Outcomes (EO), originally employed by the company to recapture its mine from RUF marauders in November 1995.[85]

Russia

More than seventy Russian and international NGOs in 2000 called on the Bank not to support environmentally sensitive projects – including mining operations, following abolition by Vladimir Putin, the country's new President, of Russia's main environmental agency. Despite this, MIGA went ahead to grant US$27.2 million of political risk cover to Canada's Bema Gold for construction of the Julietta gold and silver mine in Magadan province.[86] No information on the project or its social and environmental impacts was released by MIGA before issuing the guarantee. A technical expert in early 2001 found that Bema had already violated good practice principles. The tailings dam was precariously located on a land area which was "far larger than needed... stripped down to the permafrost level [with] the insulating and moisture-absorbing layers of soil, tundra and organic material removed". The dam was "less than 50 yards from a stream and two kilometres from a major river which could be affected by seepage or a larger cyanide spill".[87]

Friends of the Earth International took up these issues in *Risky Business*, its critique of MIGA's policy and performance.[88] MIGA brusquely denied the allegations, without offering any supporting evidence. Retorted FOE: "[R]ather than aspiring to uncover the situation at the Julietta mine in Russia, you [MIGA] disparage... people who risk their lives going public with information that exposes the government and its allies... MIGA seems to be content that no disaster has yet happened, rather than attempt to find out whether the project design has the potential to lead to a major disaster and to avert this possibility... We have found MIGA to be unduly resistant to reform and find MIGA's progress in reform efforts to be wholly inadequate. This has led many organizations to conclude that MIGA has little interest in conforming its policies and practices with the World Bank's mission of poverty alleviation, and... to conclude that MIGA should therefore no longer function as part of the World Bank Group."[89]

Papua New Guinea

The IFC has also ignored strictures, made by a fellow investment guarantee agency, in the case of two major mine projects. In 1995, the US government's Overseas Private Investment Corporation (OPIC) – the world's second largest export credit agency – refused to underwrite the Lihir gold project in Papua New Guinea, because Rio Tinto intended employing Submarine Tailings Disposal (STD) in violation of at least one international treaty to which the US was a signatory. The following year OPIC also accused Freeport-Rio Tinto of violating its PRI cover for the vast Grasberg copper-gold mine in West Papua, by doubling production rates and thus enormously increasing the burden of contaminating wastes ejected into the Ajkwa river system. The companies angrily rejected the accusation and OPIC removed its insurance cover, but MIGA refused to do so.[90] (See chapter 1 for more on OPIC.)

Zaire/DRC

Finally, the IFC seems to have violated its own guidelines on conduct. As bloody conflicts over resource control raged in Zaire during the nineties, American Mineral Fields (AMF) became the chief vehicle used by its founder and major shareholder, Jean-Raymond Boulle, to expand into Africa and create a personal fiefdom, specifically in Zaire (now the Democratic Republic of Congo or DRC).[91] Boulle gained the lucrative Kolwezi mineral workings in 1997, as a reward for lending then-rebel leader Kabila his private jet and donating US$1 billion to Kabila's campaign against the dictator Mobutu.[92]

Later, AMF was accused of links to two London-based paramilitary forces: International Defence and Security (IDS), a spin-off from the notorious Executive Outcomes mercenary force, and British-based Defence Systems Ltd, also active in appropriating mineral resources from conflict areas.[93] Just before the IFC backed Boulle's Kolwezi project,[94] AMF was condemned by a UN panel of experts, investigating companies operating in the Democratic Republic of Congo for violations of the OECD Guidelines for Multinational Enterprises. Yet these rules are themselves invoked by the Bank as a basis of its own human rights guidelines.

Conclusion

Optimists hope that the World Bank may still reverse its recent backward trends, which involve diluting safeguards, reducing capacities for oversight, and denying community rights to project pre-emption. Unfortunately there is overwhelming evidence that the institution is neither structurally capable of doing this, nor willing to seriously consider doing so.

While ignoring numerous peoples' hand-on experience and some compelling research, the Bank has adopted – virtually wholesale – the mining industry's contention that it contributes directly to sustainable community development, provided companies can make a profit. This was a key rationale behind reforming state mining codes in favour of foreign private capital, and dismantling many state-owned mining companies, instead of seeking to render them democratically accountable and environmentally secure. In this process, many thousands of mineworkers have lost their jobs, and manifestly self-serving companies have been allowed to usurp Indigenous and national patrimony. Bank-supported mines have created social divisions, increased environmental contamination and deepened the insecurity of succeeding generations. Most unforgivably, the World Bank has contributed to the very impoverishment it pledges to annul.

Notes

1   For a summary of these reservations, see *Civil Society Concerns Regarding Extractive Industries Review*, Letter to Dr. Emil Salim, Indonesian Biodiversity Foundation, Jakarta, November 7 2001, signed by Marcus Colchester (Forest Peoples Programme), et al; see also Alan Beattie, "World Bank advised to pull out of oil and coal financing", *Financial Times* (*FT*), London, November 20 2003. On alleged pressure by the World Bank to fashion the Review to its own design, see

"World Bank advised to pull out of oil and coal financing", *FT*, November 20 2003.

2   See *Livelihood: Statement for the World Bank Extractive Industries Review (EIR)*, signed by Indonesian NGOs: The Indonesian Forum for the Environment (WALHI), the Indonesian Mining Advocacy Network (JATAM), the Indigenous Peoples' Alliance of the Archipelago (AMAN) and Australian NGOs: the Mineral Policy Institute, Friends of the Earth Australia, and The Asia-Pacific Unit, Australian Conservation Foundation, Nusa Dua, Bali-Indonesia, April 26-30 2003.

3   Testimony from the April 2003 meeting with Indigenous Peoples' representatives, held in Oxford, UK, is published in *Extracting promises: Indigenous Peoples, Extractive Industries & the World Bank*, Tebtebba foundation and Forest Peoples Programme, Baguio City and Moreton-in-Mahrsh, 2003. Robert Goodland, former chief environmentalist at the World Bank, ably assisted Salim in providing information, as well as mediating the opinions of Bank critics during the whole EIR process: see Robert Goodland, *Civil Society's Top Three Priorities for the Extractive Industry Review: an informal note requested in March 2003 by Dr Emil Salim*, draft April 2003.

4   Emil Salim, *The Extractive Industries Review: Final Report*, presented to the World Bank, Washington DC, November 2003.

5   EIR Final Report, pages 34 and 59; see also *The World Bank EIR criticises mine waste tailings: Commentary by Igor O'Neil*, Mineral Policy Institute, Sydney, November 26 2003.

6   Salim, op cit.

7   *FT*, February 3 2004.

8   Nadia Martinez, Institute for Police Studies, *World Bank ignores its own advice*, Christian Science Monitor, August 16 2004.

9   *Striking a Better Balance, The World Bank Group and Extractive Industries*, the Final Report of the Extractive Industries Review, World Bank Management Response, Washington DC, September 2003, p. 5.

10 *Statement on the EIR*, Cooperaccion, Lima, Peru, August 2004.

11 See Desmond Tutu and Jody Williams, "Earth's riches should help the poor", *International Herald Tribune*, April 27 2004.

12 Nadia Martinez, Institute for Policy Studies, "World Bank ignores its own advice", *Christian Science Monitor*, August 16 2004, ibid.

13 Nadia Martinez, "More evidence of how the World Bank teams up with profit, not the poor!", *New Internationalist*, Oxford, November 2004, page 6.

14 *World Bank' Pull Out of Oil and Coal' Now Official Advice – Friends of the Earth International Media Advisory*, Friends of the Earth International, Washington DC, November 25 2003.

15 Carol Welch, *Statement on the World Bank and the extractive industries review*, Friends of the Earth International, Washington DC, September 24 2002.

16 In the first nine months of its Financial Year 2004, the IFC's overall commitment was nearly thirty per cent larger than during the same period of 2003.

Out of 1,242 projects around the world supported by the Corporation, as of March 31 2004, fifty six oil, gas and mining projects constituted 7 per cent of the portfolio, making this the third most important sector. If disbursements for primary metals production is included, then the metals-extractive industry sector as a whole ranks second only to finance and insurance as an IFC priority. IFC's commitments are greatest by far in Latin America (nearly two fifths of the global total of just over fifteen billion dollars): almost double those made to Asia, Europe and Central Asia combined, and five times those made to Africa. Of the ten largest IFC country exposures, the most critical is to Brazil (9.1 per cent of the total portfolio), followed by India (7.2 per cent of the total), Mexico (6.7 per cent) and Russia (6.3 per cent). Perhaps surprisingly, China (4.2 per cent) is rated lower than Argentina (5.6 per cent). The IFC's second largest "company exposure" is to the Baku-Tblisi-Ceyhan pipeline, in which Britain's biggest company, BP, plays the management role. Third comes the MOZAL aluminium smelter complex in Mozambique, operated by Australian-British BHPBilliton. Between them these two extractive projects comprise 1.5 per cent of the IFC's global outlay, with combined investment of US$239 million. Although this seems minor, it is actually one fifth of IFC commitments to the top ten companies in all sectors. See: Roger Moody, *Why the World Bank snubbed the EIR*, Nostromo Research, London, Special Paper, August 28 2004.

17   *World Bank Press Review*, Washington DC, October 12 2004.

18   Mining, Minerals and Sustainable Development project: Final Report *Breaking New Ground*, Earthscan Publications, London and Sterling VA, 2002, page 135.

19   *Letter to the Equator Banks – NGO concerns on IFC Safeguard Policy Review!*, Banktrack, Amsterdam, Sept 12 2004; *Two decades of environmental and social protection policies at risk*, Press release, Bretton Woods Project, September 21 2004. The World Bank claims that its Middle Income Country (MIC) strategy will be extended only to relatively stable states and "lower risk" projects, in the interests of "removing obstacles to timely quality lending": see Peter Bosshard, *The World Bank's Safeguard Policies Under Pressure: A critique of the World Bank's New Middle Income Country Strategy*, International Rivers Network, San Francisco, May 17 2004, page 1.

20   Andrew Balls, "World Bank 'weakening' social safeguards", *FT*, September 3 2004. See also "Campaigners slam World Bank 'sham' on environment", Conal Walsh, *the Observer* (UK), Sunday September 12, 2004.

21   Emily Caruso and Nick Hildyard, with Geoff Nettleton, *Background briefing for the World Bank Extractive Industries Review (EIR)*, Forest Peoples' Programme, Oxford, May 2003.

22   Caruso et al, ibid.

23   Caruso et al, ibid.

24   *FPRI and policy*, Letter to the Board of Directors, World Bank Group, from Angla Manglang Glupa' Pusaka, Philippines and 45 other Indigenous Peoples' Organisations, July 19 2004.

25   William T Onorato, Peter Fox, John Strongman, *World Bank Group Assistance for Minerals Sector Development and Reform in Member Countries*, Washington DC, December 18 1997, pages unnumbered.

26   The consequences of constructing this project and its infrastructure, are summarised in Bruce Rich, *Mortgaging the Earth: The World Bank, Environmental Impoverishment and the Crisis of Development*, Earthscan, London 1994, pages 26, 27, 29-33. Although the IFC acquired a minor equity of 7 per cent in the project, this proved to have a successful "demonstration effect" on other investors. Before long, the European Commission (EC), as well as European and Japanese steel companies, had between them secured around 60 per cent of output from the world's richest source of iron ore. Companhia do Vale Rio Doce (CVRD) was the power behind the diggers. In 1982 CVRD signed an agreement with the country's Indian Protection agency, FUNAI, to demarcate a zone of protection for the thousands of indigenous people at risk from the mine. However, the compact was ignored and the consequences were appalling. While the Bank had made the demarcation a precondition of its loan, it did almost nothing to remedy the dereliction: See: Bertram Zagema, Roger Moody, Karin Blauw, Ronald Boon, *Taking Responsibility: Metal Mining, People and the Environment*, Friends of the Earth Netherlands (Milieudefensie), Amsterdam December 1997, pps.16-18.

27   *The strategy for African Mining*, World Bank Technical Paper number 181, Washington DC 1992. See also: Felix Remy, *World Bank Financing for the Mining Sector*, Mining Unit, Industry and Energy Division, Africa Technical Dept, World Bank: Address to the International Lead and Zinc Study Group, Sao Paulo, February 7 1991. For a summary of the Bank's millennium mining policy, see: *Treasure or Trouble? Mining in Developing Countries*, World Bank and IFC, Washington 2002.

28   *Inter alia*, the mining corporations in 1988 demanded that South-based countries should guarantee "higher rates of return than in developed countries" and a "payback' (investment rate of return or IRR) between 20 per cent and 25 per cent over 2-4 years. In contrast, the companies readily accepted a considerably lower IRR of 13 per cent to 17 per cent from industrialised countries, with payback extending to six years. The risks of asset "appropriation" (principally through nationalisation), adverse exchange fluctuations, "community disruptions and general conflict," were said to account for this bias. See Remy, *World Bank Financing for the Mining Sector*, ibid, p. 44.

29   These comments were made in the specific context of Peruvian "reform," but the policy was soon to be widely applied elsewhere: see Remy, ibid, p. 47.

30   Groupe de recherche sur les activités minières (GRAMA), "The challenge of development, Mining codes in Africa and Corporate Responsibility", in *International and Comparitive Mineral Law and Policy*, Elizabeth Bastide, Thomas Wade and Janeth Warden (eds), Centre for Energy, Petroleum and Mineral Law and Policy, University of Dundee, June 2003; summarised in *MJ*, February 14 2003, p. 106.

31 GRAMA ibid, p. 106.

32 Onorato, Fox, Strongman, *World Bank Group Assistance for Minerals Sector Development and Reform in Member Countries*, op cit.

33 GRAMA, op cit, p. 108.

34 *Business Day*, February 8 2004.

35 MMSD, *Breaking New Ground: Mining, Minerals and Sustainable Development*, Earthscan Publications, London and Sterling VA, 2002, p. 167.

36 *Fiscal Regimes Supplement to MJ*, February 17 1998.

37 *MJ*, May 22 1998.

38 R Callicx, "World Bank tells Papua New Guinea its help depends on reforms", *Australian Financial Review*, May 22 1999.

39 "Philippines Road to Recovery", *MJ*, August 18 1995 pps.118-119.

40 Mineweb, August 23 2004.

41 In early 1998 Indonesia's mining regime was held up by PriceWaterhouseCoopers as "a model for other nations"; see Robert Parsons, Chairman Price Waterhouse Coopers' World Mining Group, "Indonesia's Fiscal Regime – A Model for Other Nations", *Advertisement Supplement to Mining Journal*, London February 27 1998. Later that year, however, the government announced it would change the royalties system, to provide more payments to local governments and "assuage growing resentment against foreign mining companies," (FT, December 4 1998). Although profits decentralisation has occurred, and some overseas assets have reverted to national companies, local communities have yet to see any major benefits, while in 2004, previously protected rainforests were opened up to both domestic and foreign mining companies. Papua New Guinea floated its state-owned Mineral Resources Development Company (now Orogen) to the private sector in 1995. At the same time it, too, raised royalty rates to provide higher benefits to local landowners (FT, March 22 1950), with somewhat more success than in Indonesia. The Catamarca provincial government of Argentina in 1998 came into dispute with the central government over interpretations of the 1993 Mining Act, when it demanded a 3 per cent royalty on output from the Alumbrera mine, the country's most significant earner of foreign exchange (MJ, January 9 1998). Bank-drafted minerals investment codes were imposed on Peru under the corrupt regime of President Alberto Fujimori, exposing the country to a huge minerals rush during the early 1990s. More territory was licensed to overseas mining companies, at near giveaway rates, than in all Peru's previous history. In 2000 a new government tried to temper this retrogressive legislation by abolishing the right of mining companies to reinvest profits tax-free, and by doubling the cost of holding mineral-concessions (FT, July 19 2000). The move was abandoned soon afterwards, following strident industry opposition in June 2004 ("Peru sets new royalty rates", *Mineweb*, Johannesburg, June 7 2004). At the same time the Chilean government belatedly promised to introduce royalties, for the first time in the country's history (James Rose, "Miners operating in Chile may face new tax", *Ethical Corporation Newsletter*, July 7 2004). Calls from some Chilean politicians for a minerals tax had, in fact, been made seven years earlier (MJ, September 5 1997; MJ, September 12 1997; MJ, February 27 1998).

42 World Investment Report, United Nations, Geneva, 1999; see also Bonnie Campbell's discussion of "depoliticisation" due to the changed role of the state, in "Liberalisation, deregulaton, state-promoted investment – Canadian mining interests in Africa", *Raw Materials Report, Journal of Mineral Policy, Business and Environment*, Raw Materials Group, Stockholm, vol 13 No 4, p. 15.

43 Roger Moody, *Plunder!*, Partizans and Cafca, London and Christchurch, 1991, page 113. It was chiefly under Rio Tinto's sponsorship that the Institute for Petroleum and Minerals Policy and Law – now the Centre for Energy, Petroleum and Mineral Policy and Law – was established at Dundee, Scotland to advise on, draft and introduce, new mineral codes around the world. Private consultants have also been engaged for the purpose; e.g. the UK consultancy Chris Morgan, acted for the European Union in "liberalizing" Armenia's minerals legislation in 2002 (*MJ*, January 18 2002).

44 *MJ*, August 18 1995.

45 Sintraminercol et al, *Statement from Colombia Trade Union organizations: To the Spoilers the Victory – Colombia Privatises the Mineral Industry with World Bank support*, Bogota, October 29 2003.

46 Reuters news report, Rio de Janeiro, April 30 1997.

47 *MJ*, August 30 1996.

48 See: Kathleen Anderson, "Mining, privatisation and the environment", in *Raw Materials Report, Journal of Minerals Policy, Business and the environment*, Stockholm, volume 11. No 3, p. 26.

49 Thomas Catan, "The sins of Montesinos", *FT magazine*, July 26 2003.

50 Bonnie Campbell, "Liberalisation, deregulation, state promoted investment – Canadian mining interests in Africa", in *Raw Materials Report, Journal of Mineral Policy, Business and Environment*, Stockholm, Vol 13, No 4, p. 16.

51 Campbell, ibid, p. 18.

52 C P Chandrasekhar, *Lessons from the Balco Fiasco*, Macroscan, February 22 2001.

53 Flavio E N Hegenberg, "Brazilian mining industry in the age of liberalisation", *Raw Materials Report*, vol 12, No 3, p. 8.

54 *IFC Quarterly Report on IFC Project Activities*, Washington DC, June 2002, p. 26.

55 *MJ*, October 29 2004.

56 Patricia Feeney, *The Limitations of Corporate Social Responsibility on Zambia's Copperbelt: Konkola Copper Mines (KCM): Environmental Management Plan (May 2001)*, Oxfam, Oxford, 2001.

57 Peter van der Veen, *The World Bank's role in Mineral Development*, PricewaterhouseCooper paper delivered to the Global Mining Conference, San Francisco, June 1-3 1999.

58 Placer withdrew from Las Cristinas in July 2001 after a prolonged courtroom struggle for ownership with a Canadian junior mining company, Crystallex International Corp. Placer had tried to transfer its "rights" to Vancouver-based

Vannessa Ventures, whereupon the Venezuelan government's industrial holding company, Corporacion Venezolana de Guayana (CVG) sent troops to re-possess the deposit. Soon afterwards, the Venezuelan government handed the project back to Crystallex, thus snubbing Vannessa which then threatened to drag the controversy through national and international courts if necessary. All this occurred while Las Cristinas was the subject of the tri-sector partnership study. Yet none of this conflict featured in the BPD's evaluation.

59   Programme was apparently concluded by 2005.

60   See Forest Peoples Programme, Indigenous Peoples Links, World Rainforest Movement, *Undermining the forests: The need to control transnational mining companies: a Canadian case study*, Moreton-in-Marsh, 2000, p. 15.

61   M A Thomas, *Evaluation of the World Bank Group's Activities in the Extractive Industries*, Background paper, OED-World Bank, Washington, January 2003.

62   Thomas, ibid, p. 11.

63   Thomas, ibid, p. 11.

64   Thomas, ibid, p. 20.

65   Thomas, ibid, p. 3.

66   Thomas, ibid, p. 3.

67   Thomas, ibid, p. 13.

68   IFC official document, *Enhancing IFC's Results in Response to the Millennium Challenge; Annual Review of IFC's Evaluation Findings FY 2002*, Washington DC, February 19 2003, p. 16.

69   In all categories, apart from "Economic Sustainability", the IFC's "success indicators" – including "development outcomes" – were worse in 2001 than they had been three years earlier: IFC ibid, Annex 6, p. 1.

70   *MJ*, March 14 2003.

71   See *Newmont: why are people around the world so MAD at this company?*, Report from Project Underground, Berkeley 2000, page 19.

72   *IFC Project Summary Sheet*, FY1993-2001, IFC, Washington 2002.

73   *IFC Project Summary Sheet*, ibid, p. 3.

74   *MJ*, June 23 2000.

75   Missy Ryan, *Plight of Peru town dim after mine's mercury spill*, Reuters report, July 3 2002.

76   Quoted in *Mining Environmental Management*, London, November 2000.

77   Gary McMahon and Felix Remy, *Large Mines and the Community*, Chapter One, IDRC, p. 20

78   McMahon and Remy, ibid, p. 24.

79   Roger Moody, *Five minutes to Midnight*, Minewatch Briefing on Omai, London, 1995. See also Chapter 5 of this book.

80   According to a Guyana member of parliament, MIGA told the Omai sub-commission, set up to investigate the disaster, that, if the government imposed any new environmental regulations on the mine, it would be "tantamount to nationalisation," compelling MIGA to pay compensation to Cambior and Golden Star.

See "Community Leaders of Riverain Communities Affected by the 1995 Omai Cyanide Spill", Letter to Gerald T West, MIGA, March 18 2000.

81 *IFC Monthly Operations Report*, Washington DC, October 2002, page 32.

82 FOE, *Mined Out: The environmental and Social implications of Development Finance to Rutile Mining in Sierra Leone*, London, April 1997, p. 7.

83 *Mined Out*, ibid, p. 6.

84 *Mined Out*, ibid, p. 6.

85 See Paul McGeough and Tony Wright, "The Diamond Dogs of War", *Sydney Morning Herald*, April 11 1997. Although EO finally quit Sierra Leone in early 1997, accused of major human rights abuses (Reuters report 13, November 1995), SRL thereupon engaged the services of Lifeguard, a thinly-veiled EO subsidiary.

86 E Schwartz, *World Bank Backs Russian Gold Venture Over some Objections*, Bloomberg News Service, USA, August 10 2000.

87 Personal communications to PEEC, February-March 2001.

88 FOEI, *Risky Business*, Washington DC, 2001.

89 Carol Welch and others, FOEI Letter to MIGA, Washington DC, April 2002.

90 Geoff Evans, James Goodman and Nina Lansbury (Eds), *Moving Mountains: Communities Confront Mining and Globalisation*, Zed Books, London 2002 pps.46-47. Among the instruments cited by OPIC in support of this decision were the London Convention on Dumping at Sea, the US Clean Water Act and the Marine Protection Research and Sanctuaries Act. See Roger Moody, *Into the Unknown Regions: the hazards of STD*, International Books and Society of St Columban, Utrecht and London, 2001, op cit, p. 56.

91 Boulle has been likened to "a powerful private player... with access to significant amounts of money, raw materials, military technology and even a private rapid reaction force [who] can deviously pursue his own private agenda. That is what Boulle does". (Johan Peleman, "Mining for Serious Trouble: Jean-Raymond Boulle and his Corporate Empire Project", in *Mercenaries: An African Security Dilemma*, Pluto Press, London, 2000, pps. 165-166). See also Roger Moody, "Out of Africa: mining in the Congo basin", in *The Congo Basin/le bassin du Congo*, IUCN, Amsterdam 1998, p. 137.

92 Pratap Chatterjee, "Mercenary Armies and mineral wealth", *Covert Action Quarterly*, number 62, Washington, Fall 1997, p. 36.

93 (Eds) Abdel-Fatau Musah and J Kayode Fayemi, *Mercenaries: An African Security Dilemma*, Pluto Press, London, 2000, p. 69.

94 *MJ*, October 25 2002; *MJ*, November 8 2002.

PART 2

Case Studies

CHAPTER 4

Freeloading Freeport

4.1 INTRODUCTION

Roger Moody

Gouged out of the cloud-shrouded Grasberg mountain in Indonesian-occu-pied West Papua sprawls one of the biggest man-made pits on planet earth.[1] The eponymous mine, operated by Freeport and Rio Tinto,* delivers more gold than any other single minerals venture, and is the world's third most important source of copper. Not surprisingly, it also spews out more tail-ings and waste rock than any other extractive operation. Ever since it came on stream Grasberg has been a synonym for social dislocation and environ-mental destruction. Its impacts have galvanised an unprecedented alliance of local, national and international protesters and, in 1996, it became the first major mining project to be cited under the US Alien Tort Claims Act (ATCA) – albeit the claim was later denied. There have been earlier such transna-tional campaigns, notably against Rio Tinto's Rossing Uranium in Namibia from 1975, and the Ranger and Olympic Dam uranium ventures in Aus-tralia, shortly afterwards. But only the Grasberg operations have (outside their host territory) served to mobilise lobbyists as diverse as Human Rights Watch (USA), Amnesty International, the International Chemical, Energy, and Mineworkers Union, Friends of the Earth, church leaders, academics,

---

* Officially there has never been a company called "Freeport-Rio Tinto". However, in 1985, the British company bulwarked its US partner with massive funding (and kudos) – at a stroke making itself the biggest single shareholder in Freeport Copper and Gold. People against Rio Tinto and its Subsidiaries (Partizans) coined the term at that time to emphasise the critical role in Grasberg, played by what was then the world's biggest mining enterprise. Over the following nine years, a large number of campaigners around the world followed the Partizans' lead. In early 2004 Rio Tinto sold its equity in Freeport Cooper and Gold but retained its right to 40 per cent of the Grasberg production, exploration budget, and consequent output.

anthropologists, activist shareholders and mining advocacy organisations in the US, Britain, the Netherlands, Germany, Australia and Indonesia itself.

Professor Al Gedicks is the founder of the Center for an Alternative Mining Development Policy, one of the first groups anywhere to confront the industry's *modus operandi* from the perspective of local communities. He has authored two commanding works on the mining industry: "The New Resource Wars: Native and Environmental Struggles against Multinational Corporations" (South End Press, Boston, 1993) and "Resource Rebels: Native Challenges to Mining and Oil Corporations" (South End Press, Boston, 2001). In the follolwing essay he describes the growth of various campaigns against Freeport-Rio Tinto's exploits in West Papua. Gedicks demonstrates that the granting of political risk insurance to Grasberg, though dwarfed by other investments in the mine, was the critical focal point for activists in the mid-nineties.

In turn, this repudation of PRI provoked an unprecedented counter-attack by Freeport, not only on NGOs but on the US State department itself. It also forced Freeport (doubtless under internal pressure from its higher-profile partner, Rio Tinto) to commission long-overdue environmental and social impact assessments; to appoint a Human Rights Ombudsman; and to make Tom Beanal – previously the prime Amungme critic of the mining – a company advisor. Freeport-Rio Tinto's much-reviled "1 per cent fund", set up to channel vestigial profits into village-based development and small scale businesses, has been expanded with the establishment of new trust funds. While Rio Tinto claims that these pay-outs provide "recognition of the traditional land rights of the Amungme and Komoro tribes,"[2] in fact the legal implementation of those rights *(adat)* remains as chimerical as ever.

During the same period (1999-2003), the Indonesian government dramatically increased its military presence in West Papua, mainly in the Grasberg concession areas, ostensibly to offset the growth of so-called separatist movements (in particular the Organisasi Papua Merdeka or OPM). Successive Indonesian governments have offered various forms of political "autonomy" which have been overwhelmingly rejected by many West Papuans as ill-conceived and woefully inadequate. Well-documented atrocities, illegal imprisonment, torture and forced removals, on the part of state forces, rendered West Papua the most beleaguered province in all Indonesia, with the exception of Aceh. During 2002 and early 2003, leading Papuan human rights workers were themselves receiving death-threats, widely believed to originate with the army.

Initially, this escalation of externally-imposed violence shifted domestic and international attention away from the mining operations. Both Freeport and Rio Tinto condemned generic human rights abuses and, in 2001, they even had the temerity to offer a grant to Indigenous women's leader Mama Yosefa "to promote human rights in Papua with special focus on women and children," though she was locked in earnest combat with the companies at that very time.[3]

However, if these moves provided temporary respite from criticism, Freeport-Rio Tinto was soon firmly back on the firing-line. The 2002 murders of three teachers (two of them American), based in the mining area, were initially ascribed by the Indonesian government to the OPM. But ELS-HAM, the West Papua Human Rights group, soon provided evidence that members of the military were probably the real culprits. Australian researcher, Denise Leith, has argued that the killings were a blunt and bloody warning to Freeport/Rio Tinto not to divulge the true extent of its monetary support to the army, and thereby be forced to withdraw it.[4] Under the Sarbanes-Oxley legislation, brought in by the US government after the Enron scandal, US companies are now compelled to reveal such figures. In March 2003 Freeport admitted that – in the previous year alone – it had paid US$5.3 million for such "protection".[5]

Nor have environmental issues slipped into the background. Four workers plunged to their deaths when the waste rock dump pile, at Lake Wonagaon, collapsed in May 2000. Following this disaster, Freeport/Rio Tinto agreed to limit its dumping to 200,000 tonnes of ore a day; shortly afterwards it was permitted to go to 210,000 tonnes/day.[6] One year later, however, an Indonesian court damned the company for giving "misleading" and "manipulative" statements about the nature of what the company euphemistcally dubbed a "slippage".[7] And, in June 2003, the Indonesian Minister of the Evironment himself threatened to take the Grasberg duo to court, unless they drastically reduced the impacts of tailings and rock disposal.

The environmental initiative against the companies thus appears to have been partially assumed by the government, ably informed by Indonesian NGOs, such as WALHI and JATAM. The appalling and mounting violation of villager's human rights, previously concentrated on the mining concession, has spread to other areas. While Grasberg remains a focus of discontent, it is the militarisation of West Papua and wilful suppression of self-determination for its peoples, rather than the specific legacy of resource colonisation, which now appears to have moved to international centre-stage.

Notes

1   Grasberg is an extension of the Ertsberg mine, originally worked by Freeport until ore was exhausted.

2   Rio Tinto, *Annual report and financial statements*, 2002.

3   *Business Wire*, New Orleans, April 20 2001.

4   Denise Leith, *The Politics of Power: Freeport in Soeharto's Indonesia*, University of Hawaii Press, 2002.

5   *Jakarta Post*, March 17 2003, *Time magazine*, February 17 2003.

6   *Mining Journal* (*MJ*), London, May 26 2000.

7   *MJ*, August 31 2001.

4.2 West Papua: The Freeport/Rio Tinto Campaign*

Al Gedicks

One of the most controversial mining projects on the planet is the gold and copper mine started on the island of New Guinea in the 1960s. New Guinea is the world's second largest island. In 1975, the eastern half of the island achieved independence from Australia and became Papua New Guinea; that nation now includes several eastern-lying islands as well. The western half of the island, known as West Papua, had been earlier invaded and annexed by Indonesia. Separated by 2,300 miles of ocean waters from the rest of the Indonesian archipelago, the new easternmost province under Jakarta's rule was renamed Irian Jaya.

But the incorporation into the Indonesian fold has been far from copacetic. "The people of West Papua," according to one geographer, "are different in all respects from their rulers in Java: language, religions, identity, histories, systems of land ownership and resource use, cultures and allegiance".[1] Papuan people are Melanesian, not Indonesian. Melanesians also live in Papua New Guinea, the Solomon Islands, Vanuatu, Kanaky, Fiji and the Torres Straits Islands which lie between New Guinea and Australia. Along with the other "outer" island provinces of Sumatra, Kalimantan and Sulawesi, West Papua has been forcibly incorporated into the Indonesian colonial empire primarily because of the former Dutch colony's substantial resources:[2]

> Copper, gas, oil, nickel, gold and silver and especially space in which to settle its huge surplus population are some of the attractions which led Indonesia to colonize West Papua. Mineral extraction, industrial fishing, logging and a plantation economy are all undertaken by international companies with the support and backing of Indonesian businesses.

Anthropologist David Hyndman has summarized the experience of many of the Melanesian native peoples with these projects: "As Fourth World Melanesians in the vicinity of the projects experienced ecocide, incorporation into larger regional, national, and international socio-economic networks, and conversion of their natural resources into national and transnational

---

* This essay is an updated version of "West Papua: The Freeport/Rio Tinto campaign" which comprises chapter 3 of Al Gedick's *Resource Rebels: Native Challenges to Mining and Oil Companies* published by South End Press, Boston, 2001.

resources, they responded with social protest."[3] This chapter – a case study of the Freeport mining project in West Papua – illustrates both the dynamics of the West Papuan social protest movement and its linkage with international environmental and human rights advocacy groups.

New Orleans-based Freeport McMoRan, together with Rio Tinto (formerly Rio Tinto Zinc),are responsible for the world's largest gold mine and the third-largest copper mine, Grasberg, situated in West Papua.[4] The open pit mine has been carved out of a snow-capped mountain, considered sacred by the native peoples, more than 13,500 feet above sea-level in the central highlands of the island. Freeport was the first foreign company to invest in Indonesia after General Suharto came to power in 1965 by overthrowing the Sukarno government and launching a blood-bath that led to the slaughter of at least 500,000 people.[5] Freeport's CEO, James Robert ("Jim Bob") Moffett calls Suharto a "compassionate man".[6]

Evidence uncovered after the 1965 massacre showed that the United States not only condoned the massacre but actively participated in it. Investigative reporter Kathy Kadane wrote that in 1965, high-ranking U.S. diplomats and CIA officials provided lists of Indonesian Communist Party (PKI) members to the Indonesian army. Robert Martens, a former political officer at the U.S. Embassy in Jakarta told Kadane: "[The lists were] a big help to the army. They probably killed a lot of people, and I probably have a lot of blood on my hands, but that's not all bad. There's a time when you have to strike hard at a decisive moment."[7] Noam Chomsky reflected on the absence of remorse from government officials when Kadane's revelations were published in the *Washington Post* in 1990:[8]

> The general satisfaction over the Indonesian slaughter and its aftermath helps us understand the criteria by which terror should be evaluated...We do not regard murder, torture, slaughter, and mutilation as pleasurable in themselves. To be acceptable, they must meet the condition of salutary efficacy...The only mass-based political force in Indonesia stood in the way of the goals of privileged sectors of the West. Therefore, its destruction was hailed as a great achievement, in no way inconsistent with the fabled yearning for democracy that guides our every thought, in fact, a necessary step towards achieving the blessings of democracy.

In 1967, not long after the military overthrow of the Sukarno government, Indonesia granted Freeport the right to exploit West Papua's mineral resources-two years before the so-called "Act of Free Choice" (or "Act of No Choice" as many Papuans dubbed it) ceded West Papua to Indonesia.[9] Apparently Freeport assumed that the 1969 referendum by which the West

Papuans were to determine their relationship to Indonesia was a foregone conclusion.[10] At the official opening ceremony of the mine in 1973, President Suharto renamed the territory Irian Jaya – an acronym for "Follow Indonesia Against Holland". Henceforth the Papuan, or Melanesian population, who numbered about a million would be renamed Irianese and use of the geographical name West Papua was forbidden.[11]

Both Freeport/Rio Tinto and Indonesia have benefitted from this colonial takeover at the expense of the native Papuans. The value of the Grasberg Mine exceeds $60 billion. In 1997 Freeport removed $1.5 billion of copper, gold and silver ore from Grasberg,[12] delivering a $208 million profit that year.[13] While 1998 falls in copper and gold prices dented profits appreciably, the mine has since expanded dramatically, reaching a daily throughput of up to 240,000 tons of ore by mid-1999.[14] The company's intention is to increase this rate to 300,000 tons a day "when metal prices improve"[15] – which would make it probably the largest creator of mineral wastes of any mine on the planet.

But while the mine has been very profitable for Freeport and Rio Tinto, it has been an unmitigated disaster for the Amungme, the 13,000 native people who live around the mine, the Komoro, who live downstream from it, and others who live in the company's vast exploration lease, some of which borders on the famed Lorentz National Park.

Anti-Colonial Resistance

Indonesia invaded West Papua in 1962 as the Dutch were preparing to hand over power to the local Melanesian people.[16] The attack failed, but President Kennedy pressured the Dutch into surrendering West Papua to the United Nations on the grounds that Indonesian President Surkarno might otherwise join the communist world. Surkarno had just concluded an important arms deal with Moscow and was threatening another invasion of West Papua.[17] Washington's special UN ambassador, Ellsworth Bunker, negotiated a highly controversial New York Agreement, which provided for UN control of the territory for seven months before handing it over to Indonesia. The Papuans were never consulted during this entire process. Their right to self-determination was sacrificed on the altar of Cold War politics.

From the time West Papua was forcibly incorporated into Indonesia in 1963, the native population has resisted Indonesian authority just as they resisted their former Dutch colonizers.[18] Indonesia has responded to Papuan resistance with military force and programs of forced assimilation. One of the most important parts of forced assimilation was the transmigration program, which involved moving Javanese settlers and military units from the overcrowded island of Java to West Papua in what one geographer called "the world's largest invasion" financed by the World Bank, the European Economic Community, Asian Development Bank, the United States and the United Nations Development Program, among others.[19]

Under Indonesian law, native peoples must give up "their customary rights over land and resources [adat] to so-called national development projects, which include mines".[20] Because Indonesia declared transmigration a national priority, the traditional land rights of native people were also not allowed to stand in the way of transmigration settlements.[21] Hyndman has described the collusion between Indonesia and Freeport to mine gold and copper on native land as "nothing short of economic development by invasion".[22] Bechtel Construction paid several hundred Amungme $.10 (U.S.) per hour for unskilled construction work but, once the mine was operating, only forty continued to be employed.[23] Of the 18,000 jobs connected with the mine, only 1,500 during the early years were filled by West Papuans and only 400 filled by local people.[24]

Freeport's disregard for the rights of the Amungme sparked a protest in 1977 in which villagers, with the assistance of independence fighters from the Free Papua Movement (OPM), blew up a Freeport ore pipeline. The Indonesian military responded by sending U.S.-supplied OV 10 Bronco attack jets to strafe and bomb villagers. The retaliation was code-named Operation *Tumpas* ("annihilation"). Papuans claim that thousands of men, women and children were killed in this action; the government admits to 900.[25] Reports of the use of these counterinsurgency aircraft did not appear in the world press until a year later. These same Broncos were also being widely used in East Timor to defeat the guerrilla resistance to Indonesian occupation.[26] While the U.S.-backed Indonesian massacre in East Timor received some limited coverage internationally, the comparable massacre in West Papua received hardly any notice.[27]

After the uprising the government forcibly resettled entire communities away from the mine to the makeshift township of Timika, near the coast.[28] In 1991, when a second contract was signed between Freeport and the Indonesian regime, the government was empowered to "assist the Company in arrangements" to remove even more communities from their traditional land.[29] This cozy relationship between Freeport and the Indonesian government has made this one of the most controversial, and one of the most militarized, mining operations on the planet.

By this time, Freeport was finally acknowldeging its responsibility in dumping over 110,000 tons of untreated mine waste (tailings) into the rivers of West Papua every day.[30] This practice is illegal in the United States. The company claims that the tailings are non-toxic, but it has refused requests from the Indonesian Forum on the Environment for independent testing and monitoring. The extent of the company's concern for secrecy was dramatically illustrated when Danny Kennedy of the Berkeley, California-based mining watchdog group Project Underground was deported in February 1997 for attempting to ship samples of the river's water to the United States for analysis.[31]

Moffett once described his company's operations as "thrusting a spear of economic development into the heartland of Irian Jaya".[32] Those who are most directly affected by Freeport's operations have a far different view of the situation but must be careful about what they say and to whom. When *Tifa Irian*, a local newspaper, began reporting on the environmental destruction and negative social impacts of the mine, Irian Jaya's General Director of Conservation warned that "anyone who does anything against Freeport is also against the government".[33] In 1998, Amungme spokesperson and matriarch Yosefa Alomang wanted to address Rio Tinto shareholders at the company's annual meeting, on the plight of her people. Her personal experience with human rights abuse has transformed her into a leading critic of Freeport's impact upon her people. She was taken from her home by soldiers one night in October 1994 and locked in a police station closet for three weeks.[34] Prior to her trip to London she was visited several times by Indonesian security forces who tried to intimidate her, and when she arrived at the airport, was prohibited from leaving the country.[35]

Under these circumstances, local NGOs must find ways to circumvent their own government and seek assistance from the international human rights and enviromental community to put pressure on their government from the outside. Organizations like Amnesty International and Survival International have been doing this kind of advocacy for human rights and native rights for a long time. What is innovative is the way in which traditional human rights issues have been coupled with environmental issues in a new generation of international organizations.

Transnational Advocacy Networks

The renewed assault on resource-rich native lands has been met by a rapid increase in the number of native organizations. Native rights advocate Julian

Burger has emphasized that these organizations "are now a distinct new force in world politics and their struggles can no longer be considered marginal to the main concerns of governments and, more generally, mankind".[36] In the last several years we have seen a variety of transnational environmental and native rights advocacy networks coming together to assist native communities under siege by the international oil and mining industries. Some of the major actors in these advocacy networks include the following: international and domestic nongovernmental research and advocacy organizations, local social movements, foundations, the media, churches and trade unions.[37]

The major impetus to the emergence of these networks is the understanding that the land rights of native communities in both Third World and even in some situations in advanced capitalist countries like the United States, Australia and Canada are routinely ignored, and major mining and oil projects are undertaken on native lands without the consent of those communities. In these situations, where governments are unresponsive or hostile toward the assertion of native land rights, "the boomerang pattern of influence characteristic of transnational networks may occcur: domestic NGOs bypass their state and directly search out international allies to try to bring pressure on their states from outside".[38]

Organizations such as Project Underground in the United States have brought together native rights, human rights and environmental issues in a network bound together by shared values, a common understanding of the problem and by ongoing exchanges of information and other forms of assistance. The role of information, easily and rapidly communicated by e-mail and fax, is a critical element in the success of these networks. The strategic use of information can "generate attention to new issues and help set agendas when they provoke media attention, debates, hearings, and meetings on issues that previously not been a matter of public debate".[39] Equally important is that the demands of native peoples are "framed in terms of existing international norms by internationally famous and charismatic leaders".[40] Recent examples of such leaders would include Chico Mendes and Paulinho Paiakan of Brazil, Ken Saro-Wiwa of Nigeria and Rigoberta Menchu of Guatemala.

Environmental and native rights activists have been compiling a database of multinational mining corporations and their worldwide operations for years. Publications like Roger Moody's *The Gulliver File: Mines, People and Land: A Global Battleground* provide local communities with the track records of hundreds of mining companies so that they can "intervene against mine plans or insist on better ones".[41] Also important to the success of these networks is the dramatic testimony of the people directly affected by environmental and human rights abuses that makes the case for action "more real for ordinary citizens".[42] Shareholders in corporations may find it easy to ignore the impacts of corporate policies on native peoples if those native peoples are halfway around the globe. Bring the people suffering from corporate-sponsored human rights abuses into the annual shareholders meeting, and it is much more difficult to ignore their concerns. Finally, the international contacts provided by these networks "can amplify the demands of domestic groups, pry open space for new issues and then echo back these demands into the domestic arena".[43]

Project Underground has seen itself on the front lines of a worldwide battlefield, "exposing the environmental and human rights abuses by the corporations involved and building capacity amongst communities facing mineral and energy development to achieve economic and environmental justice".[44] The Project's Freeport Campaign acted as a catalyst for about 20 international and Indonesian nongovernmental organizations, from UK Minewatch to the U.S.-based Sierra Club, Australia's Mineral Policy Institute and the Indonesian Forum on the Environment (WALHI), which is itself a coalition of 335 organizations from all over Indonesia. The broad aim of the campaign was to target a range of interests from industry insurers and private investors to the public, in order to pressure Freeport and Rio Tinto to act in a socially responsible fashion toward the people and environment around their operations in West Papua/ Irian Jaya.

This was no small task, given the absence of U.S. media coverage of the issue and Freeport's ability to restrict media access to its remote Grasberg mining operations. When Bill Elder, a news anchor for New Orleans Channel 4, asked Jim Bob Moffett for permission to visit the mine, he was told he could do so only if accompanied by Freeport escorts and only if he agreed to use equipment provided by the company. Elder turned down Moffett's offer and went on his own. In Sydney, Australia, the Indonesian consulate denied his entry into West Papua and told him he had to get permission from Freeport.[45] A professor at Tulane Law School in New Orleans put it bluntly: "Nobody visits Freeport's operations in Indonesia without, at the very least, Freeport's permission."[46] In those cases where journalists report unfavorably about Freeport, the company threatens legal action and/or spends millions on print and TV ads trying to create a favorable public image.[47]

In the case of Garland Robinnette, a co-anchor at the New Orleans CBS affiliate, who did several stories critical of Freeport's environmental practices, the company offered him a job as Freeport's vice-president of communications. Robinette accepted the offer in 1990 and developed the Planit Communications division to sell Freeport as environmentally responsible in the eyes of the public. The company sponsored "Focus Earth" infomercials for local TV and sent speakers to the local schools to talk about recycling and environmentally-responsible corporations.[48] In 1993, Planit became an independent company but retained Freeport as its biggest customer. Ironically, it was precisely this obsession with secrecy, security and its corporate image that provided an opening for the Freeport Campaign network.

Framing the Issue

The first and most important challenge for the Freeport Campaign was how to present the issues to the public in a way that would mobilize key constituencies to take concerted action. In their survey of issues around which transnational advocacy networks have organized most effectively, Keck and Sikkink note that one of the issue characteristics that appear most frequently is that "involving bodily harm to vulnerable individuals, especially when there is a short and clear causal chain (or story) assigning responsibility".[49] While the native people of West Papua have suffered repression at the hands of the Indonesian army since the first big mine (at Erstberg) began operating in 1972, Freeport was able to maintain some distance from this activity, at least in its public image.

All this changed in April 1995 when the Australian Council for Overseas Aid (ACFOA), the largest NGO in Australia concerned with development and human rights, released a report documenting the killing or disappearance of dozens of native people in and around Freeport's 5.75 million-acre concession, at the hands of the Indonesian army, between June 1994 and February 1995.[50] In reponse to the ACFOA report, the Catholic Church of Jayapura (the capital of West Papua) issued its own report based on first-hand interviews with Amungme eyewitnesses.[51] The report documents that from 1994 to mid-1995, summary executions, arbitrary detentions and torture occurred on numerous occasions in Freeport's concession area. The church report also charged that three civilians died while being tortured by Indonesian soldiers at a Freeport workshop. Freeport denied the workshop exist and adamantly denied that their security forces were involved in any killings. "We have an excellent relationship with the chiefs of the tribes," said Freeport senior vice-president Thomas J Egan. Any reports of civil unrest are "certainly not the case," he told a *Business Week* reporter.[52]

However, critics like Danny Kennedy of Project Underground argued that Freeport was directly involved in these ongoing atrocities and pointed to

Freeport's close relationship with the Suharto regime. "The Indonesian government owns a 9 per cent share in the mine and supplies soldiers, who are fed and sheltered by Freeport, to guard the mining areas."[53] Moreover, a 1995 U.S. State Department report on Indonesia confirmed that

> where indigenous people clash with development projects, the developers almost always win. Tensions with indigenous people in Irian Jaya, including the vicinity of the Freeport-McMoRan mining concession near Timika, led to a crackdown by government security forces, resulting in the deaths of civilians and other violent human rights abuses.[54]

The publicity following the reports of human rights abuses provided a further opening for the Amungme to draw attention to the environmental devastation they were suffering from current and planned mining expansion. By the company's own estimates, the Grasberg mine dumped more than 40 million tons of tailings into the Ajkwa River in 1996.[55] Environmental groups claimed that the enormous amounts of mine waste, which contain dissolved arsenic, lead, mercury and other potentially dangerous metals, had by 1999 destroyed roughly 26 square miles of rainforest, ruining palm tress that are the source of sago, a traditional staple in the native people's diets.[56] Residents along the Akjwa River were warned against drinking the polluted water by the provincial environmental authorities.[57] Freeport's expansion plans called for dumping 300,000 tons of tailings per day into the Ajkwa River. Even before these plans were confirmed – and while the projected disposal rate was 190,000 tons a day – Freeport's own consultant admitted that, over the 40 year life of the mine, 3.2 billion tons of waste rock will have been dumped into the local river system. Much of this rock is acid-generating and has already polluted a nearby lake.[58]

Most of the capital for Freeport's plant and exploration expansion (which has now reached $1 billion) came from Rio Tinto, which, by May 1999, owned 14.5 per cent of Freeport McMoRan Copper and Gold, the parent company of PT (Limited Company) Freeport Indonesia.[59] The British company's investment came in early 1995, at a time when Freeport's cash-flow was running perilously low.[60] Not only was Rio Tinto's 40 per cent contribution to the expansion critical to Freeport's fortunes; its share of the copper from Grasberg (136,000 tons in 1998) was the main factor in boosting Rio Tinto's copper output by 17 per cent in 1998 – helping make it one the world's major producers of the metal.[61]

Freeport's expansion plans at the time threatened the relocation of an estimated 2,000 people.[62] Shortly after Rio Tinto had announced its involvement with Freeport, the London-based Partizans (People Against Rio Tinto

Zinc and its Subsidaries) called on the company not to sign the agreement until shareholders had an opportunity to discuss the implications. The involvement of Partizans added yet another transnational advocacy network to the Freeport Campaign. Formed in 1978, at the request of Aboriginal communities in north Queensland, Australia, Partizans brought the concerns of native peoples to the attention of Rio Tinto directors by buying single shares in Rio Tinto stock. From 1980 to the present, this has enabled nearly 60 native people to attend the company's annual meetings and question its board. At the 1982 annual meeting, Partizans protestors took over the platform, and, for the first time at a British company's public meeting, the police were called in to eject an Australian Aboriginal delegate and 30 supporters. The event was headline news around the world the next day. When Partizans joined the Freeport Campaign, they brought more than 15 years of experience in networking with other campaigns around the issues of multinational mining, native peoples' land rights, and the effects of Rio Tinto and other mining companies on the environment and people's health.[63]

However, the UK company refused to delay signing the agreement. Rio Tinto closed the deal just before the annual shareholders meeting that year, a move designed, according to Partizans, to preempt any attempt to block the agreement.[64] As Partizans noted when the deal was finalized, Rio Tinto's experience in neighboring Papua New Guinea did not bode well for the Amungme and other native groups. The company had operated the Panguna copper/gold mine on Bougainville island until 1989, when it was shut down as a result of a guerrilla insurgency in response to Rio Tinto's disregard for native land rights and irresponsible mine waste disposal practices.[65]

By 1995 the Freeport Campaign was able to frame the issue as the inseparable connection between protecting one of the world's most pristine ecosystems and the vulnerable people who live in it. By joining the issues of human rights abuse and environmental degradation, the Freeport Campaign enabled the Amungme to go beyond the relatively weaker human rights advocacy network and tap into the stronger international advocay network of environmental groups.[66] The first targets of the campaign included a U.S. government insurance agency and the World Bank.

Targeting Responsible Parties

Jim Bob Moffett once dismissed the pollution from his company's West Papua mining operation as "the equivalent of me pissing in the Arafua Sea"[67] (the body of water into which the Ajkwa river flows). This arrogant disregard for the devastating impact of the mine was still apparent when the Overseas Private Investment Corporation (OPIC), a U.S. federal agency that provides support for American companies overseas, cancelled Freeport's $100 million political-risk insurance policy in October 1995. The insurance – carrying an annual premium of $1 million – provided Freeport with protection against damage to its assets from war, insurrection and unilaterial breach of contract by the Indonesian government.[68] But, as a federal agency, OPIC is also enjoined to take into consideration any adverse environmental or social consequences of projects it endorses. Following OPIC's public announcement, Moffett went on live television in New Orleans saying "There's been no claim by OPIC that we have an environmental problem."[69] However, when OPIC's letter to Freeport was leaked from within the agency (supporting materials later became available under the Freedom of Information Act) , there was no question that there was an environmental problem. OPIC said that "massive deposition of tailings and the sheetflow of tailings" from Freeport's mine into the Ajkwa river "has degraded a large area of lowland rainforest," posing "unreasonable or major environmental, health, or safety hazards with respect to the rivers, the surrounding terrestial ecosystem, and the local inhabitants".[70]

The cancellation of Freeport's insurance was the first time OPIC has cancelled a client's insurance for environmental reasons. Moreover, the cancellation was confirmed despite a major lobbying effort by former Secretary of State Henry Kissinger, who was a member of Freeport's board of directors and also a lobbyist paid about $400,000 per year for his services for Freeport. President Suharto also made a personal appeal to President Bill Clinton during a meeting at the White House.[71]

Freeport immediately launched a multimillion-dollar media strategy to respond to the OPIC decision and the unfavorable news coverage that followed. In addition to buying ads in *Newsweek* and U.S. *News & World Report,* the company took out two full-page ads in the December 5 1995 *New York Times* which blamed unnamed "foreign special-interest groups" for promoting "misleading accusations about our environmental record" which the ad claimed was "a model of development". The ads also attacked the U.S. Agency for International Development (AID) for giving funds to Freeport's detractors.[72] This was a reference to the Indonesian Forum for the Environment (WALHI). Prior to OPIC's announcement, the Jakarta-based WALHI, along with the International NGO Forum on Indonesian Development (INFID), had been asking Freeport, to neutralize its tailings before dumping them into the river, and to allow independent testing of the river's water quality. WALHI also filed a lawsuit in Jakarta against the Indonesian government for failing to follow national environmental laws when it issued mining permits to Freeport.

The company responded to the WALHI lawsuit by sending a letter to AID asking that it cut off all funding to the "newly radicalized" WALHI for "openly affiliating with radical international NGOs such as Earth First!, Friends of the Earth, Global Response and Greenpeace". It was a ploy that dismally failed. WALHI was also accused of "organizing protests" and using "access to the media to manipulate public discourse," a charge that of course would never be made against Freeport for its full page ads in the *Times*.[73] OPIC's decision to cancel Freeport's insurance was not just bad publicity for the company but a vindication of the claims that had been made by a transnational advocacy network for years.

The Freeport media counter-offensive continued with an article on "environmental imperialism" in *Forbes* magazine, which featured a picture of Jim Bob Moffett standing at his desk, with the caption: "Forced to his knees by environmental control freaks." The article made the case that U.S. AID "has become a virtual partner of the environmental extremist organizations" in imposing "environmental fascism" on U.S. companies operating abroad. The article accused Lori Udall, the Washington director of the Berkeley, California-based, International Rivers Network, of being part of an international conspiracy to "hold the financial institutions that are involved in Freeport's activities in Irian Jaya accountable" and of arranging for Indonesian activists to come to Washington, D.C. to meet with OPIC officials about Freeport's environmental violations and complicity in human rights abuses.[74]

In this bizarre reinterpretation of history, the imperialists are not the multinational corporations acting in concert with Suharto and the Indonesian military, but environmental and human rights activists. In other words, what upset Freeport the most about the OPIC insurance cancellation was the ability of the Freeport Campaign network to dramatically reinforce the attack on the company's environmental and human rights abuses. In this way, it became clear to a government agency, whose primary objective was to facilitate American foreign investment, that this company had gone so far beyond the limits of acceptable capitalist profit-maximizing behavior as to threaten the political stability of an already highly militarized police state system in West Papua.

Freeport campaigners then set their sights on a World Bank affiliate that also insured the Grasberg operation.[75] The Multilateral Investment Guarantee Agency (MIGA), offers insurance against political risks to companies in developing countries. MIGA had sold a $50 million policy to Freeport in 1990 – the first contract the fledgling agency had ever made. "OPIC has done the right thing," said Danny Kennedy, who was then an activist with the Action for Solidarity, Equality, Environment and Development (ASEED). "We are calling on the World Bank, which also guaranteed Freeport's mine, to follow their example immediately."[76]

But before pressure on MIGA could become effective, Freeport's own browbeating and blustering had apparently succeeded. Following an environmental assessment by the Australian consulting firm, Dames & Moore, which identified many problems with the mine but concluded the company was striving to remedy them, OPIC reversed its earlier decision. It would renew Freeport's political risk insurance from April 1996 until the end of that year, at which point it would reassess the situation in the light of improvements effected by the company.[77] This decision regrettably had more to do with pro-Freeport political maneuvering (in particular by Kissinger Associates) than logic or consistencies within OPIC. The one essential measure Dames & Moore did not recommend was the cessation of tailings disposal in the Ajkwa river system, even though this was clearly the only way that OPIC's original objections to the Grasberg operations could be met.

MIGA had planned to send a three-member team to West Papua in late 1996 as part of its own investigation of Freeport, when the company announced that it no longer required political risk insurance – whether by MIGA or OPIC. The timing of Freeport's announcement was seen by many critics as an attempt to pre-empt a full-scale investigation of the charges against Freeport and the possible disclosure of more damaging information.

On the other hand, the cancellations occurred just months after the most serious indigenous demonstrations at West Papuan mining towns since the beginning of the mining operations. Surely this was precisely the time that insurance against political risks was most required? The revolt started following an incident when a tribal man was hit by a car driven by a Freeport employee. Survival International estimated that 6,000 tribal people attacked Freeport's offices and facilities (but not people) in three towns connected with the mine.[78] On March 12, 1996, local protestors marched to the airport to meet the incoming plane of Jim Bob Moffett. Said an Amungme tribal leader:

"Because Jim Bob Moffett and Freeport are deaf to our complaints and demands, because the Government continues to ignore the problems of the Amungme and Komoro people and all the other native inhabitants of Irian Jaya, we have been forced to use this kind of language to tell them what we want."[79]

When Moffett met with the Amungme Tribal Council, LEMASA, the executive director of the organization said that local tribes were in agreement that "Freeport operations should be shut down."

Following this meeting LEMASA was warned by Brigadier-General Prabowo, Suharto's son-in-law and commander of the notoriously brutal special forces army unit, KOPASSUS, that this was tantamount to a declaration of war.[80] Clearly Freeport and its partner Rio Tinto felt they could rely on brute force, to protect their interests, better than a U.S. government agency and a World Bank affiliate, which were coming under public pressure.

After the revolt, the Indonesian army announced that a rapid deployment force battalion from the army's strategic command had been sent to the area to protect mining company property. Freeport also invested $35 million for barracks and other facilities for this military task force.[81] In December 1996, the Indonesian armed forces (ABRI) had created a special unit of no less than 6,000 troops (more than one soldier for each adult Amungme) to "safeguard" the mining complex. It was, declared the UK-based Indonesian Human Rights organization, TAPOL, "the only task force of its kind to exist anywhere in Indonesia".[82] According to Danny Kennedy, of Project Underground, "the mining concession is now the most militarized district in all of Indonesia. The military presence surpasses even that of occupied East Timor, where invading Indonesian forces have been fighting a popular resistance for more than 21 years."[83]

But there was still a token velvet glove barely covering the iron fist. Freeport also said that it would allocate at least 1 per cent of its gross revenues for the next ten years, an estimated $15 million per year, in support of "a comprehensive social development plan based upon the input of indigenous leaders during a year-long series of meetings".[84] However, none of the "indigenous leaders" that Freeport consulted included members of LEMASA, the representative organization for the native people living in the mining area. Instead, Freeport set up seven local foundations to be the recipients of the revenues. LEMASA rejected the 1 per cent Trust Fund as any kind of solution to the grievances that led to the March revolt. They also noted that the majority of the revenues went to government and military projects.[85]

The response of the Indonesian army to the revolt against Freeport left little doubt that the grievances of the native people would not be taken seriously in Jakarta. If the Amungme and other native groups wanted to press their claims against Freeport, they would have to find a more hospitable forum than their own government. With the help of the Freeport Campaign network the Amungme shifted the conflict from the West Papuan rainforest to the corporate headquarters of Freeport in New Orleans, Louisiana.

Tom Beanal and Yosefa Alomang v. Freeport-McMoRan

In April 1996, Tom Beanal, a leader of the Amungme Tribal Council, filed a $6 billion class action lawsuit in New Orleans district court, charging Freeport with human rights abuses, the robbery of Amungme ancestral lands, violations of international environmental law "tantamount to acts of eco-terrorism," and the "planned demise of a culture of indigenous people whose rights were never considered" during the course of the company's mining operations.[86] Freeport spokesperson, Garland Robinette, strongly denied the allegations contained in the lawsuit, claiming: "There is no basis in law or in fact for the claims." Richard C Adkerson, vice chairman of Freeport, called the suit "frivolous and opportunistic".[87]

With the help of Friends of the Earth and Project Underground, Tom Beanal came to New Orleans to meet with Martin Regan, the attorney handling the lawsuit, and to provide testimony in response to Freeport's attempt to have the case dismissed. The night before his testimony he spoke at Loyola University through an interpreter:[88]

> "[G]old and copper have been taken by Freeport for the past 30 years, but what have we gotten in return? Only insults, torture, arrests, killings, forced evictions from our land, impoverishment and alienation from our own culture. Even the sacred mountains we think of as our mother have been arbitrarily torn up by them, and they have not felt the least bit guilty... During the last 30 years, we tried to find justice, but we never found it. And now comes Mr. Martin [Regan], and I can see justice. I come here to ask for justice."

Beanal found the students at Loyala University especially receptive to his message. Freeport had already been targeted by a local environmental group, the Delta Greens, for dumping radioactive gypsum waste into the Mississippi river from the company's phosphate processing plants in New Orleans.[89] According to u.s. Environmental Protection Agency records, during the 1990's Freeport was the worst polluting company in the United States, based on the quantity of toxic materials released into the air, water and soil.[90] To reverse the company's anti-environmental image, Moffett donated $600,000 to Loyola to endow a chair in environmental communications. The chair was part of Freeport's Environmental Research Consortium of Louisiana that includes the University of New Orleans, Louisiana State University, Tulane University and Xavier University.[91]

Instead of improving the company's image, the controversy that erupted at Loyola only served to focus public attention on Freeport's abysmal record.

"By using an endowed environmental chair at Loyola in his efforts to disguise Freeport's role in ecological destruction and environmental injustice," wrote Loyola University philosophy professor John Clark, "Moffett presented the university with an inescapable responsibility to confront the issue".[92]

In April 1995, Assistant Law Professor William P Quigley sponsored a resolution that the $600,000 be returned to Freeport, citing "crimes against humanity in places like Indonesia as well as Freeport's lack of commitment to preserving the environment throughout the world".[93] While administrators at this Jesuit-run university sought to delay any campus-wide discussion of the endowment controversy, news of the OPIC decision prompted Professor John Clark to organize a protest march. Protestors, including Loyola faculty and students, marched outside Moffett's house carrying signs that read "Jim Bob kills for profit." Similar protests occurred at the University of Texas at Austin, which has also received large financial endowments from the company. After the New Orleans protest, Moffett asked the university to return the $600,000 gift. A journalist for the local New Orleans paper, the *Times-Picayune*, concluded that "Moffett asked for his money back to show his displeasure at Loyola University's failure to stifle dissent".[94]

If Moffett's objective was to buy off university dissent the same way he had bought off media dissent by hiring his critics, he was partially successful. After the OPIC news broke, the *Times-Picayune* received letters, supporting Freeport's record, from the president of Loyola University and UNO's chancellor and its dean of the College of Business. Tulane University paid for a full page advertisement in the *Times-Picayune* applauding Freeport's environmental record.[95]

A year after filing the lawsuit, a federal district court judge dismissed the case but left the door open for Beanal to amend his case with more specific allegations and refile it. More importantly, Judge Stanwood Duval ruled that Beanal and other tribal people had standing to bring damage claims against Freeport in a U.S. court. At that point, Yosefa Alomang became the chief plaintiff and Freeport lost all attempts to prevent a hearing taking place.[96] Both the federal court case and Louisana state court case were ultimately unsuccessful.[97] Despite the loss, the case was an important rallying point for thousands of Papuans seeking to hold Freeport's corporate executives accountable for their behavior in West Papua. Fortunately, they did not put all their energies exclusively into the lawsuits.

Exerting Leverage over Freeport

Echoes of the human rights allegations in the Beanal/Alomang lawsuit also figured prominently in a shareholder resolution filed by the Seattle Mennonite Church prior to Freeport's 1997 annual meeting. By working with religious denominations who own minority shares in a variety of multinational corporations, transnational advocacy networks can bring controversial issues directly before shareholders and ask them to vote for actions to be taken by the board of directors to address these concerns. Even if activists are unsuccessful in getting enough votes to compel action by the company, a large number of votes, usually anything over 3 per cent, has enormous symbolic value. It represents a public criticism of the company's corporate management and forces a company to state its position on issues in a public fashion. Resolutions that garner at least 3 per cent are automatically carried over to the following year's meeting.

Taken in conjunction with the lawsuit, the shareholder resolution represented a further challenge to Freeport's ability to control public discussion and debate about its Grasberg mine.[98] The church asked Freeport's board of directors to end the company's relationship with the Indonesian military and postpone expansion of mining operations until the company can resolve ongoing disputes with tribal people. The church also asked Freeport to release all of its environmental audits and to allow independent environmental monitoring.

CEO Moffett began the meeting by noting that the Beanal lawsuit was recently re-filed and called it an effort to "intimidate and shake down" the shareholders.[99] When it came time for the Mennonite proposal, Moffett advised Bob Pauw, a Seattle immigration attorney, that he had two minutes to speak to the resolution. Before he could finish his statement, Moffett cut him off. After Pauw's presentation, Moffett told Project Underground's Danny Kennedy that he had one minute to address the Mennonite proposal. Kennedy told Freeport board members that they should support the shareholder resolution because it made good business sense. He also pointed out that the revised Beanal lawsuit was very similar to one now pending in Los Angeles Federal Court against Unocal, which has been sued for human rights violations that occurred in relation to its natural gas pipeline project in Burma. In that case, a federal judge found Unocal potentially liable if it could be shown to be "accepting benefits of and approving" human rights abuses by the military.[100]

The Mennonite proposal garnered 2.5 per cent of the shares that were voted. While this was not enough for the proposal to be carried over to the following year's meeting, it was an impressive showing, especially in the context of the unprecedented security that Freeport had employed to preempt any protest at the meeting. Meanwhile, in London, Freeport's partner, Rio Tinto, was also being challenged for its complicity in human rights abuses at the Grasberg mine. The main challenger was the World Development Movement (WDM), one of Britain's most influential development campaign organizations, which in 1996 focused on Rio Tinto and the West Papua mine as a key instance of unacceptable multinational exploitation.[101] The WDM presented Rio Tinto's board of directors with a petition calling on the company to withdraw its shareholding in Freeport unless the company addressed the claims of the Amungme and Komoro peoples.[102] Rio Tinto defended its involvement in the Grasberg mine and avoided any response to the specific claims of the Amungme and Komoro. The inability of the Freeport campaigners to engage the board of directors, of either Freeport or Rio Tinto, in a dialgoue at their annual meetings, prompted a change of tactics the following year.

Activists in advocacy networks are constantly evaluating how to exert leverage over more powerful actors. The two most common forms of leverage are material and moral ones.[103] With the publication of alternative annual corporate reports, the Freeport Campaign network was able to identify both material (financial liability) and moral (public shaming) sources of leverage.

Prior to the 1998 Freeport annual shareholders meeting, Project Underground produced an independent annual report on Freeport's Indonesian operations and distributed it to the company's top 100 institutional investors, financial reporters and members of the company's board of directors.. The report, *Risky Business: The Grasberg Gold Mine,* attempted to persuade investors that they were not being told the entire story about the company's pattern of human rights violations around the Grasberg mine, and that this exposed the company to future risks and liabilities, including the ongoing litigation against the parent company.[104] Project Underground arranged for a shareholder briefing on the report the day before Freeport's annual meeting. In addition to several shareholders and reporters, Freeport senior vice presidents Thomas Egan and Paul Murphy showed up. They were quite upset with Project Underground for charging Freeport security and police with responsibility for the beating to death of a Dani tribal person, in *Risky Business.* The company had explained the death as due to malaria and dehydration, in an internal company memo obtained by Project Underground and reproduced in the report. Egan and Murphy threatened to sue Project Underground for libel. When Danny Kennedy produced a polaroid photo of the beaten man, obtained from the man's family, there was no further discussion of the issue. However, during the annual meeting the next day, Moffett took Kennedy aside and told him "I'm gonna take you down."[105]

In Europe and Australia, the Freeport Campaign network had meanwhile secured the commitment of the world's largest miners' union, the Brussels-based ICEM (International Federation of Chemical, Energy, Mine and General Workers' Union) to publish its own alternative annual corporate report. Entitled *Rio Tinto: Tainted Titan: The Stakeholders Report*, it covered several of the company's more unacceptable operations, focusing particularly on the Grasberg mine. Copies of the report were distributed to shareholders and the public at the 1998 Rio Tinto shareholders' meeting. Rio Tinto had early access to the report through the ICEM's own website.

The report identified "stakeholders" such as native groups, trade unions, environmental groups, churches, human rights groups and aid agencies who "have raised significant concerns over the company's systematic failure to address human and workers' rights and environmental protection at many of its operations around the world".[106] The report emphasized that the cost of ignoring these concerns will affect the company's bottom line. "With respect to occupational health and safety and indigenous peoples there is an increasing risk that the company will be involved in expensive litigation over compensation."[107] Rio Tinto's directors did not have to look very far to be reminded of this fact. In 1996, Broken Hill Proprietary (BHP), Australia's largest company, settled a class action lawsuit brought by native leaders downstream its Ok Tedi mine in Papua New Guinea that would cost the company about $500 million. The settlement required the company to come up with a plan to stop mine tailings from entering the local river.[108]

When confronted with questions about the report during the meeting, Rio Tinto's chairman, Robert Wilson, announced that he hadn't seen it until just minutes prior to the meeting. Nonetheless, shareholders were given a detailed rebuttal to the report immediately after the meeting – a rebuttal that could only have been prepared in advance.[109]

One indication of the effectiveness of the Freeport Campaign's shareholder actions is the fact that Freeport moved the shareholders' meeting from its traditional location in New Orleans to Wilmington, Delaware the following year. Critics claimed that the company moved the meeting to avoid negative publicity. Lending credibility to this interpretation was the fact that neither the company's Board of Directors nor CEO Moffett attended the meeting. This did not stop Freeport Campaign activists, and shareholders representing religous groups, from attending and raising concerns about the company's Grasberg mine. The network also brought John Rumbiak, a human rights worker from West Papua. Rumbiak told shareholders: "My people are fighting against you so that you can recognize our dignity as human beings."[110] It was Freeport's failure to respond to Amungme grievances that prompted the lawsuit against the company, said Rumbiak. At the same time that campaign activists were talking to shareholders, Yosefa Alomang was protesting outside Jim Bob Moffett's mansion in New Orleans.

Just in case anyone had any doubt about the international networking capability of the Freeport Campaign, on the same day as the protests in New Orleans and Wilmington, yet another Amungme representative, Paulus Kanongopme, attended the annual shareholders meeting of ABN Amro, a Dutch bank that has been financing Freeport. He told the bankers that Freeport has adversely affected an area the size of Belgium, either through mining, or from the in-migration that the company has attracted to the region. "My people have been killed by ABN Amro's investments," said Kanongopme. A top executive of ABN Amro expressed shock at the situation of the mine and assured Kanongopme that ABN Amro would maintain pressure on Freeport to conduct an independent environmental audit.[111]

Assessing the Freeport Campaign

Has the Freeport Campaign's transnational advocacy network been successful in presenting the issues in a way that could mobilize others to take action? If one looks at the public discussion and debate that has been generated in the media, within financial institutions, government agencies, U.S. courts, and shareholder meetings on two continents, it is clear that Freeport-McMoRan is facing demands for corporate accountability that Jim Bob Moffett would have considered inconceivable prior to 1995.

Despite a well-funded public relations effort to counter the negative publicity about human rights abuse and environmental devastation, Freeport was unable to prevent an unprecedented finding of environmental recklessness by a government insurance agency, repeated, well-documented, charges of human rights abuses by respected NGOs and church agencies, well-organized protests at shareholder meetings in New Orleans and London, or a multibillion dollar lawsuit filed on behalf of thousands of native people pushed off their land to make way for Freeport's Grasberg mine.

The Freeport Campaign network was able to provide both technical information about the environmental impacts of the Grasberg mine, and dramatic first person accounts of human rights abuses, to international constituencies as part of a strategy to assist local communities in West Papua in achieving some measure of economic and environmental justice. While con-

ditions in the communities immediately around the mine have not improved
and in some respects are even more oppressive, the organizational capability
of native organizations, such as LEMASA has increased and extended its reach
into the very center of Freeport's corporate headquarters in New Orleans.

By 1997, a report by one of the largest corporate consultants on political
risk noted that international NGOs had raised human rights and environmental issues pertaining to Freeport/Rio Tinto's West Papuan/Irian Jayan operations so successfully that they are now "as much a part of the mine's political
risk profile as Arungme (sic) tribespeople".[112]

Following the Indonesian populist uprising of May 1998, and the removal
of Suharto from office, there have been increasing calls for a public accounting of Freeport's cozy ties to the former dictator and a reconsideration of
Freeport's mining contract for the Grasberg mine. The company has been
forced to agree to pay increased royalties and to a further government stake
in Freeport-McMoRan Copper and Gold.[113] Before the Indonesian general
elections in June 1999, the government also suspended the company's exploration permit in outlying areas for "political and security reasons" – a euphe-
mism for the antagonism of local communities.[114] For a period, between
mid-1998 and early 1999, the Indonesian press and parliament rung with
accusations of complicity between ex-President Suharto and his cronies,
including a former mining minister, the timber tycoon Bob Hassan, an
investor group led by Aburizal Bakrie, and Freeport, in particular Jim Bob
Moffett. Bakrie and Freeport were accused of corruption in dealing in Freeport shares, contributing to the fiction that the U.S. company was divesting
to Indonesians, when it was actually consolidating control.

A checklist of these accusations appeared in the *Wall Street Journal*, which
also summarized the history of environmental problems and human rights
abuses at the Grasberg mine.[115] Although Freeport vehemently denied these
claims, it did not prevent the Indonesian House of Representatives from calling Moffett to defend the company's reputation in Jakarta.[116] More important
– though given less attention – was the fact that a parliamentary commission
had reported the month before that Grasberg "has not proved to be of sufficient benefit to the local people".[117]

"Freeport got away with murder," allegedly declared Mohammad Sadli,
Indonesia's foreign investment czar at the time Freeport signed its first mining contract in 1973.[118] What is certain is that the company, and its essential
helpmate, Rio Tinto, continue to get away with practices which would not
get past an initial social and environmental assessment in much of the rest
of the world – in particular the countries where the two companies are registered, and to which they return their fattest profits.

While the Freeport Campaign cannot take credit for the popular uprising against Suharto, it can certainly take some credit for the intense scrutiny of Freeport's Grasberg mine in a post-Suharto Indonesia. The international connections provided by the Campaign network did indeed overcome the media blackout on West Papua, provide new venues where environmental and human rights issues could be addressed, empower native communities to challenge Freeport's policies, and mobilize key constituencies to put pressure on Freeport to act in a socially responsible fashion. The Freeport Campaign network – inside and outside the country – has so far not stopped the environmental degradation and human rights abuses, but it did make it significantly more costly and politically risky for the company to continue doing business as usual. This was dramatically illustrated by the political response to events in 2000.

Freeport McMoran in the National Spotlight

Following a May 2000 landslide from Freeport's Lake Wanagaon waste site, WAHLI launched a national campaign for an environmental audit of the Grasberg minerock and a renegotiation of the terms of environmental management and income distribution. The announcement of this campaign had been preceded by a government commission visit to the Grasberg mine. The commission's report asserted that the mine resulted in socioeconomic injustice, rampant human rights abuse, and political tension.[119] On May 8, and again on May 18, protests against Freeport in Jakarta shut down the company's offices and prevented a thousand employees, from this and several other firms, going to work.[120] The protestors attacked Freeport's environmental record at Grasberg and demanded that the company return a larger share of the profits to the communities in West Papua.

The Indonesian government of then-President Abdurraham Wahid had already ordered Freeport to cut its output from the Grasberg mine while the government investigated the May 4th landslide. The company agreed to cut its output by around 30,000 tons from its level of 230,000 tons per day (tpd).[121] Given the company's recent investment to boost production to 300,000 tpd, it risked losing money on its capital investment, no matter what level of production was permitted. The company was also ordered to clean up the pollution caused by the toxic materials dumped by the landslide, and to compensate the losses suffered by local villagers. The Indonesian government also asked a new human rights commission to investigate possible abuses by Freeport at Grasberg.[122]

The Freeport situation is not exceptional. After sponsoring a national meeting to discuss the problems caused by gold mining, the Mining Advocacy Network (JATAM), an Indonesian non-governmental organization, called for the immediate cessation of all mining activties in Indonesia. According to JATAM, "Indonesia is standing at the verge of a massively serious ecological disaster, created largely by the mining industry."[123] U.S. AID responded immediately by cutting funding for JATAM. The group had received $75,000 to protect the rights of communities to manage their natural resources, and also assist in monitoring the impact of mining operations. Newmont Mining, a Denver-based U.S. mining company, had complained to the U.S. Embassy that taxpayer funds were being used to fund a campaign against a U.S. company. The issue came to a head after the director of JATAM attended Newmont's annual meeting and told shareholders about the company's dumping of toxic mine tailings directly into the rivers and coastal waters in North Sulawesi, yet another of Indonesia's outer islands.[124]

Indonesia's Minister of Environment Sonny Keraf assured reporters for the *Wall Street Journal* that President Wahid had no intention of shutting down Freeport's mining operations, though he wouldn't rule out a renegotiation of its contract. The chances that President Wahid would take any drastic measures against Freeport were, in fact, very slim. After taking office, President Wahid invited Henry Kissinger, former U.S. Secretary of State and Director Emeritus of Freeport's board, to be an unpaid adviser to the Indonesian government. Kissinger's trip to Jakarta coincided with the increasing demands for renegotiating Freeport's mining contract. His first piece of advice to the president was to honor the Freeport contract negotiated under the Suharto dictatorship. "Investors also expect an assurance of law enforcement," Kissinger told a legislative defense commission.[125] The reference to "law enforcement" was a reminder that Freeport McMoran expected the same level of military assistance for its operations as the Suharto dictatorship had provided.

However, the political upheavals in Indonesia had made investors nervous. In April 1999, Standard & Poor lowered its rating on $3.3 billion worth of Freeport debt and preferred stock, citing the firm's ties to Suharto and the possibility it could face "retribution and reprisals".[126] After the May 2000 landslide, investors' concern over the future of the company's Indonesian mining operations caused Freeport's stock price on the New York Stock Exchange to fall more than 50 per cent, from above $21 at the start of 2000, to $10.375 in May that year.[127]

From Revolt to Secession

The May 2000 environmental disaster at Freeport's mine also spurred the demands of the Papuan peoples for complete independence from Indonesia. Former governor of West Papua, Freddy Numberi, noted that the conflict between the local people and Freeport was the primary factor that had triggered the demand for independence.[128] Following the historic June 2000 Papuan People's Congress, Tom Beanal, deputy chairman of the Papuan People's Presidium Council, said there was now unanimity and determination to separate from the Indonesian Republic and to become a fully sovereign state.[129] Over 6,000 West Papuans gathered in the provincial capital of Port Numbay, formerly known as Jayapura, for the largest pro-independence gathering in over 30 years.

While rejecting the demand for independence, Indonesian President Wahid warned the military against resorting to violence in West Papua. Referring to military massacres in East Timor, following the August 1999 independence vote, and to the more recent massacres of independence supporters in Aceh, another exploited outer island, Wahid said the military must not act as they did on those occasions. At the same time that the president urged calm, he warned that security forces would act to maintain order. In December 1999, Indonesian soldiers arrested Yosefa Alomang, the class action plaintiff, as part of a general political crackdown.[130] Indonesian troops were increased from 8,000 to more than 12,000 just before the June 2000 Papuan People's Congress.[131] Since November 2000, the Indonesian government has "systematically closed down the political freedoms that had emerged in Papua since the fall of Suharto".[132] This has included the arrest of pro-independence leaders on charges of subversion, the military occupation of Jayapura in December 2000 on the eve of an independence rally, and the systematic repression of peaceful flag-raising ceremonies by independence supporters.

The Papuan people have asked for negotiations to settle the question of West Papua's political status through just and democratic means. They have also called upon the international community to provide protection to the Papuan Nation while this issue is being negotiated. Based upon Indonesia's response to similar independence movements in East Timor and Aceh, and the military occupation of West Papua today, there is still every reason to fear a blood-bath.

The response of the u.s. government will be critical for the Papuan Nation. The u.s. Embassy in Jakarta said that Washington didn't support "independence for Papua or any other part of Indonesia".[133] As in the recent past, the

U.S. government can be counted upon to defend the interests of U.S. mining companies in Indonesia.

A Code of Conduct for Mining and Oil Corporations?

In response to the escalating violence by Indonesian military and police in West Papua and Aceh, Representative Cynthia McKinney (D-GA), and eight other Congressional representatives, wrote to former Secretary of State Madeline Albright that "...it is imperative that the U.S. refrain from all re-engagement with the Indonesian military at this time".[134] Despite repeated warnings from the international human rights community, about the possibility of another East Timor-style blood-bath, U.S. military assistance and training of the Indonesian military continues as before. Similar demands to stop the flow of British military assistance to the Indonesian military have been largely ignored.

While U.S. Secretary of State Albright and British Foreign Secretary Robin Cook were not willing to admit complicity in the Indonesian violence, they were enthusiastic about the joint U.S. State Department and U.K. Foreign Office initiative, announced in December 2000, aimed at curbing human rights abuses at mining and oil facilities in places like West Papua, Colombia and Nigeria. Seven leading U.S. and U.K. oil and mining companies announced their support for a set of voluntary principles, to ensure that companies act to stop abuses by public or private security forces protecting company operations. The seven include five oil companies – Chevron, Texaco, Conoco, BP, Amoco and Shell – and two mining corporations, Rio Tinto and Freeport McMoran. Noticeably absent from the list were Exxon-Mobil, Unocal, Occidental, and many others with a history of human rights abuses. "The initiative," according to the London *Financial Times,* "arises out of numerous incidents in the past decade in which large oil and mining companies have come under sharp criticism from human rights groups for killings carried out by security forces in states such as Nigeria and Colombia".[135] Among the principles agreed to are the following: instructing security personnel hired by companies to use only the minimum force necessary to protect company property, pushing for investigation of alleged abuses by security people or local government forces, noninterference with peaceful demonstrations, and tolerance of collective bargaining efforts by workers.[136]

Robin Cook said the pact should "greatly reduce the scope for human rights abuses associated with the way companies protect themselves and their employees overseas".[137] These principles are completely voluntary and there is no commitment to monitor compliance with them. Nonetheless, they do provide a standard against which independent human rights groups can measure corporate compliance and apply the pressure of international public opinion.

However, these standards do not address the systematic relationship between the activities of multinational mining and oil corporations in Third World countries and the flow of u.s. and u.k. military aid, equipment and training of repressive military forces. Companies like Freeport-McMoran not only employ private security forces to protect their mines (as in West Papua); they also lobby Congress and the president for increased u.s. military aid to Indonesia.[138]

Between 1975 and 2000, the u.s. arms industry sold an estimated $1.1 billion worth of weaponry to Indonesia's military. Following Indonesia's invasion of East Timor in December 1975, u.s. military aid more than doubled, from $17 million to $40 million, and u.s. arms sales jumped from $12 million to $65 million.[139] u.s. Secretary of State Henry Kissinger, who personally approved the sales, had earlier given the green light to Suharto's invasion while attending a state dinner in Jakarta with the dictator.[140] Mr. Kissinger used his government connections to lobby on behalf of Freeport-McMoRan in Washington and Jakarta. However, if one is to believe the editors of the *New York Times*, companies like Freeport just happen to find themselves in "violent places" with no particular responsibility for the preexisting violence:[141]

> "Oil and mining companies do not have the luxury of relocation. They often find themselves working in poor and violent places where protecting a mine or pipeline is a challenge. Occasionally the security forces hired by American or European corporations have gone too far. In the Indonesian province of Irian Jaya [West Papua] in the mid 1990s, military men hired as guards at Freeport-McMoRan's Grasberg gold and copper mine were accused of killing civilians. The security forces contracted by British Petroleum in Colombia, and Shell and Chevron in Nigeria, among other companies, have been accused of similar abuses."

What the *New York Times* could not admit is that these places *became* violent as a direct result of the extractive activities of these corporations. Culturally insensitive, environmentally hazardous, and economically unjust, resource exploitation provoked local resistance that was then repressed with massive military force made possible by imperial powers like the u.s. and the u.k. No amount of voluntary compliance with ethical guidelines will address the systemic violence of U.S. and U.K. military aid to repressive regimes in resource-rich countries in the Third World.

Notes

1   Bernard Nietschmann, "Economic Development by Invasion of Indigenous Nations", *Cultural Survival Quarterly*, Washington DC 10:2:2-12, 1986, p. 5.

2   A Whittaker (ed), *West Papua: Plunder in Paradise*, Indigenous Peoples and Development Series, Anti-Slavery Society, London, Vol 6, 1990, p. 5.

3   David Hyndman, "Melanesian Resistance to Ethnocide and Ecocide: Transnational Mining Projects and the Fourth World on the Island of New Guinea", in John H Bodley (ed) *Tribal People and Development Issues: A Global Overview*, Mountain View, CA: Mayfield, 1988, p. 281.

4   *Engineering and Mining Journal*, 1999, p. 16. Rio Tinto sold its equity stake in Freeport in early 2004 but retained its right to fund and access 40 per cent of the company's exploration budget and minerals production.

5   Jeffrey Udin, "The profits of genocide", *Z magazine*, May 9 1996, p. 21.

6   Eyal Press, "Jim Bob's Indonesian Misadventure", *The Progressive*, June 1996, p. 32.

7   *In These Times*, 1990, p. 5.

8   Noam Chomsky, "A gleam of light in Asia", *Z magazine*, September, 1990, p. 21.

9   Under threat of execution, 1,025 representatives, pre-selected by the Indonesian government, were allowed to "choose" Indonesian rule on behalf of 800,000 people. See Carmel Budiardjo and Liem Soei Liong, *West Papua: the obliteraton of a people*, TAPOL, UK, 1988, p. 33.

10 *Freeport Indonesia: Briefing Sheet no. 11*, Minewatch, London, 1990, p. 1.

11 Nietschmann, op. cit., p. 6.

12 Peter Waldman, "How Suharto's circle and a mining firm did so well together", *Wall St Journal*, New York, 1998.

13 *Mining Journal*, London, February 6 1999.

14 *Indonesian Observer*, June 16 1999.

15 *Jakarta Post*, June 16 1999.

16 George Monbiot, "Another massacre is on the way", *Guardian*, London, November 30 2000.

17 Budiardjo and Liong, op. cit. p. 9

18 Budiardjo and Liong, op. cit. p. 4.

19 Nietschmann, op. cit., p. 7.

20 Carolyn Marr, *Digging deep: the hidden costs of mining in Indonesia*, Down to Earth and Minewatch, London 1993, p. 4.

21 Nietschmann, op. cit., p. 7.

22 Hyndman, 1988, op. cit., p. 285.

23 Ibid.

24   Curtis Runyan, "Indonesia's discontent", in *World Watch*, May 1998, p. 18.

25   Robin Osborne, *Indonesia's Secret War: The Guerilla Struggle in Irian Jaya*, Allen and Unwin, Sydney, 1985, p. 5.

26   Matthew Jardine, *East Timor: Genocide in Paradise,* Odonian Press, Tucson, 1995.

27   Budiardjo and Liong, op. cit. p. 69.

28   Marr, op. cit. p. 74

29   *1991 Contract of Work between Freeport Indonesia and the Indonesian government, Article 18, clause 3.*

30   P.T. Freeport Indonesia.

31   *Development by Invasion: mining and human rights in Melanesia: Briefing sheet no. 23,* Minewatch, 1993, p. 2.

32   *Far Eastern Economic Review*, Hong Kong, July 4 1991.

33   *Rio Tinto critic gagged*, Survival International media briefing, London 1998.

34   Danielle Knight, *US aid cut to Indonesian environmental groups that criticized US mining corporation,* Inter Press Service, Washington DC, May 16 1998.

35   Survival International 1998, op cit.

36   Julian Burger, *Report from the Frontier: the State of the World's Indigenous People*, Zed Books, London 1987, p. 44.

37   Margaret Keck and Kathryn Sikkink, *Activists Beyond Borders: Advocacy Networks in International Politics*, Cornell University Press, Ithaca, 1998, p. 9.

38   Ibid. p. 12.

39   Ibid. p. 25.

40   Donna Lee Van Cott, *Indigenous Peoples and Democracy in Latin America,* St Martin's Press, New York, 1995, p. 30.

41   Roger Moody, *The Gulliver File: Mines, People and Land: a Global Battlefield*, Minewatch-London, WISE-Australia, International Books Utrecht, 1992, p. 13.

42   Keck and Sikkink, op. cit., p. 21

43   Ibid. p. 13.

44   Project Underground, *Mission Statement*, San Francisco (undated).

45   Robert Bryce, "Spinning Gold", *Mother Jones*, October 1996, p. 67.

46   Oliver Houck, "Major money influence in Freeport-Indonesia affair", *New Orleans Times-Picayune*, February 29 1996, p. B7.

47   Both Robert Bryce and Daryl Slusher of *The Austin Chronicle* received threatening letters from Freeport. See *Austin-American-Statesman,* December 14 1995, p. B1.

48   Eyal Press, "Freeport McMoran at home and abroad", *The Nation*, July 31-August 7 1995, p. 130.

49   Keck and Sikkink, op. cit. p. 27.

50   *Trouble at Freeport: Eyewitness accounts of West Papuan resistance to the Freeport McMoran mine in Irian Jaya, Indonesia and Indonesian military repression, June 1994-February 1995,* Australian Council for Overseas Aid, April 1995.

51   *Violations of human rights in the Timika area of Irian Jaya, Indonesia,* Catholic Church of Jayapura, August 1995.

52   Michael Shari, "Gold rush in New Guinea", *Business Week*, November 20 1995, p. 66.

53   Danny Kennedy, "US mine gouges for gold", *Earth Island Journal*, Spring 1997, p. 24.

54   *Report on Indonesia*, U.S. Department of State, 1995.

55   Bryce, op. cit. 1996, p. 66.

56   Press, op. cit. 1996, p. 34.

57   "River Ajkwa polluted", *Jakarta Post*, March 27 1997.

58   *PTFI (Freeport) Environmental Audit Report*, Dames & Moore, 1996, p. 36.

59   Terry Brookes "Freeport and RTZ: complicity and crime in West Papua", *Higher Values*, Minewatch, London, April 1996.

60   *Parting Company*, Partizans, London, Spring, 1995.

61   *Rio Tinto: Report and Accounts*, London, 1999.

62   "West Papua: Indonesian military torture and murder at mining site", *Urgent Action Bulletin*, Survival International, 1995.

63   "Special Report on the RTZ 1990 Annual General Meeting", *Parting Company*, Partizans, 1990.

64   Roger Moody, personal correspondence, June 26 1999.

65   Roger Moody, *Plunder!*, Partizans and Cafca, London 1991, pps.70-71.

66   Van Cott, op. cit. p. 35.

67   Bryce quoting the *Australian Financial Review* in *Texas Observer*, November 17 1995.

68   *South East Asia Mining Letter*, London, November 30 1995.

69   Cited in Bryce, op. cit. p. 67.

70   Press, 1996, op. cit. p. 34.

71   Bryce 1995, op. cit.

72   Bryce 1995, ibid.

73   Press, 1996, op. cit. p. 34.

74   Brigid McMenamin, "Environmental Imperialism", *Forbes magazine*, May 20 1996, pps.124-136.

75   Freeport conducted a massive lobbying effort in Washington, D.C. to get OPIC to reinstate the company's insurance. In April of 1996, the agency reinstated the company's insurance through to the end of 1996. In exchange for the reinstatement, Freeport agreed to create a $100 million trust fund to be used for remediation of the site after the mine closes. See Robert Bryce and Susan A. Brackett, "Controversy at the Grasberg mine in Indonesia", *Clementine,* Mineral Policy Center, Washington DC, Spring-Summer, 1996, p. 12.

76   Pratap Chatterjee, "Indonesian mining project posed 'unreasonable hazard'", Inter Press Service, November 3 1995.

77   *Drillbits and Tailings,* Project Underground, San Francisco, September 18 1996.

78   "Freeport's mine incites wrath of tribal peoples in West Papua", *Bulletin*, Survival International, August 1996. p. 2.

79   TAPOL Bulletin, 1996, p. 1.

80 Ibid p. 3.

81 John McBeth, "Global human rights activists have a new target: Freeport", *Far Eastern Economic Review*, December 4 1997.

82 TAPOL, 1997.

83 Kennedy, op. cit. p. 24.

84 Paul S Murphy, personal correspondence, 1998.

85 LEMASA, Tembagapura, July 5 1996.

86 *Beanal v. Freeport-McMoRan, Case no. 96-1474,* US District Court, Eastern District, Lousiana 1996.

87 *Texas Observer*, June 14 1996.

88 John Clark, "Freeport and the conscience of the University", *Maroon*, Loyola University, New Orleans, April 11 1997

89 Pratap Chatterjee, "The mining menace of Freeport McMoran", *Multinational Monitor*, April 1996, p. 13.

90 Press, 1995, op. cit.

91 Julia D Fox, "Leasing the Ivory Tower at a Social Justice University", *Organization & Environment*, 1997, p. 268.

92 Clark, op. cit.

93 C Bonura, "Knoth delays forum to discuss money", *Maroon*, October 6 1995, p. 1.

94 James Gill, "Unendowing of a University chair", *New Orleans Times-Picayun*, November 12 1995.

95 Houck, op. cit.

96 *Freeport-McMoRan Inc. and Freeport-McMoRan Copper and Gold, Inc. v. Yosefa Alomang and others, the Supreme Court of the State of Louisiana, case No. 98-C-1352,* July 2 1998.

97 Abigail Abrash, "The Amungme, Kamoro & Freeport: how Indigenous Papuans have resisted the world's largest gold and copper mine", *Cultural Survival Quarterly* Spring 2001, p. 41.

98 Freeport tried to persuade the Securities and Exchange Commission (SEC) that the Mennonite resolution should be dismissed because the request to end company cooperation with the military would violate its contract of work with the Indonesian government. The Mennonites argued otherwise and the SEC allowed the resolution to go before the shareholders.

99 Robert Bryce, "Freeport shareholders are secured", *Austin Chronicle*, May 9-15 1997.

100 Project "Freeport faces challenges from all sides", *Drillbits and Tailings*, Project Underground, April 21 1997.

101 *Protests and profit: mining in West Papua,* World Development Movement, London 1996.

102 Danny Kennedy, "Freeport follies" *Down to Earth Newsletter*, London, August 1997.

103 Keck, op. cit. p. 23.

104 Danny Kennedy, with Pratap Chatterjee and Roger Moody, *Risky Business: the Grasberg gold mine: an independent annual report on PT Freeport Indonesia*, Project Underground, Berkeley, CA, 1998.

105 Personal interview with Danny Kennedy, June 22 1999.

106 *Rio Tinto: Tainted Titan: the Stakeholders Report, 1997*, International Federation of Chemical, Energy, Mine and General Workers' Unions (ICEM), Brussels 1998, p. 1.

107 Ibid. p. 18.

108 "BHP's dirty deeds", *Multinational Monitor* 1996, p. 5. See also: Aviva Imhof, "The Big Ugly American goes to Ok Tedi", *Multinational Monitor,* March 1996, pps.15-18.

109 Moody, personal correspondence, 1999.

110 "Human Rights activists protest Freeport gold mine in Indonesia", *Drillbits and Tailings*, Project Underground, June 1 1999.

111 Ibid.

112 John Bray, *No Hiding Place: Business and the Politics of Pressure*, Control Risks Group, London 1997, p. 45.

113 *Indonesian Observer*, June 16 1999, op.cit.

114 Agence France Press, Jakarta, June 4 1999.

115 Waldman, op. cit.

116 Agence France Press, Jakarta, October 23 1998.

117 *Indonesian Observer*, Jakarta, September 4 1998.

118 Waldman, op. cit.

119 *Jakarta Post*, February 4 2000.

120 *Independent Annual Report on Newmont,* Project Underground, San Francisco 2000.

121 Andrew Marshall, "Indonesia says Freeport agrees to cut output", Reuters, May 24 2000.

122 Jamie Tarabay, "Indonesia may probe US mining company", Associated Press, May 25 2000.

123 *Independent Annual Report on Newmont*, Project Underground, 2000, op. cit.

124 Danielle Knight, "US Aid cut to Indonesian environmental groups that criticized US mining corporations", Inter Press Service, Washington DC, May 16 2000.

125 Terry Allen, "With friends like these: Kissinger does Indonesia", *In these Times,* April 17, 2000, p. 12.

126 Adam Zagorin, "Freeport's lode of trouble", *Time,* June 7 1999, p. 62.

127 Puspa Madani and Jay Solomon, "Indonesia orders Freeport to reduce mining output", *Wall Street Journal,* May 24 2000.

128 Kompas, Jakarta, June 7 2000.

129 *Suara Pembaruan*, 2000.

130 John Otto Ondawame, "Self determination in West Papua (Irian Jaya)", *Indigenous Affairs*, International Workgroup for Indigenous Affairs (IWGIA), Copenhagen, January/February/March 2000, p. 35.

131 Andrew Kilvert, "Machete militias clash as self-rule tensions heat up", *Sydney Morning Herald*, June 8 2000.

132 Richard Chauvel, "Indonesia's dead end", *The Age,* Melbourne, December 27 2000

133 "us Embassy supports Indonesia's position on West Papua", *Dow Jones Newswires*, June 5 2000.

134 Cynthia McKinney et. al., *Letter to Madeline Albright,* October 30 2000.

135 Edward Alden and David Buchan, "Oil groups back initiative to guard human rights", *Financial Times*, December 21 2000.

136 "Investing in Human Rights", *Christian Science Monitor,* December 28 2000.

137 Ibid.

138 Eyal Press, "The Suharto lobby", *The Progressive*, May 1997.

139 Jennifer Washburn, "Twisting arms: the us weapons industry gets its way", *The Progressive*, May 1997, p. 26.

140 Jardine, 1995, op. cit. p. 10.

141 Editorial, *New York Times,* December 29 2000.

CHAPTER 5

Omai: Poison in the Jungle

5.1 FIVE MINUTES BEFORE MIDNIGHT

"We're turning a mud land into a gold land!," declared Guyana's President Cheddi Jagan, on opening Omai Gold Mines Ltd [OGML]'s mine in early 1993. But, two years later, the mine's waste dam fissured, causing millions of gallons of cyanide-laced effluent, sediment and biologically active wastes, to pour into the Omai and Essequibo Rivers. Within forty-eight hours, Jagan was calling this "the country's worst environmental disaster". The mine's Canadian operators – Cambior Inc and Golden Star Resources Inc [GSR] – merely dubbed it "an industrial accident".[1]

What happened at the Omai mine site on August 19th – just five minutes before midnight – is not in dispute. The tailings pond – a huge pit into which are piped cyanide liquids, other chemicals and mill wastes – developed cracks on two sides, two hundred metres across and six metres deep. Over the next three days, much of the contents of the dam cascaded into the adjacent Omai river, then rushed in a massive plume down the Essequibo, the country's largest waterway. Several hundred thousand fish died instantly. A few hours later, engineers managed to bulldoze a pathway for the polluted torrent, into the mine pit itself. But seepage into the rivers continued for another hundred hours. It was not until Thursday August 22, that OGML claimed to have stemmed the tide completely.

However, most other facts about the disaster *are* in dispute. Just how much waste ended up in the rivers and along their banks? OGML said, on August 22, that there were "only" two million cubic metres of effluent in the tailings dam.[2] Yet, consultants brought in by the company to assess the damage, two days later spoke of 3.2 million cubic metres "having been released into the receiving environment".[3] By late August, the government was quoting an even higher figure of 3.5 million cubic metres.[4]

How toxic were these tailings as they flowed one hundred miles down-stream towards the major town of Bartica and the Atlantic ocean? OGML told a sceptical Guyanese public on Wednesday August 23, that the Essequibo was safe to drink. Yet, by then, Amerindians, traders and miners along the river banks were reporting not only dead fish, but also wild hogs floating belly-up within the effluent. Two months on, and residents of the Middle Mazaruni River (near the confluence with the Essequibo) were complaining about itching and burning of the skin and blistering of the mouth when they used the water.[5]

Criticism, in those crucial first days, was also made of the validity of OGML's water testing. The World Health Organisation representative in the capital Georgetown, commented: "We don't know where the company has been sampling. We don't know what the mix of the sludge is. We have no idea how fast the river will cleanse itself".[6]

These are vital points in any assessment of long-term damage. Gold tail-ings contain a potent toxic cocktail of heavy metals, chemically-bound with the cyanide, and present as suspended solids. In every major similar accident in the past, they have entered the marine environment, where they latch onto micro-organisms. These get ingested by fish and other invertebrates, and then bio-magnify and bio-accumulate. Arsenic, copper, cadmium, lead, mercury – the heavy metals – become more poisonous over time, and as they travel through the food chain, ending up concentrated in the human con-sumer.

No report from OGML focussed on the potential for such longterm heavy metal pollution. Instead, the company issued numerous assurances that the cyanide had broken down, under the twin action of the fast-flowing Esse-quibo waters and the tropical sunlight. This may be true; but heavy metals are impervious to such factors, nor did the assurance that the river was fit to drink – or bathe in – have any relevance in this context.

On August 31, OGML announced that it accepted full responsibility for the disaster and would "establish arrangements to assess any justifiable losses suf-fered by persons because of the accident and [to] evaluate claims for compen-sation".[7] However, proving causality is notoriously difficult in mining-related cases. (Victims of the biggest tailings dam collapse before Omai, at the South African Harmony gold mine in early 1994, waited two years to have their claims recognised by the courts, and only after powerful and sophisticated lawyers took up their cases.)[8]

The long-term effects of both the heavy metal poisoning and siltation of the Essequibo River could take years to register. By then OGML may have left Guyana. We might also ask how a poor Amerindian is going to prove that reduction in his/her fish catches, or inexplicable intestinal illnesses, were caused by the Omai deluge – rather than other forms of mining (such as the mercury-using missile dredges which have afflicted Guyana's rivers over the past forty and more years).

In March 1995, OGML did announce a plan to dispose of cyanide effluent directly from the tailings dam into the Essequibo River after passing it through a treatment plant. The company claimed that the technology to be used was "well established... and [has] been implemented successfully around the world".[9] The announcement was greeted with cries of alarm, from both inside and outside Guyana. After the government sent a mission to investigate the plan, the scheme was postponed for up to a year. Barely two months later, on May 15, an unauthorised discharge of cyanide, directly into the Omai river, killed several hundred fish; many of the corpses were thrown into nearby bushes, and the "incident" was not reported to the government by OGML for six days.[10]

These events not only raised major doubts about the integrity of Omai's management but – more importantly in the light of the August 1995 disaster – they focussed attention on the state of the tailings dam. Why did OGML need to discharge any effluent into the river at all, if it was following the industry's "best possible practice"? Many gold mines in north America now have to adopt a "zero discharge" policy, recycling all waste water through the mill and processing complex. In 1995, Chile introduced legislation to ensure that all such effluents remain within mine-sites.

In fact, in March 1995, OGML had already admitted that the current tailings dam was reaching capacity, while Brian Sucre – Guyana's Geology and Mines Commissioner – said that "the tailings pond is filling up faster than the company had originally projected".[11]

Was the dam critically overloaded in the period leading up to the August calamity? Confirmation that this was the case came on August 24th from a surprising source. Knight Piesold, the Canadian engineers who built the dam, claimed that they had "built hundreds of dams and this is the first time something happened like this". Added Knight Piesold director, Bruce Brown:"[W]e are certain the failure is in a part of the dam we did not deal with." Brown went on to point out that OGML had increased the dam height to some 45 metres above the lowest point on the foundation, without agreement from his company.[12]

In other words: the dam was too full, too high or too unstable – probably all three. And knowledge of this had (so to speak) been "written on the dam wall" several months before it finally gave way.

Although the Omai disaster swiftly become a byword for mining's worst case scenario, probably securing more media publicity around the world than any similar event before or since, the palpable results of the large number of protests and critiques which followed have, in reality, been minimal.

The mine re-opened; no government crashed down; mining regulations were not radically overhauled; new foreign ventures were still encouraged. And political risk insurance was continued as if merely a breeze had wafted down the middle of Guyana, that fateful night in August 1995, snatching a few leaves along the way.*

MIGA and Omai

Of the numerous articles and several major reports on "the country's worst environmental disaster" relatively few have focused on the specific responsibility of the World Bank, whose MIGA along with Canada's EDC provided vital political risk insurance covers (worth US$ 49.8 million) for the partners in Omai Gold Mines Ltd (OGML): Cambior and Golden Star Resources (both Canadian companies) and the Guyana government itself.

MIGA dismally failed to properly assessing the standards of mine construction. Although the company claimed to have observed North American standards, these were set in Quebec rather than the higher ones followed in Ontario or by the US Environmental Protection Agency (EPA). The partners failed to line the tailings dam with HDPE (high density polyethylene) covers to protect groundwater resources. Worse, they permitted the dam's capacity to rise far above limits set in the original Environmental Impact Assessment, doubtless contributing to the "massive loss of core integrity resulting from internal erosion of the dam fill," almost certainly the key factor in ensuring that wastes would overwhelm the dam's capacity to contain them.[13] As the scenario for disaster developed during 1994 and early 1995, several observers pointed out that a collapse was virtually inevitable. There had, in fact, been three "spills" already in the previous six months, when cyanide poisoned fish swimming in the Omai creek. These, combined with an admission by Cambior that the dam was filling to its brink, led OGML to petition the Guy-

---

* The first part of this introduction was originally published in 1995, as a Minewatch Briefing paper. A slightly different version also appeared in the London-based Afro-Caribbean newspaper, *The Weekly Journal*, on September 7 1995, entitled "The golden goose that turned rotten".

ana government to be allowed to discharge treated wastes directly into the river. The government refused on environmental grounds, but the mine continued to operate until the dam's collapse in August that year. Throughout this critical period, MIGA failed to monitor mine safety, let alone insist on a precautionary closure of its operations. The United Nations Development Programme (UNDP) later concluded that the "baseline and continuous monitoring at Omai have largely been inadequate".[14]

On January 8, 1996, a five-member commission of inquiry, with ties to the government, military, banking and business issued its report on the Omai disaster. The mine was cleared to re-open, albeit with several new technological improvements. Remarked lawyer S Dennison Smith:

> "It came as no surprise to many Guyanese that the January Commission failed to find the cause of the spill. This means no one is liable, with the assumption being that it was an 'accident.' A month after the spill, the company [had] boasted that they'll be back to work in six months, and sure enough, they were. In the first week of February, OGML got permission from the government to go ahead and dump waste from the Fennel [mine] Pit (named after David Fennel, the CEO of the company) directly into the Essequibo river, with the condition that they warn local residents before they do so. "OGML started dumping the same concentrated cyanide-tainted water that was part of the August spill into the Essequibo from March 1 1996 to May 1996. OGML officials claimed they told local people of the discharge, but many local residents said they did not receive any warning."[15]

The World Bank, from its early promotion of Guyana's "structural adjustment" programme based inevitably on privatisation, had regarded Omai as a tangible example of the large-scale minerals-related investment which must be imposed upon a highly-indebted country. It was certainly not going to argue that the disaster proved the mine to be unacceptable and should therefore be closed. Indeed, two months after the dam collapse, Gerald T West, MIGA's Senior Advisor for Guarantees, offered his opinion that the damage had been grossly overestimated. According to a Guyanese member of parliament, MIGA told the ensuing Omai inquiry that, if the government imposed any new environmental regulations on the mine, the agency would consider this "tantamount to nationalisation", compelling it to pay compensation to Cambior and Golden Star.[16]

Despite the fact that many Indigenous, and other, families, living along the banks of the Essequibo, alleged they had suffered major losses of their fish, pollution of their crucial freshwater supplies, and adverse health effects, they have not been adequately compensated. Several attempts to bring claims against OGML partners in Guyana and Canada have failed.

The first came in May 1996 when the National Committee for Defence Against Omai, an umbrella organisation of Guyanese grassroots and Indigenous organizations, and Public Information Resource Associates (PIRA), a Montreal based public relations firm, sought C$226.7 million to be divided among 155,000 persons.[17]

Ten months later, a group set up by Guyanese citizens in Montreal, called Recherches Internationales Quebec, brought Essequibo resident, Judith David to Canada to file a class action suit against Cambior. Ms. David demanded C$69 million dollars on behalf of the 23,000 Guyanese she claimed were affected by the disaster.[18]

In 1999, another case was filed, this time in Guyana, with Judith David once again a lead plaintiff. Key extracts from the statement of claim are reproduced here. The case has not yet been heard.

Notes

1   *Financial Times* (FT), London, September 1 1995.
2   Cambior press release, Montreal, August 22 1995.
3   Report by Technitrol Eco Inc, August 24 1995.
4   *FT*, September 1 1995, op cit.
5   *Catholic Herald*, Georgetown, Guyana, October 15 1996.
6   Peter Carr, World Health Organisation, quoted in *The Guardian*, London, August 8 1995.
7   OGML statement, Georgetown, August 31 1995.
8   See Roger Moody *Into the Unknown Regions: The hazards of STD*, Society of St Columban and International Books, London and Utrecht, April 2001, p. 48.
9   Alexander Kozak, Chief Metallurgist, OGML, *Environmental Management Perspectives at Omai Gold Mines Limited*, paper delivered at the Third International Gold Symposium, Caracas, Venezuela, October 2-4 1994.
10   *Stabroek News*, Georgetown, Guyana, May 29 1995
11   *Guyana Chronical*, Georgetown, Guyana, May 10 1995.
12   *Toronto Globe and Mail*, August 25 1995.
13   The preliminary report of the tailings dam review team contained the following assessments:
     "3.2 Proximate cause of failure
     It is our current judgement that failure of the dam was caused by massive loss of core integrity resulting from internal erosion of the dam fill, a process also known as piping. Internal erosion in this context means simply that finer particles from one soil moved freely under the influence of seepage forces into and through the

interstitial voids of adjacent coarser soil due to excessive disparity between particle sizes of the two soils. We believe this process began at the interface between the filter sand and the compacted rockfill. Loss of filter sand into the rockfill left the overlying saprolite core material unsupported and subject to the development of cavities, softened zones, and cracks as its particles too moved into the rockfill. Cavity development in the core fill is likely to have propagated undetected for some period of time until reaching the reservoir at and above the slimes level. The final breakthrough of these cavities formed "pipes", or tunnels, in the core fill at multiple locations that allowed uncontrolled flow of water into and then longitudinally through the rockfill zone of the dam. There are believed to be two primary physical defects in the dam, one related to filter incompatibility between the sand and rockfill zones, and another involving the diversion conduit. Both were produced by known or suspected deficiencies in design, construction, or construction inspection, either singularly or in combination. Moreover, defects related to filter incompatibility and the diversion conduit may not be mutually exclusive, and may have interacted in complementary ways not yet fully understood. It is apparent that the transition zone rockfill was never included in the dam during construction in any complete or systematic way. Even if properly designed, meticulous adherence to transition rockfill gradation specifications at each and every location within the dam would have been mandatory to ensure its safety against internal erosion. By contrast, construction documentation and existing conditions on the dam crest indicate that pit-run rockfill of essentially unrestricted gradation was placed directly against the filter sand, without adequate construction control of this critical feature.

Rockfill placement was supervised during construction of the initial stages of the dam and is believed to have been inspected or observed by several geotechnical engineers on various occasions. Such gross disparity of particle sizes between the filter sand and adjacent rockfill as can be currently seen on the dam crest should have been visually evident to any experienced geotechnical engineer, along with equally clear implications for filter incompatibility between the two materials. However, we have been provided with no information to indicate that any such supervision, inspection, or observation sufficiently recognized the severity of this condition, adequately warned of its potential consequences, or undertook measures necessary to correct it.

In basic terms then, the rockfill adjacent to the filter sand was simply too coarse to prevent the sand from washing into and through it, and both potential and actual problems this produced appear to have gone unrecognized or uncorrected throughout the sequence of design and construction until the failure occurred. There is the possibility that deformation incompatibility between the rigid grouted section and the deformable open section may have caused structural failure, or that the combined fill, slimes, and water loads may simply have exceeded the structural capacity of the culvert in the critical region beneath the Stage 1A starter dyke. Any such structural failure would have produced a void or allowed soil to enter the conduit, providing a direct path for concentrated seepage and cavity formation within the fill. Even so, structural failure of the conduit would not necessarily have been required for concentrated seepage and internal erosion to initiate and propagate along the outer surface of the conduit, a common occurrence without adequate safeguards.

3.5 The failure was caused not by some "hidden flaw" but by inadequate application and execution of sound practices for design, construction, supervision, and inspection that are well understood in current embankment dam and tailings dam technology. Respectfully submitted, Dam Review Team, November 16 1995. See Report of the tailings dam sub-commission, Prelimary Report on Technical Causation. Omai Tailings Dam Failure, Georgetown, Guyana, November 16 1995.

14   UNDP, *Institutional Strengthening of the Environmental Division of the Guyana Agency of Health, Science, Education, Environmental and Food Policy* (GUY/90/009), 1996.

15   "The Cyanide Spill continues", in *Saxakali Magazine*, Volume 2 number 2, revised July 11 1997, http://saxakali.com/saxakali-magazine/saxmag3e1.htm). The article is based on a June 1996 interview with Gustav Jackson, a Guyanese geologist, from Rainforests Consultants Association (RAFCA) of Maryland, USA. See also: "Omai pumps cyanide tailings into Essequibo River", *Platt's Metals Week*, May 6 1996, p. 13.

16   *Community Leaders of Riverain Communities Affected by the 1995 Omai Cyanide Spill*, Letter to Gerald T. West, March 18 2000.

17   Press Release: *Guyanese Environmental Community: Development Must Not Be At The Expense And Lives of Indigenous Peoples*, signed by the National Amerindian Council (NAC), the Guyana Organization of Indigenous Peoples (GOIP), Amerindian Peoples Association (APA), Red Thread, Rainforests Consultants Association (RAFCA), Canadian-Guyana Legal Defence Fund, Public Interest Research Associates (PIRA), May 18 1996.
       See also: "Guyanese group takes action against Cambior", *Globe and Mail*, Toronto, May 10 1996; "Cambior dismisses activists case", *Montreal Gazette*, May 10 1996; "12 clauses of Omai contract with Guyana government violated!", *Kaiteur News*, Guyana, May 17 1996; S. Dennison Smith, "Chronicle of a Disaster Foretold: The Omai Gold Mine", in *Mining Issues*, number 1, LAMMP, Bromley, Kent, January 1999.

18   Pratap Chatterjee, *Canadian Mining Company Muzzles Activists*, Inter-Press Service, San Francisco, August 24 1997; *Montreal Mirror*, March 27 1997.

5.2 Liability

S. Dennison Smith

The Plaintiffs contend that in the premises, the Disaster was caused totally by the diverse acts or omissions of the 1st, 2nd and 4th Defendants, by themselves, their servants or agents, and was, negligent, wrongful and unlawful. Further and/or in the alternative the Plaintiffs contend that in the premises, the Disaster was caused by breach of statutory duty of the 1st, 2nd and 4th Defendants, by themselves, their, servants or agents.

Further and/or in the alternative. the Plaintiffs contend that in the premises, the Disaster was caused by the breach of contract of the 1st and 4th Defendants, by themselves their servants or agents, for which the Plaintiffs are entitled to sue by dint, *inter alia*, of the doctrines of agency and/or claims in tort and/or breach third party beneficiary rights.

Further the Plaintiffs aver that the 4th Defendant has admitted liability for the August 19th Disaster in "Jardim Holdings Ltd. and others v Omai Gold Mines Ltd., Case number 3155 of 1996," filed in the High Court of the Supreme Court of Guyana.

Particulars of negligence, breach of statutory duty and breach of contract

I   The 1st, 2nd and 4th Defendants, and each of them, failed to so design, construct and/or to maintain the tailings dams so as to prevent a breach of such dams.

II   The 1st, 2nd and 4th Defendants and each of them failed to design and/or construct and/or to maintain the tailings dams so as to prevent the escape from the said tailings dam of toxic waste into the Omai and/or Essequibo rivers and/or surrounding environment.

III   The 1st, 2nd and 4th Defendants and each of them did not take any or any suitable precautions to ensure that the contaminated water in the tailings dams would not escape from the tailings dam to the Essequibo and/or Omai rivers and/or surrounding environment.

IV   The Plaintiffs will further rely on the discharge and/or release of the contaminated water from the tailings dams as evidence of negligence, breach of statutory duty and breach of contract.

v   The 1st and 4th Defendants and each of them failed to adopt a safe system of managing their gold mining operations by sampling and monitoring the tailings, release and ground water during its gold mining operations in order to ensure that the Plaintiffs, the people they represent and the eco-system of the Environmental Disaster Zone were not harmed.

vi   The 1st and 4th Defendants and each of them failed to comply with the standards applicable to the international gold mining industry.

vii The 1st and 4th Defendants and each of them adopted and misapplied the incorrect/inappropriate standards.

viii The 1st, 2nd and 4th Defendants and each of them failed to use impermeable liners in the design, construction or maintenance of the tailings dam at the Mine to prevent leaching and seepage from and/or ruptures of the tailings dam.

ix   The 1st and 4th Defendants and each of them failed in the following respects:

   a to build the tailings facility to a design to accommodate a 10 year, 24 hour storm, plus 1 meter for spill way free board.

   b to maintain the tailings facility at an elevation difference of at least 6 meters between the embankment crest and the tailings elevation at the embankment.

   c to implement an on-going monitoring of the tailings elevation and the volume of water in storage, to ensure sufficient freeboard stability at all times and to plan for future embankment raises and raising said embankment.

   d to implement a program of ongoing monitoring of the tailings deposit to indicate the final height of the tailings embankment.

   e to implement a tailings management program consisting of geotechnical instrumentation for the tailings dam and monitoring instrumentation.

   f to monitor the performance of the tailings dam as against the original design of the dam, with a view to modification of the dam by raising it as a result of the instrumentation readings.

   g by discharging and or allowing the discharge of contaminated water into the Omai River.

   h by discharging mine tailings pond water into Essequibo River before the natural degradation processes had acted to lower the concentration of cyanide and copper to levels at, or below, the acceptable limits of these elements in discharged water.

i to meet even the (incorrect and misapplied) North American receiving water quarterly guidelines for the protection of aquatic life by the use of a sub-surface outfall diffuser to take advantage of the dilution capacity of the Essequibo River.

j to devise, and/or adopt, and/or implement, a contingency plan as part of the management of the gold mining operations, so as to deal with seepage from, and/or ruptures of the tailings dam, and/or unplanned discharges from the tailings pond into the Essequibo and Omai rivers [which are] above the acceptable levels for cyanide and copper discharge, [and] in order to minimise environmental degradation and safety hazards associated with said seepage, ruptures or discharges if or when they occurred.

k to devise and/or adopt and/or implement a contingency plan... to contain and/or recover spills on land to minimise safety hazards, and reduce infiltration and migration to bodies of water.

m to devise and/or adopt and/or implement a contingency plan [by] providing a list of all equipment and/or basic inventory of useful equipment both for containment and safety purposes, to be kept on site, that would be required should such seepage, rupture or discharge occur [in order] to ensure worker safety.

n to devise, and/or adopt, and/or implement, a contingency plan... containing a plan for a rehearsed series of actions to be carried out in the event of such seepage, ruptures and discharges, with each members' responsibility being clarified.

p to devise and/or adopt and/or implement a contingency plan...

   i [failure in] placing the protection and well-being of personnel as the prime consideration at a seepage, rupture or discharge site

   ii [failure in] recognising that such seepage, rupture or discharge places workers in a hazardous environment and seeking to avoid such hazardous environment

   iii [failure in] giving special consideration to the unique safety problems associated with such seepage rupture or discharge

   iv [failure in]appointing and designating in advance as part of the contingency plan, a supervisor at the commencement of discovery of the seepage rupture or discharge containment and recovery operation, who had received extra safety training

q [failure] to monitor the tailings facility's water balance, the aquatic mass balance parameters, a comprehensive system of water quality monitoring and [monitoring] the cyanide concentration in the tailings pond as part of its environmental monitoring program, in the monitoring of the effluent quality and quantity.

     r [failure] to continuously monitor and assess worker exposure to the various toxic and hazardous agents available at the site.

x   The 1st and 4th Defendants by themselves, their servants or agents, continuously and unlawfully discharged toxic waste from the tailings pond to the Essequibo River above acceptable levels.

xi   The 1st and 4th Defendants, by themselves, their servants or agents, issued statements during and after the Disaster minimising or ignoring the harmful effects of the escape of the toxic waste.

xii The 1st and 4th Defendants failed to warn the Plaintiffs adequately or at all about the danger of using or drinking or coming into contact with the water of the Essequibo River.

xiii The 1st and 4th Defendants failed to warn the Plaintiffs adequately or at all about the continuing danger of using or drinking or coming into contact with the waters of the Essequibo River and such breach continues.

xiv The 1st and 4th Defendants failed to provide any or any sufficient alternative sources of water, for any of the purposes aforesaid, and such breach continues.

xv   The 1st and 4th Defendants carried out no, or no adequate, research on the entire ecosystem that would have been affected by any escape from the Mine.

xvi No, or no sufficient, study was done by 1st and 4th Defendants to establish a reliable background information base on the entire ecosystem.

xvii The 1st and 4th Defendants established no or no adequate ground water monitoring networks at the Mine.

xviii The 1st and 4th Defendants established no or no adequate surface water monitoring systems at the Mine.

xix The 1st, 2nd and 4th Defendants failed to ensure that in the design and/or construction of the tailings dams there were redundancies and over-designs sufficient to prevent the escape of the toxic waste in to the Omai and Essequibo Rivers.

xx   The 1st and 4th Defendants failed to ensure that in the design and/or construction the tailings pond, there was any or any sufficient overdesign so that no extension over the Omai River would have been needed.

xxi The 1st and 4th Defendants failed to adopt a zero cyanide discharge policy as part of their long term effluent management plan.

XXII There were no point or non-point sources of effluent discharges, adequately identified or at all, at or contiguous with the Mine.

XXIII More details of negligence, breaches of statutory duty and breaches of contract will be provided upon discovery. The 1st and 4th Defendants were, and are at all material times, engaged in large scale gold mining based on amalgamation and cyanidation, ultra-hazardous activities and a non-natural use of the land, and the toxic waste [has] escaped therefrom into the environment and damaged the same. In the premises, the Plaintiffs contend that the 1st and 4th Defendants by themselves, their servants or agents, are strictly liable for such injury and damage suffered by the Plaintiffs and those they represent (i.e. without the Plaintiffs having to establish want of care on the part of the 1st and 4th Defendants by themselves, their servants or agents). Further, and/or in the alternative, the Plaintiffs contend that said toxic waste constituted a nuisance caused or permitted by the 1st, 2nd and 4th Defendants by themselves, their servants or agents. The Plaintiffs will seek exemplary damages on the grounds that the conduct of the 1st and 4th Defendants by themselves, their servants or agents, after 24th August 1995, was calculated by them to make a profit for themselves which may well exceed that payable to the Plaintiffs. As to the particulars hereunder the Plaintiffs aver that such a motive can be properly inferred from the matters hereinbefore set out... Further the Plaintiffs will seek aggravated damages on the basis that their feelings of outrage and indignation were justifiably aroused by the highhanded and cavalier manner in which the 1st and 4th Defendants by themselves, their servants or agents, dealt with the Disaster... and further the Plaintiffs continued and/or started to use the water of the Essequibo prematurely and for more than would have been the case had the 1st and 4th Defendants, reacted properly, promptly, frankly and efficiently.

Wherefore the plaintiffs claim against the 1st, 2nd and 4th defendants:

a   Damages in excess of $17,800,000,000 (seventeen thousand, eight hundred million dollars)

b   A declaration that the Plaintiffs and the persons they represent have suffered damages and loss by reason of the Disaster.

c   An assessment and payment of the damages and loss suffered by the Plaintiff and the people they represent for the loss suffered by them by reason of the Disaster, including damage to the eco-system of the Environmental Disaster Zone.

d   A declaration that the 1st, 2nd and 4th Defendants knew and/or ought to have known that unplanned/uncontrolled seepage from and/or rupture in the tailings dam releasing toxic waste to the Environmental Disaster Zone would cause irreparable damage and loss to the Plaintiffs and the people they represent and the eco-system of this said zone.

e   A declaration that the 1st and 4th Defendants and each of them, deliberately caused the discharge into the Environmental Disaster Zone of the toxic waste.

f   A declaration that the 1st, 2nd and 4th Defendants and each of them were negligent in failing to use impermeable liners to prevent seepage from and/or ruptures of the tailings dam.

g   A declaration that the 1st, 2nd and 4th Defendants and each of them were negligent in the design and/or construction of the tailings dam as part of their waste and effluent management of their gold mining operations.

h   A declaration that the 1st and 4th Defendants and each of them failed to adopt a safe system of managing their gold mining operations by sampling and monitoring the tailings, release and ground water during the gold mining operations, in order to ensure that the Plaintiff, the people they represent and the eco-system of the Environmental Disaster Zone were not harmed.

i   A declaration that the 4th Defendant breached paragraph 2(13) of the Licence by polluting the surface and/or sub-surface freshwater supply and/or failing to comply with the Regulations made under the Mining Act of Guyana number 20 of 1989 and/or failing to comply with the EIS.

j   A declaration that the 1st, 2nd and 4th Defendants and each of them under and by virtue of the Act, and/or the Regulations and/or the Licence and/or the Agreement and/or the EIS are bound by and/or required to comply with the standards applicable in the international gold mining industry.

k   A declaration that the 1st, 2nd and 4th Defendants and each of them failed to comply with the standards applicable to the international gold mining industry.

l   A declaration that the 1st and 4th Defendants and each of them used the incorrect/inappropriate standards, i.e. the North American receiving water quality guidelines for the protection of aquatic life, within a short distance of the outfall by the use of a sub-surface outfall diffuser to take advantage of the dilution capacity of the Essequibo River, with respect to the effluent from a gold mining operation using amalgamation and cyanidation.

m   A declaration that the 1st and 4th Defendants and each of them should have adopted a zero cyanide discharge policy as part of their long term effluent management plan at the Mine.

n   A declaration that the 1st and 4th Defendants and each of them were negligent and/or in breach of duty and/or in breach of contract and/or failed to comply with the EIS. [There then follow twenty six instances in which the EIR is alleged to have been breached, as mentioned earlier in the claim. (RM)]

o   A declaration that the said toxic waste has settled and remains along the length and breadth of the Essequibo river and continues to pollute the Plaintiffs environment in diverse bio-available forms.

p   A declaration that the 1st and 4th Defendants and each of them, since the Disaster has continuously and unlawfully discharged toxic waste from the tailings pond to the Essequibo River in concentrations above acceptable levels.

q   An assessment and/or account of the damages suffered by the Plaintiffs (and the persons they represent) by reason of said unlawful discharges of toxic waste into the Essequibo River and other waters since the Disaster.

r   A declaration that by reason of the 1st, 2nd and 4th Defendants ' negligence and//or breach of statutory duty and/or breach of contract the Plaintiffs have sustained personal injuries and physiological shock and trauma and have suffered loss and damage.

s   A Declaration that the 1st, 2nd and 4th Defendants are liable for all damage to the Plaintiffs, their environment and to the eco-system caused by the Disaster.

t   A Declaration that the 1st and 4th Defendants are liable for all damage to the Plaintiffs, their environment and to the eco-system caused by the continuing discharge of toxic waste, into the said environment.

u   A Declaration that the Plaintiffs are entitled to specific performance of clause 6. 9 of the said Agreement.

v   Specific performance of clause 6. 9 of the said Agreement.

w   The provision, by the Defendants of safe, constant and easily accessible water for all Plaintiffs, for the following purposes:

     i   drinking water,

     ii   cooking water,

     iii   bathing water,

iv   drinking water for livestock and game,

vi   water for agriculture,

vii water for recreational purposes,

viii water as a source of food in the form of riverain life such as fish and other aquatic life.

x   The provision by the Defendants of scientific monitoring of the environment to ascertain precisely the extent and longevity of all damage, of whatsoever nature, caused by the said Disaster.

y   The provision by the Defendants of scientific monitoring of the environment to ascertain precisely the extent and longevity of all damage of whatsoever nature, caused by the continuing discharge of toxic waste into the said environment.

z   The provision by the Defendants of a scientifically proper, thorough and complete clean-up of the toxic waste deposited into the environment by the Defendants negligence and/or breach of statutory duty and/or breach of contract.

aa   The provision by the Defendants of medical monitoring of the effects of the Disaster on the Plaintiffs (present and future), their livestock and game.

bb   The provision by the Defendants of medical monitoring of the present and future effects of the continuing discharge of toxic waste, into the said environment.

cc   The provision by the Defendants of medical treatment and facilities and personnel therefor, for all Plaintiffs (present and future) injured or damaged by the said breaches of the 1st, 2nd and 4th Defendants.

dd   The provision by the Defendants of alternative, comparable sources of economic activity for all Plaintiffs, their communities and the region.

ee   Such further accounts and enquiries which as to the Court shall seem just, inter alia, for the purpose of ascertaining the amount which the Defendants should pay to the Plaintiffs by way of compensation and/or damages for the breaches of duty.

ff   Such further or other relief as is deemed fit by this Honourable Court

gg   Costs

Attorneys-at-Law for the Plaintiffs. Dated at Georgetown, Demerara
This 16th day of August, 1999.

5.3 The Case against Omai

SCI1998 No. 867-W Demerara

In The High Court of the Supreme Court of Judicature Civil Jurisdiction

Between: – Judith David & Elizabeth David (suing in their individual capacity and on behalf of all persons residing, using, working, fishing or possessing property within the Riverain area of the banks of either and/or the Omai and/or Essequibo rivers and their tributaries in Guyana, ranging between the area from the Omai Gold Mines to the Atlantic Ocean (the "Environmental Disaster Zone") including all people, approximately twenty three thousand (23,000) persons drawing and using water from these rivers. Plaintiffs Individually, Jointly and

Severally,

– and –

1 Cambior Inc. (a legal person within the meaning of the Civil Code of Quebec, having its Head Office at 800 Rene-Levesque Blvd, West, Suite 850, in the City and District of Montreal, Province of Quebec (H3B 1X9)

– and –

2 Golder & Associates (a legal person within the meaning of the Civil Code of Quebec, having its Head Office at 63 Place Fontenac, in the City and District of Montreal, Province of Quebec)

– and –

3 Home Insurance (a legal person within the meaning of the Civil Code of Quebec, having its Head Office at 1 Place Ville Marie, Suite 4000, in the City and District of Montreal, Province of Quebec).

– and –

4 Omai Gold Mines Limited – OGML (a company duly incorporated under the Provisions of the Companies Act Chapter 89:01, situate at Lot 176 D Middle Street, Georgetown).

Defendants
Individually, Jointly and Severally

Summary

Before the commencement of OGML's mining operation, the water resources and land, in and around the area of the Essequibo, combined to form the foundation of an almost pristine ecosystem, extraordinarily rich in biodiversity and life, including, for example, more than 50 aquatic organisms below fish in the food-chain. The watershed, rivers and groundwater, comprising the Essequibo water resources are vital to the continued health and safety of all the fauna and flora and the people of the area, particularly the Plaintiffs.

The Plaintiffs and the persons they represent, being residents, occupants and persons using and living in the areas of the Omai and Essequibo rivers, are members of riverain communities, of which the said rivers are and were at all material times, literally the very lifeblood. The rivers were being used constantly by such persons and all other members of such communities for, *inter alia*, the following purposes:

a   in some cases the only available and/or feasible source of drinking water and, in others, a major source of drinking water.

b   in some cases the only available and/or feasible source of cooking water and, in others, a major source of cooking water.

c   in some cases the only available and/or feasible source of water for bathing and, in others, a major source of bathing water.

d   in some cases the only available and/or feasible source of drinking water for livestock and game and, in others, a major source of drinking water for livestock and game.

e   in some cases the only available and/or feasible source of water for washing clothes and other items and, in others, a major source of washing water.

f   in some cases the only available and/or feasible source of water for agriculture and, in others, a major source of water for agriculture.

g   in some cases the only available and/or feasible source of water for recreational purposes (such as swimming) and, in others, a major source of water for such recreational purposes.

h   in all cases a major source of food such as fish and other aquatic life.

i   in all cases the only available and/or main means of transportation in boats and other aquatic vessels.

6   Further, the said rivers were and are one of the main economic resources of the area and the single major potential resource for developing and diversifying the economy of the Essequibo region, eg. into eco-tourism.

7 From, on or about, August 19th to 24th 1995, the Plaintiffs entire lives and livelihoods were devastated by the wrongful and unlawful discharge by the Defendants, by themselves, their servants or agents, of approximately 3.2 billion cubic litres of water contaminated with cyanide and other noxious compounds and metals from a ruptured reservoir at the Mine, into the Omai and Essequibo rivers and surrounding area, (hereinafter "the Disaster").

"Treating gold as more valuable than water"

By reason of the Disaster, the area referred to in paragraph 1 above was included in a region declared a "Disaster Zone"by the government of Guyana in the week of August 19th, 1995.

This case is brought by the Plaintiffs for the devastation and damage to their lives, the water resources and the eco-system of the Environmental Disaster Zone, caused by the 1st, 2nd and 4th Defendants by themselves, their servants or agents, in calculated pursuit of profit, by treating gold as more valuable than water.

The Background

Cyanide, a powerful poison potentially lethal to plants, animals, and very dangerous to human beings, is usually used in conjunction with water, in most gold mining operations, as it was at the Omai mine, to separate the gold from the gold ore: processes, known as amalgamation and cyanidation, which result in an effluent by-product, or waste, of a slurry of a lethal and corrosive mixture of highly toxic chemicals, including cyanide, cyano-metallic complexes, and other heavy metals such as copper and mercury and other substances (hereinafter known as "the toxic waste").

The harmful effects of toxic waste and mining pollution on the environment have been studied and well-documented by the mining industry, and are subject to extensive regulation in all industrialized countries. The Defendants knew or should have known about the said studies and regulations. Toxic waste has both direct and indirect harmful, and indeed potentially life-threatening, effects on all forms of plant and animal life. When not properly contained, controlled, recycled, or disposed of, these chemicals can kill and/or damage practically all living organisms.

Toxic wastes, when released into the environment, also become bioavailable – i.e. available to be inhaled, ingested or absorbed by living organisms. When so inhaled ingested or absorbed, these chemicals can have, *inter alia*, the following harmful effects: carcinogenic – cancer-causing, and harmful to living organisms; teratogenic – harmful to foetal development and resulting in malformed foetuses; mutagenic – inducing defective genetic mutations which might manifest in subsequent generations, even while skipping intervening generations. Cyanide itself can produce the following effects in humans, whether contact is by inhalation, or by oral or skin exposure:

a In high enough doses:
   i   Convulsions,
   ii Coma, and
   iii Death.
b Lower doses can produce:
   i   Skin irritation and sores,
   ii Breathing difficulties,
   iii Pain in the heart area,
   iv Vomiting,
   v   Blood changes,
   vi Headaches,
   vii Enlargement of the thyroid gland,
   viii Harmful effects to the nervous system,
   ix Weakness in the fingers and toes,
   x   Difficulty in walking,
   xi Damaged vision, including blindness, and
   xii Deafness.

Cyanide is also present in many foods, especially, *inter alia,* cassava and casreep, and the use, for example, of cassava as a primary food, has led to high blood cyanide levels and some of the above symptoms. Further, cassava and casreep are staple foods of, and used extensively by, many of the Plaintiffs.

Further, cigarette-smoking, another common source of cyanide in humans, is fairly widespread among the Plaintiffs.

Thus, many of the said Plaintiffs are peculiarly predisposed to the above symptoms. These primary and secondary effects, along with the factors outlined above, are of concern to the gold-mining industry and the 1st, 2nd and 4th Defendants either knew, or should have known, about them.

The management of toxic waste (ensuring that noxious and toxic chemicals are safely contained and/or rendered innocuous at the site) and the prevention of pollution of the surrounding environment, is essential to maintaining a safe and efficient mine and a major duty and/or responsibility of any gold mining operation.

Tailings Dams

In the management of toxic waste at mines using large scale cyanidation and amalgamation, tailings dams are specifically designed and constructed as reservoirs in order to contain, *inter alia*, the toxic waste on site, prior to disposal.

Specific elements of over-compensation in the design of tailings dams, (known as redundancies and overdesigns), and in the waste and effluent management systems, are essential for maintaining good environmental protection. The 1st, 2nd and 4th Defendants knew, or should have known, about the said redundancies and overdesigns in the waste and effluent management systems which, when properly designed, constructed and maintained, act as an important mechanism for the protection of the environment.

In addition, impermeable liners may be used in the tailings dams, line the reservoir to ensure that groundwater does not become contaminated by infiltration, seepage and leaching. The 1st, 2nd and 4th Defendants knew, or should have known, about impermeable liners, which when properly designed, constructed and maintained, act as an important mechanism for the protection of the environment.

The OGML Mine

For each ounce of gold produced (and OGML declared a production of 251,000 ounces for 1994), OGML will have processed approximately one tonne of ore. Water is an integral part of the amalgamation and cyanidation processes and OGML has altered the course and flow of the Omai River in order to siphon off a huge volume of water to facilitate gold production at the Mine.

OGML used the tailings dam at the Mine to store, at its highest, some 5 billion plus cubic litres of toxic waste.

The Mine never has used, and does not use, impermeable liners in the tailings pond but instead stores its toxic waste in direct contact with the earth. Thus the said toxic waste continues to infiltrate, seep and leach into the land, ground water and surrounding environment, polluting and continuing to pollute the surrounding land and rivers and causing damage to the eco-system and the Plaintiffs.

Further, the tailings dams do not have any, or any sufficient, of the specific design elements, known as redundancies and over-design as part of its effluent management systems which are essential for maintaining good environmental protection. The 1st, 2nd and 4th Defendants knew, or should have known, about the necessity [for these].

As a pre-condition of owning and operating the mine, the 1st and 4th Defendants were required to adhere to environmental protection guidelines promulgated, *inter alia,* for the purpose of ensuring a clean and potable water supply for the region and preventing pollution. Consequently, the 1st and 4th Defendants were required by the Government of Guyana to submit an Environmental Impact Statement detailing the effects of their operation on the environment, particularly the water resources in the area.

These Defendants were also required to sample and monitor the tailings, releases, and groundwater, during operations, in order to ensure that people and the environment were not being harmed.

On or around January 1991, the 1st and 4th Defendants submitted an Environmental Impact Statement which was accepted by the Government of Guyana. The 1st and 4th Defendants also submitted an addendum to the original Environmental Impact Statement, requesting permission for a new discharge event during August 1995, which was not allowed by the Government of Guyana. The 1st and 4th Defendants' rate of gold production increased significantly from the beginning of production, and particularly the beginning of 1995, until August 1995.

There were two earlier "unplanned" and wrongful discharges in March and May of 1995 which caused injury and damage to diverse residents, occupiers and other users of the land and water resources in the area. By virtue of the said discharges, the 1st, 2nd and 4th Defendants knew, or ought to have known, that any subsequent discharge would cause injury, loss and damage to the Plaintiffs.

The Environment

The topography of the Mine site is inhomogenous: because of subsurface structures and attitude of the underlying geological formations, the ground water flow patterns are varied and complex, reflecting the complexity of the subsurface structures. The hydrology of the site – the heterogeneous nature of the Essequibo River basin into which the effluent is being discharged – is characterised by the presence of terraces, bays, sand banks, lagoons, wetlands, natural levees, flood-plains and tidal influences from the Atlantic Ocean up to and beyond the Mine.

The nature of the sediments, rocks, fauna and flora which line, form and live in the banks and beds of the river, is such that the said toxic waste, especially including as it does heavy metals and other cyano-metallic compounds, is readily absorbed, entrapped and retained in the said banks and beds of the rivers. Further the pH of the Essequibo River water is acidic, normally between pH 4 and 6.

The effluent is reported by OGML to be alkalinic. Discharging such effluent into the Essequibo has the effect of increasing its toxicity. The fact that the Essequibo is tidal, as stated above, results in the toxic waste not only remaining in the Essequibo River, but also in its being transported into the various tributaries (and their tributaries) of the Essequibo, both upstream and downstream of the Mine, thereby affecting the entire watershed of the region.

All the above will have significant and complex impacts on the dynamics of the distribution and end-states of the various elements in the toxic waste after they leave the Mine. Essentially, far from the toxic waste being allowed to drain rapidly and harmlessly away, the *in situ*/local environmental factors, detailed above, all combine to trap, retard and retain the toxic waste, in various bio-available forms, in the rivers and riverbeds, for several decades.

The Legal Background

The 1st and 4th Defendants' mining activity in Guyana is governed by, and is subject, to the following:

a   The Mining Act, number 20 of 1989 of the Laws of Guyana (hereinafter "the Act");

b   The Regulations made and/or saved and incorporated under the Act (hereinafter "the Regulations");

c   A Mining Licence granted by the Government of Guyana to OGML under section 44 of the Act (hereinafter "the Licence");

d   The Mineral Agreement dated 16th August 1991 (hereinafter "the Agreement") made between the Co-operative Republic of Guyana, expressly as represented by the Government and, *inter alia*, the 1st and 4th Defendants;

e   The Environmental Impact Statement, dated January 1991 (hereinafter "the EIS"), prepared by a third party known as Rescan Inc. on the instructions, *inter alia*, of the 1st Defendant.

The Plaintiffs at the hearing of this action will rely on the full terms of the Licence Agreement and the EIS, for their true meaning and effect. OGML (the Licensee) is granted the said Licence subject to, *inter alia*, the following covenant:

"The Licensee shall preserve and protect the natural environmental conditions of the Mining Area, and shall take corrective action from time to time, before the said Mining Area or part or parts of the said Mining Area are surrendered, as may be reasonably necessary for soil conservation, site restoration and the prevention of stream and air pollution. The Licensee shall conduct the Mining Operation so as not to unlawfully pollute any surface or subsurface freshwater supply, keep soil erosion and flood damages to a minimum, keep terrace and landscape waste disposal areas in a reasonable manner and replant them in an economical way and minimize air pollution and shall comply with all applicable regulations made by the competent Government authorities. More particularly the Licensee shall comply fully with the EIS (as defined in the Mineral Agreement). The Government will cause its relevant departments or agencies to issue the necessary permits so that the operations can be carried out in accordance with the EIS.

In the Agreement, the 1st and 4th Defendants, *inter alia*, agreed, *inter alia*, that:

"6.1 The Company shall conduct Operations in a good workmanlike and responsible manner in accordance with good mining practice using standards applicable in the international gold mining industry.

"6.4 The Company shall use reasonable efforts to minimize the negative impact of its operations on forest, land quality, wildlife and human settlements. In particular it shall take care to avoid fires and soil erosion on the land.

"6.7 The Company shall subject to section 16. 6 hereof, preserve and protect the natural environmental conditions of the Mining Area and take such corrective action from time to time before the relinquishment of the Mining Area as may be necessary for soil conservation and to reduce stream and air pollution. In particular, the Company shall conduct Operations so as not to unlawfully pollute any surface or subsurface freshwater supply, to hold erosion and flood damages to a minimum, to maintain terrace and landscape waste disposal areas in a reasonable manner and replant them in an economical way and to minimize air pollution. Timber operations conducted as contemplated in 6. 5 hereof shall be held to standards at least as stringent.

"6.9 The Company shall not be entitled to materially diminish the quality or quantity of any existing source of water being used for domestic or livestock purposes without making reasonable efforts to provide the users of such water with a comparable supply and source.

"6.10 The Private Parties shall not unduly disturb, and interfere with, the living conditions of indigenous populations presently settled in the Mining Area, if any. The Government shall not require, encourage or permit any additional settlements in the Mining Area during the term of this Agreement. Subject to the foregoing, the Private Parties shall comply with the provisions of Amerindians Act and shall respect the customs of indigenous populations. If at any point a resettlement appears to be absolutely essential, the Company shall move with the utmost caution, with the consent of the Government and in consultation with the authorities of the settlement in persuading the settlers to resettle and provide a fully adequate resettlement program at its expense in accordance with the directions of the responsible Minister.

"6.16 Guyana (represented herein by the Government) and the Commission, ereby acknowledge having reviewed and hereby accept and approve the EIS together with all provisions set forth in the study relating to environmental matters. The Company shall conduct Operations substantially in accord with the terms of the EIS and shall comply with all applicable laws and administrative policies of the Government relating to environmental matters which are presently in effect. Guyana (represented herein by the Government) and the Commission hereby agree to take such Corrective Action (as defined in section 15. 5 hereof) as may be necessary to ensure that any Unilateral Action (as defined in section 15. 5 hereof) shall not result in the imposition of more stringent environmental obligations on the Project, or on the Private Parties in connection with the Project, than those in effect from time to time in the Province of Quebec, Canada.

Some of the relevant terms of the Terms of Environmental Impact Statement, are to the following effect:

"*5.1.2 Water Balance*
To build the tailings facility to a design assuming an active pond volume of up to 500,000 cubic meters with an additional allowance of 100,000 cubic meters to accommodate a 10 year occurrence, 24 hour storm plus 1 meter for spillway freeboard. (p 5-3);

To ensure the containment of a free water volume of 500,000 cubic meters plus runoff of 100,000 cubic meters, an elevation difference of at least 6.5 meters must be maintained between the embankment crest and the tailings elevation at the embankment. (p 5-41)

[The implementation of an] on-going monitoring of the tailings elevation at the embankment and the volume of water in storage [must] ensure that freeboard stability and storm storage requirements are met. (p 5-42)

The implementation of ongoing monitoring of the tailings elevation and the volume of water in storage [must] ensure sufficient freeboard is maintained at all times and to plan for future embankment raises. (p 5-5)

"5.5.3.3 Tailings Discharge

[There must be] implementation of a program of ongoing monitoring of the tailings deposit to indicate the final height of the tailings embankment so that maximum use could be made of inexpensive in-pit tailings storage. (p 5-32)

"5.5.3.7 Instrumentation

The implementation of a tailings management program, including for tailings storage and effluent treatment, shall be carried out consisting of geotechnical instrumentation for the tailings dam and monitoring instrumentation. The type of geotechnical instrumentation shall include piezometers, settlements gauges and inclinometers. (p 5-42)

[There must be] [m]onitoring of the performance of the dam... with a view to modification of the dam [by raising it] as a result of the instrument readings. (p 5-42)

"5.5.7 Subaqueous Discharge from Aeration Pond

Following natural degradation in both the tailings and aeration pond, effluent will be discharged through a pipeline and through a 4 port diffuser located at the deepest section of the main channel of the Essequibo River. Under average conditions it is estimated that a dilution of about 2,000:1 will be achieved in the mixing zone, within 100m of the diffuser.

Given that natural degradation has brought the total cyanide concentration in the effluent to 2 mg/L this dilution will yield a cyanide concentration in the river of approximately 1µg/L, which is well within North American standard receiving water guidelines (see section 4. 3. 2). Similarly, a copper concentration of 2 mg/litre would also be reduced to 1 µg/L. This too meets North American receiving water standards.

Thus it appears that the Essequibo River always has sufficient flow to provide dilutions which will yield very acceptable cyanide concentrations well within 100m downstream of the diffuser.

A "Conceptual Spill Contingency Plan" was also contemplated to minimize environmental degradation and safety hazards associated with contaminant spills at or near the mine site if they were to occur. It was also contemplated that the final plan would include an assessment of the worst possible scenario and details of how to deal with such a situation. The contingency plan should detail efforts to contain and recover spills on land, to prevent soil and vegetation damage, to minimize safety hazards, and to reduce infiltration and migration to bodies of water. Spills of liquid on land to be commonly contained by either berming or ditching. (p 5-66)

"5.6.2 Containment Method for Spills on Water
The contingency plan should detail methods to contain spills on water. (p 5-68)

Spill Response Plan

The contingency plan should contain a plan for a rehearsed series of actions to be carried out in the event of an accidental spill. Each member's responsibilities to be clearly defined. The spill response plan should be optimized through the use of practice drills and these drills should occur at regular intervals. (p 5-70)

"5.6.6 Safety Considerations
The contingency plan should place the protection and well being of personnel as the prime consideration at a spill site. Actions that place workers in a hazardous environment should be recognized and avoided. Special consideration should be given to the unique safety problems associated with each different variety of spill. As part of the contingency plan, a supervisor should be appointed at the commencement of the spill containment and recovery operations. This person should be designated in advance and should receive extra safety training. (p 5-70)

"6.1.2 Surface Water Quality
It was never intended to discharge contaminated water into the Omai river. The planned discharge of mine tailings pond water into the Essequibo was only to occur after natural degradation processes had acted to lower the

concentration of cyanide and copper to levels at, or below, the acceptable limits of these elements in discharge water. (p 6-3).

The North American receiving water quality guidelines for the protection of aquatic life were to be met within a short distance of the outfall by the use of subsurface outfall diffuser to take advantage of the dilution capacity of the Essequibo river. (p 6-3)

"8.2 Environmental Monitoring

It was contemplated that the main environmental monitoring program would revolve around the tailings impoundment. Of critical importance was to be monitoring the final effluent quality and quantity. To facilitate this it would be necessary to establish a program to monitor the tailings facility's water balance. (p 8-1)

Monitoring these aquatic mass balance parameters was to facilitate the estimation of the unrecoverable seepage losses from the tailings impound-ment to the groundwater and residual water content of the tailings solids. The water balance was to be important in tracking the rate at which the tail-ings pond filled. (p 8-2)

Because the primary dispersion of contaminants would be into the river-ain system, a comprehensive system of water quality monitoring would be necessary. (p 8-2)

The cyanide concentration in the tailings ponds was to be regularly moni-tored in order to assess the efficacy of the natural degradation process in reducing cyanide content to an acceptable level. (p 8-2)

Should any spills of hazardous material occur, the water in the immediate vicinity of the spill was to be sampled and the Omai river near the mouth to be monitored to facilitate an estimation of non-recoverable losses. This is accounted for in spill contingency planning. (p 8-2)

The final aspect of the monitoring program was to be the human aspect [i. e. the industrial hygiene monitoring] especially for silica dust and HCN gas. The monitoring program after abandonment was to be primarily of a geotechnical and hydrological nature, to ensure the continued stability of the tailings impoundment, waste rock dumps, and the exposed pit wall. (p 8-3)

Counter Claims

It is averred that, contrary to the above assertions (in paragraphs 5.5.7 and 6.1. 2) the Canadian Water Quality Guidelines, as promulgated by the Task Force on Water Quality Guidelines of the Canadian Council of Resource and Environment Ministers, dated March 1987, are not blanket values but must be modified for local conditions.

Further, the guidelines should not be used to impair water of superior quality. It is averred that the Essequibo was a waterway of superior quality prior to the Disaster.

Further, the United States Environmental Protection Agency has adopted a zero discharge standard for all mines using Cyanidation. The only exception is where net precipitation exceeds net evaporation and discharge is allowed only to the extent of the difference between the two and is subject to national limitations established on a case-by-case basis.

The Disaster

The Disaster on or about August 19th, 1995 whereby the tailings dam at the Mine ruptured, discharging approximately 3.2 billion cubic litres of toxic waste (representing approximately 60 per cent of the original amount held inside the dam), resulted in the escape of an unknown but substantial amount of toxic waste into the Omai and Essequibo Rivers, causing vast plumes of toxic waste to discolour the surface and the body of the rivers.

The toxic waste has settled and remains along the length and breadth of the Omai and Essequibo Rivers, their tributaries and thus the entire watershed, continuing to pollute the Plaintiffs' environment in diverse and complex bio-available forms.

The immediate impact on the environment and the community was immense. By, on, or about, 22nd August 1995, when the Government declared a Disaster Zone, visible proof, and word, of the Disaster had already spread all along the rivers. Ambiguous, confusing and contradictory warnings about using, drinking or touching the water had been passed along the river and... widespread confusion, trauma, alienation, worry and concern descended upon the Plaintiffs.

An almost total cessation of all economic activity, associated with and supported by the Essequibo River, resulted. Large fish kills had been reported floating downstream. No one would purchase any fish or aquatic game. The Caribbean Common Market soon thereafter declared an embargo on imports of all fish products from Guyana. Some inadequate alternative sources of water were provided by the 4th Defendants, the Government of Guyana and other agencies, and diverse Plaintiffs attempted to make their own arrangements.

In numerous cases, with no fresh water, or fresh water only sufficient to drink, the Plaintiffs were very soon driven to sporadic, tentative and desperate contact with the Essequibo and the other polluted waters. Most people had been warned not the play in the water but parents had to constantly watch their children to enforce the ban. The inevitable failures only served to heighten the general sense of worry, concern, anxiety and foreboding.

Immediately thereafter there were widespread instances of itching, sores and burning eyes, after contact with the water. Itching became sores, and sores became lesions on the skin of babies and adults alike. Diverse Plaintiffs started to experience aching joints, feelings of lassitude, loss of libido, vomiting, loss of memory, burning eyes and eye infections, diminished vision, hearing problems and sundry aches and pains, which symptoms continue to date.

The Defendants, by themselves their servants or agents, issued no, or no proper, warnings to the Plaintiffs. Some Plaintiffs were not told anything and some were told simply not to drink the water. Some were told not to touch the water. No, or no proper, warning was give by the 1st or 4th Defendants as to the true extent and severity of the problem.

Diverse Plaintiff fishermen were told that it would be safe to fish and eat the fish after three – and then after six – weeks. However, fish stocks dwindled or disappeared. What fish were caught had sores, lesions and strange discolourations about their bodies. Fields of produce and entire herds of livestock were devastated, entire families economically ruined, communities destroyed.

At least two people have died as a result of bathing in and/or drinking the waters of the Essequibo. In all the riverain communities of the Plaintiffs, the Essequibo River (and other waters), which had once been such a fecund life-source and considered a friend and ally, became a poisoned river, a source of death and despair.

A substantial remainder of the contaminated water that did not enter the Omai and Essequibo rivers was diverted into the Fenell pit, an open pit and source of gold ore at the Mine. This pit was not lined properly, or at all, and thus the said toxic waste continues to infiltrate and/or seep and/or leach into the land and surrounding environment, continuing to pollute the eco-system and causing damage to the Plaintiffs.

The toxic waste that was directed to the Fenell Pit contained contaminated groundwater and was not disposed of properly before the restart of operations in February of 1996. After an involuntary closure due to a special resolution of the parliament of Guyana, the Mine resumed gold mining operations from February of 1996.

The Continuing Effluent Discharge

Upon restart, the 1st and 4th Defendants further increased gold production to much higher levels than immediately before the August 19th Disaster, and the Mine continues to discharge toxic waste directly into the riverain environment. Increased production has been accompanied by increased water pollution.

By reason of the 1st, 2nd and 4th Defendants' negligence and/or breach of statutory and/or other duties and/or breach of contract as aforesaid, the Plaintiffs have sustained personal injuries and psychological shock and trauma, and suffered loss and damage.

CHAPTER 6

Come to Grief: the Kumtor Gold Mine in Kyrgyzstan

6.1 CHRONOLOGY OF A DISASTER 1995-2000

12 January 1995

The Kyrgyzstan government says it hopes to increase gold production from more than 2 tons in 1994 to more than 20 tons by 1998.[1]

7 July 1995

Canada's CAMECO Corp signs an agreement to develop the Kumtor gold field, working with a syndicate of seven banks, CAMECO owning one-third of the joint venture and the Kyrgyz company, Kyrgyzaltyn, the other two-thirds.[2] The joint venture Kumtor Operating Company (KOC), is scheduled to start gold extraction in 1997 but, before that, a million tons of glacial ice must be removed from the area. The target figures for gold extraction are 12.4 tons in 1997 and 15.5 tons in later years.[3]

10 October 1995

A search party finds the bodies of seventeen passengers and the crew of a helicopter that crashed on October 4th.[4] The helicopter was carrying twelve foreigners, including nine Canadians from CAMECO, returning from Kumtor when it encountered bad weather in the Tien-Shan mountains.[5]

31 January 1996

CAMECO says that KOC will invest $160 million in the Kumtor gold field in 1996.[6] CAMECO had already invested US$215 million in the project in 1995 and production is scheduled to begin in 1997.[7]

7 January 1997

Gold extraction starts.

6 March 1997

Jalgap Kazakbayev, director of the Kara-Balta state mining company, and Leonard Homenyuk, president of KOC, sign an agreement whereby gold extracted at Kumtor will be refined at the Kara-Balta complex.[8] Some 12 tons of gold are expected to be refined at Kara-Balta that year. Earlier reports that gold would be refined abroad had led to an outcry from opposition groups in Kyrgyzstan.[9]

17 November 1997

The Kumtor joint venture announces it has exceeded its goal of producing 12.7 tons of gold this year;[10] production is expected to reach 20 tons annually by the end of the century.

15 April 1998

Mamat Aibalaev, the head of Kyrgyzstan's parliamentary commission on corruption in the gold industry, tells the RFE/RL correspondents in the Kyrgyz capital, Bishkek, that the government should ask a foreign company to conduct an audit of the industry. A four-member parliamentary commission had requested information on the gold industry from the Kumtor joint venture in February but only just received it. The Kumtor facility had far exceeded its budget in January, while Apas Jumagulov's sudden resignation as Kyrgyzstan premier, in March, had followed media reports alleging his involvement in illegal sales of Kyrgyz gold through a company in Austria.

20 May 1998

After a "traffic accident", a consignment of sodium cyanide en route to the mine ends up in the Barskoun river. It appears that the driver lost control on a curve in the road, some eight km from Barskoun village. An estimated 1,762 kg of granular sodium cyanide are lost in the waters.[11] The truck and its cargo are removed from the river within six hours of the accident, but not before one of the packages ruptures, spilling some of its contents. "The source of the spill (sic) has been contained and monitoring of the river continues in order to assess the environmental impact of the incident," CAMECO says, adding: "At this time, the impact is believed to be negligible".

Water supply to Barskoun village is shut off, in cooperation with the local authorities, as a "preventive measure" according to the company, since it is near Issyk-Kul lake, Kyrgyzstan's biggest tourist attraction.[12]

Reports vary on the extent of damage to the environment. A spokeswoman for President Askar Akayev says there are no "environmental consequences". But the newspaper *Komsomolskaya Pravda* on May 22 reports that eight tons of sodium cyanide was spilled into the river. Independent ecological experts tell RFE/RL correspondents in Bishkek that the Kumtor gold mining company refuses to allow them on the site.

According to later analysis, cyanide concentration in the waters at the place of the disaster is 1590 mg/litre (as opposed to the country's permissible level of 0.035 mg/litre), while soil samples evince a concentration more than 70 times North Kyrgyz's limits. It takes a day for the level to return to its legal level.[13]

25 May 1998

Kyrgyzstan's Deputy Environmental Minister, Tilekbai Kyshtobayev, announces at the scene of the accident that "there are no grounds for panic. No ecological disaster is expected,"[14] a viewpoint echoed by Gerhard Glates, the head of Kumtor. Glates says there will be no serious environmental consequences and that his company will cover all expenses for the cleanup.

However, both ITAR-TASS and RFE/RL correspondents report that dead fish and cattle have been found near the scene of the accident. They also say that residents of the area have been warned against drinking un-boiled water and swimming in the river or lake. The Minister of Ecology, Kulubek Bokonbayev, tells RFE/RL correspondents that, since the 20 May accident, some 250 residents of the Issyk-Kul region have sought medical help.

27 May 1998

Four hundred and seventy five people around Kumtor have become sick and sought medical treatment, according to Interfax. Of these, 68 have been kept in the hospital. Officials from the Kyrgyz government and the Kumtor company continue to claim that the effects of the spill will be negligible.

28 May 1998

Deputy Premier, Boris Silayev, accuses Kumtor Mining Company of being "irresponsible".[15] Kyrgyz premier, Kubanychbek Jumaliev, announces that more than 1,000 residents of the southern Issyk-Kul area have sought medical treatment and at least 93 have been kept in the hospital. Two people have died, while eight are in a serious condition and have been moved by helicopter to better facilities in Bishkek, he says.[16]

29 May 1998

The heads of the Kumtor gold mining project visit residents of the disaster area. Dastan Sarygulov and Gerhard Glates say the company will pay for all medical costs of the more than 1,000 people affected by the spill, and will install a water system to villages on the south shore of Lake Issyk-Kul. The residents have demanded that there should be no further shipments of sodium cyanide along the lake's southern road. ITAR-TASS reports that more than half the tourist reservations for the summer season on Lake Issyuk-Kul have been cancelled.

3 June 1998

A woman allegedly dies from cyanide poisoning in a hospital in the eastern town of Karakol, according to a report by RFE/RL correspondents. These reporters also comment that, at the end of May, tourists on the north shore of Issyk-Kul had received little, if any, information about the toxic spill and were still swimming in Issyk-Kul. Michel Bernard, president of CAMECO Corp, tells a press conference in Bishkek that the reporting of the incident has been exaggerated. He says that "well-respected experts" had concluded that the spill will not present environmental hazards to the residents of the area or to the lake.

4 June 1998

Boris Silayev declares that 3,500 residents of Barskoun area will be evacuated to the northern shore.[17] Concerns have also been expressed about the storage of 2,000 tons of sodium cyanide in the town of Balykchy, on the western shore of Issyk-Kul. Government officials continue to say that it is safe to swim in the lake.

9 June 1998

Doctors claim that, according to a preliminary finding, the death of a 71-year-old man from the Issyk-Kul area on 6 June was from sodium cyanide poisoning following the spill the previous month.[18]

Meanwhile, Interfax reports that 40 people assisting in the clean-up of the area have been taken ill and brought back to the capital for treatment.

9 June 1998

According to Kyrgyz Minister of Health Care, Naken Kasiev, the evacuation of the Barskoun area has been completed.[19] The authorities have temporarily relocated 4,800 people to the northern shore of the lake, while 5,349 sick people from the affected area have sought medical help. Two experts from the World Health Organization (WHO) state at the same press conference that the level of sodium cyanide in the water and ground is now at acceptable levels and present no danger to the population.

10 June 1998

The following day, President Askar Akayev seeks to confirm that there are no longer any dangers posed by the accident.[20] "The lake is alive and well and is looking forward to tourists," he declares, adding that Issyk-Kul is "absolutely not contaminated" since the chemical "dissolves into harmless components" when mixed with water.

At the same news conference, the president of KOC, Len Homeniuk, and the head of Kyrgyzstan's state gold company, Dastan Sarygulov, admit that the spill of sodium cyanide was Kumtor's fault and that the company was negligent in informing the population of the area as to the possible danger. However, opinions differ over who should pay for the cleanup and compensate residents of the area. Kyrgyzstan officials, including Akayev, announce that CAMECO Corp will pay all compensation. CAMECO officials apparently retort that, since the company has only a one-third share in the project, it will pay only one-third of the costs.

15 July 1998

New questions arise over the clean-up process.[21] Two weeks after the spill, calcium hypochlorite was used in the cleanup. Reports from hospitals in the area say some local residents have developed a rash, possibly related to the chemical. Moreover, independent experts from the U.S. have been unable to reach the Kumtor gold mine to inspect conditions. The experts were informed that the plane assigned them by the government was unable to fly owing to "technical reasons".

21 July 1998

The Vecherni Bishkek daily newspaper carries an interview with Viktor Grinenko, Deputy Minister of Health Care and Chief Sanitary Inspector of Kyrgyzstan. He says that the "rescuers" from the Kumtor Operating Company had extensively worked the soil and the water on the accident site with calcium hypochlorite in extended volume on 21 May, one day after the accident, as a result of which local people and the soil had now been poisoned. According to Grinenko, the KOC did not co-ordinate its action with the Health Ministry.

The presidential press service announces that President Akayev will, the following day, open the country's first international tennis tournament, to be held the resort town of Cholpon-Ata, on the Issyk-Kul lakeshore. The aim is to demonstrate that the lake is not contaminated.

22 July 1998

The driver of the truck which spilled the sodium cyanide into the Barskoun River on 20 May is charged with violating rules for transporting chemicals.[22] He faces a maximum of 10 years in prison if found guilty. All other drivers who transported sodium cyannide on the day of the accident have been fired. The Kyrgyz parliamentary commission investigating the spill reports that the management of the Kumtor Gold Mining project has not repaired bridges leading to the mining site, which were built 20 years ago and not intended for cargoes exceeding 13 tons. The company's trucks regularly transport 40-ton cargoes across such bridges.

5 August 1998

Two foreign toxicologists, invited by the management of KOC to examine its findings on the consequences of the 20 May spill, are denied access to the appropriate data.[23] The Kyrgyz Health Care Ministry claims that the U.S. citizen, Allen Holl, accompanied by Russia's Yurii Ostapenko, do not have authorisation from the World Health Organization and are therefore not allowed to talk with people who were hospitalised following the event.

7 October 1998

Deputy Prime Minister Silayev gives a preliminary costing of the damage caused by the sodium cyanide spill as 91 million soms (about $4 million).[24] The estimate does not include agricultural losses. An RFE/RL journalist who visited the village most affected by the spill finds that, although a medical center has been established there, residents have not received compensation for their losses and humanitarian aid to the village amounted to one notebook, one pen, and five pieces of candy per inhabitant.

15 December 1998

The Kumtor Gold Mining Company announces it will open a diagnosis and monitoring center in Barskoun,[25] paying for all its construction and the first year's running expenses.

14 January 1999

Kyrgyzstan's Ministry for Emergency Situations says it will assume control over the transportation of poisonous chemicals.[26]

26 March 1999

The Movement of Kyrgyzstan claims in Bishkek that some 80 people have died as a direct consequence of the spill in May 1998.[27] Parliamentary Deputy Jeksheev says neither the Kyrgyzaltyn state gold company, nor the Canadian Kumtor Operating Company (KOC), have kept their promises to pay compensation for all damage resulting from the spill.

8 May 1999

The governmental press service says a special governmental commission is now inspecting the activities of the Kyrgyzaltyn state gold company, following its release of a major report on its recent activities. According to this, $122.9 million of foreign investment was made in the Kyrgyz economy between 1994 and 1996, while $47.5 million was given to the state budget from the gold industry between 1997 and 1998.

4-8 May 1999

Residents of Kyrgyzstan's Issyk-Kul region blockade roads leading to the Kumtor gold mine and destroy two trucks belonging to the KOC.[28] The picketers protest the disappearance of some 780,000 soms (US$22,000) allocated by the KOC as compensation for victims of the Barskoun disaster. Five police and two picketers are hospitalized following clashes, when police try to disperse the picketers, 34 of whom are detained. Other demonstrators then take three local officials hostage, not releasing them until the night of 9-10 May when their fellow protestors are freed. Criminal proceedings have been brought against one of the local officials accused of embezzling the relief funds.

20 May 1999

Some 1,000 residents of Barskoun hold a meeting to mark the first anniversary of the sodium cyanide accident.[29] No local or national officials attend the ceremony.

21 May 1999

Parliamentary deputy Jeksheev declares that the conciliatory agreement between the Kyrgyz Government and CAMECO, signed in New York the previous January, should be cancelled. He says that the Kyrgyz Government and the Kumtor Operating Company should pay all the compensation promised to the victims of the spill. He promises to present documents on the accident, including several video documentaries, to international organizations and international courts.

Mid-May 1999

Jengish Jylkybaeva, a physician at the National Hospital in Bishkek, tells RFE/RL that she recently visited Barskoun, where local records indicate that 22 people have died in the village over the past year, compared with a total of 40 deaths in the preceding four years. In two cases, the cause of death was given as cyanide poisoning. Speaking at a press conference in Bishkek on 24 May, First Deputy Premier Silayev defends as "adequate" the compensation agreement, signed in January 1999 between Kyrgyzstan CAMECO Corporation.[30]

4 June 1999

The Soros-Kyrgyzstan Foundation says it will hold an international conference on the accident at the resort town of Cholpon-Ata on 8-12 June. On 10 June participants of the conference will visit the village of Barskoun, close to the site of the accident.

2 July 1999

Inhabitants of Tosor and Tamga villages, in Jeti Oegyez, continue blocking the Barskoun-Kumtor road leading to the gold mine. They also ask to meet with the head of the government commission into mitigating the consequences of the spill, Vice-Prime Minister Boris Silayev. KOC's Foreign Relations officer, Tynara Shajdyldajeva, confirms that, over four days, lorries were prevented by the blockade from reaching the mining site, causing many difficulties.

11 October 1999

An official of the Kumtor project tells an RFE/RL correspondent that an independent British organization will examine the impact of the project on the ecological situation in Kyrgyzstan. This will be financed – to the tune of $190,000 – by the European Bank for Reconstruction and Development (EBRD), while the British based Flora and Fauna International has won an "international tender" for the study.

30 November 1999

KOC agrees with the government to pay around $6 million in taxes, despite the "holiday" earlier granted to the company.

20 January 2000

The Ministry of Emergencies says that a KOC truck, carrying chemicals, overturns on a bridge along the road between Barskoun village and the Kumtor mine. About 1,500 kilograms of ammonium nitrate are spilled. KOC workers supposedly collect all the spilled chemicals the same day.

5 February 2000

Statements by representatives of several international ecological and human rights organizations, are released in Bishkek on February 4. They call for an independent audit of KOC's development of the Kumtor gold mine. They also demand that the World Bank/IFC and Cameco release an emergency response plan for the mine.

Notes

1 Interfax, January 11 1995, citing Prime Minister Apas Dzhumagulov.

2 Reuters report, July 7 1995.

3 Bruce Pannier, OMRI, Inc; EBRD *press release*, July 7 1995.

4 ITAR-TASS, October 10 1995.

5 Bruce Pannier, OMRI, op cit.

6 Kumtor Operating Company President Len Khomenyuk *press release*, January 30 1996.

7 Bruce Pannier, OMRI, op cit.

8 RFE/RL report, March 5 1997.

9 Naryn Idinov, *Kyrgyzstan: Gold To Be Refined Locally*, March 6 1997.

10 RFE/RL correspondents, November 20 1997.

11 Jozsef Feiler, *Kumtor – the poisoned gold*, May 2000, p. 35.

12 RFE/RL correspondents and ITAR-TASS, May 20 1998.

13 OCEI 2000 quoted in Feiler, *Kumtor – the poisoned gold*, op cit, p. 35.

14 ITAR-TASS, May 25 1998.

15 RFE/RL reports, May 28 1998.

16 RFE/RL reports, ibid.

17 RFE/RL reports, June 4 1998.

18 RFE/RL reports, June 9 1998.

19 RFE/RL correspondents, June 10 1998.

20 Interfax and RFE/RL, June 11 1998.

21 RFE/RL, *Kyrgyz Service report*, July 15 1998.

22 Interfax, July 22 1998.

23 RFE/RL correspondents, August 5 1998.

24 Interfax, October 7 1998.

25 RFE/RL December 15.

26 RFE/RL, January 14 1990.

27 RFE/RL Bishkek bureau, March 30 1999.

28 RFE/RL Bishkek bureau, May 13 1999.

29 RFE/RL Bishkek Bureau, May 21 1999.

30 RFE/RL *Newsline*, May 24 1999.

6.2 KUMTOR GRIEF

Roger Moody, with the Bank Information Center

"The fabulously wealthy but cruel khan who ruled the area fell in love with a beautiful girl of lowly origins who refused to marry him. The girl, who loved another, began to weep and eventually her tears filled the whole valley. This is how Lake Issyk-Kul was created." (From a Kyrgyz creation story)

It scarcely seemed possible. Just two years after the Omai disaster (see chapter 5), another gold mine – also operated by a Canadian company and backed by MIGA and the EDC – suffered yet another disaster which several observers swiftly declared to be both unprecedented and avoidable.

The Kumtor mine is managed by the world's biggest uranium producer, CAMECO Corp. (through the Kumtor Operating Company, or KOC). Just like its counterpart in Guyana, this project carried a promise to boost the impoverished economy of Kyrgystan, employ many local people, and float a raft of social benefits. On the surface (literally) the project could scarcely be more different than Omai. While the latter lies deep within primary rainforest, close to the country's main river, Kumtor is one of the highest and most exposed mines in the world. It sits precariously on the crest of a mountain range where temperatures regularly dip below zero, machinery is liable to freeze-up, and the atmosphere is so rarefied that employees must regularly be decanted from the minesite to recover their strength.

Nonetheless, similarities between the two operations run uncomfortably close. No pre-project provision was made to strengthen bridges on roads leading to Kumtor and some type of "accident" was easily predictable. Sure enough, one occurred in May 1998, when a consignment of sodium cyanide (such as employed for gold processing at Omai) toppled into the river Barskoun, quickly entering the tourist-resort lake of Issyk-Kul. Non-Kyrgyz experts were impeded in reaching the site and inappropriate palliative chemicals were dumped indiscriminately in the affected waters, where dead fish were soon observed floating belly-up.

Thousands of residents in the area believed they had been poisoned. And (like Cambior and Golden Star, the corporate culprits behind Omai) KOC representatives dismissed local and national fears by claiming that little untoward had occurred, even before any damage assessment was mounted.

The failure by IFC/MIGA and the second PRI provider, OPIC, to act in line with their avowed policies of due diligence and adequate disaster response was arguably less excusable in Kyrgystan than it had been earlier in Guyana. Hiding behind the Kyrgyz government's obstructive policy towards independent disaster assessment, they ignored demands for an exhaustive and objective investigation. The IFC compounded these earlier errors of judgment by later issuing a bland "Project Brief". This not only ignored the persistence of local peoples' contentions that they had been misled, but propagated manifest inaccuracies.

CAMECO, claimed the IFC, "...is in full compliance with all World Bank Group policies and guidelines".[1] Apparently the company's refusal to impart its full emergency response plans was not considered a material breach of those guidelines – even though it was the IFC which "required" CAMECO to refashion them. Seeking to minimise the likelihood of a major disaster the IFC blandly ascribed the spill to "human error on the part of the truck driver".[2] "All material and containers met international standards for transporting cyanides," declared the IFC, adding – with dubious relevance – "Kumtor road traffic accident frequency is lower than that of Canada's".

The stability of the cyanide packages was not in chief contention; the method of transporting them, the overloading of the carrying vehicles, and the failure of the company to resurface and upgrade the approach routes, certainly were. According to CEE (Central and Eastern Europe) Bankwatch policy coordinator, Jozsef Feiler, the Kumtor Operating Company (KOC) had initially contracted the Kyrgyz Ministry of Transport to do this essential work.[3] However, the agreement was cancelled by KOC in January 1995 and several further appeals for finance made by the Kyrgyz Ministry of Transport, to both company and government, were rejected.[4]

The European Bank for Reconstruction and Development (EBRD) put up something of a defense of its financing for this dubious project, while MIGA and OPIC – the providers of political risk insurance to Kumtor – have remained almost silent. Yet, it is precisely a more fundamental – and community-defined – concept of risk that the project required from its outset. If this had not been denied it might conceivably have resulted in the project being halted, or at least fundamentally re-designed.

Consider first the environmental hazards associated with constructing a mine in permafrost and – against all best practice – relying on "nature", in the shape of a glacier, to contain the tailings.

Second, there was an indisputable threat to workers' health. No matter that an impressive 1,621 people were employed at the mine by the end of 1999, with "cumulative benefits" to employees and the economy totalling just under US$28 million[5]: a significant proportion of the workforce was likely to suffer the long term effects of labouring under oppressive climatic conditions, dogged by lack of oxygen.

Third, as pointed out by Joszef Feiler, there was the prospect that the tailings retention could be disastrously impacted by global warming.

> "It is not clear what will happen with all [this] highly toxic content when the melting of glaciers will increase. In addition, significant climatic changes are [expected] for the years 2040-2050. The Environmental Impact Assessment of the mine site deals only in general terms... and takes the sub-zero temperature as an important factor for the eternal storage of toxic materials. It does not assess the possible climatic fluctuations and the change of precipitation and water-flow from melting. If material from the tailing disposal basin enters the watercourse via the Kumtor River, it would poison the main water resources of Central Asia, which are already under stress."[6]

Most important in a catalogue of deficiencies was perhaps, the near-total absence of thorough examination of (not to mention community debate about) the wisdom of imposing such a large, externally-financed, undertaking on a country laden with debt. Kyrgystan is only just becoming conversant with democratic procedures and the very institutions which should have provided alternative models for development, abjectly failed to do so. Kumtor was quite simply dumped on the people of Kyrgyzstan.

A Show of "Stakeholder" Participation

In 1999 the EBRD initiated a Monitoring Advisory Group (MAG). This was supposed to address the lack of credibility of monitoring data released until then, and the increasingly cynical, often hostile, declarations by various local, national and international critics. MAG was later transformed into the Community and Business Forum CBF), managed by Fauna and Flora International, to be an agency for "stakeholder" dialogue. The Forum does not appear to have contributed much to a reduction in criticism – on the contrary. Jozsef Feiler says that the establishment of CBF prompted "the watering down of the original stakeholder dialogue on Kumtor-related issues" into general "collaboration". Local NGOs raised serious concerns about the usefulness of the process in this form: "It is perceived by them that the forum is used to divide the NGO community with the tools of small grants, and monopolize further the information flow..."[7]

Belatedly following the May 1998 disaster, the IFC set up purchasing centres to assist residents in selling their local produce, in an atmosphere coloured by public perceptions of widespread cyanide poisoning. It also launched a US$66,000 "marketing campaign" to "reassure potential visitors of the safety of the location". But these inadequate responses seemed to have served only to compound a growing sense of alienation between many citizens and the mine.

Kumtor has not just been beset by "mishaps". Rather, the Kyrgyzstan mine has been blighted by a series of ecological and social problems. These in turn have been nuanced – and surely compounded – by the rise of new political and economic forces. Between 1997 and 2000, various Kyrgyz leaders jockeyed with each over the power to make decisions about the project and dispose of its gold. Heads rolled amid accusations of corruption; external investigators had the door opened by one faction, then closed by another; medical sources were quoted making wildly divergent claims about the casualties of the May 1998 event. (Perhaps it is indicative that there is not even an agreed westernized spelling of "Barskoun" among the documents examined for this chapter variously cited are "Barskon", "Barskoon", "Barskaun" – and even "Barksoun" or "Barkon".)

Such internecine rivalry has characterised most of the resource-rich regions of the former Soviet Union. Indeed, Russia itself has seen bloody wars break out over the ownership of privatised assets and, whatever the post-communist rhetoric of liberalisation, the control of several key mineral producing companies lies firmly with capitalist oligarchs.

It is only fairly recently that "free-world" enterprises, supposedly bringing with them high standards of transparency and shareholder democracy, have begun courting (and being courted by) these dubious entrepreneurs. Backing for these projects by international finance institutions (IFIs) will become increasingly critical to their advancement. While exact parallels cannot be drawn between Kyrgyzstan and the other newborn states of Central and Eastern Europe, the Kumtor story is surely an object lesson in failures of project appraisal and mis-management, abject lack of corporate transparency, and the cavalier snubbing of community concerns.

What follows is an attempt to tell the Kumtor story by drawing on several studies, accompanied by a chronology for 1997-2000 which provides insight into how various key events were regarded by the Kyrgyz press and the ubiquitous US-controlled Radio Free Europe.

The Hills Are Alive with the Sound of Mining

Kyrgyzstan's Kumtor gold mine is poised at 4,400 meters along the north-western slopes of the Ak Shirak mountain ridge, in the interior of the Tien-Shan range adjacent to China. The mine is owned two-thirds by the Kyrgyz Republic and one-third by CAMECO, Canada's biggest uranium (also a major gold) producer, through the Kumtor Gold Company (KGC). It is managed by the Kumtor Operating Company (KOC), a subsidiary of CAMECO.

The project is funded by an array of loans and guarantees from private and public financial institutions, while CAMECO by mid-2000 had provided $167 million of its own funding. The partners are:

- European Bank for Reconstruction and Development (EBRD, an international public institution) $40 million loan. [The EBRD also provided a $30.1 million loan to the Kyrgyz Republic for electricity upgrades in order to supply the mine complex with electricity.]
- International Finance Corporation (IFC) of the World Bank Group (international public institution) $40 million loan (US$30 million "senior" and US$10 million subordinated loan).
- Multilateral Investment Guarantee Agency (MIGA) of the World Bank Group (international public institution) $45 million for political risk insurance.
- Overseas Private Investment Corporation (OPIC: US public institution) $192 million for political risk insurance.
- Export Development Canada (EDC: Canadian public institution) $50 million loan.[8]

Two eight year loan packages were provided by several banks led by Chase Manhattan:
- The Republic National Bank of New York: $13.48 million.
- ABN-AMRO Bank of Canada: $16.61 million.
- Bank of Nova Scotia: $14.39 million.
- Royal Bank of Canada: $28.79 million.[8]

Claimed at the time by KOC to be the largest western-managed mining project in the former Soviet Union, it cost $452 million to construct, and initially enjoyed a 10-year exemption of profit tax. The company pays royalties to the Kyrgyz government at $4 an ounce, plus a further royalty variable on the gold price. Between 2 and 4 per cent of the profits go to local community organisations.

CAMECO also obtained – in contrast to other gold ventures in Central Asia – a licence to export the gold, asserting that this was a key requirement for obtaining finance. If the National Bank of Kyrgyzstan wanted to exercise its first option on buying the gold it had to pay the full going London bullion market rate. CAMECO controls the venture's gold account, which means it has the last word in any gold sales.

Though Soviet geologists concluded, in 1989, that mining Kumtor was not commercially feasible, soon after the collapse of "state capitalism" in the USSR CAMECO signed an agreement to take a stake in the mine, as well as assume management responsibility.

As Joszef Feiler explains it:

> "The collapse of the Soviet Union left the Kyrgyz Republic with little foundation for economic development. The backward technologies, inappropriate management skills, cash flow problems and limited access to world markets, among other factors, hindered the process of the economic and social stabilisation of the country. As a result, the Gross Domestic Product (GDP) fell by 10 per cent in 1991, by 16.5 per cent in 1993, and by more than 20 per cent in 1994. ... According to the recommendations of various development agencies, including the World Bank and EBRD, the mining and metallurgical industry [had] great potential [to promote] economic development."[9]

By 1998 the bulk of foreign direct investment (around 66 per cent) in Kyrgyzstan was concentrated in two gold mines, Kumtor and Jero,[10] although the following year the figure had dropped to a reported 21 per cent.[11]

A Blemished History

Mining in the Republic carries a distinctly chequered history. Kyrgyzstan's 1999 National Report on the Environment notes that the mining and metallurgy sectors had become the main sources of the country's air and water pollution. By 1995 the amount of land directly damaged by mining activities reached 3,000 hectares;[12] with tailings dumps contained about 100 million m^3 of waste, including two million m^3 considered to be radioactive.[13] According to Torgoev *et. al.* these wastes occupied more than 195,000 square metres, affected by significant dyke failures, breakdown of drainage systems, and water and wind erosion.[14]

Torgoev and his colleagues pointed, *inter alia*, to:

"The generation and accumulation of a great amount of mining waste in areas prone to dangerous natural disasters, such as earth quakes, tectonic active zones and land-slides, which are not properly maintained;

"Movement of earth and deformation of earth surfaces due to both underground and open pit mines;

"Cryogenic physic[al]-geological processes in mines situated at high altitudes (thermosetting phenomenon and salt out cropping), glacier destruction that, in turn, may lead to glacier pulsation, land slides and the over-flooding of glacier lakes."[15]

The scientists were doubtful that a new, environmentally sound technology to avert these dangers, could be developed in the near future.

The mine's location presented several major challenges. Machinery operates at only 70 per cent percentcapacity because combustion engines lack oxygen at high altitude in sub-zero temperature. The venture has to send home roughly one in 12 workers within days because they cannot stand the thin air.

Moving-in supplies – such as some 17 tons of steel grinding balls consumed every day by the mills – takes three to four months. These are delivered by trains and then trucked through Russia and Kazakhstan to Kyrgyzstan, past the giant Issyk-Kul lake up a steep, serpentine, road 60 kilometres from the Chinese border. They also have to cross eleven bridges – most of which were only re-inforced for such unprecedented heavy traffic after the May 1998 cyanide spill.

The mine tailings are heaped upon a glacier which, according to the company, enables process by-products, including unrecovered cyanide, to freeze and supposedly neutralize. After 1999, treated effluent from the tailings facility was being discharged to the Kumtor river, a tributary to the river Naryn.[16]

However, the company's faith in this method of disposal has been strongly questioned. According to Feiler, although

"[g]lacier pulsation in the Tien-Shan Mountains has not caused any significant damage yet... ice landslides can occur at any time and cause massive destruction. Due to changes in the type of ore encountered after mining operations began, KOC found that even very low cyanide concentrations interfered with the gold recovery process. [Therefore] approvals were sought and received to allow the company to use fresh water rather than recycled water, as in the feasibility study. A complete water balance was [carried out] to determine the effect of fresh water use on the Kumtor River and Petrov Lake, but this technolog[ical] change increases the environmental risks."[17]

A comprehensive Environmental Impact Assessment (EIA) for Kumtor, together with an audit of previous exploration, was allegedly drawn up following the EBRD's procedures for high-risk category A/1 projects. However, Feiler declares that there was insufficient public input into this process,[18] let alone observance of the principles behind "fully informed prior community consent". Torgoev and Aitmatov asserted that long-term potential environmental impacts, due to geo-ecological changes, were not considered in this phase.[19]

Despite the considerable depth of permafrost (up to 250 meters), and the mine's high altitude, the potential effects of global warming, due to strong solar radiation (more than 25 kkal/sm), are far from neglibile. Significant heating of the soil, including that lining the tailings impoundment, could produce "swelling, congelifraction, thermokarst, and soil flow". Morever, said Torgoev and Aitmatov, dust levels at Kumtor can, and do, rise to 20 microns per cubic metre, against the national permissible concentrations of 0.5 mg/m for suspended particulates in the atmosphere.[20]

Rehabilitation?

The Master Agreement between the state and CAMECO,[21] laid down that mine reclamation and de-commissioning should conform to the Land Code of Kyrgyzstan. The open-pit will be allowed to fill with ground water, surface run off and ice from the Lysyi Glacier. Demolished buildings are to be thrown into the pit, while waste rock dumps will not be reclaimed, in the belief that there will be no long-term acid rock drainage.

Environmental monitoring is to be carried out in two phases. Over the first three years monitoring will be continuous, until tailings discharges meet with defined limits. During the next three years, seepages from the waste, tailings and site run-off, will be monitored to ensure conformity with run-off requirements.

Feiler maintains that this plan provides
"no clear delineation of the roles and the responsibilities of the various parties, including the mining company, the government, and the lending institutions. In addition, it is difficult to determine whether the [reclamation] fund of US$5.4 million is an adequate sum... how it was calculated and whether it will be available by the time the mine closes, or who is going to be responsible for managing [it]."

"Moreover," he adds, "the [lack] of transparency becomes evident… particularly when IFC rejected disclosing the whole decommission[ing] and reclamation plan for the Kumtor mine, as was requested by Kyrgyz NGOs."[22]

The 1998 Disaster and its Aftermath

On May 20 1998, at 12.15 p.m., on a point 78 kilometers from the mine site and 8 km from Barskoun village (population 7,000), a truck rolled over on the road adjacent to a bridge crossing the eponymous river, causing a container with sodium cyanide packages to fall into the water. The container was damaged and seven of the packages were punctured. An estimated 1,762 kg of sodium cyanide was lost in the river.

Cyanide concentration in the water at the site of the accident was 1590 mg/litre whereas the country's permissible concentration (PC) in water is 0.035 mg/l. In other words the river became roughly fifty thousand times more toxic than was allowable under law. After the container was recovered from the river, the concentration sharply decreased, reaching 10 PC – still around 300 times the legal limit. By May 21, the concentration had declined to the permissible level.[23]

The KOC's laboratory registered concentrations in Issyk-Kul Lake, near the mouth of Barskoun River, at 0.36 mg/l. Soil samples taken near the bridge revealed cyanide-in-soil levels at more than seventy-seven times permissible limits for the Kyrgyz Republic (at 4.6 mg/kg, as against 0.06 mg/kg).[24]

Although there were conflicting reports of the number and extent of casualties (see Chronology), the Kyrgyz Ministry of Health admitted that two people had died due to cyanide exposure, while 2,577 people suffered some form of illness.[25] However, the international committee of experts formed by the Mining and Mineral Sciences Laboratories (MMSL), strongly questioned the Ministry of Health's findings,[26] claiming that the majority of these cases had been wrongly diagnosed. The committee said that the cyanide concentrations (in air – 7.3 mg/m^3; in soil – 1.0 mg/kg) were below Canadian guidelines. Moreover, patients had been mis-diagnosed and existing acute pathology or disease overlooked.

While the IFC argued that the commission's assessment failed to confirm a direct link between the cyanide spill and reported deaths, it nonetheless acknowledged that, because the Kyrgyz government restricted access to autopsy and medical records by outside parties, the commission's findings were inconclusive.[27] Meanwhile, the Washington-based Mineral Policy Center (MPC) recorded on film a physician, on duty at the Barskaun hospital, asserting she was directed by higher government authorities to limit her documented, cyanide-related deaths, to just four.

A case study of the effects of the spill, carried out by Dr. Robert Moran for the MPC, pointed out that cyanogen chloride, a cyanide-related compound, is toxic to aquatic organisms: as a heavy gas it would also have spread through local villages, causing throat and eye irritation. Moran concluded that these compounds, along with the presence of gaseous ammonia, might have adversely affected the health of local people.[28]

Moran also claimed that analytical techniques, used to detect cyanide, were applied only to the free cyanide form, failing to report metal-cyanide complexes, toxic cyanide breakdown products (cyanates, thiocyanates, cyanogen), or concentrations of ammonia and chloramine.[29]

Still the Ministry of Environment blithely asserted there had been no significant environmental damage[30] and that free cyanide concentrations in the soil had never reached a level sufficient to threaten serious harm.[31] In a few cases, conceded the Ministry, low cyanide concentrations in the soil did have an adverse impact on earthworms and other soil invertebrates, as well as on the growth of radishes, lettuce and bush beans.

KOC Responses

The Kumtor Operating Company sprung to its own defence. It claimed that, within minutes of the accident, it had sent emergency response teams and environmental and safety personnel, as well as doctors and nurses, to the site.[32] Nonetheless, it seems that KOC delayed for five hours in informing local people and local authorities about the spill – by which time many villagers had already been using contaminated water.[33]

Perhaps even more culpably KOC had used calcium hypochlorite as a cyanide antidote, which inevitably led to the formation of other toxic chemicals, including cyanogen chlorine and cyanate.

A May 29 1998 Cameco press release maladroitly attempted to calm intense public concern by stating that cyanide "occurs naturally in most stone fruits". For good measure, three weeks later on June 22, in a letter to several financial institutions backing the joint venture, KOC President, Len Homeniuk, described local reaction to the spill as "media sensationalism, political opportunism and medical misstatement".

KOC also said that the cyanide at Barskoun dissipated rapidly into the environment, so it could not be blamed for the skin rashes, sores and other ailments reported by local residents for weeks after the spill.[34] However, the application by Kyrgyz authorities of excessive amounts of calcium hypochloride to the main irrigation canals could, according to the government, have "poisoned [residents] by cyanogen chloride which could have been formed as a result of the treatment of watered plots with calcium hypochlorite". The Kyrgyz State gold mining company, Kyrgyzaltyn, admitted that "10 per cent calcium hypochlorite solution, and not (the usual) 1 per cent solution" was applied, and that in places "20 per cent solutions, and later 50 per cent solutions, were prepared, and in some places even dry lime of chloride was scattered around. It was an inadmissible overdose."

In January 1999, KOC reportedly reached an agreement to pay the Kyrgyz government $4.6 million in compensation for the estimated costs of the spill, in accordance with the Law on Environmental Protection.[35] Total damage was estimated at US$4,663,914. Deputy Prime Minister Boris Silayev retorted that this figure did not cover agricultural and tourism losses. Others have put the tangible financial losses from the spill at closer to $20 million, while government estimates have run as high as $42 million. It is also questionable whether complete compensation from KOC ever reached the affected institutions and individuals. In May 1999, a local government official was charged with embezzling portions of the funds intended for affected villages.[36]

Blockades

Feeling frustrated, isolated and powerless, in the aftermath of the accident, local people took matters into their own hands. Between July 10 and 12, 1998, residents of Barskoun and Tosor villages blockaded am approach road to Kumtor, seized company vehicles, and clashed with Kyrgyz militia, as they demanded cancellation of the government's contract with the mining company. Periodic demonstrations in front of company and government offices in Bishkek also ensued. Kyrgyz NGOs, specialising in rural community health, visited local villages to ascertain the impact of the accident and contacted international NGOs in order to research the role of international finance institutions (such as the IFC) in supporting the Kumtor project.[37]

Some overseas experts also offered their services in monitoring other environmental problems at the mine site, such as the potential increase in toxic discharge into the watershed. However, KOC consistently denied such visitors access.

University of Kyrgyzstan pathologist, Dr. Kalia Moldogazieva, was summarily fired in January 1999 and her Institute of Human Ecology at the University closed down. Ms Moldaziewa had published, in the country's national press, results of a study she conducted on the impact of the Kumtor accident, which differed from the official version. In response, an international NGO letter of protest was sent to Kyrgyz President Askar Akayev and International University of Kyrgystan president Asylbek.

The IFC Response

Since the original "accident", IFC has insisted that it is improving the Kumtor situation through project monitoring, on-site inspections and audits, the development of a revised Emergency Response Plan, and "proactive engagement" of the KOC. However, despite the need to rebuild public trust in the safety of its projects, IFC has consistently backed KOC's refusal to publicly disclose the revised Emergency Response Plan. According to the Kyrgyz NGO, Bureau for Human Rights and Rule of Law, this is a violation of the country's freedom of information Act. In refusing to disclose the plan, IFC said that its information disclosure policy allowed project sponsors to withhold documents they deemed of a business confidential nature. IFC also refused to disclose its own project monitoring documents and consultants reports, upon which some of its assurances of project improvements were based.

IFC claims that it has improved KOC's emergency response capabilities. Yet there was no immediate notification to the Kyrgyz authorities, following another spill in January 2000. Moreover, IFC has not addressed some of the underlying weaknesses in the government's emergency response and medical services – for example, those that led to the excessive application of sodium hypochloride and cyanide antidote following the accident. With regard to the latter, IFC has stated:

> "(KOC) has pointed out to us that they know of no jurisdiction in the world that permits a corporation to interfere with the independence of government-operated medical services or to dictate the level, method, or training of medical professionals within that jurisdiction. Therefore the medical training of Kyrgyz authorities was not, nor could it be, part of the Kumtor's emergency response plan. In the days and weeks following the spill, specific advice, support, and resources were offered by Kumtor to the medical community in Kyrgyzstan. In most cases, however, these were rejected as interference."

Why then did the IFC approve a loan for a project where infrastructure to mitigate the consequences of a potential major accident, was not even in place?

The Kumtor mine has increased export earnings, employment opportunities, and has led to the North-South transfer of some management and technical skills. However, given the estimated eleven year lifespan of the mine, this development is hardly "sustainable". Some citizens argue that the majority of project benefits flow to the Kyrgyz government in Bishkek and CAMECO in Canada, and that any positive local development impact is coincidental.

A project that poisons citizens, then conceals from them important information on their safety and well being, offsets any positive development impacts. Indeed, IFC's defensive and evasive response after the spill probably contributed to local hostilities and an environment of distrust.

In with the EIR – but not Conclusively

The Extractive Industries Review (EIR) was established at the beginning of the new millennium, when the World Bank could no longer face down demands that it should cease all investment in oil, gas and mining. Headed by an "eminent person," the former Indonesian environment minister, Emil Salim, set up several regional policy workshops. The second of these, for Eastern Europe and Central Asia, was held in Budapest, Hungary in June 2002. The Kumtor case was high on the agenda for many of the eighty delegates, who were also informed by the cyanide disaster at Baie Mare, Romania, which occurred in February 2000.[38]

Other testimony to the workshop concerned the World Bank Group's preliminary discussions to support the development of an open-pit gold mine at Rosia Montana, also in Romania.

Twelve case studies, submitted to the EIR, documented experiences of extractive industry projects in Eastern Europe and Central Asia from the perspective of civil society, industry, government, academia and other organizations. No less than four of these

"... raised issues relating to the cyanide spill at the Kumtor Gold Mine... Major concerns regarding the circumstances of the spill included the operating company's failure to implement an emergency response plan, the low degree of public consultation and transparency, and the effects of cyanide contamination on public health and the local environment. More general concerns related to the long-term impact of the mine, including its inadequate preparations for closure and questionable security of its frozen tailings dam. Due to the mine, local farmers had reduced water supplies for irrigation, and communities were concerned that dust particles from the mine explosions would contaminate future water supplies from the glacier above the village. A representative from the local Community and Business Forum (CBF), set-up after the Kumtor spill, documented longer-term social concerns, including the communications gap, sustainability of benefits from projects and support for small, local projects. Their work was aimed at improving public access to information, increasing employment opportunities, and supporting new, local enterprises."[39]

The Consultation drew up a list of imperatives, should the World Bank agree a

"scenario [to] phase out [its] involvement in the extractive industries." Delegates demanded that the Bank "avoid financing new coal mining capacities, including open pit extraction. In mineral mining, the Bank would observe a ban on all new mines in sensitive areas, such as near mountains, national reserves, indigenous people, and subsistence communities. Its projects would ban the use of cyanide and other toxic technologies, and an objective criteria would be developed to identify 'no-go zones', which would be respected."

Meanwhile the Bank Group

"… should target the development of effective legal and regulatory frameworks prior to privatizing oil, gas and mining industries. The Bank would help to formulate and finance close-down strategies for non-profitable state companies. Micro-finance schemes, training programs and proper pension schemes would have priority in Country Assistance Strategies. The World Bank Group should promote anti-corruption campaigns and link such action to loan agreements with host governments."[40]

The Consultation demanded that

"environmental and social impact assessments should be fully disclosed, as well as annual monitoring reports. Disclosure would also cover environmental action plans, emergency response plans, accident and response reports. Product sharing agreements should also be released to the extent feasible. Disclosure of all government revenues should be incorporated into environmental and social impact assessments and actual payments recorded in annual monitoring reports. Disclosure would also track the impact of revenues flowing to local communities. There would be a base-line from which to track human development indicators at both the local and national level, independently validated by civil society experts."[41]

In summer 2004, the World Bank dismissed almost all the recommendations of Emil Salim's final Extractive Industries Review. What happened at Kumtor from 1997 onwards provided an important barometer against which the Bank should have both evaluated and admitted the critical failings in its programme of minerals-related investment.

It did neither.

Notes

1   IFC, *Kumtor Gold (Kyrgyzstan) Project Brief*, Washington DC, undated.

2   IFC Project Brief, op cit.

3   Jozsef Feiler, *Kumtor – the Poisoned Gold*, May 2000.

4   Feiler, op cit, p. 10.

5   IFC Project Brief, op cit.

6   Feiler, op cit, p. 14.

7   Feiler, op cit, p. 13.

8   Feiler, op cit, p. 2.

9   Jozsef Feiler, *Mountains of Gold*, (www/bankwatch.org/downloads/Kumtorgold. pdf), op cit, p. 17.

10   OECD, *Investment Guide for the Kyrgyz Republic*, Paris, 1998.

11   The Economist Intelligence Unit, *Kyrgyzstan Country Profile 2000*, London.

12   Kyrgyz Republic, MEPKR, 1995.

13   MEPKR 1995, ibid.

14   Torgoev, I, Aleshin U, Moldobaev, B: *Geoecologisheskaya bezopasnost i risk prirodno-technogenykh katastroph na territori Kyrgyz Repubica*, EKA Ltd, 1999. ("Assessment of man-made disaster risks in the territory of the Kyrgyz Republic: Methods and means of risk reduction.")

15   Torgoev, et al, op cit.

16   Feiler, *Kumtor – the Poisoned Gold*, op cit, p. 4.

17   Feiler, *Mountains of Gold*, op cit, p. 32.

18   Feiler, op cit, p. 31.

19   Torgoev, I, Aitmatov, I, *Vozmozhyne geokologischskie posledstviya zolotoddobychi v usloviyakh vysokogortya: Ekogolicheski Dokland*, Bishkek, 1999. ("Possible geo-ecological consequences of gold mining in uplands: Environmental Report.")

20   Torgoev, et al, op cit.

21   *Generalnoe soglashenie mejdu Praviltelsvtom Kyrgzkoi Republika i Canadskoi CAMECO Corporation*, Bishkek, November 19 2001. ("Master Agreement between the Government of the Kyrgyz Republic and the Canadian CAMECO Corporation.")

22   Feiler, *Mountains of Gold*, op cit, p. 34.

23   *Ecologicheskij Informatzionnyj Buleten* (Ecological Information Bulletin) Obshestvennyj Center Ecologicheskoi Informatzi (OCEI), Bishkek, 2000.

24   OCEI 2000, ibid.

25   OCEI 2000, ibid.

26   Mining and Mineral Science Laboratories, *The International Scientific Commission's Assessment of the Impact of the Cyanide Spill at Barskoun*, Kyrgyz Republic, May 20 1998, MMSL 08-039, 1998.

27   Doug Norlen, *The Kumtor Gold Mine: Spewing Toxics From On High*, Pacific Environment and Resources Center, San Francisco, USA, September 2000.

28   Robert Moran, *Cyanide uncertainties. Observations on the chemistry, toxicity and analysis of cyanide in mining-related water*, Mineral Policy Centre, Issue Paper No 1, p. 12, Washington DC 1998.

29   Moran, op cit.

30   OCEI 2000, op cit.

31   MMSL 1998, op cit.

32   Kumtor Operating Company, *Preliminary Statement of Circumstances Surrounding May 20 1998 Incident*, Bishkek, 1998.

33   OCEI 2000, op cit.

34   Norlen, op cit.

35   *Kyrgyz Republic Law on Environmental Protection*, Chapter 10, Article 54, 1999.

36   Norlen, op cit.

37   Norlen, op cit.

38   Roger Moody: *Into the Unknown Regions: the hazards of STD*, SSC and International Books, London and Utrecht, 2001, p. 49.

39   *Draft Report of EIR Review, Eastern Europe*, World Bank, Washington DC, 2002.

40   EIR Review Draft Report, ibid.

41   EIR Review Draft Report, ibid.

CHAPTER 7

Lihir: a Case to Answer

7.1 INTRODUCTION

Roger Moody

After being accused, for many years, of ecological desecration and blatant violation of Indigenous rights, the world's then-most powerful mining company finally came up with its model project in 1995. The gold mine on Lihir island, off the coast of Papua New Guinea would, according to Rio Tinto (then RTZ), not only be one of the largest of its kind, representing the triumph of technology over nature. It would also provide a social and environmental blueprint for others to follow.

Certainly the Lihir deposit is huge by any standard, although the island itself is only 20 square kilometres and the population has barely reached 7,000. Initial ore reserves were put at well over a million tonnes, grading a high 4.37 grams per tonne (14.6 million ounces), and would be processed over a projected 37 years:[1] other deposits were also to be vigorously explored. The gold, lodged in a "geothermally active" volcano – though "virtually" extinct[2] – would be extracted after "pumping down" the water table, using sea-water to cool the burning-hot ore. This would then be discharged back to the marine environment to within 100 meters of the coast.

The most controversial aspect of the project has proved to be its use of STD (Submarine Tailings Disposal). The discharge pipe ends at a depth of 125 metres; the tailings (which could eventually exceed 90 million tonnes) are supposed to spread on the sea bottom at a depth between 125 and 1600 meters. By 2003, twenty million tonnes of overburden were also being annually tipped by barge into Luise harbour, and expected to accumulate to more than 340 million tonnes over the project's lifetime.

Rio Tinto was adamant that STD was the only method that could cope with the huge amounts of mill wastes generated. Riverine disposal (practised by the Grasberg mine in West Papua) was clearly out of the question (there are no large rivers on Lihir); and so was conventional valley or dam containment on the island itself.

As former World Bank environmental advisor, Robert Goodland, puts it: "[Lihir] is volcanic with earthquakes up to 7.5 on the Richter scale having been recorded since 1900, frequent tremors, fumaroles, hydrothermal gas (e.g., H_2S), solfataras and hot springs. This is the first mine to mine in the caldera of an active volcano. Active tectonics is one of the reasons [for] deciding against land-based waste disposal, as the waste dam might rupture."[3]

The Cyanide Question

When defending its decision to use STD, in July 1996 Rio Tinto claimed that "around 90 per cent" of cyanide would be "detoxified" from the tailings before disposal.[4] However, in an internal memorandum just two months earlier, the World Bank had promised detoxification "exceeding" 90 per cent.[5] And, to confuse matters (if not the critics) even further, Rio Tinto's operating company, Lihir Gold Management, admitted that the 90 per cent limit may not in fact be reached. In a minor gem of linguistic presdigitation, the company told Peter Bosshard of the Berne Declaration: "[T]he laboratory work could not be done with an accuracy which would allow the company to translate those results into a claim that some precise degree of detoxification in excess of 90 per cent will be achieved."[6]

Heavy metals, although admitted to be present in large quantities (the ore being unusually high in sulphides), were predicted to plume their way down to the ocean bed through alakaline water, "well below the ecologically important upper 30-60 metres of the water column in the project area and at a level in which it can readily be mixed by wave and current action".[7]

However, critics of STD – including Robert McCandless, an acknowledged Canadian environmental expert[8] – were far from convinced. They pointed out that there was virtually no experience of the consequences of dumping such huge amounts of wastes into a pristine and biologically important marine environment in the southern Pacific. The impacts were also bound to intensify, if mining were extended to new ore reserves, or there was any substantial reduction in the cut-off grade of milled ore. Furthermore, the company itself admitted that discharged mine water, geothermal water, and stockpile leachate, would destroy seven kilometres of coral reef, and a major nesting zone for the Melanesian Scrubfowl.[9]

A Little History

Lihir Gold started up under the management of British-Australian Rio Tinto (RTZ), along with its immediate partner, Vengold. Other shareholders were Niugini Mining (then wholly owned by Battle Mountain of the USA),[10] the Papua New Guinea government (holding 8.55 per cent), the Lihirian land-owners (also with 8.55 per cent), the Australian public (13.99 per cent), Australian institutions (10.8 per cent), and international institutions (11.8 per cent).[11]

While this was not quite a "shotgun marriage," the main project partners certainly had a stormy courtship. Inheriting Lihir from British Petroleum (via Kennecott) in 1989, RTZ resisted pressures to proceed, for nearly four years. Although junior partner, Niugini Mining, had claimed in 1992 that Lihir would be among the cheapest 20 per cent of all global gold producers,[12] the British mining giant retorted that the mine wouldn't meet its mandatory 12 per cent return on investment.[13] If Niugini wasn't happy with RTZ twiddling its thumbs, the Papua New Guinea government – desperate to get the huge project quickly underway – was furious. It threatened to compulsorily purchase 50 per cent of Rio Tinto's stake[14] and, in early 1994, Papua New Guinea mining minister, John Kaputin, accused the company of intolerable delays and "appalling behaviour".[15]

Both parties appeared mollified when Rio Tinto finally recovered its $100 million – plus exploration costs – following the 1995 share flotation in Australia, USA and Papua New Guinea.[16] Rio Tinto argued that all the project costs must be covered by external debt finance. The company was uncharacteristically candid in admitting itself still haunted by the ghost of Bougainville, another mineral-rich Papua New Guinea island (where its Panguna copper-gold mine had been forcibly closed by armed nationalists in 1989).[17] In March 1995, Lihir's Special Mining Lease was granted. The Lihir landowners, who had been holding out for a 20 per cent equity, settled for 15 per cent. As projected operating costs went up[18] so did estimated reserves.[19] A public relations bandwagon literally hit the road (there was, indeed, a "Lihir Road Show" visiting key global investment centres). It was designed to flash an irresistible glitter into the eyes of banks and private institutions.

By the end of that year the promotion had paid off. Lihir Management (Rio Tinto) raised a US$300 million loan, co-ordinated by Union Bank of Switzerland (UBS) as lead financier, accompanied by ABN Amro, the Australian Investment Development Corporation (AIDC), Citibank, and Dresdner Australia; ABN Amro's partner NM Rothschild was the financial adviser.[20] In the

final event the loan was guaranteed by the Papua New Guinea government
– thus adding to pressures on the state to endorse the project, whatever its
negative impacts.[21]

Enter MIGA, EFIC and EDC...

The package was critically dependent on political risk insurance, confidently
expected to come from EFIC, the Australian government's export credit and
political risk insurance agency, with MIGA and Canada's EDC following suit.[22]
However, EFIC initially baulked at the idea: in February 1995 it had rated
Papua New Guinea a "D" state – the riskiest category for country exposure.[23]
EFIC stated that a final decision would have to wait on the World Bank/IMF
and Australia's Reserve Bank which, though agreeing to a Aus$220 million
structural adjustment package for the south Pacific state, had not yet dis-
pensed it. By summer that year Papua New Guinea had swallowed the World
Bank conditions[24] – a decision which sparked off enormous and prolonged
protests from national NGOs.[25]

This meant that MIGA would almost certainly fall into line behind EFIC.
The 1995 US$450 million public flotation which followed, on both Austra-
lian and New York stock exchanges, was one of the most spectacular of its
kind that year, with Papua New Guinean investors being given first bite at
the cherry.[26]

At the end of this speculators' flurry, Lihir Gold's equity had been re-
arranged, cutting new stakes for (among others) the US investment banks,
Goldman Sachs International, JP Morgan, Bankers' Trust, British-based
HSBC, and four insurance companies: Australian Mutual Provident (AMP),
National Provident, Prudential, and County/Natwest (the last three being
British).[27]

Political risk insurance now quickly followed. EFIC guaranteed US$250
million, Canada's EDC cast in US$27 million, and the World Bank's MIGA
another US$76.6 million (US$10 million of which was for Rio Tinto's own
investment in the project). Although MIGA's limit on PRI is US$50 million per
project, because of the US$27 million re-insured by the EDC, the World Bank
affiliate did not break its own rules.[28]

MIGA's PRI provision was stridently criticised by environmental organisations in Europe and the USA. Their anger was compounded when, in a meeting with Swiss parliamentarians in May 1996, the recently-appointed Bank
President, James Wolfensohn, reportedly commented that the Lihir project
would be "disastrous".[29]

...Out with OPIC

Although later denied by the World Bank, Wolfensohn's comment rings true. He must have been aware that the US government's own export credit and PRI-dispensing agency, the Overseas Private Investment Corporation (OPIC) had, only the year before, refused to back the project after engaging an environmental consultant to assess the project's liabilities.[30] In August 1997, the reasons for OPIC's stand were clarified when the agency (under some pressure from Friends of the Earth USA) finally released a summary of its assessment of Lihir's potential environmental risks. Pointing out that "World Bank guidelines and international law and policy are ambiguous," OPIC relied instead on US environmental laws "for guidance". (This it was obliged to do under the US Foreign Assistance Act.)[31] OPIC decided that the US Federal Water Pollution Control Act prohibited the oceanic dumping of untreated cyanide wastes "as contemplated in the project proposal," and that the US Marine Protection Research and Sanctuaries Act of 1972 made it illegal to dump "industrial waste" into the ocean. There also was the London Convention of 1972 on the Prevention of Marine Pollution by Dumping of Wastes and Other Matter (the "London Convention"). This did not specifically ban the discharge of wastes from land-based outfalls (as by STD). Nonetheless, said OPIC, the Convention was designed to protect the marine environment from such material. Moreover, the Convention covered waste rock containing trace amounts of cadmium and mercury, dumped from vessels, as at Lihir.[32]

Equally important, the 1990 Convention for the Protection of the Natural Resources and Environment of the South Pacific Region, and the Protocol for the Prevention of Pollution of the South Pacific Region by Dumping, did proscribe the tossing of land-derived wastes into the sea.[33]

OPICs conclusion was unequivocal: "Any project that does not meet the standards provided in [these Conventions and Protocol] could not receive OPIC support as [they] contravene accepted US environmental policy."[34]

Greenpeace Intervenes

In late 2002, Greenpeace International delivered a sideswipe against the Lihir mine, with a submission to the 24th conference of the London Convention. Its allegations were based on the analysis of samples, collected a year earlier (in November 2001), from the soft clay overlying the company's gold reserves, and the coarse overburden from around the deposits, which were about to be loaded onto barges. The samples were sent to the Greenpeace

Research Laboratories at Britain's University of Exeter and analysed for concentrations of metals and metalloids.

Reflecting OPIC's judgments five years earlier, Greenpeace concluded that
"the elevated levels of the toxic metals copper and mercury, and metalloid
arsenic, combined with the acidic nature of the wastes... confirm that the
material cannot be classified as 'uncontaminated inert geological materials, the chemical constituents of which are unlikely to be released into the
marine environment'."

Instead they are "clearly industrial wastes, the dumping of which is prohibited under Article IV of the London Convention (1972), to which Papua
New Guinea is party".[35]

Although Greenpeace conceded that the levels of heavy metal could "not
be assumed to be representative of average concentrations for either material," they nonetheless "confirmed concerns raised by the original Environmental Plan".

Appendix 14 of the plan had highlighted "arsenic and copper as being particularly enriched, as well as cadmium and antimony, while lead and mercury were enriched in some samples".

The organisation pointed out that "(t)he nature and composition of this
solid waste has previously been described in the Environmental Plan prepared for the mine in 1992 by NSR Environmental Consultants Pty Ltd. (Australia)".

It cited NSR's conclusion that the "[w]aste rock comprises both barren
and mineralised soil and rock. Most of the waste rock is mineralised to some
extent but the mineralised portion is neither economically nor technologi-
cally recoverable. ... Some of the fine material would form a turbid surface
plume, particularly during dumping of soft waste."[36]

Analyses, conducted in preparation of the plan, showed that a substantial
proportion of the waste would be "naturally acidic" and would "release filterable metals when mixed with seawater". Therefore, even before the mine
came on stream, environmental assessments had highlighted major concerns:
"Each time a barge load of acid producing hard waste rock or soft waste
is dumped, a column shaped halo of acidic water and filterable metals is
expected to form around the descending solids."[37]

Greenpeace went on to issue several demands, one of which unfortunately
evinces the studied elitism for which the group has sometimes been criticised. Instead of calling for an immediate halt to sea-dumping, it asked the
Papua New Guinea government to "develop contained and controlled land-
based alternatives for the Lihir mine and for other such mines within its territory".[38]

Of course Rio Tinto had found this purported "alternative" technically, environmentally, and culturally, unacceptable for Lihir island. It was also partly because of rapidly growing community resistance to terrestrial dumping that STD was proposed for Lihir and other large scale Asia-Pacific mines during the 1990's.[39] To ship the overburden and tailings, spewed from Lihir, to the mainland would clearly be unacceptable, both economically and politically.

If Greenpeace had intended to force the Papua New Guinea government into canceling Lihir's license (which is doubtful) it should surely have come right out and said so.

For Rio Tinto, Lihir provides a narrative of great success against considerable odds, despite the fact that the company on several occasions delayed implementation of the project, and has more recently rumoured that it will sell its stake. For one or two anthropologists it comes as close as one can get to a "best case" reconciliation between the conflicting interests of extractive industry and bona fide landholders. This is also the view which some other mining companies have come to hold. For example, in 1995 Golden Star (one of the Omai corporate culprits – see Chapter 5) cited Lihir's compensation and benefits package as an example to follow, were it permitted to mine the Gros Rosebel gold deposit in Suriname.

Unanswered Questions

There is also no doubt that, for successive Papua New Guinea governments, income derived from the venture has been regarded as a lifeline, in the wake of the Bougainville project's dissolution and growing disquiet about environmental impacts of the Ok Tedi copper-gold mine.

However, out of the case studies in this work, it is Lihir – a storybook quest for the golden chalice buried deep within a fiery furnace (even the technical term "caldera" carries mystical connotations) – where declaration and reality prove most difficult to disentangle. This is partly because, as one of the most ambitious and long term mining operations of recent years, several assumptions about its permanent impacts remain speculative. These were recognised by researcher, Peter Bosshard, some time before mine construction began (see "Tainted Gold" below). Partly it is because Lihir has become central to an increasingly volatile public discourse in Papua New Guinea over dependency on extractive industry, as the country bogs deeper down in debt.

The crude core of the debate appears to be between "modernisation" and "tradition". If so, it is an argument relatively simple to apostrophise, but fiendishly difficult to synthesise. Has the Lihir landowners "rights" package (uniquely generous as it was at the time) in truth become its opposite: a continual reminder that what has been sacrificed can never be compensated for by cash? Whereas the Lihirians (in contrast to the landowners of Bougainville, confronted by Rio Tinto almost 25 years earlier) almost unanimously welcomed the project in its early days, they are now fiercely divided. If the livelihoods they previously enjoyed have been sacrificed for ever, then who is to blame? Is it successive Papua New Guinean administrations avid for royalties and foreign exchange; an hubristic and venal mining company; the World Bank/IMF obsessed with "structural adjustment"? Or might it be Lihir islanders themselves, who appeared to rush for "stakeholdership," while ignoring warning signals already posted along the way?[40,41]

To help answer these questions, the last document in this chapter was put together by three Papua New Guinean women, whose spokeswoman Matilda Koma is a Lihirian formerly employed by Rio Tinto on the island. It is a plea for the imparting of truths which many islanders consider have been kept from them, as they continue to ask: who is monitoring the mining impacts, why have their reports not been divulged, how are the findings to be interpreted?

The document might also seem to be grasping for – but not quite attaining – an evaluation of what has been lost (territory, gardens, fishing, cultural traditions, women's social centrality, sobriety, socio-economic exchange), against what might have been gained (waged employment, technical training, housing, access to medical care, improved literacy).

The authors do not deny that some Lihirians are "better off" as a result of the benefits agreement bestowed on a significant proportion of the islanders. Nonetheless, they point to the discriminatory nature of this "package," the implementation of which has increasingly been socially divisive. Above all, there is the awful spectre – visible each day – of the physical consequences of accepting the largesse in the shape of a mounting volume of mine wastes being dumped and siphoned offshore. Scientists may debate the intrinsic toxicity of these wastes; environmentalists may deplore their very existence; the company may seek to allay all anxieties; the World Bank will nod its concern – but that is all, since MIGA's involvement is now over, with the successful repayment of corporate debts.

And still the Lihirians have this massive discharge on their doorstep, in their once-sheltered bay. Hour by hour, thousands of tonnes of their territory is being converted into dross and minuscule amounts of gold "recovered", then sent many miles offshore into an alien world of market speculation.

And all this frenzied movement is essentially beyond their control.

Notes

1 *Mining Annual Review*, Mining Journal (MJ), London, 1997.

2 *MJ*, December 3 1993.

3 Robert Goodland, Draft *Background Paper for EIR*, May 2003

4 Lihir Gold Ltd, *letter to Peter Bosshard, Berne Declaration*, July 25 1996.

5 *World Bank Office Memorandum, MIGA to Peter Bosshard, Berne Declaration, Zurich*, May 5 1996.

6 Lihir Gold Ltd, Washington DC, *letter to Peter Bosshard, Berne Declaration*, July 25 1995.

7 MIGA *Office Memorandum to Lihir Gold Ltd*, Washington DC, May 16 1996.

8 Robert McCandless, personal communication to Minewatch Asia Pacific, London, 1996.

9 *South Asia Mining Letter (SAML)*, London October 15 1993; *SAML* October 29 1993, *Lihir Gold Prospectus*, Lihir Management Ltd, August 1995

10 *Financial Times*, London, November 11 1996.

11 *Mining Environmental Management*, London, March 1996.

12 *Australian Financial Review*, May 1 1996.

13 *SAML*, London, March 27 1992.

14 *Guardian*, London, August 6 1993.

15 *SAML*, May 27 1994.

16 Richard Harkinson, "Papua New Guinea – Under the Volcano", in *Higher Values*, Minewatch, London, number 7, January 1996.

17 *SAML*, May 13 1992.

18 *SAML*, June 16 1995; *Mining Monitor*, MPI Sydney, February 1996.

19 *SAML*, October 15 1993; *SAML*, October 29 1993.

20 *SAML*, May 20 1995.

21 Peter Bosshard, *Tainted Gold*, Berne Declaration, Zürich, 1996.

22 *SAML*, May 12 1995.

23 *Post-Courier*, Port Moresby, Papua New Guinea, July 5 1995.

24 *SAML*, May 12 1995.

25 Pacific Research Bulletin, Fiji, 1995-1996, *passim*.
     The so-called "macro stabilisation" and structural adjustment packages included "reducing business restrictions on foreigners; replacing import bans and quotas by tariffs, removing price controls; [and] ceasing government approval requirement, except for safety, for private investments". R Callicx "World Bank tells Papua New Guinea its help depends on reforms," *Australian Financial Review*, May 22 1999; see also: P Cook and J Faulkner, *EFIC support for the Lihir gold project in Papua New Guinea – joint media release*, EFIC, July 31 1995.

26 *SAML*, October 13 1995.

27 *Post Courier*, Port Moresby, Ocober 16 1995.

28 Bosshard, *Tainted Gold*, op cit.

29 Personal communication, Peter Bosshard to Roger Moody, 1995.

30   OPIC, *Overseas Private Investment Corporation: Environmental Summary of Lihir Gold Project, Papua New Guinea*, (undated); see also correspondence between OPIC and FoE Washington, August 18 1997.

31   OPIC *Lihir Environmental Summary*, ibid, p. 2.

32   OPIC *Lihir Environmental Summary*, ibid, p. 4.

33   OPIC *Lihir Environemntal Summary*, ibid, p. 5.

34   OPIC *Lihir Environmental Summary*, ibid, p. 6.

35   *Sea dumping of wastes from the mining industry: the case of the Lihir gold mine, Papua New Guinea*, submitted by Greenpeace International to the London Convention 24th Meeting, November 2002. One extract from the submission reads: "At 135 mg/kg and 387 mg/kg respectively, arsenic concentrations in the clay and rock waste are 3-7 times higher than the maximum which might be expected for uncontaminated soils in non-mineral bearing deposits. Copper was present at more than 1 g/kg in the clay waste. Both wastes contained mercury at levels 4-5 times higher than the highest concentrations which may be expected for uncontaminated soils (3.3 and 2.6 mg/kg respectively)."

36   NSR, *Lihir Project Final Environmental Plan, Volume B: Main Report*, NSR Environmental Consultants Pty Ltd, Hawthorn, Australia, April 1992.

37   NSR, *Lihir Project Draft Environmental Plan, Volume C: Appendices (Part II:11-17), Appendix 14: Geochemical Characteristics of the Leinitz and Minifie Deposit Materials*, Hawthorn, November 1989.

38   *Sea dumping of wastes...*, Greenpeace Summary, op cit.

39   See Roger Moody, *Into the Unknown Regions*, Utrecht, The Netherlands, 2001; and *The Manado Declaration*, Jatam and other NGOs, Manado, Indonesia, 2001.

40   Colin Filer, *Lihir Project Social Impact, Mitigation, Issues and Approaches*, December 1992. Colin Filer, *Participation, Governance & Social Impact*, PNG National Research Institute, Port Moresby, October 1995.

41   The anthropologist, Professor Colin Filer, had issued such warnings in his early social impact study on the project (see note 40 1st). In a follow-up study Filer pointed to the unequal distribution of income, the subordination of women, the influx of outsiders, and the project dependency syndrome. *Inter alia*, Filer claimed that a process of strengthening local custom to cope with unprecedented impacts had not been sufficiently addressed while effective monitoring and grievance/mediation procedures had not been put into place (see note 40 2nd). Lihir is a major gold producer, but annual output is well under a million ounces each year; its economic "virtue" may be in its longevity but, therein lie various long term threats. In addition, both tailings and waste rock contain small amounts of metallic materials which could one day be of economic value, were the "wastes" stored on land for future possible recovery. By being consigned to the ocean floor, these resources – which belong of course to the Lihirians – are almost certainly lost for ever.

Twin Poles

Lihir is a classic case of polarization. The proponent, mainly Rio Tinto, strongly defends its STD, backed up by eminent scientists. Even Australia's CSIRO agency cannot find much wrong. On the other hand, civil society is deeply concerned, claiming that Lihir will be worse than Ok Tedi and Bougainville long before the 36 year project duration. Lihirians disrupted the mine in December 1995, shut it down in 1998, and threatened to shut it in March 2002 because they will lose their land, coral reefs and its resources, their ecosystem, their sea; and their environment will be destroyed by pollution. Lihir's ocean is one of the most biologically diverse in the world. Lihirians have reputable scientists on their side too. The head of the [Australian] Commonwealth Environmental Protection Agency, Barry Carbon, concluded that STD off Lihir was unacceptable in 1995. The proponent's own prospectus admits that "sediment on coral will reduce biodiversity and fish". The Deutsche Bank refused to invest in Lihir in December, 1992. US OPIC refused political risk insurance in 1995 because it concluded that STD would not comply with US waste disposal standards, and would violate the UN London Dumping Convention of 1972 and its 1996 Protocol, as well as the 1976 UN treaty "Convention on the Conservation of Nature in the South Pacific". On the other hand, the European Investment Bank invested 46 million ecus in Lihir in July 1996, but ducked questions on compliance with environmental standards.

Robert Goodland

[This text is taken from a draft background paper prepared by Dr Goodland in May 2003 for the World Bank's Extractive Industries Review (EIR)]

7.2 Tainted Gold

Peter Bosshard

A 1996 piece of private research was one of the first to examine a dubious mining project, primarily by analysing the consequences of its funding and the motives of its institutional backers. The author, Peter Bosshard, was then head of the *Berne Declaration* – a highly respected Zürich-based NGO which has worked for nearly thirty years to effect equitable relationships between Swiss citizens and peoples in the South. He was drawn to the issue when the Union Bank of Switzerland (UBS) became the lead financier of the Lihir mine. The original paper was partially updated in 1999 and is published here with some further revisions by Roger Moody.

Critical Questions

The Lihir Island goldmine project is a case study in unbalanced power relations between private corporations, multilateral institutions, national governments, and civil society. It raises critical questions about the policies of the Bank's Multilateral Investment Guarantee Agency (MIGA), the International Finance Corporation (IFC) and national guarantee agencies regarding environmental assessment and access to information.

The Lihir consortium will use a complicated open-pit process for a first mining phase of almost 15 years, with an average yield of 18.2 tonnes gold per year. In a second phase of 21 years, stockpiled lower-grade ore will be processed to yield a further 7 tonnes of gold per year. The relatively high gold content and the complicated mining process will account for an average production cost of US$234 per ounce over the 36 year lifespan of the mine. The project will be run by Lihir Gold Ltd., a consortium involving foreign private corporations, the government of Papua New Guinea, and the landowners of Lihir. The annual production of the open-pit mine will place the company among the 15 largest gold producers in the world.

Gold was discovered in Lihir in the early 1980s. Over several years various governments in the capital, Port Moresby, debated whether mining rights should be given to Western corporations or to a state-owned Malaysian company. Finally, Prime Minister Julius Chan, who assumed power in August 1994, issued exclusive mining rights for an Anglo-American consortium for 40 years (see below). Chan is a wealthy entrepreneur from the Lihir region.

In 1987 he was involved in a large gold scandal, when an official commission of inquiry discovered that he had made about 2 million dollars through illegal meddling in a float of gold mine shares.

Goldmining and the Environment

Gold is found in such low concentrations in the earth's crust that whole mountains may have to be destroyed to obtain a few thousand ounces. The 2,200 tonnes of gold produced globally in 1992 left a waste residue of around 550 million tonnes. Today the ore is usually won by the relatively cheap cyanide leaching process. Either cyanide solutions are poured several times over slag-heaps of ground-up ore until the gold separates out. Or the cyanide may be used in a carbon-in-pulp process (as at Lihir) whereby the cyanide/gold mix is precipitated on carbon columns. Even when the chemicals are carefully removed, the tailings will be polluted with diluted cyanide and other residual solutions.

Cyanide is highly toxic. A solution of 2 ppm (parts per million) can prove fatal for humans. Late August 1995 saw one of the biggest environmental disasters in the history of South America, when 2.5 hectolitres of liquid residue from the Omai goldmine leached into the Essequibo river in Guyana. This led to temporary mine closure. Like Lihir, the Omai mine had received political risk insurance from the World Bank's MIGA. (See Chapters 3 and 5.)

Social Aspects

During three days in early April 1995, the people of PutPut, on Lihir Island, bid farewell to their village. Fifty six roasted pigs, countless chickens, coconuts, and yams were served up. The remote village near Luise Caldera was one of the settlements which had to cede to the new gold mine. Lihir Island has a population of about 5,500. Most inhabitants live from subsistence agriculture. After six years of extensive negotiations, the mining consortium and the Lihir Landowner's Association concluded a so-called "Integrated Benefits Package" on April 26 1995. The company agreed to provide 22 million dollars for the development of social and technical infrastructure on Lihir Island, and average annual compensation and other payments of approximately one million dollars per year. (A study in 1989 estimated the average cash income of Lihirians to be around 100 dollars per year.)

In addition to the compensation payments, the landowners successfully negotiated a 15 per cent equity share in the project. According to an agreement with the government, this share would be held "directly or indirectly for the benefit of the Lihirians". It was paid for by a loan from the government, to be repaid from the dividends of the shares over a minimum of twelve years. In March 1995 the landowners had refused to sign a first benefits package which did not include such an equity share. The comprehensive final package was a direct consequence of the protracted conflicts over the Bougainville and Ok Tedi mines. (See "7.3 A View from the Land".) But the landowners in Lihir had to agree not to bring future claims against the mining company.

The Lihir goldmine promised to create around 1,200 jobs, of which one third to one half were supposed to go to local people. The landowners also created an umbrella firm called the Lakaka Group of Companies, with around 2,500 shareholders, to do business with the mining consortium. By late 1995 about eighty companies on the island were providing goods and services to Lihir Gold Ltd. The estimated turnover of the umbrella company was around 50 million dollars per year, though expected to decline to half this amount after the initial construction work was completed.

In spite of the rapid influx of money into the island economy, disenchantment with, and opposition to, the mining project has grown. Members of a local youth group, and of a mission station, criticised the environmental and social impacts of the gold mine in letters to the government in Port Moresby. A local leader warned that payments by the company were going to create sharp class conflicts between the haves and the have-nots on the island. In December 1995, frustrated landowners disrupted the mine's construction work.

The arrival of workers and job-seekers from other areas, and the resettlement of part of the population, inevitably caused social problems. "Male alcohol abuse had already become much more prevalent since exploration activities began," according to the project's 1992 Environmental Plan, "with attendant problems of neglect of gardens and the physical abuse of wives". In December 1995 the District Manager of Lihir suspended the issuing of liquor licenses for an indefinite period. Lihir Gold Ltd. agreed to provide a temporary police cell until a new police station for the island was built.

Environmental Aspects of the Lihir Project

In 1992 Kennecott Explorations Ltd., with the assistance of Australian based NSR Environmental Consultants Ltd., completed an environmental assessment of the Lihir project. (Kennecott is a wholly-owned subsidiary of Rio Tinto, formerly RTZ corporation, the main investor in Lihir.) The creditor banks commissioned the Canadian engineering firm, Micon International, to do a technical review of the project, including environmental aspects. The prospectus of the Lihir share offering covered environmental risks too. It was considerably more straightforward than the main report of the Kennecott/ NSR Final Environmental Plan. (The Environmental Plan, which conspicuously appeared without the Kennecott label, was eventually made public. It was, however, a restricted document and brought out of Papua New Guinea illegally.)

The Southwest Pacific Ocean, near Papua New Guinea, belongs to those marine areas richest in species diversity worldwide. Paul Chatterton of WWF South Pacific has listed the Lihir area as among the country's six key biodiversity areas. An official government report in 1993 stated that the area "may be very important for endangered vertebrates such as sea turtles". The Lihir mine threatened to affect the environment in several ways, including the stockpiling of huge amounts of lower-grade ore over a long period, the disposal of waste rock and, most importantly, through the disposal of toxic tailings. The mine, the processing plant, and the corresponding infrastructure, would require some 7.3 square kilometers of land in Lihir, most of which is in, or around, Luise Caldera. The mine threatened to destroy the most revered religious site in Lihir, culturally important hot springs, graveyards, and the breeding grounds of most Melanesian Scrubfowls on the island. The Environmental Plan pointed out that such losses were "an unavoidable consequence of the project".

Sixty four per cent of all ore from Lihir would not be processed immediately, but be stockpiled for later use. The long stockpiling period would generate liquid runoff, containing iron, copper, arsenic, zinc, aluminium, manganese, cadmium, lead, and possibly mercury and chromium. This runoff, and additional wastewater from the normal mining operations, would be discharged into the ocean. Runoff temperatures would vary between 30 and 80 degrees Celsius. "Because of the chemical interaction between input streams," the Kennecott/NSR study reports, "the available data does not permit estimation of the actual filterable metal concentrations" at the mouths of the drainage channels. Still, the channels were "expected to be significant contributors of metals to the surface waters of Luise Harbour". While many metals should be adsorbed by sediments, "some metals, such as cadmium, are likely to be stabilised in the liquid phase".

According to the share-offering prospectus, "runoff from construction and operations will result in sedimenation effects to coral reefs" along the island's east coast, and reduce "the diversity of coral species and fish". The document agrees with Kennecott/NSR that "it is not possible to predict the expected water quality with great certainty". It further indicated that lime neutralisation of the stockpile runoff, prior to discharge "would be a requirement in most North American jurisdictions".

According to the prospectus, Lihir Gold Ltd. did "not know whether or to what extent the [planned] practice would be permitted in other jurisdictions".

The processing of 104 million tonnes of proven and probable ore reserves was estimated to create 341 million tonnes of waste rock. While some rock would be used to extend the land area near Luise Caldera, most material would be disposed of in the ocean about 1.5 kilometers from the shoreline. Up to four barges would continuously dump between 1,400 and 4,600 tonnes of rock per hour. According to the Kennecott/NSR report, "it is expected that concentrations of metals [from the waste rock] in the water column are unlikely to exceed the standards outside the immediate dumping area," and "are likely to be attenuated by the processes of precipitation and adsorption". The prospectus, in turn, predicted that the main impacts of rock dumping would damage the coral reefs, due to increased turbidity of the water and the smothering of sea floor benthos. In November 1990, the government in Port Moresby asked that the waste rock from Lihir be backfilled into the mine pit, or be dumped farther ashore. These requests were turned down by the mine consortium as being too costly to implement.

The gold from the Lihir mine was to be extracted by a carbon-in-pulp process involving cyanide. The investors expected that 1,785 tonnes of highly toxic sodium cyanide would be utilised annually. During the mine's lifespan, at least 89 million tonnes of toxic tailings would be produced. The tailings would be partly detoxified by reaction with iron-rich, counter-current, decantation (CCD) washwater. After this treatment they would be discharged into the sea by a pipeline, at a depth of 125 meters. They were then expected to spread on the ocean floor at a depth of between 125 and 1,600 meters. The tailings would have a free cyanide concentration of 1,220 microgram/liter at the discharge level, and 70 microgram/liter at their equilibrium depth. Within a mixing zone, with a radius of 2.3 kilometers, the concentration was expected to exceed the Papua New Guinean national standards of 10 microgram/liter.

The Final Environmental Plan of Kennecott/NSR argued that there was not enough space on the rugged Lihir Island for a land-based tailings deposition, and that in any case, this would pose an accident hazard for the population and the environment. (Land-based tailings disposal would also be more expensive.) The Plan argued that submarine tailings disposal (or STD) would not constitute such a hazard. First, the document maintained, "ocean water is naturally alkaline and the combined tailing stream (sic) will be acidic. Therefore, when tailing is discharged to the ocean, the natural alkalinity of seawater would neutralise the acidity of the tailing." Secondly, since the density of seawater increases with depth, this would prevent any tailings disposed of at 125 meters below sea level "from entering the [upper range] mixed layer under worst-case conditions".

It was expected that the CCD washwater process would detoxify at least 90 per cent of the cyanide. "Conceptually," the share offering prospectus indicated, "tailings could be further treated to detoxify the contained cyanide and/or to precipitate heavy metals". Yet, this would not be performed at Lihir since "neither of these procedures is presently required by the Papua New Guinea government". The Environmental Plan admitted that benthic macroinvertebrates would be exposed to high concentrations of cyanide and metals in the area of the tailings sediments, and toxics could bio-accumulate in the food chain. The degree of metal accumulation, according to the Plan, "cannot be predicted with certainty". The prospectus was more straightforward: "There may be the potential for bioaccumulation of metals within the marine ecosystem over time," it said, although "the potential for bioaccumulation of metals (if any) was not assessed in the Environmental Plan".

In its section on monitoring, the same document dismissed routine water testing near the tailings deposition as "inefficient, logistically difficult and expensive". Instead it proposed a cheaper "short-term intensive investigation" to validate the assumptions regarding tailings disposal. After this, argued the Kennecott/NSR Plan, "monitoring can be confined to measurement of key parameters in the tailing or treated sewage effluent prior to discharge". In other words, the composition of the tailings and the runoff would be examined, but not the actual impacts on organisms in the sea. The prospectus also refered to the monitoring program, indicating that "if a significant increase in metal content develops, mitigation strategies and compensation will be considered". One is left wondering how bioaccumulation of toxic metals could be mitigated, once milions of tonnes of tailings had been dumped, and how a long-term threat to biodiversity could be "compensated"?

Lihir Island is considered a region of "moderate seismic activity". According to the Environmental Plan, earthquakes of a strength reaching 7.5 on the

Richter scale have been recorded since 1900. The share prospectus modestly indicates that Luise Caldera "is believed to be a no longer active volcano". The Plan estimated that the main consequences of a major earthquake would be the rupture of vessels or pipelines. According to the prospectus, such events could cause a "severe environmental impact", although the mine slopes and structures could "resist without causing major damage or injury," with earthquake shaking estimated to have a "10 per cent probability of being exceeded during the Lihir Project's design life".

Opposition to Submarine Tailings Disposal

Environmental and human rights' organizations from Papua New Guinea and Australia strongly opposed submarine tailings disposal at Lihir. They referred to the planned mine as "Ok Tedi by the sea". "Miners would not be allowed to dump this material in the Rhine or four miles off the coast of California," argued Max Henderson of the Pacific Heritage Foundation in Papua New Guinea, so "why expect to do it in Papua New Guinea?" In late October 1995, Bougainville provincial politician Parara Ahewa publicly appealed to the national government to make sure that the adjoining Atolls islands would not be affected by tailings from the Lihir mine. The government should "prove beyond doubt what the effects of dumping waste in the sea will have on the Atolls people," Ahewa demanded. A few days later, Barry Carbon, the head of the Commonwealth Environmental Protection Agency, declared at a mining conference in Canberra that it was unacceptable to dump waste contaminated by cyanide into the ocean off Lihir. MIGA and IFC in turn did not seem to be concerned.

The Environmental Politics of Lihir Gold Ltd.

The Final Environmental Plan, and the share offering prospectus, indicated that the normal operations of the Lihir mine and the hazardous stockpiles would have significant impacts on the environment. The submarine tailings disposal carried the risk of heavy metals being accumulated in the food chain. The dimensions of the different impacts were therefore a matter of considerable uncertainty. John Kola, an inorganic chemist from the University of Papua New Guinea, pointed out (in the *Post-Courier* newspaper) that the sea is "a complex mixture" while "no one [can] really understand what

[is] going to happen unless an experiment based on the conditions at the Lihir area [is] conducted".

Environmental impacts are a technical and scientific challenge. Financial, political, and legal, considerations also play a critical role. Further detoxication of the tailings, a safer design of the mine pit slopes and stockpiles, the dumping of waste rock farther ashore, and a more reliable monitoring of the submarine environmental impacts, would all have been technically feasible. The mining company decided to forego such measures for simple financial reasons.

In fact, the share offering prospectus admitted that "submarine disposal of tailings is not accepted practice in certain parts of the world and a number of jurisdictions have declared a moratorium on the practice". The document tried to reassure potential investors that, according to the Micon engineering firm, "it is unlikely that policies from other jurisdictions will influence this aspect".

Lihir Gold Ltd. seemed to consider environmental damage as a problem, only insofar as it inflicted a financial burden: the risk section of the share offering prospectus typically analysed environmental risks in terms of possible costly new legislation and government regulations. The mining company chose to minimize environmental risks, not by using maximum safety standards, but by legal and political pre-emptive measures. It required the landowners in the vicinity of the mine to contractually refrain from future legal compensation claims, through such as those brought against the Ok Tedi mine.

According to the prospectus, the Papua New Guinea government had to agree "that, while borrowings under the Loan Agreement are outstanding, it will not initiate any amendments to the Environmental Plan which will materially increase the cost of the Lihir project." (The reference to the loan agreement indicated that such assurance could have resulted from pressure from the creditor banks.) Finally, the prospectus mentioned that, while the national government was considering "potential changes to its water quality standards," the company "was involved in discussions with the Papua New Guinea Government concerning these potential changes".

The Financing of the Mine

On March 17 1995, the government of Papua New Guinea granted a Special Mining Lease to Lihir Gold Ltd. to mine the Luise Caldera over forty years. The company also received an Exploration Lease which gave it exclusive exploration rights over the whole of Lihir Island. The investment costs – including exploration, pre-production development, construction, replacement, and capital costs – were estimated to be US$962 million dollars over the 36-year lifespan of the mine. To raise capital, Lihir Gold Ltd. floated shares worth 450 million dollars on the capital markets of Europe, North America, Australia, and Papua New Guinea, in early October 1995. Within a short period the float was oversubscribed more than fourfold, with 7,000 residents of Papua New Guinea buying 4.3 per cent of the shares. On August 18 1995, Lihir Gold Ltd. signed an agreement in London for a loan of US$300 million dollars, which was syndicated by the Union Bank of Switzerland (UBS), ABN AMRO of the Netherlands, the huge US-based Citibank, Germany's Dresdner Bank, and AIDC Ltd. The loan agreement contained a long list of conditions on drawdowns and default, including references to the country's political violence. The loan would only be disbursed after the company had spent at least US$400 million of its own funds on project development costs. It would bear an interest rate of between 1.5 and 1.875 per cent over LIBOR (London Inter Bank Offered Rate), due to be repaid in 2003.

In December 1992, the Lihir joint venture tried to secure a loan from Germany's largest bank, the Deutsche Bank (DB), but to no avail. The Bank had long been supportive of many mining projects. However several German companies were targeted in 1992-93 by an NGO campaign because of their investments in the controversial Ok Tedi mine. Since Deutsche Bank held major investments in these companies, this is likely to have been why DB refused to fund the Lihir project.

UBS had also been an active credit provider to many gold mining companies or ventures, including Ashanti Goldfields (Ghana), La Coipa (Chile), Carachugo and the Maqui Maqui mine in Peru (see Chapter 8). Several mines financed by the bank have received political risk insurance from MIGA. Together with two other Swiss banks, UBS forms the Zürich gold pool which takes a leading role in the worldwide trade of physical gold.

Political Risk Insurance

The Lihir mine offered attractive future profits. Yet, in October 1990, the *Financial Times* reported that bankers deemed it "virtually impossible to raise project finance for schemes in Papua New Guinea following the closure of the Bougainville copper mine". Lihir had therefore to be insured at several levels. The Papua New Guinea government guaranteed the loan repayment by the mining consortium to the banks. EFIC decided on July 31 1995 to guarantee 90 per cent of the syndicated UBS loan up to a maximum of US$ 250 million for the principal; and US$120 million for the interest. The coverage of principal was tied to procurements from Australia, with the government in Canberra claiming that this would generate up to nearly a billion Australian dollars in exports of domestic mining and infrastructure equipment and services. A further US$26.6 million of the loan was guaranteed by the Canadian Export Development Corporation (EDC).

In mid-August 1995, just after this loan agreement was concluded, MIGA issued guarantees of US$66.6 million for the UBS loan, and US$10 million for the RTZ (Rio Tinto) investment. The premium for the different political risk insurances would come to a total of approximately 2.6 per cent per annum on the outstanding loan principal. RTZ also applied for a guarantee from the U.S. Overseas Private Investment Corporation (OPIC). But OPIC refused to issue insurance because of the unsustainable use of submarine tailings disposal.

Unlike the loan, the investments of Lihir Gold Ltd. *per se* are not covered by any public political risk insurance. (The share offering prospectus did not completely correspond with information obtained from MIGA in this regard.) The company did arrange various private insurances against losses or damages due to factors such as sabotage, strikes, earthquakes, volcanic eruptions or floods. Interestingly, according to the share offering prospectus, there was only limited coverage for damage which might be ascribed to environmental destruction, while "losses relating to seepage, pollution or contamination, suffered as a result of claims brought against the Company in the United States or Canada" were completely excluded.

The political risks of the Lihir loan were thus guaranteed threefold: by the Papua New Guinea government, by the governments of Australia and Canada, and by MIGA. EFIC's guarantee depended on Papua New Guinea's acceptance of a controversial IMF/World Bank structural adjustment program. In July 1995, the International Monetary Fund approved a stand-by credit for the government in Port Moresby of US$ 110 million. On August 28 1995, the World Bank approved a loan of US$80 million. The adjustment program was to be co-financed by Australia and Japan (US$50 million each) and the Asian Development Bank (US$40 million).

The structural adjustment package encountered massive opposition for several reasons: the government was told to shed the jobs of 3,000 public servants; price controls should be abolished; and hospital fees must be introduced. There were also growing fears that all customary land might have to be registered. Thirty five trade unions, church groups, student, women and other community groups, formed the National Coalition for Socio-Economic Justice in order to prevent the implementation of these measures.

The Environmental Policy of the UBS

Lihir provides a test-case for the environmental policies of creditor banks like the Union Bank of Switzerland. In 1988 UBS was the first Swiss bank to create the position of an environmental officer. In June 1993, the Bank's top management approved an internal environmental policy which was, however, not released to the public. It dealt with environmental aspects of in-house business practices (such as energy and recycling) as well as with the different sectors of UBS's banking activities. The bank consciously did not create specific environmental products (green investment funds etc.) for a market niche. This might be considered acceptable so long as the record of the UBS' overall business practices is effectively improved. The bank is a signatory to the environmental charters of the UN Environmental Program (UNEP) and the International Chamber of Commerce (ICC).

The environmental policy includes guidelines on the domestic and international lending of UBS. When assessing the credit-worthiness of a project, UBS managers are supposed to apply economic as well as ecological criteria. If projects seem to be problematic, internal bank experts check them in detail. This new policy was motivated, among other factors, by the development of the legal liability of creditors for their projects. UBS general director, Hans Heckmann, in June 1994 confirmed that the Bank considered mining to be one of the environmentally risky lending areas. Public controversies and unstable legal and political conditions are also considered to be risk factors as well.

Despite its weak international standards, the environmental approach of UBS may be regarded as progressive. Given the criteria mentioned above, the Lihir gold mine must have been considered a risky venture which deserved special attention. Sven Hansen, the head of the UBS environmental office, indicated that the bank had been advised on the project by a Canadian engineering firm – obviously Micon International. UBS had made sure that MIGA, IFC and the national environmental authorities accepted the environmental plan. "In certain areas," Hansen claimed (but without giving further details), "stronger environmental measures were implemented, upon instigation by the banks, than were originally envisaged". The UBS officer concluded that "social and environmental aspects were integrated into the Lihir goldmine project to a very large extent".

The Association of Concerned UBS Shareholders has advocated stronger environmental policies for the Bank over a long period. It is evident that, in the case of Lihir, the bank did consider ecological aspects as part of the overall project assessment. Nonetheless, it did not seem to bother about the submarine disposal of toxic tailings. It also seemed likely that the loan providers put pressure on the Papua New Guinea government not to strengthen its environmental guidelines while the Lihir loan was outstanding. But UBS apeared to a large extent satifised that national authorities and World Bank agencies had given the project environmental clearance. (John Faulkner, the Australian Minister for the Environment, also cited MIGA's environmental review as a reason for his support of Lihir.) This trust placed increased responsibility on institutions like MIGA. "The present project will comply with the most recent requirements of the World Bank," Sven Hansen of UBS told the Berne Declaration.

MIGA and Lihir

On May 10 1995, the Executive Board of MIGA approved guarantees of 76.6 million dollars for the Lihir Island project. MIGA's Swiss representative, Pietro Veglio, raised a series of critical questions on environmental and social problems but, reportedly, was not supported by other members. In the end, the guarantee was unanimously approved: 66.6 million dollars were authorized as coverage for the UBS loan, and US$10 million for the RTZ investment. As the Canadian agency EDC reinsured the UBS guarantee to the tune of US$26.6 million, MIGA's total liability for the project remained within the Agency's guarantee limit of 50 million dollars. Board approvals authorize the MIGA management to guarantee specific projects, but do not preclude subsequent negotiations and agreements with the investors. The guarantee for the Lihir project was effectively issued in mid-August 1995, immediately after the loan agreement was signed.

The IFC Environment Division rated Lihir an 'A' project. Site visits were conducted by both IFC and MIGA staff members (unusual for MIGA). Martyn J. Riddle and Harvey Van Veldhuizen respectively, head of the Environment Division and Environmental Specialist of IFC, discussed the project with the Berne Declaration and other NGO representatives in Washington during October 1995. They claimed that the IFC management had openly presented the trade-off, between ecological problems and economic benefits, to the MIGA Board in May 1995.

In spite of this they denied that any environmental problems existed when they discussed the project with the NGOs. Van Veldhuizen argued that submarine tailings disposal could only impact on Lihir's environment in the case of a volcanic eruption. "And then," the Environmental Specialist maintained, "Lihir would have other problems". He did not refer to any of the critical issues and legal double standards which had been revealed by the share offering prospectus.

In their meeting with NGO representatives, Riddle and Van Veldhuizen stressed the long process of negotiations which had taken place between the Lihir joint venture and the local landowners. They claimed that the completion of the Final Environmental Plan was announced in various national media, and that all interested NGOs could receive copies of the Plan and make comments, at consultations in the regional capital and in Port Moresby. Nonetheless, the national NGOs with which the Berne Declaration cooperated in preparing this briefing paper had great problems obtaining copies of the Environmental Plan. Furthermore, many critical issues were not discussed in the Plan proper, but in technical studies which were themselves not made public. The Union Bank of Switzerland incidentally confirmed to the Berne Declaration in August 1995 that the Lihir Environmental Plan was a confidential document.

The research for this briefing paper demonstrated that MIGA's information policy did not fulfill any standards of accountability. When interested NGOs asked for information about the project, Senior Advisor Gerald T. West, on July 5 1995 claimed that "MIGA ha[d] not issued any guarantees" for it. This was almost two months after the Executive Board approved a guarantee for Lihir, and four months after the environmental assessment had supposedly been released to the public. Using a vague omnibus clause in its constitution, MIGA refused to inform NGOs, or the public at large, about any project decisions until a guarantee was issued by its management. The Agency ostensibly did not feel accountable to the public from which it ultimately receives its capital.

In the case of Lihir, MIGA proved to be more secretive than both the Union Bank of Switzerland and the responsible Swiss authorities.

Conclusion and Recommendations

The Lihir Managment company used political leverage and legal obligations to ensure that it could externalise damage to the environment which might occur in the future.

It is not surprising that a private mining company tries to avoid strict environmental measures and to externalize costs in this fashion. But national and multilateral guarantee institutions are supposed to respect and defend the public interest, including addressing environmental concerns. The U.S. Overseas Private Investment Corporation (OPIC) denied a guarantee for the Lihir loan on international legal and environmental grounds. EFIC and EDC did not seem to be concerned. Neither did IFC and MIGA which, unlike these institutions, need not defend national export interests.

Our analysis revealed the following problems:
- There are no indications that IFC or MIGA, or the national guarantee institutions, applied pressure on the investors to improve the environmental standards of the Lihir mine;
- MIGA and IFC concealed critical information about the Lihir project from interested NGOs, and defended the project throughout the public debate;
- MIGA deployed utmost secretiveness regarding the project, which even exceeded the normal commercial confidentiality of the lead creditor bank. It is shocking that potential investors were informed about the risks of the Lihir goldmine by the share offering prospectus, while such information should be withheld from the public. After all, it is the public which is affected by any damage, and/or which provides the capital to the national and international guarantee institutions;
- Finally, MIGA and IFC did not seem to have the institutional capacity to regularly monitor the implementation of a project like the Lihir goldmine.

The demand for IFC loans and investments, and for MIGA guarantees, is bigger than the supply. The two institutions can thus afford to be selective. "By exercising the latitude to say no," the Corporation stated in a 1992 report, "IFC can influence governments to change policies that impede capital market developments". IFC and MIGA should use this influence to change social and environmental policies as well. This responsibility is all the greater since national authorities and commercial investors often base their decisions upon project assessments by IFC or MIGA.

National authorities, private investors, and creditor banks, can no longer delegate the responsibilities for project assessments to MIGA or IFC. In-house environmental offices, like the one created by the Union Bank of Switzerland, are steps in the right direction. Private companies and banks should uphold the same standards for their domestic and international business, and should allow public reviews of their environmental record.

Peter Bosshard, Berne Declaration, February 1996 (updated by Roger Moody, May 2004).

[This paper was based upon information and support from Brian Brunton (ICRAF), Cindy Buhl (BIC), Pratap Chatterjee (IPS), Paul Chatterton (WWF South Pacific), Alison Cleary (Community Aid Abroad), Andrea Durbin (Friends of the Earth/US), Greenpeace Switzerland, Chris Harris and Matthew Jamieson (Mineral Policy Institute), Max Henderson (Pacific Heritage Foundation), Aviva Imhof and Carol Sherman (AidWatch), Roger Moody (Partizans), and Alex Wilks (Bretton Woods Project). Mark A. Constantine, Martyn J. Riddle and Harvey Van Veldhuizen (IFC), Sven Hansen and Conrad Lerch (Union Bank of Switzerland), Matthias Meier (Federal Office of Foreign Economic Affairs), and Gerald T. West (MIGA) took their time to answer questions on the Lihir project. An early German draft of the paper was translated by Irvin and Herta Imhof (AidWatch).]

7.3 A VIEW FROM THE LAND

Jacklyne Membup, Matilda Koma & Augustine Hala

The following is a slightly-revised and shortened version of a case study on the effects of extractive industries in Papua New Guinea, in particular of the Lihir mine. It was presented by Ms. Koma in May 2003, at a forum convened by the Tebtebba Foundation of the Philippines and the Forest Peoples Programme, to allow Indigenous Peoples to make critical input to the World Bank's Extractive Industries Review (EIR) (see Chapter 3).

Introduction

Mining has been an integral part of Papua New Guinea's development, and the highest revenue generating industry in the country – particularly in the late 1980's. However, there was a paradigm shift in the mid 1990's, when exploration and mine development peaked, and then began to decline.

Papua New Guinea's population is almost 100 per cent Indigenous, with over 800 local tribes. The people traditionally own about 95-97 per cent of land, about 3-5 per cent of which is used for other development or by the government. Nevertheless, common resources, such as minerals and water, are state-owned by law. The people of Papua New Guinea say that, without land, there is no life! Developers, however, have in the past found it difficult to deal with land issues in Papua New Guinea, and sometimes refer to them as a hindrance to progress.

The social and environmental problems associated with extractive resource exploitation increased during the late 1980's and early 1990's, as mine wastes were directly dumped into rivers and oceans at an alarming rate. Exploration and mine development began declining rapidly in the mid-1990's for many reasons, including the fact that mine-affected communities began challenging the companies and government in a more aggressive manner, when they failed to address their concerns.

A Chronology

1989 – War broke out in Bougainville when landowners and affected communities took control of the Panguna mine, then Papua New Guinea's largest copper mine, operated by Bougainville Copper Ltd., itself 54 per cent owned by the British-Australian Rio Tinto (then RTZ). Between 1972 and the cessation of mining on May 15, 1989, Panguna produced 3 million tonnes of copper, 306 tons of gold and 784 tons of silver, with a value of PGK5.2 billion (around US$5 billion), representing approximately 44 per cent of Papua New Guinea 's exports during that period. The war cost the lives of over 20,000 people – partly through a blockade – and even now the struggle for peace has not been fully accomplished.

1994 – Controversy over ownership of minerals led to the closure of the Mount Victor gold mine, owned by Niugini Mining (a junior partner with Rio Tinto in the Lihir mine). Local people allege that over 30 people have died since the mine closed because the tailings were not properly neutralised.

1994 – A rupture occurred in the tailings pipeline at Placer Pacific's Misima gold mine. The local water source dried out in 1996 and a hydrological report by the Papua New Guinea Environmental Agency confirmed a drop in the water table had occurred, because of borehole extraction for mill processing.

1995 – Affected communities within, and downstream, of the Porgera Gold Mine (also operated by Placer) lodged demands for compensation, relocation and environmental damage. The communities in early 2003 started preparing legal documents for reparations.

1996 – A law suit alleging environmental damage was launched against BHP (now BHPBilliton), the company responsible for the Ok Tedi Gold and Copper Mine. Although a settlement was reached out of court, some aspects of the agreement have yet to be satisfactorily settled.

1997 – Following the announcement of a Papua New Guinea-Queensland gas pipeline project, landowners along the pipeline corridor began to organise and negotiate for reasonable compensation. This caused several delays in approval and construction. Up to early 2003 the project had not started.

2002 – Landowners from a gas development project area disturbed the operations of the Porgera mine by damaging a power pylon. This put a halt to mining operations for several weeks.

Community Consciousness

As people became more aware of issues surrounding extractive industries, many of them were vocal about the mal-distribution of benefits and compensation, for loss of resources or because of environmental damage. Their actions added to the increasing costs of exploration and government taxes. This, coupled with a declining national economy, meant companies began to lose confidence: from 1995 to 2003, there were no new mines. However, existing mines continue to dump waste directly into the environment – and so the pressure from affected communities continues.

In response, the government of Papua New Guinea and the mining industry have been taking action to revive the ailing industry. Through the Department of Mining, the government secured a US$10 million Technical Assistance Loan (TAL) from the World Bank for a project entitled: "Papua New Guinea Mining Sector Institutional Strengthening Technical Assistance." The TAL will be used to strengthen the capacity of the Department of Mining and the Internal Revenue Commission. A US$7 million loan was also provided by the World Bank to the petroleum sector, under the "Petroleum Utilisation and Technical Assistance Project," in 2000. However, the Lihir Gold Mine has been the only PNG private sector mining project supported by the World Bank, through MIGA.

Environmental and Social Accountability

The state owns all minerals at six feet or more below the earth, as laid down in Section 5 of the 1992 Mining Act, thus provoking inevitable conflicts of interest between state and local peoples. By law, all the water in Papua New Guinea also belongs to the state, giving the government the right to issue water licenses – be it for domestic or industrial use; the disposal of waste; the diversion of water for industrial purposes and for storage, as in dams to generate hydropower.

Existing mines have been allowed to dispose of mine tailings directly into rivers and oceans. Ok Tedi discharges 80,000 tonnes per day and Tolukuma (managed by the South African company Durban Roodepoort Deep Ltd, or DRD) disposes daily of 300-400 tonnes. In their "mixing zones", used to dilute mine wastes, Ok Tedi, Porgera and Tolukuma have employed 200, 150 and 7 kilometres of rivers respectively. Environmental NGOs in Papua New Guinea have been campaigning against such double standards, which allow multinational corporations to behave in Papua New Guinea in ways they could not in their own countries.

Compensation for environmental degradation associated with mining is a major social demand, though usually complex to resolve. Each community, with its own culture and customs, has its own way of dealing with these issues, making it difficult for implementing agencies to develop general policies and regulatory frameworks. An attempt to register land, in order to properly identify landholders, has failed. Another system – based on the creation of "Incorporated Land Groups" – is still not widespread.

Benefits from mines are also not equally distributed. People located within the Mining Lease Areas get more than those outside – notably people living downstream of waste disposal sites – even though they are also profoundly affected by the development of a mine.

The Lihir Case

The Lihir gold mine is located on Niolam Island, in New Ireland Province, 700 km northeast of Papua New Guinea's capital Port Moresby. Niolam is often referred to as Lihir since it is the principal island in the Lihir Group. It is a volcanic seamount that rises steeply from sea level to approximately 600 metres. At its widest points, the island measures 22 kilometres from north to south and 14.5 kilometres from east to west.

All statutory documentation was completed in 1995 for the opening of the mine and inauguration of Lihir Gold Pty, incorporated in Papua New Guinea that August, and known as the Lihir Management Company (LMC).

Lihirians Attempt to Monitor the World Bank

Until the World Bank loan was paid off in 2000, MIGA and the IFC visited the mine each quarter, to monitor its performance. According to Geoff Day, Lihir's Environmental Manager, the company has been in compliance with MIGA's conditions, in terms of governance as well as environment and social accountability. However, the local people of Lihir Island – themselves shareholders in the mine – are not aware of any World Bank monitoring.

In March 2003 a survey was conducted by the Environmental Watch Group (NEWG) among the Lihir Islanders, to discover whether they were aware of the World Bank's involvement in the project, and to determine how the Bank's policies on transparency, social and environmental accountability,

and poverty alleviation affected them. Those questioned included representatives of the Lihir Area Landowners Association, Lihir Management Company (LMC), Niramar Development Authority, local level government, the
local church, the local women's group, and community leaders. It was made
possible primarily through the support of the women of Lihir.

The research showed that almost all those interviewed at community level
knew nothing about the involvement of the World Bank, or MIGA's role.
Most discussions centred on the impacts of the mine.

NEWG: How about you? Are you aware of any World Bank involvement in
the Lihir Project?

PWA: No! Not at all.

NEWG: Well, I'm told that one of the World Bank Group, MIGA, financially
supports the project's political risk. I thought you might have heard somet-
ing about it.

PWA: I have never heard of them and when I asked around here, no-one
seems to know about it as well. Anyway they are also asking what MIGA
stands for.

NEWG: It stands for Multilateral Investment Guarantee Agency. Could you
please ensure leaders of the negotiation of the project, particularly church
leaders, Landowners Association and even company officials, attempt to
answer the questions?

PWA: Allright, I will try to talk to the community leaders, church leaders and
the company about this.

NEWG: Have you had any chance to talk to the company about this?

PWA: Yes. In fact we did, we will let you know about all the findings soon.

Environmental Issues

The Lihir area is listed among the country's six high biodiversity areas, according to experts working for Papua New Guinea WWF (Papua New Guinea
World Wildlife Fund). Its reefs provide – or rather did provide – a habitat
for a variety of oceanic species, as well as being a magnificent diving hot spot.
The naturally rich volcanic soil provides for good cultivation of crops, at
both subsistence and commercial values. There was a Melanesian shrub-fowl
habitat before it was destroyed in order to build the mine. Several culturally

and socially important areas, such as hot springs and graveyards, have been transformed into construction sites to support the mine.

The mine pumps 110 million cubic metres of waste, contaminated with diluted cyanide and other toxics, into the sea each year through a pipeline 125 meters beneath the surface. Another 20 million tonnes of rock waste are annually dumped into Luise Harbour from a barge, while stockpiles of low grade ore are heaped in the sea along the shoreline of Luise Harbour.

Parties involved in the Lihir Project have failed to honour the London Convention, which obliges signatories not to dump industrial waste by barges or ships into the sea. Countries signing the Convention include Australia, the UK, and Papua New Guinea itself.

In its "Environmental Fact Sheet No. 3", LMC tried to explain what it called a "misconception" about the London Convention, Deep Sea Tailing Placement (DSTP), and the Dumping at Sea Act. It claims not to be in breach of the agreement, since it uses land-based structures to transport the tailings, while wastes are dumped into the internal waters of Papua New Guinea, not international waters.

Management and Monitoring

Natural Systems Research (NSR), an Australian consultancy for extractive industries, has developed Environmental Plans (EPs) for mining and petroleum projects throughout the Asia-Pacific region, including the major mines in Papua New Guinea. It consistently recommends direct disposal of mine waste into Papua New Guinea waters – both by river and sea – and it developed the EP for Lihir, including Submarine Tailings Disposal.

"The company visits our villages sometimes to tell us about the environment. They give us flashy reports, which many people cannot read. They tell us that there is no problem with the environment. They try to explain the science that nobody on this island really understands or believes. We have naturally grown up here and we believe that we know the environment better. When there is a change, we can tell straight away. We don't necessarily need scientific explanation. We have been zoned as affected communities and we believe this has been done for a reason. We in Malie, would like a very independent monitoring of the environment by an independent institution.

"This system of waste management only hides the truth about the reality that occurs on the ocean floor beneath the sea. It is the cheapest means that causes massive environmental destruction that is unseen."

(Statement by a community leader from Malie Island, one of the Lihir group of Islands directly facing the mine.)

The company monitors the wastes, and findings are presented to the government (Department of Environment and Conservation) on a periodic basis. The department is supposed to evaluate the monitoring reports, but lacks the skills and capacity to do so. There is no independently funded regular review, or monitoring of the environment, to verify the company's position. There have been numerous complaints of environmental pollution by local people but little, or no, independent investigation of them has been carried out.

Social Challenges

Life on Lihir Island has changed dramatically since the mining began. There has been a rapid transformation of both the physical and social environment.

The concerns of the silent majority are seldom heard, despite what is in their hearts. For five years and more, a picture has been painted of Lihir being the best mine possible, delivering necessary services and the best environmental performance. But this is only one side of the coin.

The people have become increasingly divided. On the top of a hill in Londolovit sits the LMC Mine Township, overlooking the sea towards the outer Lihir group of islands, Luise Harbour and the parts of Niolam Island on which the mine is located. The township contains sporting facilities, a hotel, national government staff houses, and the residence of the Chairman of the Landowners Association's (LMALA), all of higher quality than in other areas. The social club, with its barbecue area, swimming pool and other entertainment facilities, is open to members only: fees are PGK150.00 for township residents, but three times that for those living outside.

Along the foot of this hill, and barely visible from the LMC township, is the local Lihir township; sparsely populated, with some land divided among clan groups that operate small businesses using containers brought ashore during development of the mine. This township also has a marketplace, built by the company and managed by the Petztorme Women's Association (PWA).

There are two reasonably big supermarkets, a department store, the community affairs office, a police station, and few contractors' workshops. The PWA office (newly built without a toilet facility), and the Tutorme hall (where LMC embroidery is performed), are located on the waterfront beneath the hill. We understand that residents of the LMC township hardly ever shop in the Lihir township supermarkets, since they purchase their food items through an advance special orders mechanism, established for delivery to their camp.

"I am a prisoner"

One thing I find hard to understand is why they (LMC) live in a bigger and differently designed house than I, enjoy the luxury brought about by the gold found in my very own soil. I was given a house without any toilet, showers and kitchen compartments. Why can't I also enjoy that privilege is sometimes what I ask myself. I was relocated from Kapit where the mine now stands. I lost everything, my land and the sea where I used to freely move around and get whatever I wanted. Now I am a prisoner. I got relocated onto a clan land, which means that I cannot use that freedom anymore. Now I am bound by decisions of Clan leaders. It is not the same as when I was on my own land.

My biggest worry now is my children's future! I have lost my land and my children will never own and enjoy that land as I did before. Maybe I was a fool! Even today I have to struggle to meet the school fees for my four children (thank god that a brother helps meet the cost for two), while the company allow their children to go through nearly free education at my cost of my lose.

(Words of a relocated Kapi man, Lihir.)

There has certainly been some improvement, including a coordinated effort by local groups and the company to build over 500 houses, as well as upgrade and construct some community schools, and assist in the improvement of the health facility. The LMALA, and the Community Affairs office of LMC claim much development has taken place since the mine came on stream. And more is planned as part of a five-year review, including the Integrated Benefits Package.

But, while many Lihirians are benefiting, there also negative impacts. The majority of Papua New Guineans depend on subsistence farming, growing and harvesting food from gardens, and gaining protein by hunting in the bush. Lihirians are no exception and they enjoyed a similar lifestyle until the advent of the mine. They depended on garden food, hunted wild animals, collected srubmegapod eggs, and fished in the seas and rivers for fish and prawns. The environment was pristine: clean waters, clean beaches, clean air, plenty of food, and fewer people producing less noise.

When the company leased and occupied the land on which the mine now stands, local communities had to relocate. Their most respected sacred site was demolished. Although the company promised compensation for the losses, in the form of cash and the building of much better permanent houses for the displaced locals, how does this really compensate for the losses? How can we measure the satisfaction of the indigenous people who don't seem to have much say anyway? In the accompanying boxes we hear some of the things the people of Lihir have to say.

I live in Londolovit village which is in the heart of the mining area but I do not benefit at all. Please, don't think that all Lihirians benefit from this mine! Those who are lucky and have a job earn a bit of money to support their family. Those of us living in Londolovit who are not employed, are very much affected. When the mine began its development, all our natural creeks were polluted, our sea was polluted, our bush fowls were chased away, our bushes stripped off. We were left here without a thing except for a cheap house and a company water supply facility. We don't believe that what we are getting is worth what the company is making. The gold, the sea, the rivers and our land are god-given gifts (for us, Lihirians) which no man should take away from us that easily.

(Words of village church leader's from Londolovit village, Lihir.)

Communities were traditionally confined to their part of the island, or group of the islands, despite the natural interactions that occurred between them through family ties and big gatherings, such as sports, church and traditional events. The mine has caused a sudden transition from subsistence to a monetary-based lifestyle. It has introduced a mixed and more educated community of all cultures and races, representing a shift from traditional ways to a modern lifestyle and increased basic government services. However, this does not mean happiness has arrived.

The Lihirian leaders may be preparing for future challenges (not least the eventual closure of the mine) through a sustainability programme, focused on agriculture and other resource developments apart from mining. Even so, people still feel strongly about the loss of traditional values and their simple way of life.

Before we used to go to Londolovit to collect sago leaves, ropes and bamboos for our houses. Through an agreement, a piece of land was provided for Malie people where we could make our gardens as well. Today, the land is a public land. We are now stuck here. We do not know where to go, particularly in future.

(Words of a women from Malie Island, Lihir.)

Traditionally, women have led through a matrilineal regime of governance; ownership of land on Lihir is also through women. They therefore decide on issues relating to land. But did this happen during the process of negotiations for the mine? It appears not.

As a women's leader puts is: Before the mine the matrilineal system was well respected. But, when the mine came into operation on the island, women were never given any space in areas of decision-making. We have little contribution, or even nothing at all, over land matters today. Our traditional way has lost its true meaning by the introduction of the mine.

The World Bank and Transparency

The World Bank's involvement in PNG's mine, oil and gas industries raises some critical questions among different groups of actors: some NGOs and local people describe it a virus, others say it is frightening and others just simply say "we've already sold ourselves as a commodity". The government encourages the World Bank's involvement. There seems to be a conflict of interest. We need to ask: "What do the government and the World Bank know that the civil society doesn't know?"

Conflicts of interest are a result of inadequate awareness, mistrust and corruption. Our research indicated a society that was ill-informed with regard to the World Bank, or International Financial Institutions' involvement in extractive industries. There has clearly been a lack of transparency. It seems the government and the investors work well together, and usually do not disclose a lot of information to the third major stakeholder, the landowners. Only recently we heard that the loan has been re-paid because of good project performance on social, environmental and governance grounds. But we did not know whether all the loan had been re-paid, or whether there were still some loans to be repaid through the government. Without true transparency how can some of the replies we have received be trusted?

It is not so easy for ordinary citizens, affected communities and informal organisations, to have access to information on the environment. A company usually does environmental monitoring, sending the report for evaluation to the responsible government agency (in this case the Department of Environment and Conservation). Whether this report is circulated, and to whom, is not very clear. On top of that, it is believed that the report is biased in favour of the company – especially when the company frequently reports good performance, and yet people can see negative consequences all around them.

Future Expansion

It has been reported recently by LMC that exploration on Lihir is showing promising reserves on the island, and thus there is a possibility of expanding the mine through a possible US$200 million–US$250 million investment expansion which could increase ore throughput by two-thirds from mid-2006.

Such expansion could mean more grave environmental consequences if the submarine tailings disposal and the dumping of overburden material at sea continue. This will result in the destruction of a large area of marine habitat. In the thirty years of estimated operation, at least 104 million tons of ore reserves will be exploited, producing 341 million tons of waste rock.

The World Bank is now providing Technical Assistance Loans (TAL) to Papua New Guinea, to strengthen the capacity of the Department of Mines and the Internal Revenue Commission, as well as the petroleum sector, in order to fast-track exploration and mine development, in an attempt to alleviate poverty. Or so it claims. Training provided under the TAL for the staff is commendable. But, as Indigenous People, we believe that the World Bank has betrayed us. It is encouraging mining through a review of the current Mining Act, development of the mining policy, and other regulatory frameworks. The affected communities find it hard to believe that this is aimed at alleviating poverty.

The people of Papua New Guinea are not starving to death for food and clothing. Papua New Guinea needs support to upgrade basic provisions, such as health, education and infrastructure developments. Promoting extractive industries will not help: in fact they make the situation worse.

The country's resources are being taken at an alarming rate, and the benefits are hardly seen, particularly in the rural areas where the companies are based and two thirds of Papua New Guinea's population live.

If we had been given the chance to air our views on Lihir, we would have asked for diversion of the funds to a more realistic project, to assist the development of Papua New Guinea and enable poverty reduction.

Conclusion

More mines, oil pipelines, and refineries will do us no good, as our livelihoods are based on the living things of the land, the rivers and the seas.

The people of Papua New Guinea, affected by mining, cry out to their government and the World Bank to realise that, over the past decade or more, mining has been more disastrous to their livelihood and way of life than anything else. Increasing the number of extractive industries cannot alleviate poverty. Lowering taxes on the industry cannot reduce poverty. Mining and petroleum industries are there only for a very few rich people.

- Our rivers and oceans have been polluted. Riverbeds and ocean-floors have been destroyed by the deposition of sediments that eliminate aquatic and marine life.
- Our livelihood is in danger, as fish numbers decrease rapidly, our water is poisoned so we cannot use it for drinking, cooking, washing, fishing and other recreational uses any more.
- Our societies are fragmented. We no longer live and practice our communal Melanesian way of life. Instead we have become self-centred and greedy.
- No mining town today is as cheap as the markets in the capital, Port Moresby. Living standards for the overseas workers are high in mining towns, thus raising prices and causing locals to become poorer than they should be.
- Social problems trail the industry as it enters into very remote areas, where people have very limited exposure to so-called civilisation. This causes sudden transitional changes that are sometimes very detrimental to their

traditions and cultures. Respect for elders and women no longer exists. Womanising, marriage break-ups, new diseases, alcoholism, and drug abuse are on the rise.

— At the end of the day, when the developer leaves, we go back to where we started and try to reprogram ourselves, just to realise that we were taken for a ride to a destination which is foreign. We have to put ourselves back together again, without the aid of the companies that have left.

Recommendations

We, as indigenous communities of Papua New Guinea, recommend that:

1 The World Bank ensures that any review, development, or change made to the mining law of Papua New Guinea and its management tools or regulatory framework, should be the business of every individual Papua New Guinean. This should be done through the engagement of a civil society representative on the steering committee of the IDA project or direct engagement with National Umbrella NGOs to which we are affiliated.

2 The Department of Mining and the World Bank Team make it their business to conduct forums and meetings, to discuss the changes of regulatory framework with as many people as possible.

3 Changes in any legal framework should always consider social, environment and economic concerns from the viewpoint of the local people.

4 The World Bank should be prepared to fund research into problematic projects to which they have been party in the initial stages, and hence support an independent environmental monitoring or research project for the Lihir mine. The research should be funded by the World Bank and the monitoring team should stay with local people rather than the LMC.

5 No new mines should be encouraged until we are assured that our basic rights have been respected, and the industry is not going to put waste directly into our rivers and oceans.

CHAPTER 8

A Sink not a Spring – the Yanacocha Mine, Peru

8.1 INTRODUCTION

Roger Moody

Project Underground was a leading US non-governmental organisation (NGO) which unfortunately had to suspend its operations in 2003, due to lack of funding. It set the pace in supporting communities adversely affected by US resource extraction companies, both in minerals and oil. During the late nineties, it took on Newmont – now the world's biggest gold producer – publishing an illuminating corporate "anti-report" in 2000.[1] Project Underground concentrated its fire on three of the company's mines: two in Indonesia and one in Peru: Minera Yanacocha S.A. (MYSA), located in the Cajamarca province. With Newmont holding just over half the equity, the Peruvian company Buenaventura almost 44 per cent, and the remaining 5 per cent in the hands of the World Bank's IFC, this has become the premier gold producer throughout all Latin America, occupying the biggest single mining concession in the subcontinent.[2]

The Yanacocha project was already provoking considerable alarm among Cajamarcas Indigenous communities when its modest first gold was poured in 1993. Shortly afterwards, another Northern NGO – Minewatch (London) – was approached by community advocates to gain international support.[3] Protests mounted during the next twelve months when the World Bank, after financing the start-up of Yanacocha, put in US$15 million and a 'swap facility' towards exploitation of the Maqui Maqui pit. Five years later, the IFC pledged up to another US$ 110 million as a credit facility for yet a third "development" – that of the La Quinua deposit. The majority of this loan was co-arranged by the London based investment bank, Dresdner Kleinwort Benson, underwritten by its German parent, Dresdner Bank AG. It was syndicated to eight other lenders, including London-based NM Rothschild & Sons and the Standard Bank.[4]

Between May 1993 and June 1999, the IFC's funding and promises reached US$151.7 million.[5] By the end of 2002 gold production had leaped to 2.5 million ounces a year.[6]

After more than a decade, the IFC remains unabashed about financing the project. It was not that the mine or its host country were risk-free. On the contrary, the IFC specifically undertook to provide 'political comfort' to Newmont and its domestic partner, in the face of distinct investor reluctance to back Peruvian mining.[7] The World Bank's private lending arm also played an important role in enabling the project to "hedge its long term currency risks".[8] Further, the IFC intended that Yanacocha would provide a "demonstration" of competence and viability for other foreign mining companies to follow. (Demonstration there undoubtedly was, though not of the kind the World Bank anticipated.)

Minerals Rush

This, then, was the World Bank's Latin American "flagship", in the woeful absence of any other during the early 1990s. However, the Bank was not just intent on proving that Peru could be an investors' safe haven; it wanted to show that quick returns could be made at little cost. The World Bank demanded the privatisation (in some cases, asset stripping) of the country's state-owned mining companies; World Bank-drafted minerals investment codes were imposed under the corrupt regimen of President Alberto Fujimori; the country was exposed to a minerals rush. Over the space of a few years, more territory had been licensed to overseas mining companies, at near giveaway rates, than in all Peru's previous history.

Not surprisingly, MIGA political risk insurance was also enlisted to cover, not only Newmont's, but also the Union Bank of Switzerland's investments (in the Maqui Maqui exploit), against the risks of expropriation, war, and civil disturbance. Among all the examples of MIGA-backed projects studied for this book, unpredicted (if not unpredictable) mishaps, miscalculations, and a clear abdication of the World Bank's own rules of oversight and mitigation, could not have been more graphically portrayed. Thanks in large part to Project Underground's zealous and careful investigations, the Yanacocha case encapsulates the most contentious, and – for many observers – least acceptable, elements of World Bank Extractive Industries policies.

A Plague of Protests

In the year following the IFC's heaviest investment and expression of confidence in Yanacocha, MYSA was dogged by bad publicity. June 2000 saw an uncanny replay of the notorious cyanide disaster at the Kumtor mine two years previously.[9] One hundred and fifty-one kilogrammes of mercury spilled from a truck leaving the Yanacocha mine, causing eight people to be hospitalised.[10] By mid-2002, some 1,000 residents and municipal authorities had filed lawsuits against Newmont in Colorado, alleging injury as a result of this disaster.[11] The company was fined half a million US dollars by Peru's Mining and Energy Ministry. The IFC/MIGA's newly-appointed Compliance Advisor/Ombudsman (actually a Papua New Guinean woman called Meg Taylor) acknowledged a failure by MYSA to avoid the accident, saying the Peruvian government had "no relevant regulations regarding the transportation of mercury or *other hazardous materials* (editor's italics)".[12]

But, while recommending some twenty-five new operational procedures, the IFC did not explain why it had backed the project, knowing of these glaring deficiencies.[13]

In early 2001, as they released its year-end 2000 financial and operating results, Newmont and Minera Buenaventura were accused of having paid Fujimori's notorious "spy chief", Vladimir Montesinos, "millions of dollars" to take their part in a 1998 legal dispute with another company over Yanacocha's ownership. The claim, made by French businesman, Patrick Maugein was hotly denied by the US company, but attracted international attention.[14] Then, in March, five thousand townspeople and several mayors from around Yanacocha blockaded an approach to the mine, in protest at the death of fish in trout farms, fed by a river they claimed was contaminated with mine run-off.[15]

Judging for Oneself

These are just some of the most apparent and newsworthy aspects of a funding commitment which, instead of being continually examined and critiqued, has been pushed by the World Bank further and further out to sea, like some expeditionary force determined to capture an enemy hilltop. More and more dollars have been injected into what has increasingly become a sink, rather than a long term spring for sustainable development. The economic "value" of the mine has taken precedence over virtually all other considerations, in particular the self-identity and integrity of its indigenous neighbours. And, while the IFC continues to declare that Yanacocha has promoted large scale employment, economic spin-offs and wellbeing (its familiar mantra), even World Bank personnel themselves have thrown strong doubt on some of these claims.

Gary McMahon and Felix Remy in a late 2001 study pointed out that "in Peru substantial taxes from a mining operation [also] should go to the local and regional levels but it is unclear if they actually have, as the case of Yanacocha illustrates".[16] While the authors tried to quash fears that mining results in increased costs to local consumers (inflation), they conceded that "there were some problems (at Yanacocha) primarily concerning rents and real estate values".[17] Examining the rise in prostitution, "related diseases" and alcohol abuse, McMahon and Remy also found that, among the six mines they investigated, these problems were "most evident in Cajamarca (near Yanacocha)".[18]

The two contributions below are drawn from several, made by Project Underground between 1999 and 2002, as the organisation committed itself to representing the views of the women's organisation, the Federation of Rondas Campesinas Feminas of Northern Peru (FEROCAFENOP) to the outside world. The first article outlines the failings of the World Bank to observe its own (albeit dilute) policies on Indigenous Peoples and environmental protection.

The second is a detailed submission to the IFC/MIGA's Compliance/Advisor Ombudsman (CAO), following the Bank's failure to adequately address three previous complaints made by FEROCAFENOP between June 1999 and June 2001. This closely alalyses the proceedings of a "dialogue table" (*mesa de dialogo*), set up under the World Bank's auspices ostensibly to promote constructive engagement between what are now commonly called "stakeholders" in an extractive project. In reality, declared Project Underground, this "stagnant and self-limiting" process had undermined community resistance.

In fact community dissent was to dramatically revive the summer of 2004, when Newmont and its Peruvian partner attempted to stake out Cerro (Mount) Quilish for exploration and possible exploitation. This region had been specifically excluded from the *mesa de dialogo* and, no doubt partly for that reason, the opposition seemed broader-based and more vocal than ever before. As a result Newmont announced that it would not proceed with the Mount Quilish extension – at least not for the time being: a response hailed as a victory by the Yanacocha communities.[19]

Notes

1   *Newmont: why are people around the the world so* MAD *at this company?*, Report from Project Underground, op cit, Berkeley 2000.

2   *Newmont: why are people ...?*, ibid, p. 19.

3   See correspondence between Jaime Llosa Larrabure, Coordinador Grupo de Apoyo, Lima, and Erich Schoepe, Arbeitskreis Peru, Heidelberg, and Minewatch, London 1994-1995.

4   *Mining Journal* (MJ), London, November 28 1999.

5   *IFC Project Summary Sheet*, FY1993-2001, IFC, Washington 2002.

6   *MJ*, March 14 2003.

7   *IFC Project Summary*, ibid, p. 3.

8   *IFC Project Summary*, ibid, p. 2.

9   See Chapter 6 of this book, *Kumtor Grief.*

10   *MJ*, June 23 2000.

11   Missy Ryan, *Plight of Peru town dim after mine' mercury spill*, Reuters report, July 3 2002.

12   Quoted in *Mining Environmental Management*, London, November 2000.

13   Press release from Meg Taylor, IFC/MIGA CAO, June 21 2000.

14   *MJ*, February 8, 2002; see also *New York Times*, February 3 2001.

15   *Bretton Woods update*, number 22, London, April/May 2001.

16   Gary McMahon and Felix Remy, *Large Mines and the Community*, Chapter One, IDRC, p. 20.

17   McMahon and Remy, ibid, p. 21.

18   McMahon and Remy, ibid, p. 24.

19   See *Statement by Social Organisations*, Cerro Quilish, September 17 2004.

8.2 Peru's Yanacocha Gold Mine: The ifc's Midas Touch?

Shanna Langdon (Project Underground, September 2000)

This case raises significant questions about the IFC as a development institution, the rationale for its involvement in certain projects, and its capacity to ensure that the local people benefit from the projects it supports. To the extent that a development rationale exists for this project, it seems to be based on the assumption that investment will lead to growth which will then reduce poverty. As this case study demonstrates, such an assumption fails to examine the effects of IFC financing on the lives of the people directly impacted by its projects.

Project Overview

Minera Yanacocha is a huge open pit gold mine spreading over a concession of about 25,000 hectares, and approximately 47 kilometers by road,[1] to the town of Cajamarca, about 850 kilometers from the capital, Lima. The rock containing the gold is loosened by daily dynamite blasts, and then piled up and sprayed with cyanide solution. The solution that runs off is then processed to remove the gold. The mine produced 1.66 million ounces of gold in 1999 at a cost of $103 per ounce,[2] making it one of the largest and lowest-cost gold mines on the planet.

ifc Development Rationale

According to the IFC, it got involved in Yanacocha "to support a project promising to generate substantial revenue, employment and foreign currency flows".[3] In an otherwise high-risk context, IFC believes that its participation facilitated access to long-term capital and mobilized funding from other lenders. The IFC says that its involvement was also to ensure high standards in environmental and social practices. It "sees its role and impact to be in facilitating, where necessary, relations between the company, local community and government on social and environmental issues".[4]

Overview of Key Problems with the Project

According to the IFC, Yanacocha has led to significant reforms and privatization in the mining sector, and become an example of private sector leadership for mining and other sectors in Peru.[5] However, many local residents have asserted that the Yanacocha mine has caused so much environmental harm and social dislocation that they are now opposed to any further development of the mine, and many would like it to be shut down completely. Problems with the mine include water quality and quantity, circumstances surrounding land transfers, inadequate consultation, social dislocation, questions regarding indigenous peoples, and the adequacy of emergency response measures.

Water Quality and Quantity

Since the establishment of the mine in 1992, the local people have reported serious degradation and contamination of their water sources, affecting irrigation practices and their food supply. In recent interviews, the local people described the water flowing downhill from the mine as having a foul odor and taste, appearing yellow or brown, carrying surface contaminants such as trash or sewage, and causing sickness to both animals and people. Mine waste flows directly into waterways that are the only source of water for several campesino communities.

An investigation into the water quality in the mine area's rivers and streams found that the mine consistently breaches World Health Organization and Peruvian Ministry of Energy and Mines standards for a wide range of potential contaminants.[6] Of major concern are fecal coliforms and copper present in, respectively, 160,000 times and 10 to 20 times higher levels as compared to WHO standards. The acidity of the water is also extremely high, with a PH of 3.3 as compared to 6.5, which is the highest acidity considered drinkable.[7] These pollutants have resulted in situations where villages have been without potable water for two months at a time. According to local communities, fish and frogs have disappeared from the river, both of which were previously a food supply for the rural communities.

It is not just the quality of water sources, but also the quantity, that have adversely affected the communities around the mine.

Campesinos living downstream from the mine assert that the quantity of water in the streams and canals that flow from the mine site has diminished. For many the result has been a reduced capacity to irrigate their crops and therefore a reduced agricultural yield. The plots of land possessed by many campesino families are already small and marginal, and any reduction in yield is likely to exacerbate poverty.

Land Transfer Issues and Inadequate Consultation

Social problems associated with the mine started with the process of land acquisition by MYSA. Campesinos have explained[8] that the practice of selling land was almost unknown in their communities before the advent of the mine, although the practice of transferring land for land and negotiating for different uses of land was common. Many families said they had not fully understood that "selling" their land would prevent them from any further use.

Moreover, many local people believe they have been deceived by the promises that were given at the consultation about the benefits that would come to them from selling their land and from the mine itself.[9]

Company employees assured campesinos that they would be able to return to their lands in a few years time. There appears to be a widespread perception, not dispelled during consultations, that the mining would consist of a few holes in the ground, around which normal agricultural activities could continue.

Consideration and Protection of Indigenous Peoples

The IFC, like the rest of the World Bank Group, is subject to policies and procedures that are supposed "to ensure that the local indigenous people do not suffer adverse effects during the development process and that they receive culturally compatible social and economic benefits".[10] To accomplish this goal, project plans must include an indigenous peoples development plan that, among other things, is designed to ensure the culturally appropriate and informed participation of affected groups, identify local preferences, incorporate indigenous knowledge into project approaches, and to use experienced indigenous peoples specialists.

In the Yanacocha case, the local people were not recognized as indigenous peoples in the environmental impact study analysis,[11] prepared by the MYSA for the IFC.

Therefore, none of the measures required by the IFC to protect indigenous peoples were applied in this case. Contrary to MYSA's assessment, the rural communities of Cajamarca meet the definition of indigenous peoples under the IFC policy. They both self-identify as indigenous peoples and are recognized as such under the Constitution of Peru. They have a close attachment to ancestral territories and the mountains in particular, speak Quechua as a primary language, produce primarily for subsistence, and have their own social and cultural institutions (land exchanges, campesino justice for example). The failure to define the rural communities as indigenous peoples, and to apply the indigenous peoples policy, may well have aggravated the adverse social and environmental impacts of the mine.

Increased Poverty and Social Dislocation

The development of the Yanacocha mine has lead to significant social dislocation in the area.[12] Families displaced by the mine move into the city of Cajamarca where they have no way of making a living. The migration into the city is tearing the social fabric of the indigenous communities as men leave to find work, as traditional practices of the indigenous people of the area are being forgotten, and as families lose their community support structures. Many families, unable to support themselves, are left to depend on social services for food and shelter.[13]

The Federation of Rondas Campesinas Femeninas of Northern Peru (FEROCAFENOP) has documented a nearly 20 per cent increase in family problems since the Yanacocha mine began operating, including non-recognition of children, abandonment of families, failure to pay child support and domestic abuse. Similarly, debt problems have skyrocketed.

The Mercury Spill and the Adequacy of Emergency Response Measures

In addition to the impact of the mine's normal operations, a recent mercury spill, related to the mine, raises questions about the adequacy of emergency response measures. On June 2 2000, a truck carrying mercury from the mine to Lima spilled between 80 and 151 kg of its load while passing through the small town of Choropampa. It was reported that the driver of the truck did not inform local residents of the dangers the mercury posed, and continued on to Lima. People gathered up the mercury, believing it to be a valuable metal, and many kept it in their homes.

Symptoms of mercury poisoning emerged a few days later among approximately 50-70 local residents, including many children. Several of them were hospitalised.[14]

According to the IFC, Yanacocha and Newmont informed the IFC that the spill was promptly reported to the local community, regional and national mining and environmental authorities as well as officials in Choropampa and Cajamarca.[15]

According to FEROCAFENOP, people started exhibiting symptoms a few days after the spill, and initially doctors were unable to determine the cause of their illness. This would suggest that those affected had not been informed that they had been exposed to mercury or of the symptoms of mercury poisoning.

Local Resistance to the Project

In 1999 the IFC approved a loan of approximately $100 million for further expansion of the mine (the La Quinua Pit), something the local indigenous communities are adamantly opposed to because of the problems associated with the existing mine operations. According to Segunda Castrejon, President of FEROCAFENOP, the mine has changed the lives of thousands of indigenous campesinos: "Before the mining company came, we lived a clean, healthy life. That's no longer true. Now all of our flora and fauna are gone. To us, our mountains are sacred. They brought us good luck. But now those mountains are gone because of Newmont."[16]

An assembly of FEROCAFENOP affiliates held in Cajamarca on September 20, 1999 unanimously passed a motion opposing mine expansion, resolving to support upcoming demonstrations against the mine.

At the same time, the Federation organized a series of demonstrations and marches over the past year, which drew as many as 10,000 people.[17] These have all been peaceful on the part of the campesinos and their supporters, but in January 2000, the police turned violent and beat and arrested protestors. Several leaders of the Federation were arrested and charged with terrorism as a result.

FEROCAFENOP, with the support of the affiliated grassroots bases it represents, is also organizing capacity building workshops to inform the local communities about the reality of selling land to the mine, and the impacts the mine is having on their environment. As the land is the self-identified indigenous campesinos' home, tied to their community, and the only source of livelihood, they must understand the possible impacts of selling it before they do so. The Federation sees educating people as a way to prevent future problems – instead of protesting when the mine expands, they hope that people will understand the long term implications of selling their land to the mine and decide to avoid any further damage to their communities. The high level of poverty makes the balancing of today's necessities with tomorrow's a difficult decision. The local people understand clearly, however, that such a project does not improve their lives or reduce their poverty.[18]

IFC's Response to External Criticisms and Demands

In March of 2000, the IFC environmental specialist for this project recognized that the consultation process has been flawed and agreed that the process had to be much more inclusive of the affected communities in the future. However, since this communication little has happened to make the communities believe that the consultation process has improved.[19]

The IFC supervision mission in May did meet with the affected communities for four hours, but they did not visit the problem areas, leading the communities to question whether the visit was simply perfunctory.[20] The IFC mission had promised to answer a series of questions in writing, but, at the time of writing [September 2000], the local groups have still not received any communication. In accordance to the IFC's disclosure policy, the mission's assessment report will not be released to the public, leaving the communities without any information.

In response to charges that the mine has adversely impacted water quality, the IFC asserts that the baseline data show that the rivers in the area had some pre-existing sediment loads, acidity, and presence of heavy metals. While the Environmental Impact Assessment identified impact on water quality and quantity as a potential problem,[21] the subsequent investigations mentioned above show that this situation has been severely exacerbated since the advent of the mine. The fact that IFC was aware of the poor water quality brings into question why IFC would approve a loan that would exacerbate the water quality problem, which directly impacts the lives and livelihoods of local residents. As a development institution, concerned about "improving people's lives", the IFC should have proposed adequate measures to safeguard and improve the water quality.

Regarding the indigenous peoples issue, this project illustrates the sponsoring company's perverse incentive not to recognize local peoples as indigenous, given the additional obligations and associated costs involved. It also brings into question whether the company should be responsible for this assessment, especially in cases where identification may be difficult, and whether the IFC has adequate safeguards in place to verify these critical issues in a sponsor's environmental assessment.

Conclusion

The Yanacocha mine has been a disaster for the thousands of indigenous people who traditionally inhabited the land in the vicinity of the mine. This case study demonstrates several important points about IFC lending. First, that the IFC's assumption that economic growth equals poverty alleviation is fundamentally flawed.

The Yanacocha mine has brought much environmental and social disruption for the local people, exacerbating poverty for many.

Second, the IFC's consultation procedures are severely deficient, and have led to people signing away their lands and livelihoods without understanding what they were doing. The campesinos were not given access to information about the Yanacocha mine, let alone information presented in a culturally appropriate way.

Third, the IFC does not have adequate mechanisms in place to ensure compliance with the indigenous peoples policy. The local campesinos were not treated as indigenous peoples, despite the fact that they fit the definition of the indigenous peoples policy. The IFC must address these issues if it truly wants to promote private sector investment that improves peoples' lives.

Notes

1   IFC *Summary Project Information*, for Peru – Yanacocha III.
2   *Newmont Mining Corporation Annual Report*, 1999.
3   *IFC chart compiled by* IFC *personnel*, IFC, June 21 2000.
4   *IFC chart ...*, ibid.
5   *IFC chart ...*, ibid.
6   *Audit and Inspection Report*, Minera Yanacocha S.A., First Quarter 1999, file 1168938 MEM, Peruvian Ministry of Energy and Mines; *Informe de Ensayo O/L ECO-900464*, October 1999, SGS del Peru; *Carachugo/Maqui Maqui Water Quality Data 1997 & 1st quarter 1998*, file 1168938 MEM, Peruvian Ministry of Energy and Mines; MYSA *Water Quality Data*, file 1168938 MEM, Peruvian Ministry of Energy and Mines, 1998; *Aprobacion del Estudio Complementario de Impacto Ambiental del Proyecto Carachugo Minera Yanacocha sa.* Informe no. 222-94-em-dgm/dpdm, file 1168938 MEM, Peruvian Ministry of Energy and Mines.
7   For more details, see *Newmont report*, Project Underground, May 2000.
8   Interviews were conducted with 70 campesinos from the Cajamarca region by Alison Gibbins and Andrew Burke for Project Underground between September and December 1999.
9   Interviews ..., ibid.
10   Operational Directive 4.20 on Indigenous Peoples, para. 6. At the time of writing, the IFC had no specific policy on Indigenous Peoples or resettlement, two key elements protecting the local peoples. In the absence of its own, the IFC defers to the World Bank Policies, according to the IFC website, www.ifc.org/enviro/EnvSoc/Safeguard/Indigenous/indigenous.htm.
11   *Minera Yanacocha*, la Quinua EIS addendum, March 1999, p. 27.
12   26 families according to the IFC, 2,500 people according to the Federation of Rondas Campesinas Femeninas of Northern Peru, FEROCAFENOP. FEROCAFENOP is a constitutionally recognized federation that represents the rural, indigenous

population in the Andean region of Northern Peru. It represents 14,000 affiliated bases in the seven departments of Northern Peru.

13 Pers. Comm. with representatives of FEROCAFENOP, November 1999.
14 "Vida de 30 Campesinos de Choropampa Corre Peligro por Derrame de Mercurio", *La República*, June 14 2000.
15 IFC *statement on the mercury spill*, June 22 2000.
16 Quoted in "Newmont Mining Protested", by Steve Raabe, *The Denver Post*, May 4, 2000.
17 Pers. Comm. with Julio Marín of FEROCAFENOP, February 2000.
18 Pers. Comm. with Julio Marín of FEROCAFENOP, November 1999.
19 Pers. Communication with Mauricio Athie, March 29 2000.
20 Pers. Comm. with Julio Marín of FEROCAFENOP, May 2000.
21 *Environmental Action Plan*, La Quinua Project, prepared by Minera Yanacocha for the IFC, March 1999.

8.3 The Path of Least Resistance

An Assessment of the Compliance Advisor Ombudsman's Handling of the Minera Yanacocha Complaint

Project Underground, July 2002

Executive Summary

For the past year and a half, the Compliance Advisor/Ombudsman (CAO) for the International Finance Corporation (IFC) has attempted to resolve the complaint filed by the Rondas Campesinas (FEROCAFENOP) concerning an IFC-financed gold mine in Peru. The CAO's handling of the complaint has been limited to the creation and oversight of a local dialogue process. The ongoing dialogue process has made few concrete achievements and has deteriorated into a bureaucratic corporate engagement exercise that avoids grappling with most of the substantive issues raised in the complaint.

The dialogue's progress has been hindered by an ineffectual team of mediators hired by the CAO to facilitate the process. The mediators, as well as the CAO itself, are overtly hostile to criticism of the team's performance and have sought to exclude Project Underground as an international observer, by cutting Project Underground out of the communication loop.

The primary beneficiary of the dialogue process is the mine, which has usurped the process as a public relations forum and heralded it internationally as an example of its good corporate citizenship. As the principle financial contributor to the dialogue process, the mine appears to be getting what it pays for.

Introduction

The mine has caused a number of devastating environmental and social problems, ranging from severe water contamination and a major mercury spill, to an upsurge in prostitution, alcoholism and domestic violence. In short, the mine has destroyed the way of life of thousands of campesinos and impacted the health and safety of the entire *Cajamarquino* community.

In March, 2001, Project Underground assisted the Rondas Campesinas in filing a complaint with the Compliance Advisor/Ombudsman (CAO) of the IFC.* The complaint alleges numerous, egregious, violations of IFC and World Bank social and environmental safeguard policies, most notably the mine's failure to consult with the affected community as part of the environmental impact assessment process, and its refusal to recognize the campesino community as an indigenous people entitled to special protection under the World Bank Policy on Indigenous Peoples.

The CAO accepted the complaint and, since September, 2001, has sponsored a "stakeholder" mediation process called the "*mesa de diálogo*" or "dialogue table". *Mesa* participants represent many sectors of *Cajamarquino* civil society, including the mine, the Rondas, the municipality, government agencies, the university and, until recently, non-governmental organizations (NGOs). The CAO hired a team of private mediation consultants to facilitate and oversee the *mesa de diálogo*.

A Project Underground representative has attended all but one of the meetings of the *mesa*. In April, 2002, Project Underground facilitated a campesino community evaluation of the mesa. This report is based on the evaluative feedback of community members, as well as Project Underground's own observations of the process.

The Rondas' complaint was the third complaint accepted by the CAO and is the furthest along in the resolution process. How the CAO handles this complaint provides IFC-impacted communities and NGOs with their first case study of the CAO's ability to hold the IFC accountable to project-affected communities and to increase the IFC's compliance with its social and environmental safeguard policies.

Mesa de Diálogo's Lack of Substantive Focus

The *mesa de diálogo* has been meeting for nine months now but has discussed, much less achieved, little of substance. Instead, the CAO team has directed the *mesa*'s attention toward bureaucratic issues, such as a protocol for the process, a logo for the *mesa* "capacity-building" workshops, the creation of dysfunctional working groups and the logistics of opening a *mesa*

---

* The CAO was established in 1999 to address complaints by people affected by IFC and MIGA projects and to "enhance the social and environmental outcomes of projects in which these organizations play a role". (CAO Operational Guidelines).

office in Cajamarca. As a mayor of a rural community said at one of the
mesas: "After six months of meetings, we haven't achieved any benefits, well,
a little. We are not here to just drink the mineral water and then return to
our communities."

For several months *mesa* participants engaged in a series of "capacity-
building" workshops. During these workshops, no issues of substance were
discussed; instead, the participants were led through a series of role-plays
that sought to illuminate the nature of conflict, and constructive conflict
resolution techniques. It was difficult for the many illiterate and less educated workshop attendees to fully participate because of an over-reliance on
written materials and highbrow lectures. Minera Yanacocha's participation in
the workshops was extremely spotty, leading many participants to question
the mine's commitment to the process. Also, the hypothetical disputes, that
were the subjects of the role plays, usually involved family or interpersonal
squabbles that in no way mirrored the vastly unequal and impersonal relationship between the world's largest gold mining company and the citizens
of Cajamarca.

Although a long list of critical issues was created and prioritized at the
first meeting of the *mesa* in September, 2001, it was not until the March
mesa, at Project Underground's urging, that this list of issues was ever again
referenced. Even after the priority list was revived, there was no discussion of
substantive issues during the next two *mesas*. Without explanation, the CAO
team skipped over the "Review Agenda" item at the top of the April *mesa's*
agenda.

One of the agreements, made at the first meeting in September, was that
the CAO would hire an independent team of medical experts to conduct a
study of the lingering effects of mercury contamination in Choropampa. (A
large mercury spill occurred there in June, 2000, and the victims suffer ongoing and, in some cases, worsening medical problems. This situation was the
subject of a separate complaint, presented to the CAO by Choropampa residents in late 2000. The issues presented by the Choropampa complaint are
handled by the *mesa de diálogo* alongside the issues presented in the Rondas'
complaint). Nine months later, as of the writing of this report, the medical
team still has not been sent to Choropampa. The CAO has vaguely alluded to
"bureaucratic delays" posed by Peruvian government officials, but it remains
unclear what efforts the CAO has made to overcome the red tape and fulfill its
promise to the neglected and disappointed Choropampa community.

Another agreement made at the October *mesa* was that the CAO would
conduct an independent biodiversity study of the mine's impact on the flora
and fauna of the area. When a *mesa* participant reminded others of this

agreement months later, the CAO team said it had no money for further studies, and that a governmental body was considering conducting a biodiversity study. Similarly, an agreement to conduct an independent study of air pollution has been removed from the *mesa's* purview, due to the CAO's "limited resources". Thus, biodiversity and air pollution, two issues identified by the community as top priorities, have been effectively removed from the *mesa's* agenda.

Before the *mesa* even began, the CAO decided that the controversial issue of the mine's planned expansion to a watershed area, called Cerro Quilish, would not be a subject of discussion. There is nearly unanimous opposition, across all sectors of *Cajamarquino* civil society, to the mining of Cerro Quilish. The municipality of Cajamarca passed an ordinance declaring Cerro Quilish a nature preserve off-limits to mining. Rather than respecting the clear will of the people of Cajamarca, Minera Yanacocha is challenging the ordinance in court.

Several groups and individuals demanded, as a condition of their participation in the *mesa,* that the mine agree to a moratorium on the development of Cerro Quilish. The mine did not agree and these groups have boycotted the *mesa.*

The removal of Cerro Quilish from the *mesa's* purview was a significant victory for the mine, which has chosen to pursue an aggressive legal strategy, rather than engage in community consultations. It also set an important precedent for the *mesa* that participants must check their opposition to the mine, at the door, as a condition of entry.

Mine's Exploitation of Mesa as Public Relations Platform

The *mesa* facilitators have allowed the *mesa* to be used as a public relations forum for Minera Yanacocha to tout its commitment to economic development and environmental protection. Although *mesa* participants adopted a ten-minute speaking limit as one of their ground rules, mine representatives are routinely permitted to speak at great length and make PowerPoint presentations seeking to convince the participants of the mine's generosity and goodwill.

Underlying the mine's privileged position in the *mesa* is a tacit assumption that the mine possesses technical knowledge that uniquely qualifies it to formulate development proposals, and that the community's experiential or traditional knowledge is of no relevance. The role of the community is to make brief, on-the-spot, comments in response to the mine's presentation, thus, and to be grateful for the mine's patronage.

Even after the formation of a small business development working group, the mine still came back to the *mesa* seeking rubberstamp approval of the mine's unilateral small business development plan. The working group never in fact got off the ground – the group never met because the mine's representative failed to return the phone calls of the working group's point person. When the point person voiced frustration about the mine's lack of participation, the CAO team accused him of making an unwarranted personal attack against the mine representative. At no point did the CAO team acknowledge the fact that the working group was completely non-functional due to the mine's non-participation.

Community participants have pointed out, time and again, that the development proposals put forth by the mine are the same top-down proposals it has been floating for many years, and that nothing that transpired during the *mesa* has resulted in any substantive changes. Campesino participants are aware that the mine's ideas for economic development are unlikely to benefit campesino communities equally, if at all. As one campesino from the village of Chamis said in response to a mine' presentation on its community development foundation: "This development is for others. The potable water and electricity that reach the communities usually benefit the companies more than the campesinos. We are denied our own resources. Instead of making our clothes with our resources, we need to buy cloth made in factories. The new Francisco Pizzaro[1] has arrived. Before, he had horses and weapons, now he's got pretty machines."

In response to criticism of the mine's domination of the *mesa's* development agenda, the CAO team began substituting the word "dialogue" for "presentation". This semantic sleight of hand has had no actual impact on the platitudinous tenor of the discussion.

False Premise of Equal Bargaining Power in Mesa de Diálogo

Another disturbing aspect of the workshops, and in the *mesa* overall, is the lack of acknowledgement of the power imbalance between the mine and the affected community. The conflict resolution techniques demonstrated in the workshops assume equal bargaining power among the parties to the conflict. Such techniques are of dubious value in mediating a conflict between the world's largest gold mining company and a campesino federation.

Instead of a community that has suffered all of the externalized costs, and enjoyed none of the benefits of mining operations, and has a right to be outraged about it, the community is transformed into a generic stakeholder that must hold its anger in check and be ready to agree to a "reasonable" compromise. In reality, of course, the mine is a corporate entity, not a person with feelings and moral rights. Yet, the false premise of equal bargaining power, positions the mine as a member of the extended family and forces the community to treat it accordingly, thereby robbing the community of one of the only resources it has left – moral indignation.

Ineffective Facilitation of Mesa de Diálogo

The CAO retained an international team of five private consultants to mediate the *mesa de diálogo*. Although the credentials of these consultants are impressive, their performance in Cajamarca leaves much to be desired.

The most disappointing aspect of the *mesa* has been its lack of substance, as discussed above. The facilitators contribute to this problem by failing to include and, in some instances, actively blocking, the iteration of substantive issues on the *mesa*'s agenda, and by allowing the mine to co-opt the *mesa* as a public relations forum.

The CAO mediation team appears to be unfamiliar with CAO, IFC and World Bank guidelines. For example, the Rondas and Project Underground have spent months trying to make the team understand the significance of recognition of the Rondas as an indigenous people under World Bank safeguard policies. Though the CAO finally promised to respond to this issue, it still has not. Although the *mesa* arises from the filing of the Rondas' complaint, which is premised on the violation of various safeguard policies, there is no discussion, or even bare acknowledgement, of these policies during the *mesa*. It is unclear whether this is a function of the team's ignorance of, or conscious disregard for, these policies.

One of the CAO mediators has repeatedly voiced his personal opinion that the poor water quality in Cajamarca may well be attributable to factors other than mining contamination. Even as the *mesa* eagerly awaits the findings of an independent water study, conducted by internationally renowned experts, the CAO mediator continues to use his supposedly neutral position of power to express his scepticism of the community's belief that the mine has contaminated their water.

There have been several instances of cultural insensitivity, on the part of North American as well as non-indigenous Latino and Latina CAO mediators, toward campesino participants, particularly during bi-lateral meetings between CAO mediators and the Rondas. There is also a significant imbalance in the participation of women, with insufficient effort made to ensure that women's voices are heard. At the June *mesa*, the CAO team leader told the women not to bring their children to the next one, impairing the ability of women to even be physically present at future *mesas*.

The *mesa* elected a Coordinating Committee to set the agendas for each meeting of the *mesa*. But, the mediation team has, at times, unilaterally changed the agenda after it was approved by this committee.

After each meeting of the *mesa*, the mediation team prepares a report documenting what transpired. The team originally promised to distribute these reports to participants well in advance of the next meeting, so that they could share the contents with their constituencies. In practice, the team hands out the report on the day of the *mesa* and allows no time during the *mesa* for participants to review or discuss it.

Perhaps most indicative of the quality of *mesa* facilitation is the deterioration in the level and quality of community participation. Discussion during the *mesa* has increasingly become dominated by a small handful of participants, few of whom are women. Most participants sit quietly throughout the day without saying a word. Even the members of the Coordinating Committee have grown increasingly passive, deferring to the CAO team, rather than seriously engaging in the task of "coordinating" the *mesa*.

Although several local and international NGOs participated in the *mesa* early on, they have all withdrawn, citing many of the same criticisms discussed herein. These NGOs plan in the near future to release their own letter to the CAO, setting forth their reasons for not participating.

The CAO team has demonstrated a total lack of professionalism in responding to criticisms lodged by Project Underground and *mesa* participants. Project Underground wrote a letter to the CAO critiquing several aspects of the *mesa,* and provided courtesy copies to the mediation team. The CAO's Operational Guidelines provide for the confidentiality of communications with the CAO in the course of mediation processes. The mediation team's response to Project Underground's letter was to disclose its contents to the full, and lash out at Project Underground for writing the letter. Although Project Underground's representative was present, and several participants requested that he respond, the mediation team refused to allow him to speak. Rather than discussing the merits of the points made by Project Underground, the mediation team defended the usefulness of the workshops, which had given rise to only one of many of Project Underground's points of criticism.

After the *mesa*, mediation team members told the Project Underground representative that they felt hurt and betrayed by Project Underground's letter. They acted as though they had never, in their professional lives, been subject to criticism, nor should they be subject to scrutiny here. One mediator referred to Project Underground's criticism as "the most unfounded and harsh criticism of her life," and accused its representative of distorting events that occurred during the *mesa*. When reminded that Project Underground had videotaped the *mesa*, the mediator (who has never watched the videos nor arranged for professional documentation of the *mesa*) made the preposterous suggestion that the video camera recorded events in an inaccurate manner. The CAO team's defensive attitude, counter-attacks, and the inappropriate response to Project Underground's letter, evince a shocking absence of professional integrity.

The CAO team's tendency to personalize conflict also led them to rush to the defense of one of the mining representatives, criticized by Project Underground for spending most of the workshop in the hallway on her cell phone. The day after a Project Underground screening of a Friends of the Earth-Peru/LABOR film on World Bank involvement in mining in Peru, a mine representative expressed her personal feelings of betrayal to the CAO team (based on the anti-mining message of the film, and Project Underground's earlier criticisms of her workshop attendance). The CAO team responded sympathetically, extolling her efforts to attend the workshop, despite her busy schedule, and accusing Project Underground of making intentional, bad faith misrepresentations in both its written and videotaped documentation of the *mesa*.

Institutionalization of Mesa de Diálogo

The CAO mediation team will phase out its on-site involvement by the end of this year. Thereafter, the *mesa* will be conducted under the auspices of a local "office of the *mesa*", established by the CAO. The stated goal of this project is to establish a system that, after a two-year transition period, will be permanent and self-sustaining without further CAO involvement.

Many of the *mesa* participants have grave doubts about the ability of a locally-run *mesa* to reach and/or implement any meaningful agreements. They believe that, only with the direct oversight of the CAO, will the mine negotiate in good faith and follow through on its promises.

The long term institutionalization of the *mesa de diálogo* raises serious concerns. Given the unsuccessful track record of the *mesa*, it is doubtful that the *mesa* over time will achieve any significant tangible outcomes. Instead, it is likely to become an ineffective bureaucratic entity, mired in complicated procedures that serves only to preserve the status quo. With so many sectors of *Cajamarquino* civil society putting their hopes and resources into the *mesa*, their ability to pursue other channels of redress against the mine is gradually drained away. The only entity that benefits from such a long term corporate engagement is the mine, which will continue expanding and destroying, while at the same time claiming to be a good citizen engaged in consultations with the community.

CAO's Response to Criticism

Like the mediation team, the CAO does not take kindly to criticism. Project Underground sent a series of letters raising questions and concerns about the CAO's handling of the complaint in general. After months of silence, the CAO finally responded with a defensive letter that addressed some, but not all, of Project Underground's concerns. The CAO refuted Project Underground's criticisms, based on inaccurate information provided by the mediation team. For example, the CAO led off by claiming that no one in Peru was aware of the alleged concerns, a patently false assertion belied by extensive written and videotaped documentation, including the official minutes of the Coordinating Committe; and it went on to deny other documented problems.

The CAO did not even respond to Project Underground's complaints that the mediation team had breached the confidentiality provision of its Operational Guidelines, and appeared to be unfamiliar with that, and other CAO and IFC, guidelines.

The CAO, relying on inaccurate reports from its field team, also sought to dismiss Project Underground's criticisms, by contending that the affected community does not share in Project Underground's concerns. Again, Project Underground's documentation of the *mesa* shows that most of the concerns it has articulated are widely shared.

The CAO's unwillingness to exercise oversight over its own consultants raises serious questions about the competence and integrity of the CAO office.

CAO Hostility Toward Project Underground

The CAO's Operational Guidelines allow for a complaint to be made by a representative on behalf of, or jointly with, the community affected by the project. Project Underground and the Rondas Campesinas filed the complaint jointly, and the CAO accepted the complaint without challenging Project Underground's authority to represent the Rondas.

After informing Project Underground that the complaint had been accepted, the CAO broke off communication. The CAO made a series of visits to Cajamarca giving last minute, or no, notice to Project Underground. The CAO only provided Project Underground with its reports of these trips after repeated requests. Eventually, the CAO ceased providing Project Underground with reports altogether, and it was forced to obtain copies from other sources. The CAO also ceased providing Project Underground with courtesy copies of its correspondence with the Rondas.

At the *mesa de diálogo*, the CAO team did not allow Project Underground's representative to sit at the table with the Rondas, even after the Rondas made clear their strong desire to have a Project Underground representative close at hand. The CAO team initially tried to prevent Project Underground from videotaping the proceedings, but allowed it to do so when it became clear that there was no stakeholder opposition. However, on two separate occasions, CAO team members accused Project Underground of selectively filming only those portions of the proceedings it wished to have recorded.

To a certain extent, the CAO's failure to communicate with Project Underground could be a function of the woefully inadequate staffing level within the CAO office. However, the CAO has made it clear that it does not feel obliged to communicate with Project Underground, and has evinced an attitude of disregard and disrespect for Project Underground's role. The CAO frequently cites its primary responsibility to communicate with the affected community, but conveniently overlooks the fact that, in this case, the affected community has consistently demanded that the CAO respect Project Underground's role as its representative, and keep Project Underground fully informed.

The CAO's hostility toward Project Underground may in large measure be a reaction to the NGOs strong critique of the *mesa de diálogo*. Project Underground has lodged criticisms in a straightforward and blunt manner, and a style typical of North American NGOs. By contrast, for reasons relating to Peruvian cultural norms, the power imbalance between *mesa* participants and the CAO and the feel-good corporate engagement style pervading the *mesa*, participants tend not to directly criticize the CAO or the *mesa*, and they temper any criticism with polite reassurances. The CAO takes refuge in the local people's reluctance to criticize, as a means to avoid addressing Project Underground's criticisms.

The CAO has made it clear that it would rather Project Underground not be involved in this process. One might have expected that the CAO would see the value of involvement by an international organization which has the resources to assist the affected community in framing the allegations and demands of the complaint. The CAO's hostility toward Project Underground suggests that the CAO wishes to have unequal power in its relationship with its "client". Because Project Underground serves to equalize the balance of power, the CAO finds ways to exclude and marginalize it from the process.

Mine Funding of Mesa de Diálogo

Project Underground sought clarification from the CAO of the specific expenses paid for by the mine. The CAO says that it has invoiced the mine for "services performed to date," but refuses to disclose these invoices. The CAO says that its accounts will be disclosed in its next annual report for the fiscal year that ended in June, 2002. In the meantime, the issue of the extent and nature of the mine's patronage of the *mesa* remains open.

Project Underground has serious reservations about the integrity of a dialogue process that is heavily financed by the most powerful stakeholder. Although *Cajamarquinos* are accustomed to the ubiquitous financial leverage of the mine in all sectors of civil society, such leverage is outside international norms, and raises questions that should be fully considered by the CAO and *mesa* participants.

Benefits of Mesa de Diálogo

Despite the fundamental problems that have plagued the process, the affected community has realized some small, but important, benefits.

The CAO is overseeing an independent study of water contamination. The mine has for years denied that there are unsafe levels of contaminants in the water and that it bears responsibility for any "naturally occurring" contamination. The results of the water study will establish the causation of the poor water quality; however, even if it is shown that the mine is largely, or fully, responsible for the contamination, it is unclear what impact this will have – i.e. whether the mine will pay for clean-up, improve its pollution controls, and/or refrain from further expansion.

As a result of the *mesa*, the mine has agreed to make certain infrastructure improvements in the villages closest to the mine. For example, the mine has agreed to allow the public to use certain roads, and to provide villages with potable water. These are important concessions that will directly improve the quality of life of many affected people; however, they in no way address the ongoing damage to the environment and the campesinos' way of life.

CAO Overlooks IFC Misconduct

The CAO's oversight of the *mesa de diálogo* is the only action it has taken in response to the Rondas Campesinas' original complaint. Conveniently for the IFC, the CAO has entirely overlooked the numerous IFC and World Bank policy violations that are the core of the complaint. So completely has the CAO let the IFC off the hook that the IFC actually touts the *mesa* as an example of how it constructively addresses the impacts of its investment on the community.

The CAO office was established as a mechanism for IFC accountability to the communities affected by the projects it finances. The CAO's failure to address the IFC policy violations raises a fundamental question about the purpose of the CAO and its willingness to challenge IFC management.

Lack of Transparency and Independence

The CAO's Operational Guidelines state the CAO's commitment to the principle of transparency. In practice, however, very little is disclosed to the complainant. Even documents that are supposed to be disclosed are not. For example, the CAO has never disclosed to Project Underground or the Rondas its preliminary assessment of the complaint.* It is Project Underground's understanding that the assessment report was prepared, but held up for review by World Bank officials, and then never disclosed. The CAO has never proffered any explanation as to why it has not disclosed this report.

The Bank has no business reviewing, much less suppressing, the CAO's preliminary assessment of a complaint. The fact that it did so makes a mockery of the CAO's claim to independence and impartiality.

Moreover, without a preliminary assessment, the complainants have no idea what the CAO's broader view is of the complaint and its ability to resolve it. It is unclear whether the *mesa de diálogo* is the sum total of the CAO's efforts to resolve the complaint, or whether it is part of some larger plan. Without the preliminary assessment, the complainants also have no knowledge of the IFC's response to the complaint. Does the IFC admit or deny the allegations? Has the IFC provided the CAO with information that confirms, or refutes, the information set forth in the complaint? Without access to such information, the complainants have lost the ability to prosecute their complaint and, instead, must wait indefinitely for the CAO to reveal what, if any, next steps will be taken in the process.

As the CAO itself explains: "Although the CAO cannot force outside bodies to change their behavior or abandon existing practices, she or he can call on the leverage of the IFC and MIGA in urging parties to adopt recommendations."[2] In this case, the CAO has shown no inclination to hold the IFC accountable to its own safeguard polices, much less to leverage the IFC in urging Minera Yanacocha to adopt recommendations. Absent a preliminary assessment, it is unclear whether the CAO has plans to urge the IFC to take any action at all.

Conclusion: CAO Process as Corporate Engagement Exercise

Corporate engagement involves the construction of a space and a discourse which set the parameters of debate in a way that is favorable to the corporation; that is, that evades criticisms of fundamental substantive issues involved in the corporation's practices. As Bob Burton explains:

> "Engagement, as the mining industry uses the term, is about shifting the forum of debate away from open public spaces to smaller more private venues where social pressure can be subtly mobilised to moderate more critical views. It is about subtly shifting debates away from conflict between fundamental values to discussing the "common ground". It pursues a lowest common denominator approach that seeks to shift debate away from "should we mine uranium against Aboriginal wishes in a National Park" to "how would you like the uranium mine to operate".[3]

Burton draws much of his analysis from a speech given to the 1998 annual environmental workshop of the Minerals Council of Australia by the public relations consultant, Peter Sandman. Sandman, whose clients have included Rio Tinto, BHP Petroleum, Exxon and Shell, gave the following advice to the mining industry representatives present at the workshop:

> "The experience of breaking bread with company representatives, chatting with them before and after meetings encourages many CAP [Community Advisory Panel] members to feel that harsh criticism would be somehow rude. CAP members who don't respond this way are likely to feel some social pressure from their fellow members to conform or quit. [Thus], the embattled company has a great deal to gain from visible collaboration with activists."

The *mesa de diálogo* closely follows the corporate engagement model Sandman encourages, one that poses many risks, and few positive opportunities, for the affected community. What began as a spirited attempt to force the mine to meet the community's demands has been transformed into a static, drawn out, bureaucratic process premised on the notion that the interests of the community and the mine are one. Although it has established elaborate protocols designed to give the appearance of full and fair community participation, the CAO has in reality established a process in which the community's subordination to the mine is guaranteed.

The CAO team has fostered the notion that the *mesa de diálogo* is a substantive achievement, an end in, and of, itself rather than a means to an end. The fact that parties in conflict sit in one room and talk politely to each other is heralded as a substantive achievement, regardless of the content of the dialogue or its outcome.

The *mesa* is premised on the assumption that environmental protection and economic development are common ground for dialogue. This assumption glosses over the fundamental issue of whether the mine should continue to be the pillar of the *Cajamarquino* economy, and whether it has a social license to operate in Cajamarca at all. At no point during the *mesa* has there been a space in which to discuss the short and long term political, social and environmental implications of the mine's domination of the local economy. At no point during the *mesa* has there been any acknowledgement of the incompatibility of the mine with the campesino way of life or the promotion of sustainable development in the area. If these more fundamental themes were broached, issues such as mine expansion and duration and alternative models for economic and social development would be discussed. Instead, the discussion is limited to mitigation of the harmful effects caused by the mine and how the mine's development foundation will allocate its resources.

By stanching and ignoring criticism, redirecting the *mesa*'s focus away from substantive issues, allowing the mine to exploit the *mesa* as a public relations forum, failing to address the unequal participation of women and refusing to acknowledge the power imbalance between the mine and the affected community, the CAO has facilitated the mine's agenda of using a corporate engagement strategy to undermine community resistance. As long as the community and the mine are engaged in dialogue, however superficial, the community remains distracted and disinclined to engage in more confrontational tactics and is rendered a passive participant in a process effectively controlled by the mine.

The *mesa* simultaneously creates and circumscribes the space for public expression on all matters relating to the mine. A year ago, the mine was challenged by an active resistance movement that engaged in strikes, blockades, marches and rallies. Today, the mine boasts to its shareholders that it is engaged in a constructive dialogue process with its former opponents while the IFC touts the CAO process as an example of how it responsibly addresses the impacts of one of its extractive industry projects. The long term institutionalization of the mesa promises more of the same – community embroilment in a stagnant, self-limiting process that, at its best, encourages the mine to sprinkle a few flecks of gold dust on the community that lives under its shadow.

The challenges presented by the Rondas' complaint illuminate the fundamental incompatibility of poverty eradication and resource extraction. As the World Bank continues with its Extractive Industries Review, it should be mindful that the social conflicts caused by projects like Minera Yanacocha are, at their core, incapable of just resolution. The limited success of the CAO in resolving the Rondas' complaint is as much a function of the inherent destructiveness and unsustainability of the mining industry as it is a reflection of the CAO's institutional competence, autonomy and integrity.

Notes

*   "Once a Complaint is accepted, the cao will undertake a preliminary investigation in order to assess the Complaint and determine how it should be handled. The assessment should conclude with a decision whether or not to proceed and a clear outline of the course of action proposed. An assessment will normally be completed within 30 working days of the decision to accept the Complaint." (CAO Operational Guideline 3.3.1). "The CAO's decision at the conclusion of the assessment will specify the course of action to be adopted and the timetable to be followed in implementing it. A copy of the assessment will be provided to the complainant and other relevant parties On occasion the President [World Bank] may be informed at this stage." (CAO Operational Guideline 3.3.7).

1   A reference to the notorious Spanish conquistador.

2   *CAO Operational Guidelines*, IFC/MIGA.

3   Bob Burton, When Corporations Want to Cuddle, in Geoff Evans, James Goodman and Nina Lansbury (eds.), *Moving Mountains: Communities Confront Mining and Globalization*, Zed Books, London and New York, 2002, Chapter 7, pps.109-124.

CHAPTER 9

Bulyanhulu: Massacre or Deadly Error?

9.1 INTRODUCTION

Roger Moody

The Lawyers' Environmental Action Team (LEAT), a public interest environmental law organization based in Dar es Salaam, Tanzania, has been involved in research and advocacy work in relation to the mining industry in Tanzania since April 1999. In particular LEAT has been investigating allegations of serious human rights abuses at the Bulyanhulu Gold Mine, when the security forces of the Government of Tanzania and employees of Kahama Mining Corporation Limited (KMCL) moved in to acquire the area in late July and early August 1996. KMCL was then a wholly-owned subsidiary of Sutton Resources, based in Vancouver, British Columbia, Canada. Since March 1999, it has been a wholly-owned subsidiary of one of the world's biggest gold mining companies, Barrick Gold Corporation (BGC), headquartered in Toronto, Canada.

In this chapter, LEAT's human rights lawyer, *Tundu Lissu*, suggests a pattern of systematic and deliberate non-disclosure of material facts; distortion or misrepresentation of key information; peddling of outright falsehoods; and attempts to cover up serious allegations of human rights abuses or suppress independent investigations. He contends that Barrick Gold Corporation and its Tanzanian subsidiary KMCL are primarily responsible for perpetrating these acts or omissions.

Nonetheless, both the Multilateral Investment Guarantee Agency (MIGA), and the Canadian Export Development Corporation (EDC), provided the mine with vital political risk insurance, totally US$345 million – the largest guarantee for a single project in MIGA history, according to the World Bank. They did not investigate the accusations of human rights abuses (and forced evictions from customary land) which emerged from late 1996 onwards, although these had prompted the Tanzanian press and prominent NGO's (notably Amnesty International) to call for a full public investigation. To this date (February 2005) neither MIGA nor EDC have acknowledged their grave negligence in failing to carry out "due diligence" studies of their own.

The Bulyanhulu "massacre" may eventually prove to be a terrible miscalculation on the part of police, companies – perhaps even the small-scale miner themselves – rather than the concerted destruction of a group of defenceless workers. More likely the full truth will never emerge, especially as most of the forensic evidence must by now be lost or destroyed. But this should not detract from another key accusation made by Tundu Lissu: that the Bulyanhulu mine, though potentially highly lucrative for its owners, will not contribute significantly to Tanzanian government income, and certainly not to the sustainable livelihoods of its citizens.

What distinguishes Bulyanhulu from the other case studies in this book is the large presence of artisanal miners in the concession area. They had, it would appear, been earning a reasonable living before the evictions occurred. It is true that conditions for many such miners are often charaterised as chaotic, dangerous and unhealthy. Yet this need not be the case, as the World Bank has itself belatedly conceded. Instead of determining how these Tanzanian citizens could be assisted in organising cooperatives, to exploit the country's enviable precious metal resources, the Bank has indiscriminately backed overseas companies. The tragic events at Bulyanhulu may be exceptional, but they are not unique. And local resistance to foreign "invasion" is far from over.[1]

Note

1   See "Locals resist the foreign invasion", *Financial Times,* December 17 2001; also: "Tza's mining dilemma", in *African Business,* January 2002.

9.2 Bulyanhulu: Robbing the Poor to Give to the Rich

LEAT

Human Rights Abuses and Impoverishment at the Miga-backed Bulyanhulu Gold Mine, Tanzania*

1 Introduction

In August 1996 the Tanzanian government authorities, in collaboration with a Canadian-owned company called Kahama Mining Corporation Ltd. (KMCL), forcibly removed hundreds of thousands of artisanal miners, peasant farmers, small traders and their families, from an area called Bulyanhulu in Shinyanga Region, central-western Tanzania. The removals were the culmination of a two-year struggle pitting the miners against the company over the control of gold deposits at Bulyanhulu. Within days of the operation to remove the miners, serious allegations emerged that over 50 artisanal miners were killed, buried alive in mine shafts, when the authorities and company officials decided to backfill the shafts. KMCL was then a wholly-owned subsidiary of Sutton Resources, based in Vancouver, Canada.

The Bulyanhulu area is a collection of many villages and minor settlements. It is located approximately 127 kilometers southwest of the lakeside city of Mwanza and about 850 kilometers northwest of Dar es Salaam. It is 45 kilometers south of Lake Victoria and 42 kilometers by road from the railhead at Isaka to the south. Kakola town is the area's largest settlement within the 52 square kilometers license area that now forms part of the Bulyanhulu Gold Mine. As the most populous centre of the artisanal gold mining boom that began in Bulyanhulu in the 1970s, the town survived the destruction visited upon the area in July and August 1996. Eight of its satellite settlements and localities – Stamico, Kabale, Namba Tatu, Namba Mbili, Namba Tisa, Bariadi, Bushingwe and Mwabagikulu – were at that time razed to the ground.

---

* Submission to the Extractive Industries Review of the World Bank, Maputo, Mozambique, January 13-17 2003. Prepared by Tundu Lissu, on behalf of the Lawyers Environmental Action Team (LEAT), Tanzania.

In March 1999, Barrick Gold Corporation, a Canadian mining giant, acquired the Bulyanhulu deposits through its acquisition of Sutton Resources and its Tanzanian subsidiary. In August 2000, the World Bank's Multilateral Investment Guarantee Agency (MIGA) announced that it had issued a guarantee totaling $115.8 million to Société Générale S.A. as "an agent for a syndicate of international banks" for their non-shareholder loan investment to KMCL.[1] According to the announcement, a portion of MIGA's guarantee would be reinsured by private insurers, later identified as being Lloyd's of London and Munich Re of Germany. A few months later, MIGA's guarantee had risen to some $172 million, making it "the largest amount issued to date for a single contract," according to a World Bank press release.[2] Canada's Export Development Corporation (EDC) is co-insuring the project with MIGA, with a slightly higher exposure. The MIGA and EDC guarantees covers the investment against the risks of transfer restriction, expropriation, and war and civil disturbance.

Barrick Gold has since built an ultra-modern underground gold mine at Bulyanhulu, which was opened amid great fanfare by Tanzanian President, Benjamin W. Mkapa in July 2001. Though vehemently denied, the allegations of the 1996 killings have persisted to this day and have become the subject of a bitter international dispute involving the Bulyanhulu communities, NGOs and governments in Tanzania, Canada, the United States, Western Europe and in the World Bank Group. This submission argues that the Bulyanhulu Gold Mine is a prime example of all that is wrong with the World Bank Group's support of corporate mining investment in Africa and elsewhere in the world.

The investment stands as a monument to the plunder of the natural resources of poor countries. such as Tanzania, by the multinational corporations of the rich industrial countries of the North; and the impoverishment and further marginalization of the mostly rural communities in mineral rich areas of Tanzania and elsewhere. It is a living testimony of the proposition that where multinational corporate interests are at stake, notions of rule of law, good governance and a respect for human rights take on a secondary importance to be swept aside whenever expedient. It provides proof of the charge that the World Bank Group almost always acts against the interests of the vast majority of the poor and marginalised groups of society. The Group cannot, therefore, live up to its poverty alleviation credentials while at the same time maintaining support for socially ruinous projects such as Bulyanhulu Gold Mine. In the paragraphs that follow below we discuss these issues at some length.

2 Assault on Rule of Law and Good Governance

a The Artisanal Miners' Presence Was Legal, Sutton Resources/KMCL's Was Not!

Since 1980 the Bulyanhulu area – as indeed the entire Shinyanga Region – had been legally set aside by various ministers responsible for mining, as a designated area for the sole use and benefit of artisanal gold miners. Under section 69(1) of the Mining Act 1979, then in force, the minister responsible for mining was granted wide powers to designate areas, and prescribe minerals, for which Tanzanian citizens were to be given priority in the allocation of mining rights. The language of the provision was such as to leave no doubt that artisanal miners were envisaged as primary beneficiaries of these rights. It read: "Where the Minister considers that it would be in the public interest to encourage prospecting and mining for minerals in any area of land by methods not involving substantial expenditure or the use of specialist technology he may... designate that area and... prescribe any mineral in relation to the area."

The designation and prescription had to be done through a notice published in the Government Gazette. Almost immediately, this provision sparked considerable legislative activity regarding the rights of artisanal miners that would continue through the 1980s to the mid-1990s. The Act came into force on December 31 1979.[3] Less than three weeks later, then Minister for Water, Energy and Minerals, Al-Noor Kassum, exercised his powers under section 69 with the promulgation of the *Mining (Designated Areas) Notice, 1980*.[4] The Notice, among other things, designated the entire area of Shinyanga Region as one where prospecting and mining for gold "by methods not involving substantial expenditure or the use of specialist technology" was to be undertaken. This was the earliest and clearest legal basis for the artisanal miners' presence and operations in the Bulyanhulu goldfields.

The 1980 Notice did not, however, survive the next cabinet reshuffle that brought in Jackson Makweta as Minister for Minerals in 1982. The reshuffle coincided with the first signs of corporate interest in the Bulyanhulu gold deposits. In November 1982, the Finnish-Tanzanian consortium of Outukumpu Oy, Kone Engineering, and STAMICO was allocated a prospecting license over the Bulyanhulu area.[5] Consequently, Minister Makweta revoked the 1980 Notice replacing it with another, whose major significance lies in the fact that it removed Shinyanga Region from the list of designated areas.[6]

In late 1983, with the end of minister Makweta's tenure at the Ministry of Minerals, his replacement, Paul Bomani, promulgated yet another Notice, which brought Shinyanga Region back into the fold of designated areas[7] and Bulyanhulu back to its former status as a site for artisanal gold mining. It would remain so until the 1979 Act was replaced by the new Mining Act 1998. In between there were three other Section 69 Notices, with the last one promulgated by Dr. William Shija just two months before the Bulyanhulu upheavals brought on by Dr. Shija's order for the artisanal miners to vacate the area in late July 1996.[8] Moreover, none of these Notices in any way affected the legal status of the Bulyanhulu area as a preserve for artisanal gold miners.

This legislative history is critically important. Throughout the period preceding the 1996 removals – and since – Tanzanian government authorities maintained that the Bulyanhulu artisanal miners were operating in the area contrary to the country's laws. Sutton Resources/KMCL and the Canadian diplomats also maintained that the artisanals were nothing but squatters and trespassers illegally occupying and mining the Bulyanhulu deposits. Similar positions have been taken by MIGA and the World Bank Group as a whole and by Barrick Gold/KMCL, since its takeover of the Bulyanhulu Mine. From July 2001, when LEAT commenced the current campaign to have the removals and alleged killings thoroughly, independently and transparently investigated, these interests have repeated the same distortions.

b The Presidential Imprimatur

For the Bulyanhulu artisanal miners, the most important seal of approval came, not necessarily from legal texts on pieces of paper, but from the political establishment. Since April 1990, the government of then President Ali Hassan Mwinyi and the ruling CCM party had endorsed the artisanal miners' operations throughout the country. Not long afterwards, Bulyanhulu – by now the centre of the artisanal mining boom in the country – played host to President Mwinyi when the latter visited Kahama District on February 19 1993. Mzee Zephania Luzama, then Vice Chair of the Shinyanga Regional Miners Association (SHIREMA) and a prominent member of the Bulyanhulu Small-scale Miners' Committee, personally welcomed the President on behalf of the Bulyanhulu miners' community. In a series of interviews with this author, he vividly remembered the President's visit: "When President Mwinyi came to dedicate the Ward office building at Lunguya, I personally shook the President's hand and presented (First Lady) Mama Sitti Mwinyi with a cow. We then told him that we still had problems with the police who were still stationed at Bulyanhulu and were harassing us. The President turned on the Kahama District Commissioner, Edson Halinga, and told him: 'Governor, make sure all the policemen are removed from the mining area and the miners are free to operate in any area of Bulyanhulu and that they sell their gold to the government.'"9

That the Bulyanhulu artisanal miners were allowed to operate in the area by the President was also acknowledged, if grudgingly, by Barrick Gold/ KMCL and the Canadian diplomats based in Tanzania. In project documents submitted to MIGA, the Government of Tanzania, Canada's EDC, and Barrick Gold/KMCL assert that the discovery of the Bulyanhulu gold deposits in 1975 "attracted some small scale artisanal miners to the site". However, following a visit to the site by then President Ali Hassan Mwinyi in February 1993, "artisanal miners requested the right to resume artisanal mining in Bulyanhulu, which permission was granted by the President".

These legislative and political developments make it crystal clear that, with the exception of the period December 18 1982 to October 12 1983 when Shinyanga Region was removed from the list of designated areas, the artisanal miners operated at Bulyanhulu in accordance with the laws of Tanzania. Moreover, with the exception of that brief period, any allocation of prospecting or mining rights by methods "...involving substantial expenditure or the use of specialist technology" in the area would clearly have been illegal. This, we argue, would have been the case had Sutton Resources/KMCL been granted any prospecting or mining rights in the area. [However] the company never was allocated any such rights.

c Sutton Resources/KMCL Was Never Allocated Any Rights in Bulyanhulu
Section 31 of the Mining Act 1979 had required that any allocation of a mining concession must first properly describe the area in respect of which the allocation was made. On August 5th, 1994, the Government of Tanzania entered into an agreement with Sutton Resources/KMCL. Although a press release issued by the Ministry of Water, Energy and Minerals stated that that agreement was "...with regard to gold deposits in Bulyanhulu area Kahama District", the prospecting licence issued to Sutton Resources/KMCL, and signed by the then Minister for Water, Energy and Minerals, Hon. Jakaya Kikwete, described the area as "...Butobela Area, Geita District.".. That licence – known as PL #216 of 1994 – does not even mention the Bulyanhulu area.

Sutton Resources/KMCL's prospecting licence was twice renewed by the current Commissioner for Minerals, Mr. Gray Mwakalukwa, on July 24 1997 and again on October 6 1998. These two subsequent renewals also described the licence area as Butobela Area in Geita District. In addition, a 1996 Ministry of Energy and Minerals list of all prospecting licences granted to various mining companies, between the years 1993 to 1996, shows that the licence granted Sutton Resources/KMCL was in respect of Butobela Area, Geita District. That list is also important because it shows that no other licence was ever issued to Sutton Resources/KMCL during the period in question.

So, on the basis of available evidence, and in the absence of any evidence to the contrary, Sutton Resources/KMCL had no right whatsoever to claim ownership and access to the mineral rights of Bulyanhulu. Its presence, from 1994 through the 1996 forced evictions, to the 1999 takeover by Barrick Gold was, therefore, utterly illegal. It follows that any interest that Barrick Gold may have acquired with regard to the Bulyanhulu area was also illegal. That includes its current licence to operate the mine, since it is based on Sutton Resources/KMCL's prospecting licence.

d Illegal Entry Into and Occupation of the Bulyanhulu Area
Even assuming that Sutton Resource/KMCL had a licence over Bulyanhulu area, Section 48 of the Mining Act 1979, then in force, had required owners of prospecting or mining licences to obtain a prior written consent from the landholders in areas over which the licences were issued. This, they did not do. Instead, in late July and early August 1996, and assisted by the security forces of the Government of Tanzania, the company illegally and forcibly evicted, or caused to be forcibly evicted, hundreds of thousands of artisanal miners, peasants farmers and other property owners, old men, women and children.

e Violation of Property Rights of the Bulyanhulu Villagers
The Bulyanhulu lands were held under the customary rights of occupancy that are not only legally recognized but also protected as "property" under the Tanzanian land law and the country's Constitution (Article 24). Indeed, under section 81 of the Mining Act 1979, then in force, Sutton Resources/ KMCL was liable to pay "fair and reasonable" compensation to the Bulyanhulu land owners upon taking control of the Bulyanhulu area. We now know from the former executives of Sutton Resources, that the company's Board of Directors refused to approve the compensation package that former Sutton chairman, James Sinclair, had proposed for the Bulyanhulu artisanal miners, peasant farmers and other property holders.[10] This, too, was in violation of the Tanzania's laws and the country's Constitution.

f Violation and Disregard of the Decisions of Tanzanian Courts
In spite of the company's lack of any right with regard to the Bulyanhulu deposits, on June 20 1995 Sutton Resources/KMCL instituted legal proceedings against representatives of the Bulyanhulu artisanal miners in the High

Court of Tanzania at Tabora. The company requested the High Court to issue eviction orders against the miners. In their defence the miners objected to being removed without due process and without compensation. On September 29 1995, the High Court agreed with the miners' that the proceedings involved matters of constitutional rights that could only be decided by a special three-judge panel of the High Court. It therefore issued an order of temporary injunction, prohibiting Sutton Resources/KMCL from interfering with the miners' rights until the special panel had been constituted to decide on the merits of the case.

Regardless of that lawful order of the High Court, on July 30 1996 Sutton Resources/KMCL, with the assistance of the security forces of the Government of Tanzania, commenced the illegal and forcible evictions of the Bulyanhulu people. This was the first instance of the violation of the orders. With the illegal evictions in full swing, the representatives of the artisanal miners rushed to the High Court, asking it to intervene as a matter of urgency. And so, on August 2 1996, the High Court issued yet another order, this time prohibiting Sutton Resources/KMCL and the Attorney General, as the representative of the Government of Tanzania, from proceeding with the illegal evictions.

There is ample eye-witness testimony to the effect that the Government, and company's officials supervising the evictions, ignored the High Court court and proceeded with the illegal evictions. Newspapers of the period have also quoted Lt. Gen. Tumainiel Kiwelu, who supervised the evictions, as saying that he was not an employee of the High Court and therefore could not be bound by the Court's orders. There is, in addition, documentary evidence, in the form of internal correspondence between Sutton Resources/ KMCL executives, suggesting that the decision to ignore the High Court order was reached deliberately and not in the heat of the moment.

That evidence also suggests that the decision was reached at the highest levels of the Tanzanian Government and the police force. For instance, in a July 1997 memo to her superiors at the Department of Foreign Affairs and International Trade (DFAIT) in Ottawa, the then-Canadian High Commissioner to Tanzania, Ms. Verona Edelstein (herself a powerful behind-the-scenes force for the evictions of the Bulyanhulu miners), intimated that the evictions and subsequent filling of the mining shafts were carried out "by Sutton Resources of Vancouver under the supervision of the Shinyanga Regional Commissioner (under the direction of President Mkapa)...".

Only four days after the High Court order was issued, in a memo of August 6 1996 to the Company's President, Michael Kenyon and the chairman, Roman Shklanka, Sutton Resources/KMCL's Exploration Manager at Bulyanhulu, Jim Hylands, said that the Shinyanga Regional Police Commander was told that his orders to continue with the evictions came from the Attorney General, the Inspector General of Police (IGP), and the Shinyanga Regional Commissioner, as well as from the Director (of Criminal Investigation) of the Police Force, Mr. Kauga. According to Hylands' memo these orders "had not been changed", even after the High Court ordered the evictions be stopped. Indeed, the memo makes clear that "the IGP told 'our' RPC (Shinyanga Regional Police Commander, David Mnubi) that the police ...are to remove the miners by whatever means required; and... that there is to be no more discussion of this operation – he had his orders to carry them out – and ignore any orders he hears from the High Court." Thus the police were to remove the miners by "whatever means required", paying no heed to the decisions of the High Court.

Contemptuous disregard of the Tanzanian courts and the rule of law continued even after the evictions were effected in 1996, and became even more noticeable once Barrick Gold Corporation took over and began building the current mine. Records of the High Court of Tanzania show that, in August 1998, sixteen villagers – described in the court record as "peasants engaged in subsistence farming and cattle rearing in Kakola village, Bulyanhulu area in Kahama District" – filed a law suit in the High Court. The villagers alleged that KMCL had "decided to evict the plaintiffs from their village and grazing lands covering some 10,000 acres." The villagers complained that the company wanted to dump tailings waste in their village "which is a violation of their right to health and unpolluted environment". The same month, three villagers commenced a similar suit in the same Court on behalf of 41 other families. This complained that KMCL had grossly underpaid the complainants (an average of less than $100 per family) as compensation for all their property, including houses, agricultural crops, and as a disturbance allowance, before they were evicted. According to documents submitted by Barrick Gold/KMCL, the total compensation paid by the company amounted to slightly over $4,000.

On June 29 1998, the High Court dismissed the two cases on the grounds that it lacked jurisdiction since they raised questions of constitutional rights and freedoms. Aggrieved by this decision, the villagers appealed to the Court of Appeal of Tanzania, the country's highest court, with hearings set for May 22, June 30, November 27, and December 14 2000. However, ten days before the start of the hearings in the Court of Appeal, at the behest of Barrick Gold/KMCL – now in control of KMCL – the then-Kahama District Commissioner, Ms. Hawa Mchopa, issued a 12-hour notice requiring the villagers to vacate their settlements and farmlands. The following morning, on May 13 2000, armed police, district officials, and employees of Barrick Gold/KMCL, descended on the village, razing their houses to the ground and destroying boreholes and food crops. The villagers were then loaded into vehicles supplied by the company, and driven some miles away to be dumped in the bushes without shelter. They remain there to this day. This, too, was illegal and amounted to contemptuous disregard of due process.

3 Serious Human Rights Abuses

a Allegations of Killings

Since August 1996, the Bulyanhulu Gold Mine has faced persistent allegations of mass killings and wrongdoing that occurred in the cause of the evictions. Contemporary press reports indicate that about 52 artisanal miners were allegedly killed after being trapped in mine shafts, after Sutton Resources/KMCL and government officials decided to fill them in, beginning on August 7. Other reports indicate that about 10 other persons were killed in various localities of the Bulyanhulu area. LEAT's own investigations have established the following:

i   We have been able to compile a list of 54 persons, alleged to have died because of the 1996 evictions. The list was compiled from sworn testimony of eyewitnesses and the families of the dead miners, from newspapers reports, and from a report of the investigations carried out by the United Democratic Party, an opposition party, between November 1996 and January 1997.

ii   We have obtained pictorial evidence that there were numerous deaths in Bulyanhulu. We have obtained the sworn statements of the persons who took the evidence or directed it be taken; and these persons have vouched for its veracity.

iii We have obtained previously undisclosed videotapes taken by police investigators as well as KMCL officials. The videotapes also prove without doubt that previously undisclosed deaths occurred in the course of, or in connection with, the 1996 evictions and subsequent filling of the mine shafts. We have obtained sworn testimony of the persons who participated in rescue and/or recovery operations, including the recovery of dead bodies in some of the mine shafts, depicted in the videotapes; and these persons have testified to the veracity of the events depicted.

iv We have obtained 25 sworn testimonies/affidavits of eyewitnesses, family members of the victims, and survivors, regarding the allegations of the killings. In addition, we have written and audio or video-taped numerous other witness statement. Efforts to have these witnesses swear their testimony on oath have been hampered by police threats and intimidation, as well as repression against our members. These efforts nevertheless continue to this day.

v We have obtained hundreds of previously undisclosed documents, in the form of Government reports, official correspondence and Court records, Sutton Resources/KMCL and Barrick Gold/KMCL records, internal memoranda, and declassified documents of the Canadian Government and its diplomatic mission in Tanzania, and the World Bank Group. This documentary evidence offers ample proof of the matters averred in this submission.

b Allegations Were Not Properly Investigated

The governments of Tanzania and Canada, the companies involved, and now the World Bank Group, have vehemently denied that there were any deaths during the removals, which they have termed entirely peaceful and orderly. However, under pressure to respond to the revelations made by LEAT, the government of Tanzania has recently admitted that there were indeed some deaths during the removals. Thus, for example, a press statement released by the Minister for Home Affairs, Hon. Mohamed Seif Khatib, on September 17 2001, states that about 11 people died in the course of the evictions – although Minister Khatib attributed these deaths to mob justice or natural causes. Moreover, there is ample evidence that the allegations have never been seriously investigated in accordance with the laws of Tanzania, or in accordance with internationally accepted norms and standards for investigation of allegations of this nature.

i Under the Inquest Act 1980, the 11 deaths that the Minister for Home Affairs now admits to have occurred at Bulyanhulu should have been the subject of an official inquest in the Coroner's Court, to determine the manner and the cause of the deaths and whether any criminal acts were involved. This was never done. The Minister's statement is, therefore, based on no evidence whatever. This is especially important given sworn testimonies from eye-witnesses that the deaths were caused by police violence.

ii Under the same Act, the Minister responsible for legal affairs was obliged, upon receipt of information or reports of the allegations of the deaths of this many people, to constitute a Coroner's Court to investigate that information or those allegations. That, too, was never done, even though press reports even named the dead persons and published photographs of the dead bodies.

iii The United Nations Principles on Effective Prevention and Investigation of Extra-legal, Arbitrary and Summary Executions, recommended by the United Nations Economic and Social Council Resolution No. 1989/65 of May 24 1989, require UN member states to carry out "thorough, prompt and impartial investigation of all suspected cases of extra-legal, arbitrary and summary executions, including cases where complaints by relatives and all other reliable reports suggest unnatural deaths in the above circumstances". In addition, the principles require governments to "pursue investigations through an independent commission of inquiry or similar procedures", in cases where "the established investigative procedures are inadequate because of lack of... impartiality, because of the importance of the matter or because of the apparent presence of a pattern of abuse, and in cases where there are complaints from the families of the victim(s) about these inadequacies or any substantial reasons." With regard to the Bulyanhulu allegations, since August 1996 there have been persistent calls for the formation of an independent commission of inquiry, by the families of the dead miners, from political parties, from prominent individuals, and from local and international civil society organizations. To this day no such independent commission of inquiry has been established. On the contrary, the Government of Tanzania has not only rejected such calls but also targeted local individuals and organizations making those calls, with particularly harsh and repressive measures intended to intimidate and silence them.

We are aware of claims by the Government of Tanzania, Barrick Gold Corp, and now the World Bank Group, that these allegations were thoroughly investigated and found to be mere fabrications. Such claims are devoid of any merit for the following reasons:

i The investigations were carried out by institutions whose impartiality was anything but guaranteed. Since the Tanzanian police force was itself implicated in the allegations of the killings, its investigations and conclusions have to be treated with extreme caution and scepticism. Equally dubious are the results of any investigation that may have been carried out by the World Bank Group, or Barrick Gold Corporation or its affiliates, on account of their multi-million dollar financial interest in the Bulyanhulu mine. Indeed, a recent report, by the Compliance Advisor/ Ombudsman (CAO) for MIGA and the International Finance Corporation (IFC) has concluded that neither IFC – which had originally shown interest in funding the construction of the Bulyanhulu Gold Miner – nor MIGA, which ultimately provided millions of dollars in political risk insurance

(PRI), carried out any due diligence investigation prior to awarding the
PRI. How, then, can their pronouncements on much more complicated
human rights investigations be taken seriously?

ii The police, and the institutions that claim to have investigated the allegations of deaths, never interviewed any of the families of the dead miners.
The police refused to order the digging-up or exhumation of the pits in
which dozens of the miners were allegedly buried. There were – and still
are – credible allegations, unanswered to this day, that the police prevented
rescue and recovery operations, even where the rescuers had located the
trapped miners, some of whom were still alive.

iii There is considerable evidence that suggests police cover-up of serious
criminal wrongdoing during the evictions and subsequent filling of the
shafts. For instance, the police and senior government officials were presented with pictorial evidence of some 13 dead miners, allegedly killed
during the evictions. Furthermore, recently-obtained police and company
video tapes, show the police, company and government officials, viewing
dead bodies, some of which were recovered from mine shafts. However,
none of this evidence, nor the existence of the video tapes, was made public until very recently, when these facts were revealed by LEAT. As recently
as December 2001, senior police officers from Police Headquarters were
alleged to have tried to threaten or bribe the families of the victims to
recant their testimonies. When this failed, they resorted to bribing impos-
tors who have posed before the mass media as the alleged dead miners.

iv None of the institutions that claim to have thoroughly investigated the
allegations of killings have ever issued a public report of their investigations. In any case those investigations were contrary to the substantive and procedural laws governing investigations pertaining to sudden
or unnatural deaths (as referred to above). Therefore, the claims of these
institutions are hardly worthy of serious consideration.

c The CAO Investigation

In late August 2001, LEAT approached the CAO with a view to lodging a complaint against MIGA's support of the Bulyanhulu Gold Mine. LEAT wanted
the CAO to investigate the widespread allegations of human rights abuses,
including the alleged killings, as well as other breaches of MIGA social and
environmental safeguard policies, due diligence procedures, and provisions
of the MIGA Convention. However, the CAO made it very clear that the issue
of the killings was outside its mandate. An independent investigation of the
allegations of killings has been, and remains, one of LEAT's and the Bulyanhulu community's key demands. It therefore took months of agonised dis-

cussions, and wide-ranging consultations with community representatives and our international counterparts, before ultimately deciding to drop the allegations of killings, in order to present a complaint to the CAO.

The complaint was finally lodged on January 15 2002. It did not contain a single reference to the allegations of killings. In late March 2002 a CAO investigative team visited Tanzania to commence its investigation of the complaint. In public meetings with hundreds of Bulyanhulu villagers and affected persons, the team also insisted that it was not in Bulyanhulu to investigate the allegations of killings, in response to the villagers' testimonies that almost invariably touched on them. As result of the CAO's insistence, and believing in good faith that the CAO would not deal with the allegations of killings, neither LEAT nor the affected persons submitted the evidence that we have submitted to this gathering.

The CAO appears to have had other ideas. After months of waiting, it finally produced what was described as an "assessment report summary" of the investigations. The sole reason given for not producing a full report was "the confidentiality of... sources of information and substantiation"! Consequently, the report does not provide a single piece of evidence to support its various conclusions. However – in what can only be described as bad faith and lack of integrity and independence on the part of the CAO – it did introduce the issue of the alleged killings, despite expressly forbidding LEAT and the Bulyanhulu-affected persons from raising and submitting evidence on them. Worse still, the CAO abused our faith by concluding that we had failed to produce any evidence on the allegations. The report even concocted fictitious "facts" to back up its dubious conclusions. For example, whereas the complaint did not make any reference to the killings, the CAO asserted that the complaint "repeats allegations regarding events of late July and early August 1996 that include misconduct and murder made against government authorities and the mine". (p. 4). More specifically, "LEAT alleges that the manner in which the land was cleared on July 30 and following days resulted in 52 unnamed individuals being buried alive in the pits that they worked". (p. 5). And, at page 7, we find the following: "The complaint alleges that 52 people were killed in the process of land clearance, trapped alive in their pits by the mine and local administration staff as they plugged and filled the mine shafts...."

The CAO also mischaracterised LEAT evidence. Whereas, for example, the complaint had introduced videotapes as evidence "of the eviction of the Bulyanhulu complainants and the destruction of their settlements and immovable property," the CAO claims that: "LEAT asserts that it has new evidence, namely a video which, it states, is a contemporaneous record of bodies being exhumed from small scale miners' pits." Having created this straw man, the CAO proceeds to set him on fire: "The CAO cannot be sure that the video shows that which LEAT maintains it shows. The location, date, timing and detail cannot be verified. Therefore, it is not clear that the video shows small scale miners suffocated as a result of the clearing of the land in the days following the July 30 announcement. Further, the CAO found witnesses and other contemporaneous documentation that would refute the version of events that LEAT contends the video supports. During the field mission to Bulyanhulu small scale miners, introduced to the CAO team who knew of the video, were sure of the location where the events were filmed and took the CAO to the spot. However, they could not be sure that the miners shown being dragged from mine shafts had been killed as a result of that land clearance and were unable to support the version of events that LEAT alleged the video revealed."

Not content with misrepresentation of the contents of the complaint, the CAO invents non-existent facts. For instance, we read that "the CAO has asked for a list of the names of the 52 people who were killed in the first days of August 1996 as stated in the complaint. Neither LEAT, nor the [Small Scale Miners' Committee] have been able to supply the list of names.... The CAO is left to reflect that, if a list cannot be produced by local people, the local administration, or the Small Scale Miners' Committee, that is the complainant in this case, this casts doubt on the veracity of the allegations that these people died as a result of the filling in of mine shafts in early August 1996." Yet LEAT had already given the list to the CAO as supporting documentation in compliance with the Operational Guidelines for submitting complaints. There is, in fact, not a single shred of evidence to support the claim that the CAO ever asked for the list. Indeed, the relevant passages in the CAO summary report are similar in major respects to arguments raised by both MIGA and Barrick Gold/KMCL in their correspondence with LEAT and others, thus suggesting that the CAO plagiarised from these two sources.

On December 2 2002 LEAT wrote to the CAO requesting it to retract these and other statements and conclusions, which we deemed "outside the scope of the investigation, and... inaccurate, misleading and unfair". We professed our belief that it would not serve the concerned parties' interests, if the CAO's legacy in the Bulyanhulu matter were to be "poisoned by the inaccuracies, factual errors, unsupported claims and unsubstantiated conclusions" that had unfortunately characterised its summary report. Rather than respond to this reasonable request, the CAO has sought to justify its conclusions by arguing that, since the issue of the killings was the focus of the press and the international NGO community in contact with LEAT, "silence by the CAO ... would have been misinterpreted".

The issue is not that the CAO should have remained silent in the face of overwhelming demands for its comment. On the contrary, the CAO could – and should – have invited all those making the allegations of killings to submit their evidence on the subject. Rather than do this, the CAO did the opposite. It not only discouraged the complainants from raising the subject, thereby preventing them offering any evidence, but also made deliberately false statements and attributed them to the complainants. Rather than making amends when challenged and presented with the facts, the CAO fudged and feigned wounded innocence. This is indicative of bad faith and lack of integrity on the part of the CAO. For these reasons we submit that the conclusions by the CAO regarding the allegations of killings should not be taken as definitive findings of fact.

That MIGA should have supported this project at all is indicative of its utter insensitivity to the rights and interests of the poor and the marginalized communities. It is indicative of its callous disregard for legality and good governance, not only in poor countries such as Tanzania, but also in fulfilling its own mandate. This is all the more so since Article 12(d) of the MIGA Convention requires that, in guaranteeing an investment, MIGA shall satisfy itself as to the "compliance of the investment with the host country's laws and regulations".

4 Undermining the National Economy

a An Economic White Elephant
The Bulyanhulu Gold Mine is not only an affront to rule of law, good governance and internationally-accepted human rights norms, that we have analyzed above, it is also an economic white elephant with little, if any, benefits for the local communities and for the national economy. To understand this we must first paraphrase our submission with a discussion of the role that artisanal mining – now shrinking under the pressure of the Bank-supported penetration by foreign investors – has played in Tanzanian economic life.

The mining sector in Tanzania has historically been dominated by artisanal miners. Their operations are entirely self-financed, using simple techniques and tools. Artisanal mining is particularly labor intensive. It thus provides employment and incomes to large numbers of people who are generally uneducated, poor, and live in remote areas where no opportunities exist for formal employment.

Artisanal mining began to take off in a substantial way in the early 1970s, when the Bulyanhulu gold deposits were discovered. The deep economic crisis of the 1980s drove many poor and unemployed people into artisanal mining. However, it was government policies during this period that provided the biggest boost to artisanal mining. From the early 1980s, as we have seen, the Government of Tanzania not only recognized artisanal mining but began to earmark large areas of the country for such operations. It also began to encourage foreign suppliers of mining equipment to do business with artisanal miners. No wonder therefore that, when Sutton Resources/KMCL began its legal proceedings against the artisanal miners of Bulyanhulu in 1995, it also sued two Canadian-owned companies, and one of the companies' Canadian directors, for supplying mining equipment to the Bulyanhulu artisanal miners.

In April 1990, when then-President Mwinyi declared that artisanal miners were free to operate all over country, the modern gold boom in Tanzania began in earnest. The artisanal population in the country soared. Various studies estimate that, at its height in the mid-1990s, artisanal mining was directly employing between 500,000 and 900,000 people (Chachage, 1995a; Chachage, 1995b; Phillips et al, 2001; MMSD Southern Africa, 2002).

In addition secondary economic activities associated with the mining generated an estimated three jobs for every single person directly employed in mining. According to the most recent of these studies,[11] the sector accounted for about 46 per cent of the total middle-income jobs in 1995. The basic income in mining towns was around six times higher than rural men could earn doing farm labour. "Moreover", the researchers observed, "the money coming from artisanal mining appears to be staying local, greatly enhancing cash flow in isolated rural areas". And, while "splurging" after a rich find is commonplace, "not all of the income is going into the proverbial 'wine women and song.' Miners are building up capital to move up into a career ladder into brokering and dealing. Some are investing in more stable business such as shops, restaurants and guesthouses." The researchers' conclusion was unequivocal: "No other sector or other job-creation programme has injected dispersed incomes into the rural areas, stimulated cash flow, and reduced rural poverty on such a scale."

b Destruction of People's Livelihoods and Impoverishment of Communities
Bulyanhulu was the jewel in the crown of the artisanal gold boom in Tanzania. It was by far the richest gold deposit in the country, and maybe in Africa outside South Africa and Ghana. It is for this reason that the Bulyanhulu gold deposits attracted hundreds of thousands of people. According to proj-

ect documents submitted by Barrick Gold/KMCL to MIGA, the Government of Tanzania, and Canada's Export Development Corporation, the discovery of the Bulyanhulu gold deposits in 1975 "attracted some small scale artisanal miners to the site," However, following a visit to the site by then-President Ali Hassan Mwinyi in February 1993, "artisanal miners requested the right to resume artisanal mining in Bulyanhulu, [which] permission was granted by the President". As a result, according to these documents, that same year there was "a massive influx in which some 30,000 to 400,000 artisanal miners, associated entrepreneurs and 'opportunists' arrived".[12] Elsewhere in these documents, Barrick Gold/KMCL has repeated the same figures, stating that, although no records were kept of the number of artisanal miners, "estimates range from 30,000 to 400,000".[13]

High estimates of the Bulyanhulu population during this period find broad support in other estimates, both before and after the events of August 1996. For example, just before the removals were ordered in July 1996, the late Bhiku Mohamed Salehe, then-Member of Parliament for Bulyanhulu and the outlying areas, told a session of the Tanzanian Parliament in Dodoma that about 200,000 artisanal miners, peasant farmers and their families were threatened with evictions.[14] Two years earlier, the then-District Commissioner for Kahama had protested the apparent granting of prospecting rights over the Bulyanhulu deposits to the Canadian company [in a submission to] then Minister for Water, Energy and Minerals, Jakaya Kikwete. In the District Commissioner's opinion, the grant would result in the eviction of over three hundred thousand people from the area who were "earning a living as well as contributing to the national economy".[15]

The police force that was a major participant in the evictions has likewise provided high estimates of the people who were removed that fateful August. Following the event, the Inspector General of Police issued a press release denying the allegations of killings, but admitting that about 200,000 Bulyanhulu residents had been removed from the area in the course of about one week.[16] Extant press reports, breaking news of the killings, also estimated the artisanal population, just dispersed, at between 200,000 and 300,000.[17] These statistics make the Bulyanhulu evictions by far the biggest involuntary population displacement in peacetime Tanzania since *Operesheni Vijiji*.[18]

Barrick Gold has come to realise the historical significance of these numbers. No wonder the company does not want critics to make any reference to its own project documents. It now accuses civil society organizations, which refer to these documents, of "misleading people into thinking that the number of people who... were evicted from the [Bulyanhulu] concession was 200,000". Without expressly disowning its project documents, the company now claims that unspecified "contemporaneous documents" show "there were fewer than approximately 15,000 people on the site at the time of the events in question".[19] Jumping into the fray, perhaps to help Barrick Gold/KMCL out of the fix created by the company's own statistics, the CAO has speculated that the number of those evicted is even lower, ranging between 200 and 2000!

Whatever the correct figure, the socio-economic impacts of the removals could not be hidden. In a surprisingly frank examination of these impacts, Barrick Gold/KMCL has candidly admitted that, whereas "...it is believed that before the closure of small-scale mines, the average income in the... area was the highest in the Shinyanga region...", this has "fallen since the closure of small-scale mining". In addition "the closure of small-scale mining had a major negative effect on economic activity, population and social development, which has been felt beyond the immediate mining area".

Elsewhere in its documents, Barrick Gold/KMCL has drawn similar conclusions about the socio-economic conditions subsequent to the evictions: "The closure of illegal small-scale mining activities and related works at Bulyanhulu had an extensive impact on the socio-economic aspects of local people's lives. The mine was a source of income to a majority of people ...and made life different for many. [These] economic [activities] stopped after the closure."[20] Yet another report makes the conclusion that, "after cessation of artisanal mining at Bulyanhulu in August 1996, the income of the majority of people declined significantly, the populations in Kakola and other villages in the Ward of Bugarama decreased, and services either decreased or disappeared."[21]

c Minimal Government Revenue

Regarding its contribution to government revenue, there is ample evidence that the Bulyanhulu Gold Mine will contribute only marginally to government revenue. Whereas mineral production has risen and will continue to rise, as have foreign exchange earnings from gold exports, government revenue may indeed have fallen in both relative and absolute terms. For example, whereas – according to MIGA – the Tanzanian Government will receive US$75 million in taxes, royalties and other charges during the estimated 15-year life span of the mine,[22] Barrick Gold paid 500 million Canadian dollars (US$280 million) to acquire the Bulyanhulu area from Sutton Resources in 1999. The latter company, as we have shown, itself acquired Bulyanhulu for free, never paying a penny to the thousands of artisanal miners and other property owners whose property it took by force of arms. Barrick Gold has itself stated on numerous occasions that it expects to rake-in upwards of US$3 billion in revenue during the lifetime of the Bulyanhulu Gold Mine. These figures seem to vindicate former Canadian High Commissioner Edelstein's statement, in a July 1997 memo, that "the Bulyanhulu mine... will be very profitable for the Canadian company/stockholders".

By comparison, statistics from the Ministry of Water, Energy and Minerals show that government revenue was much higher at the height of the artisanal gold boom in the early 1990s, brought on by the government's policy shift in 1990. For example, whereas in 1989 gold accounted for slightly over $1 million, or about six per cent of the total mineral exports, in April 1990 gold exports rose to about $14 million, or about 52 per cent of total mineral exports. By 1991, gold exports had risen to over $29 million, or nearly 66 per cent of the total; in 1992 gold fetched over $40 million, over three quarters of the total. (Tanzania, 1993; Chachage, 1995a; Chachage, 1995b). That is to say, within a period of hardly three years the official gold exports had increased nearly forty times![23]

Other independent observers have, in fact, given even higher figures for Tanzania's foreign exchange earnings from gold exports during the same period. For example, in its most recent survey of Sub-Saharan Africa, the Taylor and Francis Group of Great Britain, publishers of the annual *Regional Surveys of the World*, assert that official gold exports earned $26.25 million in 1990. Exports rose sharply in early 1991, as reforms to the official buying mechanism began to take effect, with a value of $35 million in 1991, $44.3 million in 1992 and $55 million in 1993.[24]

As the contribution of artisanal miners to the national economy continued to grow, so did official recognition of the sector and its chief players – the artisanal miners. Thus, the ruling Chama cha Mapinduzi (CCM) party promised in its program for the 1990s that "small-scale miners shall be encouraged and supported with proper tools and markets for their products. ... Furthermore, steps that have already been taken to enable the small-scale miners to sell gold and diamonds to the central bank shall be maintained, for their benefits to the nation have become much clearer."[25]

CCM would acknowledge this fact again in 1998 hen it concluded in a critical self-assessment that the growth of the mining sector in the early 1990s "came about as a result of the Government's... decision, through the Bank of Tanzania and its agents – the National Bank of Commerce and the Cooperative (and Rural Development) Bank – to start buying precious minerals from small-scale miners in April 1990."[26]

d *The Lie About Job Creation*

MIGA has sought to justify its subsidy to Barrick Gold/KMCL's Bulyanhulu venture by arguing that the guarantee "taps the potential of the underdeveloped mining sector, helping Tanzania to diversify its economy and offering solid developmental benefits for the country's 33 million residents". These "developmental benefits" are allegedly also in the form of jobs. MIGA had estimated that Barrick Gold/KMCL would have created more than 1,000 new jobs to operate the mine facilities. But, when the mine was officially inaugurated in July 2001, the final figure was downwardly revised to some 900 jobs.[27] This means that MIGA would have spent an average of over $190,000 for every single job created at Bulyanhulu![28]

What is more, Barrick Gold/KMCL's jobs are out of reach of the local communities whose livelihoods and jobs were destroyed in the first place. According to the *Social Development Plan*, prepared by Barrick, "low levels of skills and literacy possessed by the local population will restrict their ability to realise employment opportunities offered by the mining development and will also reduce their ability to seize entrepreneurial opportunities".[29] Although we learn elsewhere that the Bulyanhulu mine will "indirectly provide jobs to thousands of suppliers and other businesses around,"[30] these claims have to be treated with some scepticism. As one Member of Parliament from the Lake Zone has recently argued, corporate mining operations "...employ very few local people; they build their own infrastructures, and develop their own supply chains connected to their home countries."[31] KMCL has, for instance, bragged about its "buy local" policy in its project documents. The company is, however, importing almost all supplies, including food, from outside the mine area, the district, and even outside the region and the country. So any "multiplier effect" in terms of indirect job-creation opportunities accrues outside the immediate areas that have borne the brunt of its operations.

Under agreement with the government, according to the MIGA report, Barrick Gold/KMCL was required to prepare and carry out an effective training and employment program for its Tanzanian employees in each phase and at all levels of operation. Indeed Barrick Gold/KMCL has boasted that it has spent millions of dollars to train its Tanzanian workforce in South Africa and elsewhere; that it pays some of the highest salaries in Tanzania; that a Barrick Gold/KMCL job is one of the most coveted, etc. These aspects of the "solid developmental benefits" have to be taken as public relations propaganda! What the company has not cared to tell is that, from the very earliest days of the mine's operations, Barrick Gold/KMCL has faced a dissatisfied and rebellious workforce at Bulyanhulu. According to press reports, hardly five days after the mine was officially commissioned, close to two thirds of the 26 qualified engineers quit the mine citing "low wages, discrimination and mistreatment of local professionals".[32]

The reports had it that the local engineers, all university graduates, had undergone internship training in South Africa but, upon returning, were deployed as manual workers at a monthly salary of $245. In contrast, "artisans from Britain, Canada, Australia and South Africa with lower qualifications earn $4,400 per month, besides [having] better housing".[33] More recent reports and company documents indicate that the situation has become so tense that the Bulyanhulu workforce has downed tools on more than one occasion, in protest against company policies that the workers describe as exploitative, anti-union, discriminatory, and downright racist.

In comparison to these fictitious benefits, Barrick Gold/KMCL's project documents, and other sources, have estimated that prior to the 1996 evictions, there were probably about 20,000 people directly employed in small-scale mining activities. Many thousands more were employed in auxiliary activities associated with artisanal mining. Together with dependents, the total population came to the hundreds of thousands we discussed earlier. Barrick's project documents readily admit that "the lives of the majority of the people in Kakola and the whole of Bugarama Ward became closely linked to mining activities at Bulyanhulu". Such was the boom that "significant sums of money spent in local villages, various markets and businesses, also greatly stimulated the development of a local cash economy. There has been a significant decline in such benefits since the departure of the artisanal miners."[34]

Equally significant are the candid and forthright admissions of the positive socio-economic conditions pertaining to small-scale mining operations, and the negative consequences of the miners' expulsion. A few quotations from these documents may not be out of place. According to one project document, "the artisanal mining activities had the positive effect on local households of providing additional income-earning opportunities, increasing disposable income and the number of income generators, and improving services such as transportation and shops...". Likewise, "...it is believed that before the closure of small-scale mines, the average income in the study area was the highest in the Shinyanga region. These have fallen since the closure of small-scale mining."[35]

With regard to medical services, these are almost inaccessible to the Bulyanhulu villagers. The medical center is inside the mine complex and villagers have to go through rigorous security hurdles and numerous checkpoints before they are allowed through. Villagers have also complained that the costs of medical care provided by the company is almost beyond the means of the community whose economy the company admits to have destroyed.

It is clear, on the basis of the foregoing analysis, that the Bulyanhulu Gold Mine has undermined the real national economic interests of Tanzania. It has also sabotaged the national poverty alleviation goals in that, rather than leading to an improvement in the social and economic conditions of the Bulyanhulu communities and the nation, it has in fact intensified poverty and socio-economic malaise of the area and the country as a whole. That MIGA should provide millions of dollars in political risk guarantees to such socially harmful, and politically risky, investment seems beyond comprehension. That the Agency should have overlooked or ignored the unambiguous mandate, granted it under Article 12(d) of MIGA Convention, that "in guaranteeing an investment, the Agency shall satisfy itself as to the economic soundness of the investment and its contribution to the development of the host country," is scandalous and unacceptable.

5 The World Bank Group's Responsibility

The World Bank Group shares a major responsibility for the abuses and socio-economic upheavals and dislocations that have characterized Tanzania's mining industry in recent years. Apart from financially supporting individual projects, such as the Bulyanhulu Gold Mine, the Bank, more than any other outside institution, is responsible for creating the ideological, political and legal atmosphere under which these abuses become inevitable and are rationalized. We shall explain in some detail.

As the Bank's Operations Evaluation Department (OED) points out in a recent report, the Bank has been deeply involved in Tanzania's economic policy making since the country's independence in 1961. During the first two decades of independence Tanzania, with active technical and financial support from the World Bank, pursued economic policies based on state control and ownership of the major economic enterprises. With regard to the mining sector, the government inherited, almost wholly, the legislative and policy framework that had been adopted by the British colonial state since the late 1920s, and which emphasised strong state presence in the sector. By the mid-1980s, however, the Bank changed course and started to demand the adoption of economic liberalisation policies as a key condition for its continued support of the country's economy.

The Bank's "intellectual leadership" of Tanzania's mineral policy-making began very early on. In September 1990 the Bank published a *Mining Sector Review* for Tanzania.[36] This Review, and the Bank's 1992 Strategy paper on mining, set the tone for the Mineral Sector Development Strategy for Tanzania, prepared a few years later. As part of this review, a Bank consultant was hired to carry out "an extensive analysis of the Tanzanian small-scale mining sector and ... provide a proposed plan of action towards the end of the year (1997)". According to Canadian diplomats who closely followed these developments on behalf of Canadian mining interests, such as Sutton Resources/ KMCL, the Bank would also finance the British and Tanzanian consultants who drafted the new Mining Act, which was enacted into law in 1998.[37] The British consultants were Transborder Investment Advisory Services Ltd., an investment firm based in the City of London.[38]

The new legislation that came out of these processes makes it far easier for foreign investors to gain access to, and control of, Tanzania's mineral resources and to operate mining ventures. It streamlines decision-making processes regarding the allocation of mineral concessions, by concentrating considerable powers in the hands of government bureaucrats. However, it offers investors significant protection against bureaucratic red tape, by imposing significant limitations of time within which the bureaucrats are required to act on applications for mining concessions. It further shields the investors from local or national scrutiny, by divesting local and national institutions of their powers to deal with disputes between the government and the investors. It also seeks to shield investors from having their operations challenged in courts of law by local communities. This it does by giving the Commissioner of Minerals powers to decide in such disputes. Although it provides for mandatory preparation of environmental impact assessments (EIAs) and environmental management plans (EMPs) for almost all mining undertakings, there are significant loopholes.

These reforms in the mining sector have been augmented and complemented by further reforms of the regulatory regime for foreign investment generally, in order "to provide for more favourable conditions for investors,"[39] offering them extraordinarily generous incentives in the form of tax reliefs and guarantees of unconditional transfer of capital and profits. There are also protections against expropriation, nationalization, or compulsory acquisition, and all restrictions on entry and ownership of the mineral resources have been removed from the statute book. Investors are therefore now legally able to have complete ownership of mining ventures.

Taxation laws, enacted in the early 1970s, were amended to remove liability of investors to pay income taxes, customs and excise duties, and sales taxes.[40] The new law also amended the Immigration Act 1995, to remove restrictions on employment of non-citizens. Thus, mining investors are now entitled to an unlimited number of foreign employees. (All other investors must make do with an initial automatic immigration quota of up to five persons during the start up period of their ventures; a quota which may be raised under certain circumstances).

Whereas exploration in Africa has previously tended to focus in particular on South Africa and Ghana, the year 1998 saw Tanzania attracting the most exploration expenditure in Africa.[41] According to a South African-based business magazine, Tanzania has been the major focus of Africa's gold exploration and development over the past five years, with up to 15 per cent of the continent's exploration expenditure spent in the country.[42] Consequently, the country has become Africa's third largest gold producer, after South Africa and Ghana.[43]

Thus with more money spent on non-ferrous minerals exploration than in any other African country; the first three commercial gold mines starting operations since November 1998; and the prospect of another two-to-five projects coming on-stream over the next few years, Tanzania has undoubtedly been the flavour of the past five years in African mining circles. However, the key question is whether these dramatic developments have made a difference to the lives of millions of Tanzanians, living in poverty and squalor. We have already shown what these transformations have meant to the Bulyanhulu community. Unfortunately Bulyanhulu was not an aberration. Rather it was the most egregious example of a general and sinister pattern that has emerged in Tanzania's mining sector in the past decade.

6 Conclusion: Agenda for Change

In an otherwise candid examination of its four decades of involvement in Tanzania's economic policy, the World Bank's OED claims that, wherever the Bank has put its focus in Tanzania, "the outcomes have improved," allegedly helping to "generate substantial institutional development". It seems obvious from the foregoing analysis that, whatever "improvement in outcomes" or "relevance" the OED has in mind, it is certainly not in the sphere of human rights and social responsibility of the corporate mining sector. Nor does there appear to be any improvement in the country's economic "outcomes". The Bank itself admits that, after almost four decades of its Tanzania strategy, "...

the best available estimates suggest that per capita income today is certainly no higher than it was four decades ago".

Indeed, in many respects the Bank's strategy, while helping the already rich foreign investors to get richer, has undermined any possibilities for poverty alleviation represented by artisanal mining. It has also undermined any chance of building a national economy that meets the real needs of the vast majority of the poor. Incredibly, the World Bank has continued to push for even deeper 'reforms.' According to the country impact review, prepared by the Operations Evaluation Department of the Bank's IFC, "Tanzania has been difficult for private investors. It is getting better, but many investors still describe it as hostile, particularly toward foreign investors."[44] Against this perceived hostility to foreign investors the Bank Group has sought to tie the Tanzanian government's hands even tighter. It has accomplished this through the use of political risk insurance to investors via MIGA. In this regard, the government of Tanzania dares not re-examine its iniquitous deal with Barrick Gold/KMCL, for fear of punitive reprisals from the Bank Group, and the donor community which nowadays increasingly coordinates its approach to developing countries.

a   Recommendations on Policy Reform
Given this evidence, now widely acknowledged, an agenda for reform of the mining sector must roll back the FDI-centered prescriptions currently in place, and put artisanal mining back at the centre of the sector. To paraphrase President Mkapa: it is about time we asked whether the cost of foreign investment in the mining sector is economically acceptable, unacceptable, or necessary.

An agenda for reform must also address the environmental sustainability of large-scale mining operations, compared to small-scale artisanal ones. Given the amount of natural resources required to run large-scale operations; the vast output of various kinds of waste, with varying toxicity; given the grossly inadequate environmental and waste management plans and programmes that exist; given the growing toll on human life and the environment, it is high time the environmental impacts of corporate mining activities were addressed in a sustained manner.

An agenda for reform must finally address the political decision-making structures and processes as regards the mining sector. Structures and processes that are characterized by secrecy and subterfuge; that rely more on coercion and the use of force than on negotiation, consensus-building and compromise, are too costly and must go.

b   Recommendations on Reform of CAO

Our experience with the complaint investigation and dispute resolution mechanism established for MIGA and IFC suggests that it is neither sufficiently independent of the two institutions, nor transparent in its practices. The CAO draws its funding directly from the two institutions and shares their offices. As a result, the CAO is seen as being, not accountable to the complainants and stakeholders, but to MIGA/IFC – to whose Presidents they report on the results of their investigations.

We recommend a major reform of the complaint investigation and resolution mechanism that will enhance the independence, transparency and accountability of the CAO. A structure similar to the Independent Inspection Panel for the International Bank for Reconstruction and Development (IBRD) and the International Development Agency (IDA), that has proven its independence from the IBRD/IDA on numerous occasions, would be preferable to the current structure of the CAO.

c   Recommendations on Bulyanhulu

Since nothing has been done towards alleviating or righting the wrongs done to the Bulyanhulu community, our demands remain as valid today as they were when we commenced our campaign for justice:

1 Establishment of an independent international commission of inquiry, to independently, transparently and thoroughly inquire into the facts and circumstances pertaining to the allegations of human rights abuses, including the killings, violations of MIGA's Convention, its social and environmental safeguard policies and due diligence procedures; and, where necessary and appropriate, to make recommendations for redress. This commission is even more important now in view of the CAO's failure to investigate the complaint submitted to it by LEAT and the communities.

2 An international panel of experts should be formed, to undertake a thorough and unhindered exhumation of all the mine pits that are known, or alleged, to contain the bodies of the dead miners.

3 Proper and dignified burials befitting of human beings should be carried out without let or hindrance.

4 Reparations and full, fair, and adequate compensation, should be paid to the families and relatives of all those who were killed or maimed; and to all those who lost property and whose sources of livelihoods were destroyed without recompense.

5 Full, fair, and just compensation should be paid to all people, currently or formerly residing at Bulyanhulu, who were involuntarily resettled without any resettlement plan or full, fair, and just compensation.

6 Full, fair, and just compensation should be paid to all people currently, or formerly, residing at Bulyanhulu, whose agricultural and grazing lands were expropriated; whose residential and commercial property and settlements were destroyed; and whose mining shafts, machinery, and equipment were confiscated; and employment opportunities lost.

7 Full, fair, and just compensation should be paid to all remaining Bulyanhulu residents whose property rights continue to be violated and/or interfered with by the actions of Barrick Gold/KMCL. In the alternative, the company should desist from any continuing, or future, acts that violate or otherwise interfere with the enjoyment by the Bulyanhulu residents of their property rights.

In the light of the refusal by Barrick Gold/KMCL and the Government of Tanzania to even consider these demands; in view of the recent finding by the CAO that MIGA did not carry out any due diligence investigation prior to approving millions of dollars in political risk guarantees for the Bulyanhulu mine; in view of the evidence presented herein and the company's own admissions that the Bulyanhulu investment is inconsistent with MIGA's and the Bank Group's poverty alleviation mandates; and in view of the violations of the MIGA Convention examined herein, we conclude by reiterating our demand addressed to MIGA President James Wolfensohn on August 23, 2001: That MIGA should "suspend, with immediate effect, the political risk cover that it issued (in 2000] until the [above] actions have been taken."

We are mindful of the fact that Barrick Gold Corp., the current parent company of KMCL, and MIGA did not become directly involved with this project until the spring of 1999 when most of the events complained of had already taken place. We believe, however, that there is a direct relationship between the events of the pre-1999 period and the current mining operations undertaken by Barrick Gold/KMCL in the Bulyanhulu area. The project would not have moved forward without having first to address the issue of the hundreds of thousands of people who were living and working in the disputed area.

We believe that this direct relationship exists regardless of the amount of time that passed between the events complained of on the one hand, and Barrick Gold's and MIGA's involvement in the project on the other hand. This direct relationship also exists regardless of the ownership structure of KMCL, since the current owners of the project will benefit financially from the pre-1999 events complained of. Indeed, we are aware that changes in the ownership – from Sutton Resources to Barrick Gold – have not changed the legal personality or identity of KMCL.

We therefore believe that the circumstances surrounding the pre-1999 events fall within any reasonable definition of the "scope" of the project. It is imperative, as we argued in our Complaint to the CAO, that the World Bank Group "not send the message that possible improprieties in project preparation are acceptable provided they occurred prior to MIGA's (or the Bank Group's) direct involvement, or under the ownership of an entity other than the immediate project sponsor". This is especially the case where there are very serious allegations of human rights abuses, including extra-judicial killings.

References

Barrick Gold Corporation and KMCL (1999) *Social Development Plan for Bulyanhulu Gold Mine, Republic of Tanzania*, August 1999.

CCM (1992) *Chama cha Mapinduzi Programme: Policy Directions in the 1990s*, National Executive Committee, Dodoma, December, 1992.

CCM (1998) *Chama cha Mapinduzi: Assessment of the Twenty Years of CCM, 1977-1997*, National Executive Committee of CCM, February 1998.

Chachage, C.S.L. (1995a) "Mining and Environmental Issues Under SAPs in Tanzania: Examples From Three Case Studies", in M.S.D. Bagachwa and F. Limbu, *Policy Reform and the Environment in Tanzania*, Dar es Salaam University Press.

Chachage, C.S.L. (1995b) "The Meek shall Inherit the Earth But Not the Mining Rights: The Mining Industry and Accumulation in Tanzania", in P. Gibbon (Ed.), *Liberalised Development in Tanzania*, SIAS, Uppsala.

FoE, Urgewald and CRBM (2001) *Risky Business: How the World Bank's Insurance Arm Fails the Poor and Harms the Environment*, Washington DC, July 2001.

George, S. and Sabelli, F. (1994) *Faith and Credit: The World Bank's Secular Empire*, London/New York, Penguin Books.

Halifax Initiative (2001) *Reckless Lending, Volume II: How Canada's Export Development Corporation Puts People and the Environment at Risk*, NGO Working Group on the Export Development Corporation, Ottawa, May 2001.

Hildyard, N. (1999) *Snouts in the Trough: Export Credit Agencies, Corporate Welfare and Policy Incoherence*, Briefing 14, The Corner House, June 1999.

Jourdan, P. (1990) *The Mineral Industry in Tanzania*, Harare, Institute of Mining Research, University of Zimbabwe (mimeo).

Khamsini, R.O. (1971) 'The Gold Miners and the Mine Workers on the Lupa Gold Field, 1922-1963', *MA Dissertation*, History Department, University of Dar es Salaam (mimeo).

Kimambo, R.H. (1984) *Mining and Mineral Prospecting in Tanzania, Arusha*, East Africa Publications.

KMCL (1998a) *Environmental Impact Statement, Bulyanhulu Gold Project, Tanzania, Vol. 1*: Prepared for Kahama Mining Corporation Ltd., by Norecol, Dames & Moore of Vancouver, Canada, May 1998.

KMCL (1998b) *Environmental Impact Statement, Bulyanhulu Gold Project, Tanzania, Vol. 3*: Prepared for Kahama Mining Corporation Ltd., by Norecol, Dames & Moore of Vancouver, Canada, May 1998.

Lemelle, S. (1986) "Capital, State and Labour: A History of the Gold Mining Industry in Colonial Tanganyika, 1890-1942", *PhD Thesis*, University of California, Los Angeles.

Maurer, C. and R. Bhandari (2000) *The Climate of Export Credit Agencies*, WRI Climate Notes, Washington DC, WRI, May 2000.

Oates, F. (1934) "Gold in the Lupa Field", *Engineering and Mining Journal*, Vol. 135, No. 2.

Reid, E. (1938) *Tanganyika Without Prejudice: A Balanced Critical Review of the Territory and her People*, London, East African Newspaper Publishers.

Roberts, A.D. (1986) "The Gold Boom of the 1930s in Eastern Africa", *Journal of Royal African Society*, Vol. 85, No. 341.

Tanzania, U.R. (1996), *Minerals Found in Tanzania*, Dar es Salaam, Ministry of Water, Energy and Minerals.

Tanzania, U.R. (1998) *The National Assembly: Parliamentary Debates: Official Record (Hansard) of the Eleventh Meeting, Sixth Session* – 23rd April 1998, Dodoma, Department of Official Parliamentary Record.

Tanzania, U.R. (1999) *The Speech of the Minister for Energy and Minerals, Hon. Dr. Abdallah Omari Kigoda (MP.), Submitting Budget Estimates for the Ministry of Energy and Minerals for the Year 1999/2000 to the National Assembly*, Dar es Salaam, Government Printer.

Tanzania, U.R. (2001) *Turning Idle Mineral Wealth into a Weapon Against Poverty*: Address by the President of the United Republic of Tanzania, His Excellency Benjamin William Mkapa, Dar es Salam.

Taylor and Francis Group (2001) *Regional Surveys of the World: Africa South of the Sahara 2001*, 30th Edition, London, Europa Publications Ltd.

Notes

1 http://www.miga.org/screens/projects/guarant/regions/africa.html.

2 See message from Patricia Veevers-Carter pveeverscarter@worldbank.org: "MIGA Issues Largest Guarantee Ever for African Mining Venture", undated.

3 See *The Mining Act (Date of Operation) Notice, 1979*, G.N. No. 146 of 1979.

4 G.N. No. 6 of 1980 published on January 18 1980.

5 See W. Mushi, "Major gold deposits discovered", *Uhuru*, June 3 1985; and "Kahama gold to bring [Tanzania Shillings] 350 million", *Uhuru*, June 4 1985.

6   See *Mining (Designated Areas)(Amendment) Notice, 1982*, G.N. No. 154 of 1982 published on December 17 1982.

7   See *Mining (Designated Areas)(Amendment) Notice, 1983*, G.N. No. 2 of 1984, published on January 6 1984.

8   See *Mining (Designated Areas)(Amendment) Notice, 1984*, G.N. No. 34 of 1984, promulgated by Minister Kassum and published on February 1 1985; G.N. No. 230 of 1987, also promulgated by Minister Kassum on July 2 1987 and published in the Government Gazette on July 22 1988; and *Mining (Designated Areas)(Amendment) Notice, 1996*, G.N. No. 106 of 1996, promulgated by Minister William Shija and published on June 14 1996.

9   The interviews were conducted at Kakola on April 24 2001; September 3 2001; and March 13, 14 and 15 2002.

10 In an article published by a Canadian newspaper, *National Post*, Michael Kenyon, former President of Sutton Resources is quoted as saying that Sinclair's $3 Million programme to pay for the relocation of the Bulyanhulu people did not pass Sutton's Board's "taste test". See B. Hutchinson, "Barrick's African tribulations", *National Post*, December 29 2001.

11 The USAID-sponsored joint study entitled *Tanzania's Precious Minerals Boom: Issues in Mining and Marketing, African Economic Policy Discussion Paper No. 68, March 2000*. The study was undertaken by researchers from the International Business Initiative and Harvard University's John F. Kennedy School of Government both of the United States; and TanDiscovery (a Dar es Salaam-based consulting firm), a government-owned parastatal State Mining Corporation (STAMICO), Ministry of Energy and Minerals and the Economic and Social Research Foundation (ESRF), a reputable research institution also based in Dar es Salaam.

12 Barrick Gold & KMCL, *Social Development Plan for Bulyanhulu Gold Mine Tanzania*, 1999:4 &21.

13 Ibid p. 20.

14 See *Speech by Hon. Bhiku Mohamed Salehe, MP, (now deceased) to the National Assembly*, Dodoma, July 26 1996.

15 See *Letter Ref. K.30/1 Vol. iii/54* from Edson M. Halinga, District Commissioner, Kahama, to Hon. Jakaya M. Kikwete, Minister for Water, Energy and Minerals, dated September 5 1994, re "Small-scale Miners at Bulyanhulu, Kahama".

16 See *Madai ya Maafa Katika Mashimo ya Dhahabu Machimbo ya Bulyankulu Mkoani Shinyanga* (i.e., "Allegations of Killings in Gold Shafts at Bulyankulu Mines, Shinyaga Region" – auth.), Press Release, August 21 1996.

17 See M. Islam and M. Rweyemamu, "Utata watawala maafa ya Kahama: waliokufa machimboni wahofiwa kufikia 52: Picha za maiti zapelekwa Dodoma: wadaiwa kufunikwa na magreda" (i.e. "Uncertainty reigns over the Kahama Killings: The number of those dead in the mines feared to reach 52: Photos of the dead sent to Dodoma: They were allegedly buried by graders" – auth.), *Mtanzania*, Tuesday, August 13 1996; N. Kicheere, "Wachimbaji walihamishwa Bulyanhulu kihuni" (i.e. "Miners were rudely evicted from Bulyanhulu" – auth.), *Majira*, Wednesday,

October 11 1996; N. Kicheere, "Polisi waliua watu Bulyanhulu" (i.e. "Police killed people at Bulyanhulu" – auth.), *Majira*, Saturday, October 12 1996.

18   *Operesheni Vijiji* was a name given to a massive collectivization program intended to reorder and reorganize the socio-economic, political and administrative land-scape of rural Tanzania. Begun by the British colonial state in the 1930s, it was to assume – under the post-colonial ideology of *Ujamaa* – harshly authoritarian military-style dimensions, leading to the forced removals of millions of rural dwellers into new Ujamaa Villages. Its socio-economic and political legacy, characterized by economic disintegration, incessant land tenure conflicts and political power-lessness, has continued to be felt to this day. See Tanzania (1994) for the crisis in land tenure that the programme engendered.

19   See letter by Vince Borg, Barrick Gold's spokesman, published in the letters section of the Canadian newspaper *National Post*, January 26 2002, responding to an earlier letter jointly written by the Council of Canadians and MiningWatch Canada that had cited police reports of 200,000 evictees. See "Tanzanian Mines", *National Post*, Letters to the Editor, January 19 2002.

20   Ibid., paragraph 5-1.

21   Ibid., Vol. 1, Paragraph E-6.

22   According to the MIGA statement, the project will also procure some $10 million in local goods and services per year.

23   This does not even take into account smuggling which – according to Chachage (ibid., 254) – continued to be a major problem, because the Bank of Tanzania was only able to purchase an average of around 3 tons a year out of the estimated 10 to 16 tons of gold that were being produced annually. About 80 per cent of gemstones were also being exported unofficially every year during that period.

24   Taylor and Francis Group, *Regional Surveys of the World: Africa South of Sahara*, Europa Publications, 2001:1041-1042.

25   See *Chama cha Mapinduzi Program: Policy Direction in the 1990s*, National Executive Committee, Dodoma, December 1992, paragraph 61.

26   Chama cha Mapinduzi: *An Assessment of Twenty Years of CCM (1977-1997)*, National Executive Committee, Dodoma, February 1998, paragraph 102.

27   See, Advertiser's Supplement, "Rais Benjamin William Mkapa Kufungua Rasmi Mgodi wa Dhahabu wa Chini ya Ardhi Bulyanhulu" (i.e. "President Benjamin William Mkapa to Officially Commission the Underground Bulyanhulu Gold Mine"), *Mtanzania*, Tuesday, July 17 2001; "Rais Benjamin Mkapa Kufungua Mgodi Mkubwa wa Chini ya Ardhi", (i.e. "President Benjamin Mkapa to Commission in the Country's Major Underground Mine"), Nipashe, Tuesday, July 17 2001; "Celebration as His Excellency President Benjamin Mkapa official inaugurates Tanzania's largest underground gold mine", *The Guardian*, Tuesday, July 17 2001.

28   MIGA's global average is, indeed, far higher at $1.175 million per job created, according to FoE et al. who have in fact called for its disbanding for promoting "risky business", failing the poor and harming the environment (ibid., 6, 19).

29   See SDP at page 36.

30   See editorial titled "Mining activities: What is wrong?", *The Guardian*, Thursday, July 19 2001.

31   Anthony Diallo, MP for Mwanza Rural, quoted in See L. Mwakalebela and T. Kaguo, "MPs differ on mining taxes", *Business Times*, Friday 18 2000.

32   See F. Rwambali, "17 Engineers Quit Tanzania's Giant Kahama Mines", *The East African*, Friday August 23 2001.

33   Ibid.

34   See EIS Vol. 1 paragraph E-6.

35   Ibid., Vol. 3, Paragraph 8-2.

36   Sector Review #9007 published on September 19 1990.

37   See memo dated April 14 1997, from High Commissioner Edelstein to the Department of Foreign Affairs and International Trade (DFAIT), Ottawa.

38   This is confirmed by then-Canadian High Commissioner to Tanzania, Verona Edelstein, in a fax message to Michael Kenyon, then-President of Sutton Resources of Vancouver Canada dated October 18 1996. Sutton Resources had acquired the Bulyanhulu concession that August and High Commissioner Edelstein wrote to thank Kenyon for his "very kind words to Ministers Axworthy and Eggleton for the Canadian High Commission's and my own support for Sutton's efforts here in Tanzania".

39   Preamble to the National Investment Act, 1997, No. 27 of 1997.

40   See Financial Laws (Miscellaneous Amendments) Act, 1997, No. 26 of 1997.

41   Mihayo, *"Tanzania's mining success a 'Pyrrhic Victory'?"*, op. cit.

42   D. Games, "A new dawn", *Business in Africa*, October 2000, p. 44-47

43   See Guardian Reporter, "Tanzanian investment in gold, minerals pays off", op. cit.

44   See OED Director General's "Memorandum to the Executive Directors and the President", *Tanzania Country Assistance Evaluation*, Operations Evaluation Department (OED), World Bank, September 13 2000. According to the IFC review, there are five principal obstacles to private sector development: (1) slow pace of privatisation, (2) delays in financial sector reform, (3) weak infrastructure and human resources, (4) social and governmental ambivalence toward private sector development and (5) aid dependence (op. cit.).

List of Abbreviations

AAC	Anglo American Corporation	CAP	Community Advisory Panel
ABB	Asea Brown Boveri	CAS	Country Assistance Strategies
ABN	Algemene Bank Nederland	CASS	Chotanagpur Adivasi Seva
ABRI	the Indonesian armed forces		Samiti
ACFOA	Australian Council for	CBF	Community and Business
	Overseas Aid		Forum
AI	Amnesty International	CCD	counter-current decantation
AID	Agency for International	CCM	Chama cha Mapinduzi
	Development	CDAP	Caspian Development
AIDC	Australian Investment		Advisory Panel
	Development Corporation	CDC	Commonwealth Development
AIG	American International Group		Corporation (now Actis)
AMAN	Indigenous Peoples Alliance of	CEE	Central and Eastern Europe
	the Archipelago	CEO	Chief Executive Officer
AMF	American Mineral Fields	CEPMPL	Centre for Energy, Petroleum
AMP	Australian Mutual Provident		and Mineral Policy and Law
AMRO	Amsterdam Rotterdam (bank)	CERCLA	Comprehensive Environmental
APA	Amerindian Peoples		Response Compensation and
	Association		Liability Act
ASAP	Action in Solidarity with Asia	CESCE	Compania Espanola de Seguro
	and the Pacific		de Credito a la Exportacion
ASEED	Action for Solidarity,	CIL	Coal India Ltd.
	Equality, Environment and	CIS	former USSR Newly
	Development		Independent States
ATCA	Alien Tort Claims Act (US)	COFACE	Compagnie Française
BAe	British Aerospace		d'Assurance pour le Commerce
BGC	Barrick Gold Corporation		Extérieur
BHP	Broken Hill Proprietary	CRG	Control Risks Group
	(BHPBilliton)	CSESMP	Coal Sector Environmental
BP	British Petroleum		Social Mitigation Project
BPD	Business Partners for	CSRP	Coal India Rehabilitation
	Development (initiative)		Project
BPS	Bank Procedures	CVG	Corporacion Venezolana de
BTC	Baku-Tbilisi-Ceyhan		Guyana
CAF	Corporacion Andina de	CVRD	Compania do Vale Rio Doce
	Fomento	DFAIT	Department of Foreign Affairs
CAMECO	Canadian Mining & Energy		and International Trade
	Corporation	DFID	Department for International
CAO	Compliance Advisory		Development
	Ombudsman	DoE	Division of Environment

DPC	Dabhol Power Company	FEROCAFENOP	Federation of Rondas Campesinas Feminas of Northern Peru
DRC	Democratic Republic of Congo		
DRD	Durban Roodepoort Deep Ltd.	FIPR	fully informed prior consent
		FOE	Friends of the Earth (by country)
DSL	Defence Systems Ltd.		
DSTP	Deep Sea Tailing Placement	FOEI	Friends of the Earth International
EBRD	European Bank for Reconstruction and Development		
		FPIC	free, prior informed consent
		FPP	Forest Peoples Programme
ECA	Export Credit (Guarantee) Agency	FT	Financial Times
		FUNAI	Indian protection agency of Brazil
ECG	Export Credit Guarantee		
ECGD	Export Credit Guarantee Department	FY02	Financial Year 2002 (etc)
		GDP	Gross Domestic Product
ECIC	Export Credit Insurance Corporation	GE	General Electric
		GMI	Global Mining Initiative
EDC	Export Development Canada	GOIP	Guyana Organization of Indigenous Peoples
EDC	Export Development Corporation		
		GRAMA	Groupe de recherche sur les activités minières
EDF	Environmental Defense Fund		
EFIC	Export Finance and Insurance Corporation	GSR	Golden Star Resources Inc
		HDPE	high density polyethylene
EI	Extractive Industry	IBRD	International Bank for Reconstruction and Development
EIA	Environmental Impact Assessment		
EIL	Environmental Impairment Liability	ICC	International Chamber of Commerce
		ICEM	International Federation of Chemical, Energy, Mine and General Workers' Union
EIR	Extractive Industries Review		
EIS	Environmental Impact Statement		
		IDA	International Development Association
EL-HAM	West Papua Human Rights group		
		IDS	International Defence and Security
EO	Executive Outcomes		
EPA	see USEPA		
ERD	Environmental Review Directory	IFC	International Finance Corporation (of World Bank)
ERG	ExportRisikoGarantie	IFI	International Finance Institution
ESRF	Economic and Social Research Foundation		
		IGP	Inspector General of Police
ESW	Economic and Sector Work	ILO	International Labour Organisation
ExIm	Export Import Bank		
FCX	Freeport McMoRan Copper and Gold	IMF	International Monetary Fund
		INFID	International NGO Forum on Indonesian Development

IPS	Institute for Policy Studies	MoU	Memorandum of Understanding
IPS	Inter Press Service		
IRN	International Rivers Network	MPC	Mineral Policy Center
IRR	investment rate of return	MPI	Mineral Policy Institute
ITT	International Telephone and Telegraph	MSEB	Maharashtra State Electricity Board
IUCN	International Union for the Conservation of Nature	MYSA	Minera Yanacocha S.A.
		NAC	National Amerindian Council
IWGIA	International WorkGroup for Indigenous Affairs	NEMC	National Environment Management Council
JATAM	Indonesian Mining Advocacy Network	NEWG	Environmental Watch Group
		NGO	Non-Governmental Organisation
JBIC	ECA Japan		
JEXIM	former name JBIC	NMA	National Mining Association
KCM	Konkola Copper Mines plc	NSR	Natural Systems Research
KGC	Kumtor Gold Company	OCEI	Center Ecologicheskoi Informatzi
KMCL	Kahama Mining Corporation Limited	OECD	Organisation for Economic Cooperation and Development
KMS	Keenie Meenie Services (?)		
KOC	Kumtor Operating Company	OED	Operations Evaluation Department
KOPASSUS	Special forces army unit Indonesia		
		OGML	Omai Gold Mining Ltd.
LAIGC	Latin American Investment Guarantee Company	OP	Operational Policy
		OPIC	Overseas Private Investment Corporation
LEAT	Lawyers Environmental Action Team	OPM	Organisasi/Operasi Papua Merdeka, Free Papua Movement
LEMASA	Amungme Tribal Council		
LIBOR	London Inter Bank Offered Rate	PCB	polychlorbiphenyl
		PERC	Pacific Environment and Resources Center
LMALA	Landowners Association Lihir		
LMC	Lihir Management Company	PIRA	Public Information Resource Association
MAG	Monitoring Advisory Group		
MARS	Major Accident Reporting System	PKI	Indonesian Communist Party
		PNC	Power Reactor & Nuclear Fuel Development Corporation
MEM	Ministry of Energy and Minerals		
		PNG	Papua New Guinea
MIGA	Multilateral Investment Guarantee Agency	PPA	Power Purchase Agreement
		PRI	Political Risk Insurance
MJ	Mining Journal	PTFI	Freeport Indonesia
MM	Multinational Monitor	PWA	Petztorme Women's Association
MMSD	Mining, Minerals and Sustainable Development (initiative)		
		RAFCA	Rainforests Consultants Association
MMSL	Mining and Mineral Sciences Laboratories		
		RLS	Remediation Stop Loss

RPC	Regional Police Commander	TCFB	Tanzania Central Freight Bureau
RSA	Royal Sun & Alliance		
RTZ	Rio Tinto Zinc	UAIL	Utkal Alumina International Ltd.
RUF	Revolutionary United Front		
S&P	Standard & Poor	UBS	Union Bank of Switzerland
SACE	Servizio Assicuratai per il Commercio Estero	UK	United Kingdom
		UN	United Nations
SAML	South Asia Mining Letter	UNDP	UN Development Programme
SAP	Structural Adjustment Programme	UNEP	UN Environmental Programme
		UNO	University of New Orleans
SAS	Sector Assistance Strategy	USA	United States of America
SDP	Social Development Plan	USAID	US Agency for International Development
SEC	Securities and Exchange Commission		
		USEPA	US Environmental Protection Agency
SEIA	Social and Environmental Impact Assessments		
		USSR	Union of Socialistic Soviet Republics
SHIREMA	Shinyanga Regional Miners Association		
		WALHI	Indonesian Forum for the Environment
SIR	self-insured retention		
SMXRA	Surface Mining Control and Reclamation Act	WCD	World Commision on Dams
		WDM	World Development Movement
SME	Small and Medium Enterprise		
SRL	Sierra Rutile Ltd.	WHO	World Health Organization
STAMICO	State Mining Corporation	WSSD	World Summit for Sustainable Development
STD	Submarine Tailings Disposal		
T&N	Turner & Newall	WWF	World Wildlife Fund
TAL	Technical Assistance Loan	ZCCM	Zambia Consolidated Copper Mines
TAPOL	Indonesian Human Rights Organization		
		ZEMS	Zurich Emerging Markets
		ZNA	Zurich North Americ

PRI Index

Company Index

Name Index

Geographical Name Index

Books by ROGER MOODY

The Indigenous Voice – Visions & Realities, Zed, London, 1988, revised Second Edition with International Books, Utrecht, 1993

Plunder!, Partizans and Cafca, London and Christchurch, 1991

The Gulliver File – Mines, people and land: a global battleground, Minewatch and International Books, London and Utrecht, 1992

Into the Inknown Regions – The hazards of Submarine Tailings Disposal, ssc and International Books, London and Utrecht, 2001